Reading
1 Peter, Jude, and 2 Peter

Reading the New Testament Series

Available

Reading Matthew
by David E. Garland

Reading John
by Charles H. Talbert

Reading Acts
by Charles H. Talbert

Reading Romans
by Luke Timothy Johnson

Reading Colossians, Ephesians, and 2 Thessalonians
by Bonnie Thurston

Reading 1 Peter, Jude, and 2 Peter
by Earl Richard

Forthcoming

Reading Mark
by Sharyn E. Dowd

Reading Luke (revised)
by Charles H. Talbert

Reading 1 and 2 Corinthians (revised)
by Charles H. Talbert

Reading Galatians, Philippians, and 1 Thessalonians
by Charles B. Cousar

Reading 1 and 2 Timothy, Titus, and Philemon
by Marion L. Soards

Reading Hebrews and James
by Marie Isaacs

Reading Revelation
by Joseph Trafton

Reading
1 Peter, Jude, and 2 Peter

A Literary and Theological Commentary

Earl J. Richard

SMYTH&HELWYS
PUBLISHING, INCORPORATED • MACON, GEORGIA
WWW.HELWYS.COM

99-056441

Smyth & Helwys Publishing, Inc.
6316 Peake Road
Macon, Georgia 31210-3960
1-800-747-3016
© 2000 by Smyth & Helwys Publishing
All rights reserved.
Printed in the United States of America.

Earl J. Richard

The paper used in this publication meets the minimum
requirements of American National Standard for Information
Sciences—Permanence of Paper for Printed Library Materials.
ANSI Z39.48–1984   (alk. paper)

Library of Congress Cataloging-in-Publication Data

Richard, Earl.
    Reading 1 Peter, Jude, and 2 Peter:
    A Literary and Theological Commentary/
    Earl Richard.
    p.   cm. — (Reading the New Testament series)
    Includes bibliographical references.
    ISBN 157312-314-5
    1. Bible, N.T. Peter—Commentaries.
    2. Bible, N.T. Jude—Commentaries.
    I. Title: Reading 1 Peter, Jude, and 2 Peter
    II. Title.
    III. Series.
    BS2795.3 .R53 2000
    227'.92077—dc21

Contents

Jude

2 Peter

Editor's Foreword

"Reading the New Testament" is a commentary series that aims to present cutting-edge research in popular form that is accessible to upper-level undergraduates, seminarians, seminary educated pastors, and educated laypersons, as well as to graduate students and professors. The volumes in this series do not follow the word-by-word, phrase-by-phrase, verse-by-verse method of traditional commentaries. Rather, they are concerned to understand large thought units and their relationship to an author's thought as a whole. The focus is on a close reading of the final form of the text. The aim is to make one feel at home in the biblical text itself. The approach of these volumes involves a concern both for *how* an author communicates and *what* the religious point of the text is. Care is taken to relate both the *how* and the *what* of the text to its milieu: Christian (NT and noncanonical), Jewish (scriptural and postbiblical), and Greco-Roman. This enables both the communication strategies and the religious message of the text to be clarified over against a range of historical and cultural possibilities. Moreover, a section of commentary on a large thought unit will often contain a brief excursus on some topic raised by the material in the unit, sometimes sketching OT, postbiblical Jewish, Greco-Roman, NT, and noncanonical Christian views on the subject. Throughout, the basic concern is to treat the NT texts as religious documents whose religious message needs to be set forth with compelling clarity. All other concerns are subordinated to this. It is the hope of all participants in this project that our efforts at exposition will enable the NT to be understood better and communicated more competently.

—Charles H. Talbert
General Editor

Author's Preface

Since the three works being examined in this volume have usually been overlooked in past generations primarily because they have rarely been read or been part of the Christian lectionary, it seemed a challenge to me to be offered by Charles Talbert the chance to present them in a series whose focus is precisely a literary and theological reading of the books of the New Testament. While the first of these, 1 Peter, has perhaps ceased to be a stepchild of NT study owing to increased appreciation among scholars of its theological contribution to early Christian tradition, the second and the third, Jude and 2 Peter, have only recently begun to receive the serious attention they deserve as forming part of the NT canon. All three continue to be a challenge for the modern reader who is both unacquainted with their content and finds difficulty in appreciating the early ecclesial setting and purpose of each.

Study of these documents has been a lengthy process for the author, who, years ago through the work of J. H. Elliott, became greatly interested in 1 Peter and its thought and, in more recent years, has found the studies of R. J. Bauckham and J. H. Neyrey most enlightening for reading Jude and 2 Peter as works of the early Church. Having tackled these annually in NT survey courses, having struggled to compose brief introductions to these for my study of NT christology (*Jesus: One and Many*), and having had the opportunity to focus on these three forgotten works in a recent graduate course at Loyola University, I have devoted much of my time these past three years (one of which was a sabbatical) to the serious reading of 1 Peter, Jude, and 2 Peter. I have attempted to read these consistently with the intended audience as focus, thereby allowing the extended readers through my voice to hear the messages of the original authors. Unless otherwise indicated, the text cited in the following commentary is my own translation. Many of the insights here offered I owe to those who have read these works before me. It is hoped that in the final analysis each author's voice will be heard by an enlightened modern audience.

Thanks is owed to many who have provided encouragement, assistance, and insight. The gratitude to fellow readers, though not usually acknowledged, is minimally indicated in the discussion of major issues and through suggested readings for further insight. The work is dedicated to the many students at Loyola, undergraduate and graduate, who have read these works with me over the years. Thanks also is owed Mary Ann, Elizabeth, Marie-Anne, and Joseph for support and a sympathetic ear.

Abbreviations

Ancient Texts

B	Vaticanus
Bar	*Baruch*
CD	Damascus Document
EH	Eusebius' *Ecclesiastical History*
En	*Enoch*
JA	Josephus' *Jewish Antiquities*
JW	Josephus' *Jewish War*
LXX	Septuagint
ms(s)	Manuscript(s)
NT	New Testament
OT	Old Testament
P	Papyrus
PssSol	*Psalms of Solomon*
1QH	Qumran: Thanksgiving Hymns
1QM	Qumran: War Scroll
1QpHab	Qumran: Habakkuk Pesher
1QS	Qumran: Manual of Discipline
S	Sinaiticus
SibOr	*Sibylline Oracles*
T	Testament

Periodicals, Reference Works, Serials, Collections

AJBI	*Annual of the Japanese Biblical Institute*
ANRW	*Aufstieg und Niedergang der römischen Welt*
AS	*Assemblées du Seigneur*
BAGD	W. Bauer, W. F. Arndt, F. W. Gingrich, F. W. Danker, *Greek-English Lexicon of the NT*
BBR	*Bulletin for Biblical Research*
BDF	F. Blass, A. Debrunner, and R. W. Funk, *A Greek Grammar of the NT*

BG	M. Zerwick, *Biblical Greek*
Bib	*Biblica*
BibLeb	*Bibel und Leben*
BibOr	*Bibbia e Oriente*
BS	*Bibliotheca Sacra*
BTB	*Biblical Theology Bulletin*
BZ	*Biblische Zeitschrift*
CBQ	*Catholic Biblical Quarterly*
ConBNT	*Coniectanea biblica: NT*
CTJ	*Calvin Theological Journal*
EA	*Erbe und Auftrag*
EM	*Efemerides Mexicana*
EQ	*Evangelical Quarterly*
ET	*Expository Times*
ETR	*Etudes théologiques et religieuses*
Etudes	C. Perrot, ed., *Etudes sur la Première Lettre de Pierre*
EstBib	*Estudios Bíblicos*
GRBS	*Greek, Roman, and Byzantine Studies*
FNT	*Filología Neotestamentaria*
HBT	*Horizons in Biblical Theology*
HTR	*Harvard Theological Review*
IBNTG	C. F. D. Moule, *An Idiom Book of NT Greek*
Interp	*Interpretation*
JBL	*Journal of Biblical Literature*
JETS	*Journal of the Evangelical Theological Society*
JSJ	*Journal for the Study of Judaism*
JSNT	*Journal for the Study of the NT*
JTS	*Journal of Theological Studies*
Jude	R. J. Bauckham, *Jude and the Relatives of Jesus in the Early Church*
LSJ	H. G. Liddell, R. Scott, and H. S. Jones, *A Greek-English Lexicon*
LV	*Lumière et vie*
Neot	*Neotestamentica*
NIB	*New Interpreter's Bible*
NJB	*New Jerusalem Bible*
NJBC	*New Jerome Biblical Commentary*
NovT	*Novum Testamentum*
NRSV	*New Revised Standard Version*
NTS	*New Testament Studies*
PFP	C. H. Talbert, ed., *Perspectives on First Peter*
PGL	G. W. H. Lampe, *Patristic Greek Lexicon*
PSTJ	*Perkins School of Thology Journal*
RB	*Revue biblique*
RCT	*Revista Catalana de Teología*

RE	*Review and Expositor*
REB	*Revised English Bible*
RHPR	*Revue d'histoire et de philosophie religieuse*
RivB	*Rivista Bíblica*
RQ	*Restoration Quarterly*
RSR	*Revue des sciences religieuses*
RTL	*Revue théologique de Louvain*
RTP	*Revue de théologie et de philosophie*
SBFLA	*Studii Biblici Francis eni Liber Annuses*
SC	*Second Century*
SNTU	*Studien zum neuen testament und seiner lumwelt*
TB	*Tyndale Bulletin*
TBT	*The Bible Today*
TCGNT	*B. M. Metzger, A Textual Commentary on the Greek NT*
TDNT	*Theological Dictionary of the NT*
TR	*Theologische Rundscheu*
TZ	*Theologische Zeitschrift*
USQR	*Union Seminary Quarterly Review*
VC	*Vigiliae Christianae*
VT	*Vetus Testamentum*
ZNTW	*Zeitschrift für die Neutestamentliche Wissenschaft*

Introduction

Renewed interest in the history of the early Christian movement has had a profound affect on modern biblical studies. Among other consequences, there has developed a keen interest in the less-well-known documents of the early Church in order to glean from these a better understanding of the first two centuries of its development. Relatively lengthy documents such as James, 1 Peter, and 1 John or shorter ones such as 2 Peter, Jude, and 2 and 3 John, which were neglected by earlier generations of scholars, have of late received renewed attention in an effort to situate these in their historical contexts. Ironically the abandoning of older theories of apostolic authorship has led, in recent years, to a greater appreciation of the historical value of these early "catholic" documents.

Canon

The NT list of books is the end product of a long process of dialogue regarding the Christian movement's normative literature. In effect its canon consists of books that over the centuries came to be accepted as normative of the community's beliefs and practice. Various internal and external forces had led first to the production of early Christian documents to meet the communities' needs, and still further factors figured in the continued scrutiny of these theological creations as regards their normative status.

While there is evidence that at an early stage (c. 160 AD) the Gospels ("memoirs of the apostles") are ascribed canonical status on a par with the prophetic writings of the OT (Justin Martyr, *Apology* 1.67.3), there is even earlier indication in 2 Pet 3:1-2,15-16 that various Christian letters (those of Paul and 1 Peter, presumably) are described as "scriptures" (*graphai*), precisely owing to their apostolic origin or tradition. Thus from the time of Irenaeus, bishop of Lyons (c. 180), 1 Peter is consistently accepted and quoted as composed by the apostle Peter (*Against Heresies* 4.9.2). At a slightly later date Tertullian not only includes 1 Peter within his NT canon but also the Epistle of Jude (*Women's Apparel* 1.3), which later draws some unfavorable criticism for its use of the apocryphal books *1 Enoch* and the *Assumption of Moses*. Despite such hesitation Jude is subsequently established among the community's "apostolic letters." Second Peter does not fare as well. Origen (early third century), who is the first to refer explicitly to this document, is doubtful as to its genuineness (see Eusebius, *EH* 6.25.11). Nonetheless, by the end of the fourth century, with the weight of Jerome's defense (*Epistles* 120.11) the letter was admitted fully within the list of catholic epistles.

On the one hand, it is clear that the overriding principle of acceptance of the letters in questions into the NT canon was their alleged apostolic origin. They were highly regarded by the Christian communities and assumed to bear the authority and knowledge of the eyewitnesses of the first generation. On the other hand, association with apostolic figures did not assure either quick acceptance into the canon or admittance at all. Thus Eusebius (*EH* 3.3 and 25) is quite insistent that a number of "Petrine" works are either disputed (2 Peter) or spurious (*Acts, Gospel, Preaching,* or *Revelation of Peter*) and thus not accepted by the believing community.

Pseudonymity

Despite the difficulties raised against their admittance into the canon, Jude and 2 Peter, along with 1 Peter, enjoyed the status of apostolic authority but, as often noted, not a high profile in theological discussions as did the works of the evangelists and Paul. Instead these works have figured largely in historical reconstructions of the events of the apostolic period, whether in underscoring the role of Jesus' family in the first-century Church (authorship of Jude, the brother of Jesus) or of the influence and role of Peter in the developing ecclesial structures extending to Asia Minor and Rome. Whether or not one wishes to acknowledge the fact, there has existed within Christian communities a practical "canon within the canon." In fact the three letters under consideration have over the centuries been relegated to the lesser works of the NT list.

While biblical experts have been reluctant until recently to designate these works as pseudonymous, this is not the situation currently. If earlier the primary impetus in the defense of apostolic authorship had been the concern for historical tradition, recent considerations of ancient authorship, better appreciation of the relationship between oral and written traditions, and better understanding of anonymity and pseudonymity in the transmission of tradition have provided a more solid foundation for discussions of NT authorship. In addition, critical scholarship is less wont, as earlier, to characterize a work either as authentic or as a pious fraud. Rather than judge such ancient works by modern standards of authorship, scholars more readily take into consideration the conventions of ancient writing whereby disciples often spoke and wrote in the names of their masters and where devotees are said to speak and act on behalf of their god or under the influence of the Spirit. In light of such considerations, biblical scholars have returned to these ancient works with new insights and a greater focus on the works themselves to discern what relation they have to other works of the Christian canon and to monitor more carefully how these documents fit into a renewed understanding of the first and second centuries of the Christian community's growth.

Just as early ecclesial foundations and mission fields claimed apostolic or first-generation origins as the battle for orthodoxy and communion expanded, so did contemporary leaders appeal to the authority of venerable figures either of the community at large or of their own theological circle to address the pressing problems of their time. Therefore speaking or writing in the name of one's ideological master can only seem strange to the modern person who is unfamiliar with the late OT and early NT world.

The Post-Apostolic Period

These once-neglected works have become of late a renewed area of research. This attention seems to be due to two important considerations, one related to the defense of authenticity and the other to the accusation of fraud or the capitulation to "Early Catholic" tendencies. In the first case there is less concern for an assumed apostolic authorship around which one must situate a given document and a greater focus on the document's content and occasion. In the second instance, there is considerable skepticism concerning the notion of "Early Catholicism," a concept that presumes a pristine doctrinal period that gives way to the stultifying orthodoxy of the Great Church. By laying aside these various presuppositions, scholars have allowed themselves more readily to situate these general letters in a more congenial context, namely the last third of the first century, which might more readily be described as the post-apostolic period.

All three documents, 1 Peter, Jude, and 2 Peter, address the post-apostolic Church as its members encounter the challenges of the Greco-Roman world, the variety and ferment of its own expanding membership, and the evolution of its beliefs and praxis. Freed from the imposed assumption of apostolic authorship, scholars more readily allow the texts to reveal their proper social and religious contexts. The following threefold commentary and discussion will address the specific post-apostolic setting, strategy, and message of the three documents in question.

Initially one might suggest that recent study of 1 Peter has opened the eyes of scholars to the complex world of the post-apostolic period. The writer is strikingly original and comparably creative in comparison to Paul. The letter offers a challenging discussion of sociopolitical thought. It addresses squarely the issue of Christians in a non-Christian society. In modern terms one might formulate the letter's focus as "religion and society" whereby believers are reminded that they have a duty toward the state, non-Christian neighbors, and all human creatures (2:17). In many ways it is a modern document whose strategy of nonviolent resistance or gentle defense is refreshing. The addressees of the document are particularly vexed by ostracisation, maltreatment, and slander on the part of pagan neighbors. The author is especially concerned with addressing this issue, which is seen by some believers as a satanic temptation to apostasy. The author's strategy involves the christological pattern of suffering and glory; believers are enjoined to pattern their lives on that of Christ in whose footsteps they are to follow (2:21). The letter's doctrine is balanced and original in its use of early tradition. Its paraenetic motivation, while eschatological in emphasis, is basically theological in focus and positive in anthropological terms. The model presented for Christian living is christological in empowerment, model, and intimacy, for Christ is the chief shepherd and guardian of the flock (2:25; 5:1-5). It is a life that demands holy conduct, reverent fear, and duty to society, to others, and especially to fellow believers as they face what the author calls a test to the genuineness of their faith (1:6-7; 4:12). One finds in 1 Peter an insistence on reverence for a "faithful creator," honor for all creatures, concern and love for fellow believers, and a yearning of obedient children to return to God as the source of promised glory.

The other two short documents, Jude and 2 Peter, offer a striking contrast to 1 Peter. Both are characterized by polemics against unspecified opponents within the community who are accused both of erroneous doctrine and licentious behavior. Jude, the shorter of the two and a source for the composition of 2 Peter, sheds light on early ecclesial disputes. The author's strategy and artistry suggest an effective struggle and success against opponents who are accused of denying the lordship of God and the Messiah and of abominable behavior. Beyond this polemical objective, however, the author affectionately appeals to fellow believers to remain faithful to their "most holy faith" and to extend a helping hand to the errant.

Second Peter is likewise focused on an early ecclesial battle concerning the community's eschatological beliefs. Some members within the community, whom the author calls "false teachers," have mockingly questioned the group's belief that Jesus will soon return to exercise divine judgment. The author adopts a testamentary framework to present, in the name of Peter, the community's tradition concerning Jesus' current and eschatological lordship. Despite the severity of the document's condemnation of these false teachers, its exhortation to righteous living and its defense of doctrinal orthodoxy transform it into a powerful statement about the early Church's challenge as it moved more fully into the Greco-Roman world.

Suggested Readings

Brown, R. E. *The Churches the Apostles Left Behind.* New York: Paulist, 1984.

Brox, N. *Falsche Verfasserangaben: Zur Erklärung der frühchristlichen Pseudepigraphia.* Stuttgart: Katholisches Bibelwerk, 1975.

Dunn, J. D. G. "Levels of Canonical Authority." *HBT* 4 (1982) 13-60.

Goppelt, L. *Apostolic and Post-Apostolic Times.* Grand Rapids: Eerdmans, 1970.

Meade, D. G. *Pseudonymity and Canon: An Investigation into the Relationship of Authorship and Authority in Jewish and Earliest Christian Tradition.* Tübingen: Mohr-Siebeck, 1986.

Smith, T. V. *Petrine Controversies in Early Christianity: Attitudes Towards Peter in Christian Writings of the First Two Centuries.* Tübingen: Mohr-Siebeck, 1985.

Wilken, R. L. *The Myth of Christian Beginnings.* Atlanta: John Knox, 1979.

1 Peter

Introduction

Rescued from its relative obscurity by recent scholarship, 1 Peter has emerged as a fascinating early Christian document whose content and message are of interest to the student of the Bible both in an academic and theological sense. Careful reading of this early letter offers many insights about the early community's interaction with its Roman neighbors. At the same time one is able to discern the sensitive strategy of the document's author in fostering perseverance among the Christians of Asia Minor. Before addressing in some detail the document's occasion, strategy, and message, however, it is necessary to discuss the letter, its author, and intended audience.

Author and Audience

In typical epistolary fashion the letter opens by naming the writer and addressees: "Peter, an apostle of Jesus Christ; to the . . . exiles of the Dispersion in Pontus, Galatia, Cappadocia, Asia, and Bithynia" (1:1).

Author

The author's claim to be the apostle Peter has been adamantly defended as well as denied by scholarship. The standard arguments for or against Petrine authorship are certainly ambivalent and of varying quality. But a combination of linguistic, social, and theological reasons argue strongly against Petrine authorship and in favor of pseudonymity. The author's notable command of Greek and familiar use of the Septuagint OT indicate a Hellenistic writer. Additionally, the Christian movement has undergone important transformations since the apostolic period; thus the author employs the term *adelphotes* ("brotherhood" or "family of believers"—2:17; 5:9) to describe the community, refers to its leadership as "elders," addresses explicitly the believers' relationship to the state (2:13-17), and notes that suffering as a Christian has become a common phenomenon (4:16; 5:9). Thus we conclude that the author invokes the name of Peter (employing the formulaic: "apostle of Jesus Christ"—see Titus 1:1 and the other Paulinist letters) to add authority to the document's traditional exhortations and to insure a positive response from the audience. What one finds in 1 Peter are not the reminiscences or teaching of a Palestinian eyewitness but the complex use of paraenetic materials that have undergone considerable development prior to their application to the communities' situation.

From the letter itself we learn that the author is a fellow elder (*sympresbyteros*) to the leaders exhorted in 5:1, one who, like these and other believers, is a witness to Christ's suffering (i.e., suffering as a Christian—4:16). The author exhibits a good command of Greek style and rhetoric, employs an extensive vocabulary, and handles adroitly, in a unified style, a wide range of early paraenetic tradition. In effect the author's style has often been characterized as rhythmic and poetic and, on the whole, as literary rather than colloquial. One finds in this letter an extensive use of imperatives with participles to convey a balanced yet urgent paraenesis to a troubled area of the Christian Church. One is probably justified in viewing this author as belonging to a Petrine group in Rome (that is, Babylon—5:13) who employs the name of the apostle to give added authority to the advice being given. There is much evidence in the NT (Paul, Acts, 1 Peter) and early post-NT writers (especially Clement of Rome and Papias) to postulate the existence of such a Petrine circle to which this author and that of the later writer of 2 Peter belonged. Appeal is here made to the venerable figures of Peter, Silvanus, and Mark as a mechanism to authenticate the group's advice to the communities of Asia Minor and to underscore the *koinonia* or fellowship that exists between the writer's community and those of the addressees (5:9, 12-14). In any case the author employs not the reflections of an early follower of Jesus but the diverse, evolved paraenesis of the early Church to help the addressees confront the challenge of being a minority in an often-hostile pagan environment. While the author is sensitive to the communities' hardships or sufferings and inserts an occasional personal note ("we"—1:3; 4:17 or "I"—2:11; 5:1, 12-13), the overall tone of the document is that of a circular letter that is written to several Roman provinces and allegedly delivered by Silvanus (5:12). Thus one must conclude that the author is a Hellenistic member and leader of the Roman Church who is writing in Peter's name, employing Jewish tradition (especially from the LXX) and the community's inherited soteriological and paraenetic material, to address the ecclesial and social problems that the communities of Asia Minor find particularly vexing but that are of a kind with those encountered by Christians elsewhere (5:9). Finally, the author, who is Hellenistic in culture and sympathies, firmly believes that an accommodation can and will soon be found between Christian and pagan neighbors.

Audience

Since the addressees are characterized as "exiles of the Dispersion" (see also Jas 1:1), since extensive use is made of the Hebrew Scriptures and its imagery (e.g.: "you are a chosen race, a royal priesthood, a holy nation, a people for his possession"—2:9), and since outsiders are called Gentiles (2:12; 4:3), one might be tempted to view the community as composed of Jewish converts. However, such statements as 1:14 ("desires that you formerly had in ignorance") or 18 ("the futile ways inherited from your ancestors"—see also 4:2-4) clearly point to Gentile converts. Furthermore, the letter is not concerned with typically Jewish issues such as kosher food laws, circumcision, and the Law generally. Such Jewish terminology as Diaspora, Gentiles, or OT ecclesial imagery no doubt derive from Hellenistic Jewish-Christian tradition and might even suggest an author with a related background (see earlier). Thus this choice of socioreligious imagery underscores, as does the use of "aliens and exiles" (1:1; 2:11) and a "duty code" (2:11–3:12), the author's predilection for political and communal imagery in focusing on the addressees' situation vis-à-vis their Greco-Roman neighbors.

If the term "Diaspora" in the author's designation of the audience signals Christian appropriation of Jewish terminology to represent believers as living in the midst of non-Christians, what might one say of the term "exile" (also "aliens and exiles" in 2:11; see also 1:17)? Were these Christian communities composed primarily of people from outside Asia Minor who moved there either as permanent or resident aliens (*paroikoi*) or as temporary or visiting merchants (*parepidemoi*)? Were they considered "exiles from heaven" (as in Heb 11:13—"strangers and foreigners on the earth"), or is the terminology the author's way of describing both the Christians' religious and political relation to the official culture in which they reside?

In the first case one could insist on the alien status of the group to underscore the members' limited economic resources and small-town or rural setting. Thus one would explain the importance of sheep, or shepherd (1:19; 2:25; 5:2-4), of lion (5:8), or of slave (from countryside estates or agricultural and commercial settings—2:18f) imagery. In any case one would focus, wrongly, on the literal situation of the addressees rather than on the author's choice of imagery in light of strategy. In the second case the option to see these terms as related exclusively to a "pilgrimage" theology does less than justice to the author's focus on conduct vis-à-vis governmental and social structures (see 2:11f). The third option is best suited to the author's purpose because Christians, who do not participate fully in the socioreligious life of the pagan culture, are in fact marginal or less-than-full participants ("exiles and resident aliens"—see discussion below of 2:11) in Roman society. Since on one occasion all the addressees are called "exiles" (1:1) and on another their lives are characterized as "your time as resident aliens" (1:17), one would have to conclude that the author has chosen terminology that describes not the audience's ethnic and economic status but that characterizes both the Christians' elect, exile status (and consequent innocent suffering) and their resident status vis-à-vis Roman culture (and consequent responsibility of acting honorably within Roman society—as far as Christian principles permit). See further discussion below of occasion and strategy.

Also, the addressees are said to reside "in Pontus, Galatia, Cappadocia, Asia, and Bithynia." The area so designated would encompass all the Roman provinces of Asia Minor, omitting only the areas contiguous with Syria to the south (namely Cilicia and Lycia-Pamphylia), that is, the area south of the Taurus Mountains. The sequence of names, beginning and ending with the designation of the double province of Pontus-Bithynia, seems, as usually proposed, to suggest a route to be traveled by the bearer of the circular letter, namely, arrival at Pontus from Rome, travel south and west to successive provinces, and return of the original to the point of arrival. Further information is available concerning the Christians of the area from Pliny the Younger (*Letters* 10.96), the governor of Pontus-Bithynia in 111–1113, in a letter to Emperor Trajan concerning the growth of this new movement and its threat to state-sanctioned religion. Interestingly, he mentions that, even twenty years earlier, circa 90 (the approximate date of 1 Peter), there existed many Christians in the area, some of whom, under government pressure, had even renounced their faith.

So we might conclude this discussion of the addressees by insisting that, despite the traditional association of Paul with the provinces of Asia and Galatia (see especially the narrative of Acts 15f), little is known about the evangelization of the entire area in question and that in effect Paul had minimal contact with this area, save for the provinces just mentioned. It is perhaps for this reason that well-known missionary figures such as Silvanus and Mark are invoked in 1 Peter's letter closing (5:12-13). Additionally, it is usually maintained that the addressees are newly baptized converts whose new situation as believers has brought about an intolerable conflict with the local population. Such a conclusion is derived especially from the author's use of "new birth" terminology (1:3f). Careful analysis instead shows that this language reveals more about Christian commitment and existence than about the "recent" status of the converts. 1 Peter is addressed to members who are both older and more recent in their Christian commitment (see analysis of 5:1-5) and, beyond this, addresses the complex issue of Christian and non-Christian relations. In effect the author is aware that believers are both "resident aliens" who are to live as responsible members of the Roman state and "religious exiles" who must live honorable lives among non-Christians (see 2:11 and discussion there). This document is both a letter of consolation in the midst of crisis (5:12) and an appeal to a beleaguered Christian minority to live as responsible "free people" who are also "servants of God" (2:16-17).

Composition and Content

A feature of post-Pauline writing is that documents tend to lose the personal characteristics of epistolary literature. Even in Paul, while the letter remains a means of communication with the members of the community, it becomes increasingly a vehicle of general exhortation. Likewise, the Paulinist writings, while retaining the epistolary features of the Hellenistic letter, emphasize further the letter's didactic and exhortatory functions. 1 Peter shares in this tendency. It too retains basic epistolary characteristics because it begins and ends in typical epistolary fashion with a standard opening (sender, addressee, greeting) and closing (greeting, doxology, benediction). However, though it starts with a blessing (similar to that of 2 Corinthians and Ephesians) and doctrinal statement (1:3f— the two coincide), it soon adopts the form and tone of later paraenetic epistles (1:6f, 13f). From the start, the letter alternates traditional doctrinal teaching with exhortatory imperatives and indicative statements of theological justification, motivation, and example (much use of "as or like"). As one might expect in epistolary literature, the author, besides employing the ubiquitous imperative and complementary participial construction, often addresses the audience directly (1:1; 2:11; 4:12 and especially in paraenetic sections) to offer advice concerning its particular situation.

The body of the letter has, in the past, presented problems for scholars interested in 1 Peter. It was common in the first half of the century to view the main part of this document as consisting of two sources, a liturgical tract or baptismal homily followed by a later paraenetic text about persecution. Recent redactional, structural, and thematic analyses are convincing that see 1 Peter as a unitary composition whose epistolary features are not a later addition to a primitive sermon but are integral to the document. Indeed, structural and theological examination on the one hand and vocabulary and stylistic studies on the other show that there exist numerous structural and thematic links between the sections and that various parts of the structure serve particular epistolary and strategic functions.

While there continues to be debate concerning the structure of 1 Peter, scholars readily admit that between the opening (1:1-2) and closing (5:12-14), the author has inserted several major blocks of material. Owing to structural (use of "beloved" at 2:11 and 4:12 to introduce two major blocks) and thematic (see below) considerations, I conclude that the author of 1 Peter organizes the document into three major sections: 1:3f, 2:11f, 4:12f. I therefore offer the following outline for the forthcoming commentary:

Opening (1:1-2)	exiles, chosen, Diaspora
Through Mercy, Chosen To Be God's People (1:3–2:10)	1:1, 3 vs. 2:9-10
Blessing: New Birth, Joy, Salvation (1:3-12)	born anew, test by fire, rejoice, suffer
Conduct: Holiness, Faith, Love (1:13-25)	obedient children
Growth as God's People (2:1-10)	newborn babies
Exhortation for Resident Aliens and Religious Exiles (2:11–4:11)	beloved/exhort
Honorable Conduct: Duty Code (2:11–3:12)	aliens and exiles, duty, do evil/good
Soteriological and Paradigmatic Role of Suffering (3:13–4:6)	to do you evil
Community Exhortation in View of the End (4:7-11)	end at hand
Final Considerations and Renewed Exhortation (4:12–5:11)	beloved
Sharing Christ's Sufferings (4:12-19)	fiery ordeal, rejoice
Community Code and Exhortation (5:1-5)	exhort, duty
Closing Exhortation (5:6-11)	devil, suffer
Closing (5:12-14)	likewise chosen, Babylon

In considering the stylistic and thematic unity of 1 Peter, it would be well to examine the author's iterative, indeed structural use of terms and themes, particularly the list of terms given above. For example, the initial reference to the author as "Peter, apostle of Jesus Christ" (1:1) is matched by a self-designation at the end as "fellow elder and witness to the sufferings of Christ" (5:1) and by an appeal to Petrine associates: Silvanus and "my son Mark" (5:12-13). Also the letter identifies the addressees as "chosen exiles of the Diaspora" (1:1) and associates these with the host community as "she who is in Babylon, elected [or chosen] along with you" (5:13). Thus both the writer (as member of a sister church) and the addressees (living in the Roman province) are exiles of the Diaspora.

Beyond this, the above list of terms attempts to illustrate the numerous and convincing literary and theological links that exist between various parts of the composition. Thus the first major block, which focuses on God's choice of a people (1:3–2:10), repeatedly emphasizes the theme of new life: "born anew," "obedient children," and "newborn babes" (see 1:3, 14; 2:2; also 1:23). Also the opening of the letter, which focuses on the themes of choice and birth (1:1, 3), forms an inclusio with the ending of the first block concerning God's chosen race and elect people (2:9-10). Additionally, the second and third major blocks (2:11–4:11; 3:12–5:11, respectively), which are explicitly qualified as exhortation (see 2:11; 5:11), employ peculiar, repetitive terminology to underscore their particular emphasis. In the case of the second block one hears of "aliens and exiles" (2:11; see also 1:1, 17), who "are spoken against [or maligned] as evildoers" (see 2:11; 3:16) but are encouraged to "do good" and "not evil" (2:14, 20; 3:12-13f), and to perform "honorable deeds" (2:12) as they honor or "perform their duty toward others" (use of the verb *hupotasso*). In the case of the last mentioned the author employs repeatedly the term to "do one's duty toward" or its equivalent ("likewise") to develop at length a complex "duty code" (2:13, 18; 3:1, 7). In the case of the third block one hears once again about exhortation (5:1), rejoicing (4:13; see 1:6f), a fiery ordeal (4:12; see 1:6-7), temporary suffering (5:10; see 1:6), and "doing one's duty" once more (5:5; see 2:13f). Finally, both the second and third blocks end on an apocalyptic note: "the end of all things is near" (4:7) and "the devil who prowls like a roaring lion" (5:8). In structural and thematic terms then one must speak of a unified composition and in light of this one might seek the author's purpose and message.

This last point brings us to a consideration of the letter's thematic focus as this relates to its structure and prepares for a discussion of its occasion, strategy, and message. If at an earlier date scholars proposed "baptism or new life" as the dominant motif at least for a major portion of the document and concluded from this proposal that a baptismal or liturgical source laid the foundation for the composition of 1 Peter, more recent scholarship rejects this view and instead proposes a variety of themes as providing a key to the understanding of this Petrine letter. There are in fact two basic approaches to this issue. On the one hand, a concerted effort is made to isolate the author's larger or controlling metaphor, that is, the metaphor that provides the basis for understanding the other figurative language of 1 Peter or for explaining the author's overall message. Thus one could argue for "the house of God," "the new people of God," or "the Diaspora" as the major theme or controlling metaphor. In the first case one would see the use of "house (*oikos*) of God" (2:9) as the author's way to foster social cohesion within the Christian community as a counterbalance to the "alien" (*paroikos*—2:11) status of the community's members within the greater society. In the second case one would argue that the author sees the Christian community as a new "people of God" (2:10) patterned on Israel as a chosen people (the letter's imagery is invariably explained as deriving from the OT) and constituted by Christ's suffering and so offering a pattern for the community's situation. In still another instance it is claimed that the concept of "Diaspora" (1:1—see also "Babylon" in 5:13) constitutes the author's controlling metaphor and therefore explains the letter's rich symbolic language and addresses the audience as the "sufferers of the Dispersion." One suspects that in each case an important but linguistically limited concept has been made to bear a far too great burden and that the author's text has been made to fit a given perspective. One also wonders how valid hermeneutically the concept of a "controlling metaphor" is in explaining an author's point of view, strategy, and message.

On the other hand, some scholars have taken a less literary approach (i.e., choosing a theme or metaphor that seems to explain others) and have proposed concepts that address what they perceive to be the community's problem. Thus some insist that the letter focuses on the future and gives the community reassurances or comfort for its suffering. First Peter then is seen as thematically focused on Christian living in a non-Christian society and the suffering often resulting from differing social and religious perspectives. There is, however, a broader perspective that in 1 Peter addresses not only present suffering as Christ has done in the past but also the promise of glory. There is in the search for a proper understanding of 1 Peter a need to examine more carefully the author's purpose for writing.

Occasion, Strategy, and Message

From the outset the modern reader is made aware of the addressees' situation. They are in effect "suffering various trials" (1:6), and the author is writing to offer encouragement or consolation (5:12). Thus the theme of suffering is paramount throughout, and 1 Peter is intent on developing a theology of suffering to address the situation of the provinces of Asia Minor.

Occasion

The theme of suffering has readily been recognized as underscoring the community's situation, but that situation has not always been understood in the same way. Indeed earlier scholarship has generally seen this suffering as related to persecution and has usually focused on the "fire" terminology of 1:7 and 4:12 as well as the explicit parallels drawn with Jesus' suffering ("sharing the sufferings of Christ"—4:13). Thus scholars routinely appealed to three persecution dates: the time of Nero (54–68), of Domitian (81–96), or of the Trajan-Pliny correspondence (c. 112).

More recent scholarship questions the wisdom of such an analysis and has concluded that 1 Peter focuses on Christian suffering not as a result of persecution but as the result of hostility, harassment, and social, unofficial ostracism on the part of the general populace. The author perceives the Christian reality as that of a minority culture within the Greco-Roman world. Beyond the realization of modern scholars that many references to early Roman persecutions were more imagined than real, careful analysis of the text of 1 Peter points also to such a conclusion. The "fire" imagery noted above describes not the suffering itself but its purpose, that of "purifying the believer's faith" (use of "testing or trial" terminology). Furthermore, when 1 Peter speaks of suffering at the hands of nonbelievers, the treatment is described in terms of "speaking against or maligning" Christians as "evil-doers" (2:12; 3:16) or of believers being "reviled or insulted on account of the name of Christ" (4:14), and these opponents are characterized by the term *epereazo* (3:16), people who "insult or treat with spite or abuse" (LSJ 620). The issue then is that of pagan slander or misunderstanding, and the addressees are exhorted to act honorably according to God's will and thereby "silence the ignorance of foolish humans" (2:15). Also they are advised to "always be ready with a defense to anyone who demands . . . an accounting" (3:15).

Furthermore, the author's view of Roman culture sheds additional light on the occasion for writing. On the one hand, while there are several negative references to pagan culture, these are expressed in a formulaic, Christian fashion. The believers' former pagan loyalties are described as "desires that [they] formerly had in ignorance" (1:14; see also 2:15 and 4:2) or as "the futile ways inherited from [their] ancestors" (1:18). Clearly the author wishes to underscore the Christian's new way of life as holiness and purity (1:15-16, 22). But the addressees are urged "to abstain from the desires of the flesh [natural impulses] in as much as they wage war against the soul" (2:11) and from their former Gentile "excesses of dissipation" (list of vices) and "forbidden idolatry" (4:3-4). Thus Christians have been called "out of darkness into his marvelous light" (2:9) but they are to renounce precisely those excesses and vices that challenge or attack their new way of life (see discussion of 2:11). From such a perspective certain aspects of Roman culture and behavior were precisely what believers renounced when they were converted to the Christian way of life, but they were also called upon to live among a Gentile majority and to honor all, including the emperor (2:17).

On the other hand, there is both a positive attitude toward Roman culture and a recognition that conflict with the general populace results from "malice, guile, insincerity, envy, and slander" (2:1) on its part. There is basic agreement that political institutions are for the common good and that believers are to discharge their duty toward all human beings, including governmental authorities "sent for the punishment of evildoers but the praise of doers of good" (2:14). Thus the author seeks both to encourage those who suffer unjustly (owing to harsh superiors or husbands) by offering the example of Christ's innocent suffering and to address areas of conflict by advising gentle, reverent defense (3:15-16), honorable activity in the midst of patient suffering (2:12; passim), and suitable social as well as Christlike behavior (proper acceptance of authority as well as submission to God's will—see especially 2:11-3:12).

Strategy

In view of heightened pagan-Christian conflict or tension, the author addresses first the Christian reality of new life that resulted from the Father's call, the Spirit's sanctifying activity, and Jesus' obedient submission of his life for the salvation of the believer (1:2). Thus the author speaks repeatedly in the first section (1:3–2:10) of "new birth" (1:3), "children of obedience" (v. 14), God as "Father" (v. 17), "being born anew" (v. 23), and of "newborn infants" (2:2). Such an emphasis on Christian life as the result of God's choice or call (1:1, 3, 15) and creation of a new people (2:4-5, 9-10) lays the foundation for a more concrete and extended discussion of the community's situation. It is in this part of the letter that the author emphasizes the contrast between the past and the present: the old life and the new, the darkness and the light, the time of the prophets and that of Christ (1:10-11), no people nor mercy and God's people with mercy (2:10). It is also in this part of the letter that the author underscores, in the past, Jesus' soteriological role because his death ("the precious blood of Christ like that of a lamb") ransomed the addressees from their former life (1:18-19). It is by contrast to their pre-conversion past and by appeal to the shedding of Christ's blood that the author is able to focus on the community's present reality as God's new people and in this context to address its particular situation.

In part two (2:11–4:11) the author addresses the communities' "behavior among the Gentiles," especially in response to the misguided accusations and slander that are being leveled against the community of believers (2:12, 15). It is here that one finds more specifically the author's message to the communities of Asia Minor. Before discussing that topic, however, it is necessary to focus on an interesting feature of the author's strategy.

The key to the strategy of 1 Peter is to be found in its image of Jesus and its use of the themes of suffering and glory. The writer has inherited from the early community a traditional exaltation christology, developed on the binary kerygmatic pattern of death/resurrection (1:21; 3:18b). Early Christian believers focused on Jesus' death and his vindication by God in the resurrection. However, this was but the beginning of the Christ-event because Jesus' post-resurrection activity was essential to Christian belief, whether his appearances to his followers, his "preaching to the spirits in prison," his victory over "angels, authorities, and powers," or his enthronement in glory at God's right hand (3:19, 22). Drawing from such a christological schema, involving suffering/death, resurrection/being alive in the Spirit, cosmic domination, and enthronement/glory, the author chooses to emphasize the initial and final moments within that christological progression: suffering/death and enthronement/glory.

As regards the first it is clear that the author accepts and is interested in the soteriological function of Jesus' death because it is through his death that believers are ransomed, freed from sin, and healed (see 1:18-19; 2:24; 3:18), but it is the related concept of "suffering" that receives the greater attention. Owing to the community's situation, the author speaks on occasion of Jesus' death as the basis of new life but dwells more particularly on Jesus' passion or suffering as the pattern of unmerited suffering. Thus the author's focus on death, on the one hand, relates to the soteriological foundation of the Christian community and its praxis; on the other hand, the preference for the theme of suffering relates to the reason for writing. The second element of the author's pattern (glory) is also chosen with the community's situation in mind. The author could have stressed the theme of resurrection, as does Paul in 1 Corinthians 15, to establish a foundation for Christian hope, but this author dwells on the theme of glory (*doxa*). A review of the texts where this term appears in 1 Peter shows that it refers either to the glory that God has given Jesus or that which the believer will share when Jesus returns at the final revelation. The term "glory" then is chosen to emphasize the heavenly or post-resurrection life of Jesus and its bearing upon the Christian's life as an alien and exile.

The themes of suffering and glory, representing the contours of the Christ-event, offer the framework for the author's understanding of the Christian's life in the world and allows for a paraenetic application of the Christ-event to those suffering unjustly in the provinces of Asia Minor. Having established a doctrinal basis for exhortation, the author develops the letter's major thesis: Jesus is the Christian's model of suffering and glory (2:21—"leaving you an example that you might follow in his footsteps"); between these two poles—the suffering that has ransomed humanity and the establishment in glory that is a future reality for the believer—lies an interim period of crucial importance to author and audience.

Message

A major feature of 1 Peter is the extended foundation that is laid for the following paraenetic treatment of the community's situation. Basically, the author wishes to underscore the fact that as a result of God's call through the Christ-event, mercy was conferred on humanity and a new people constituted. By means of the death and resurrection of Jesus, whether employing the imagery of ransom, purification, conversion, or new birth, the author establishes the basis for the community's unity, strength, and source of life. Though tested and in religious exile, it is nonetheless a house built of living stones, along with the rejected, chosen, and precious salvific stone. It is a chosen race, a royal priesthood, and a holy nation (2:4-5, 9). It is God's own people and so children of the Father, children whose task it is likewise to be holy (1:14-15). Through Jesus' salvific death God has given new life to humanity and has acquired a new people. This then serves as a foundation for the remainder of the paraenetic letter.

By means of the theme of suffering, chosen in lieu of death, the author addresses the community's unhappy situation. First, it should be noted that the author is neither encouraging nor preparing for martyrdom. Instead the term "suffering" is chosen because the author has in mind the pain, abuse, and ostracism that Christians as a minority group suffer in a pagan society. Indeed the reference at the beginning and end (1:6; 5:10) to suffering "for a little while" suggests that the strained relations between Christians and non-Christians have reached what is expected to be a temporary setback in the form of slander (and perhaps prosecution). Nonetheless, the harsh Gentile treatment (2:1) seems to have been provoked by mischief making (4:15) or less-than-honorable conduct (2:11) and harsh response (3:15). Instead the author appeals to the innocent Christ "who when abused did not return abuse, when suffering did not threaten" (2:23). Believers are advised to repay evil and abuse with a blessing (3:9), to make a defense with gentleness and reverence (3:15-16), to behave with honor, and to suffer only "on account of the name of Christ" (4:14). Ultimately the goal of such behavior is threefold: good days and peace (3:10-12), a heavenly inheritance (1:4; 3:9), and the acknowledgement of God's lordship by nonbelievers (2:12, 15, 23; 3:1-2,

15-16). In these extreme circumstances the Christian, like Christ, must trust "the faithful creator," "the one who judges justly" (4:19; 2:23). Thus the author relates the acute suffering of the addressees to a christological model because imitation of Christ means obedience to God's plan (1:2, 14, 11), the testing of one's faith (fire terminology), love of friend and foe (1:22; 3:8 and 2:12; 3:6), responsible living within a society that must be subjected to God on the day of visitation (2:12), and gentle, rational, and evangelistic confrontation with non-Christian neighbors (2:9; 3:15, 19, 22).

While the term "glory" in the majority of cases refers to Christ's heavenly enthronement or the future participation in this by the believer, it is important to emphasize that for 1 Peter the future reality of glory is so crucial and dynamic that it impinges on the interim period. Thus the spirit of glory rests now upon the believer (4:14) who in anticipation is to rejoice with indescribable and glorious joy (1:8) that God may be glorified through Jesus Christ (4:11). This is the reason for the author's emphasis on Christ's glory, because not only is it a goal that gives hope (the resurrection theme would have sufficed), but also it is the goal of all things to be glorified at the final revelation.

The document goes beyond the critical, immediate problem of suffering by focusing on the interim period in ethical and eschatological terms. In ethical terms the author shows great concern for the community's relations with all humans (2:13, 17): fellow members as well as outsiders. Good behavior and patient suffering are frequently encouraged. The last two sections of the letter are devoted almost entirely to moral and social exhortation, particularly the duty code of 2:11–3:12, which offers moral guidance to encourage conduct figured to nullify pagan slanders and acts as a charter for confronting inquisitive outsiders and even for encouraging an outward missionizing thrust; and the parallel community exhortations (3:8f; 4:7f) and code (5:1-5), which address community life, behavior, and relations. Thus the author hopes that husbands will be converted (3:1), that foolish neighbors might be silenced (2:15), that unbelieving compatriots might glorify God in the end (2:12), and that God's varied gifts might be shared ungrudgingly with other believers (4:7-10) who must be the object of love and respect (3:8; 4:8; 5:5). The audience is told to live in the world as Christians, not as Gentiles (4:1-6), that by their good deeds and responsible living these same Gentiles might render glory and make society itself subject to God now and on the day of visitation (2:12; 3:10-12, 15-16).

In eschatological terms the author sees the whole of God's plan as revealed in Christ who was "destined before the foundation of the world but manifested at the end of the ages" (1:20). The focus of the plan is on the audience, as the author ends v. 20 with the phrase "for your sake." Also, the prophets predicted Christ's suffering and glory as being a model for the suffering audience of the provinces of Asia Minor (1:12), a plan so marvelous that even angels longed to see it. The "now" of God's plan is focused on the community's new life, brought about by Christ's death and resurrection and devoted to following in his footsteps (2:21), while being under God's protection and awaiting the endtime (1:5; see also 5:10). The time is short (4:7), and the eschatological enemy is on the prowl (5:8); in the meantime the believer is to look to God's just judgment (2:23; 4:5-6).

We return to the author's striking use of metaphors to examine how proposals concerning these relate to the occasion, strategy, and message of the letter. There is no doubt that the theme of "people of God" is an important one for the author, particularly as it relates to other communal terms (2:4f, 9f) and provides the ecclesial foundation for the letter's paraenesis. Much the same can be said about "house(hold) of God" because it too relates to the theme of divine election and provides a socioreligious context (God as father, Christians as children or members of households—see the term *oiketai* or "household members" in 2:18) for the community's life within a Roman environment. How the themes of "aliens and exiles" and "diaspora" relate to these is debatable (see earlier). Further, does 1 Peter view Christian life as an eschatological journey of a community whose election has brought about its estrangement from the general population? Indeed the author's plea to the addressees to "live in reverent fear during the time of [their] exile" (1:17, NRSV; but see below) would seem to confirm the latter and to argue against viewing the audience as geographically displaced persons living temporarily in Asia Minor. Thus 1 Peter has been interpreted as combatting possible defection from the Christian way of life or as fostering inner cohesion for a pilgrim people. The author's purpose in writing, particularly the use of a duty code, would not indicate assimilation or outreach to Roman culture but rather would warn against conformity or accommodation to pagan practices and would stress Christian separation from outside influences, on the one hand, and unity and cohesion within its own ranks, on the other.

Several factors lead me to propose a different interpretation. First, while 1 Peter stresses Christian praxis and the disavowal of a pagan way of life, there seems to be a pervasive attempt in the letter not to assimilate pagan excesses but to find accommodation with non-Christian neighbors and Roman institutions, except where innocent suffering is concerned. The duty code and the general advice (gentle and reverent defense—3:15-16) point to the author's desire for a *modus vivendi* with the Roman populace.

Second, the perspective of 1 Peter is less that of a pilgrim people whose commitment to secular culture is tenuous or adversarial as that of a chosen race that desires to return to its maker. It is not an accident that believers are to trust God precisely as the "faithful creator" (4:19), "the God of all grace, the one who called [them] to his eternal glory through Christ" (5:10). They come from a faithful creator and return to the God who has destined them for glory; indeed their life on earth is seen not as a "time of exile" but of political and social activity (see discussion of 1:17), a time that will terminate when the Messiah "brings [them] before God" (3:18).

Third, the author's use of political-social imagery has a dual function. On the one hand, the use of "alien, exile, and diaspora" terminology underscores the journey motif of Christians who look to heaven for their "imperishable, undefiled, and unfading inheritance" (1:4) when they are brought back home by their shepherd and guardian (2:25). The time is a temporary but essential journey away from home. On the other hand, the use of this imagery, precisely as political metaphors, stresses the Christian's relationship to and responsibility toward the Roman populace and its institutions. The terms "resident aliens and temporary visitors or exiles" as describing the Christians of Asia Minor refer less to their lack of status and rights as to real, though limited, sociopolitical rights and responsibilities—with God as protector and judge. The addressees are committed as creatures, as a chosen people, and as resident aliens to see that "God is glorified in all things through Jesus Christ" (4:11) as they await the return of the chief shepherd who will bring a never-fading crown of glory (5:4) and will lead them back to the God in whom they trust (1:21; 3:18; 5:6).

Commentaries

Achtemeier, P. J. "1 Peter" in *Harper's Bible Commentary*. Ed., J. L. Mays. San Francisco: Harper, 1988, 1279-85.

__________. *1 Peter*. Minneapolis: Fortress, 1996.

Arichea, D. C., and E. A. Nida. *A Translator's Handbook on the First Letter from Peter*. New York: UBS, 1980.

Bartlett, D. L. "The First Letter of Peter" in *NIB*, 12:227-319.

Beare, F. W. *The First Epistle of Peter: The Greek Text with Introduction and Notes*. Oxford: Blackwell, 1970.

Best, E. *1 Peter*. Grand Rapids: Eerdmans, 1982.

Boring, M. E. *1 Peter*. Nashville: Abingdon, 1999.

Brox, N. *Der erste Petrusbrief*. Zurich: Benziger, 1979.

Calloud, J., and F. Genuyt. *La première épître de Pierre: analyse sémiotique*. Paris: Cerf, 1982.

Craddock, F. G. *First and Second Peter and Jude.* Westminster: John Knox, 1995.

Dalton, W. J. "The First Epistle of Peter" in *NJBC*, 903-908.

Davids, P. H. *The First Epistle of Peter.* Grand Rapids: Eerdmans, 1990.

Elliott, J. H. *I-II Peter/Jude* (with R. A. Martin, *James*). Minneapolis: Augsburg, 1982.

Goppelt, L. *A Commentary on 1 Peter.* Grand Rapids: Eerdmans, 1993.

Kelly, J. N. D. *Commentary on the Epistles of Peter and of Jude.* New York: Harper & Row, 1970.

Marshall, I. H. *1 Peter.* Downers Grove IL: InterVarsity, 1991.

Michaels, J. R. *1 Peter.* Waco TX: Word Books, 1988.

Perkins, P. *First and Second Peter, James, and Jude.* Louisville KY: John Knox, 1995.

Selwyn, E. G. *The First Epistle of St. Peter.* London: Macmillan, 1981.

Senior, D. *1 and 2 Peter.* Wilmington DE: Glazier, 1980.

Suggested Readings

Achtemeier, P. J. "Newborn Babes and Living Stones: Literal and Figurative in 1 Peter" in *To Touch the Text: Biblical and Related Studies.* Eds., M. P. Horgan and P. J. Kobelski. New York: Crossroad, 1989, 207-36.

Balch, D. L. *Let Wives Be Submissive: The Domestic Code in 1 Peter.* Chico: Scholars, 1981.

__________. "Hellenization/Acculturation in 1 Peter" in *PFP*, 79-101.

Bechtler, S. R. *Following in His Steps. Suffering, Community, and Christology in 1 Peter.* Atlanta: Scholars, 1998.

Bovon, F. "Foi chrétienne et religion populaire dans la première épître de Pierre." *ETR* 53 (1978) 25-41.

Brox, N. "Situation und Sprache der Minderheit im ersten Petrusbrief." *Kairos* 19 (1977) 1-13.

Campbell, B. L. *Honor, Shame, and the Rhetoric of 1 Peter.* Atlanta: Scholars, 1998.

Cothenet, E. "Les orientations actuelles de l'exégèse de la Première Lettre de Pierre" and "Bibiligraphie sélective sur la Première Lettre de Pierre" in *Etudes*, 13-42 and 269-74.

Dalton, W. J. *Christ's Proclamation to the Spirits: A Study of 1 Peter 3:18–4:6.* Rome: BPI, 1989.

Elliott, J. H. *A Home for the Homeless: A Sociological Exegesis of 1 Peter, Its Situation and Strategy.* Philadelphia: Fortress, 1981.

__________. "The Rehabilitation of an Exegetical Stepchild: 1 Peter in Recent Research" in *PFP*, 3-16.

__________. "1 Peter, Its Situation and Strategy: A Discussion with David Balch" in *PFP*, 61-78.

Feldmeier, R. *Die Christen als Fremde: Die Metapher der Fremde in der antiken Welt, im Urchristentum und im 1. Petrusbrief.* Tübingen: Mohr-Siebeck, 1992.

Herzer, J. *Petrus order Paulus? Studien über das Verhältnis des Ersten Petrusbriefes zur paulinischen Tradition*. Tübingen: Mohr-Siebeck, 1998.

Lepelley, C. "Le contexte historique de la Première Lettre de Pierre" in *Etudes*, 43-64.

Lohse, E. "Parenesis and Kerygma in 1 Peter" in *PFP*, 37-59.

Martin, T. W. *Metaphor and Composition in 1 Peter*. Atlanta: Scholars, 1992.

Prostmeier, F. R. *Handlungsmodelle im ersten Petrusbrief*. Würzburg: Echter, 1990.

Richard, E. "First Peter" in *Jesus: One and Many. The Christological Concept of New Testament Authors*. Wilmington: Glazier, 1988, 380-87.

__________.The Functional Christology of First Peter" in *PFP*, 121-39.

Schutter, W. L. *Hermeneutic and Composition in 1 Peter*. Tübingen: Mohr-Siebeck, 1989.

Soards, M. L. "1 Peter, 2 Peter, and Jude as Evidence for a Petrine School" in *ANRW* 2.25.5 (1988) 3828-49.

Sylva, D. "The Critical Exploration of 1 Peter" in *PFP*, 17-36.

Tarrech, A. P. "Le milieu de la Première Epître de Pierre." *RCT* 5 (1980) 95-129, 331-402.

Thurén, L. *The Rhetorical Strategy of 1 Peter. With Special Regard to Ambiguous Expressions*. Abo: Abo Academy, 1990.

Vanhoye, A. "1 Pierre au carrefour des théologies du nouveau testament" in *Etudes*, 97-128.

Opening

The opening of 1 Peter follows the stereotyped format of the ancient letter, an opening that consists of a tripartite formula: writer, to addressees, greeting. It is clear from this formula (1:1-2) and from the document's standard closing (5:12-14) that it is a genuine letter although its other features, tone, and content underscore its general paraenetic nature and support the conclusion that it was written as a circular letter to the Roman provinces of Asia Minor. In epistolary terms it compares favorably with the standard Pauline letter in its use of the letter form. It is addressed to a large though specific group of communities (see Gal 1:2), focuses on the addressees' particular situation, and employs the standard conventions of the pastoral letter.

From the outset one notices a number of stylistic and thematic features that point to the letter's cultural, theological, and pastoral sophistication. The writer's Petrine claim and alleged relation to Jesus, as stated in the letter opening, are matched by similar references in 5:1 to the author's self-designation as fellow elder and witness to Christ's sufferings and in 5:12-13 to traditional Petrine figures: Silvanus as faithful brother and Mark as son. Also, the writing formula of the opening, the designation of the addressees as chosen and residing in the Diaspora, and the greeting involving grace and peace are balanced by similar concerns in the epistolary closing because there the author explicitly speaks of writing to the addressees and of sending greetings from their sister church, which is characterized as chosen and residing in Babylonian exile. Finally appeal is made to the grace of God and to peace in Christ.

Writer

(1:1a)

The letter begins simply by claiming Petrine authorship and, although the author will return to this theme at the end of the letter, there is no attempt initially to bolster this claim except by employing the designation "apostle of Jesus Christ." Use of this traditional formula (see the openings of the Paulinist letters), besides underscoring the alleged writer's exalted status, seeks to establish the author's role, more fundamentally, as well as that of other preachers and elders, as "one sent (*apostolos*) by Christ" through the Spirit (1:12) and as witnesses of Christ's suffering and glory (5:1). It is the relationship to Jesus and his role, as one who saves by his blood and as one who suffers as obedient servant, which is paramount to the writer of the letter. The writer's role is that of presenting Jesus as the example in whose footsteps the innocent believer must follow (2:21). To this end 1 Peter's claim to be "an apostle of Jesus Christ" is essentially a claim to be sent or to be both one through whom (as foreannounced by the prophets) the good news is preached and through whom Christ's suffering and consequent glory is presented as the paradigm for innocent Christian suffering (see interpretation of 1:10-12).

But why the choice of Peter as pseudonym of a letter of consolation? While many conjectural responses can be given to such a question, it seems logical enough to point to the letter's concern about Christian relations to Roman culture as providing a solid basis for discussion. There is no doubt that one of the major issues confronting the addressees of Asia Minor was the heightened antagonism that existed between believers and their non-Christian neighbors in the eastern provinces where civic loyalty seems to have been a burning issue (see Rev 13). While the author insists both that Christian suffering be precisely innocent suffering in Christ's name (4:14) and that such maltreatment could be the lot of all Christians (5:9 as well as 3:17; 4:14-16) as a minority in a pagan culture, there is insistence on the role that Rome or Babylon plays in this crucial context. On the one hand, while Christian cultural separatism and religious praxis may have contributed to the current antagonism, the addressees are reminded of their duties as wards of the Roman government (2:13-14), as members of Roman households (2:18-3:7), and, more generally, as humans recognizing their duties toward fellow humans (see interpretation of 2:13, 17). As resident aliens within Roman society they have serious responsibilities to honor everyone, including their Roman non-Christian neighbors (2:17). On the other hand, the choice of Peter and Petrine authority (Peter's association with Rome is well established in early ecclesial tradition) as a basis for addressing Christian-pagan relations underscores both the letter's caution in stressing Christian values and goals and its optimism that the critical situation in Asia Minor can be resolved as similar problems have elsewhere, particularly in Rome itself. In spite of like suffering other churches are succeeding, and the sister church in Babylon sends greeting and wishes of peace (5:13-14). Choice therefore of Peter's authority to write from "Rome" to the eastern provinces form part of the author's strategy and the letter's enduring value.

Addressees
(1:1b-2a)

Interestingly, these are designated by two important and intriguing terms, "to the chosen exiles," the second of which is modified by a noun in the genitive and a list of five geographical terms also in the genitive ("of the Diaspora, i.e., in Pontus, Galatia, Cappadocia, Asia, and Bithynia") and the first of which is seemingly qualified later in the structure by a complex triadic formula concerning the Father, the Spirit, and Jesus Christ. While the first of these ("chosen") focuses on divine initiative and describes the addressees' privileged relationship to God (see below for discussion of the triadic formula), the second along with its modifiers speaks of the consequences of this choice in defining the believers' relation to other humans, particularly their seemingly disadvantaged status compared to their pagan neighbors. The terms are interrelated and their function determined by the author's strategy and message.

Rather than the Pauline "saints" (*hagioi*) to designate believers (though see 1:15-16 where Christians are exhorted to be "saints or holy" in conduct; also 3:5), the author employs the term *eklektoi* ("elect, chosen, or holy"; see also 2:9) to indicate separation or setting apart. The term is taken from the Hebrew Scriptures to describe the choice and creation of Israel as God's people separate from the nations (see Deut 7:6-8; 14:1-2). In effect Israel is called "my elect ones" or "my chosen people" (Ps 105:6; Isa 43:20). While the term "elect or chosen ones" is also often employed in apocalyptic literature to designate the righteous of the end-days (Mark 13:20, 22, 27; Rev 17:14), it is rather the earlier meaning of "God's chosen people" that is intended by the author of 1 Peter since the first major section of the letter concludes by calling the community "a chosen race" (*genos eklekton*, borrowed from Isa 43:20) and God's "people," among other OT ecclesial titles (2:9). The theme of election then will dominate the first major part of the letter as the author dwells upon the Christian community as God's people who have received new life through the Christ-event and a call to holiness (see 1:15 for a discussion of the author's use of "call"), which separates believers from their Gentile neighbors (4:3-4) and leads to antagonism and slander —the same is true of Christ who is also characterized as "chosen (*eklektos*), precious" (2:4, 6—see discussion below). Such separation, presumably without the extreme consequences of the Asia Minor situation, is also true of the Roman Church, also designated as "she who is . . . elected" (5:13).

The second term used to designate the addressees, along with its genitive modifiers ("the exiles of the Diaspora"), calls for some attention, particularly its relation to the election theme discussed above. The adjective engaged, *parepidemos*, a late Greek term, refers to temporary residence in a foreign setting, usually used of travelers or ethnic residents in a foreign land (Polybius, *Histories*, 4.4.1-2; 27.6.3; 32.6.4-6). The emphasis then is on being "a foreigner or stranger." Since, however, this designation is modified by *diaspora*, a technical Jewish term for residence outside of Palestine, it is often rendered as "exile, refugee, or sojourner (on earth)." Appeal is made to the earlier meaning of diaspora as the scattering or exile of Israel outside of Palestine as the result of divine judgment and the eschatological awaiting of Israel's restoration from exile (see the LXX of Deut 28:25; Isa 49:6)—the reference to Babylon in 5:13 is usually cited as supporting such an interpretation. Careful examination of 1 Peter, however, points not to "exile" as the result of divine judgment nor even of a "sojourner" status away from a real or heavenly homeland (see Phil 3:20) but rather indicates that the term has a socioreligious sense and points to divine election and its consequent separation and even estrangement from general or pagan society (a similar conception of election and separation appears in Qumran texts: CD 3.21-4.6; 6.4-5; 1QM 1.2-3). Christians have been called by God out of the pagan populace and, like the Jews of the time, as a result of divine election live in communities scattered among the Gentiles, that is, the *diaspora*, a term that has a political nuance and is a virtual synonym for *paroikos*, rendered "resident allien" (see 1:1; 2:11). They are called to a new life of holy conduct as God's "chosen race . . . (and) holy nation" (2:9). Thus the terms selected to describe the addressees (a designation that applies equally to Christians worldwide; see 5:9, 13) prepare for the author's following lengthy treatment of the new life to which the audience has been called, a life that varies considerably from its ancestral way of life (1:18; 4:3-4) but one that still has political responsibilities (see 2:11f). Additionally, such an interpretation is confirmed by structural considerations. The two terms designating the addressees in 1:1 should be rendered not "to the elect exiles" but rather "to the elect, that is, to those who are (religious) exiles living in the Diaspora." Thus the second expression describes the consequences of being chosen and separated religiously from the neighboring population, while the term *diaspora* underscores the audience's political context (see further discussion of 1:17 and 2:11).

Finally the term *diaspora* introduces five geographical areas of Asia Minor where the addressees reside. There is ample evidence, apart from 1 Peter, for early Christian missionary activity in the areas mentioned: for Pontus-Bithynia, see Pliny, *Letters* 10.96; for Galatia, see Paul in Gal 1:2; 4:13-14; for Asia, see the numerous references in Paul, Acts, and the Book of Revelation; but for Cappadocia, there is only Acts 2:9 (Pontus and Asia are also found in this Lukan list). If one can presume that Pliny's statements about the spread of Christian belief in Pontus-Bithynia apply also to the other Anatolian provinces, even to the extent that traditional Roman religious activities and temples are beginning to suffer neglect, then one would have to suggest that the addressees constituted a not-insignificant portion of the population. A vigorous and sizeable Christian movement would have brought to the fore the tension that developed between the Greek inhabitants of the region and the ever-expanding Jesus movement. For further discussion of this locale, the order in which the Roman provinces appear, and other considerations, see the introduction.

The part of the epistolary opening devoted to the addressees ends with an extended threefold structure consisting of parallel prepositional phrases that deal successively with the Father, the Spirit, and Jesus Christ. After an extended commentary on the designation "to those chosen," a commentary that addresses the audience's religious status in their provincial milieu, the author returns to the theme of election to characterize its source, its goal, and its means by employing and adapting a trinitarian formula. Not only does this passage relate to other triadic formulas of the Christian tradition, but also its particular application as related to the addressees' situation recalls the use made of these by other NT writers. Not only are functions pertinent to this author's discussion attributed to Father, Son, or Spirit, but also the order and therefore stress on the final element of the triad further indicate 1 Peter's primary emphasis. Thus Paul makes use of such a formula to stress fellowship in the Spirit in a fractured community (2 Cor 13:13) or proper use of gifts as coming from and activated by the God of gifts (1 Cor 12:4-6). Similar observations can be made for the Paulinist writers who stress the cosmic plan (Eph 4:6—"one God and Father of all") or the authenticity of their eschatological preaching (2 Thess 2:14—God "called you through our proclamation of the good news, so that you may obtain the glory of our Lord Jesus Christ"); see also Jude 20-21 on Jesus as merciful judge. In the case of 1 Peter, while each segment of the formula contributes to the discussion, the emphasis falls finally on Christ's soteriological and paradigmatic role as it relates to the divine choice.

The first part of the formula relates to God as Father (*theos pater*), a theme that is as old as Homer's epithet of Zeus as "father of both humans and gods" (*Odysseus* 1.28; 11.544; a tradition confirmed by Dio Chrysostom, *Orations* 53.12), which is a frequent title for Israel's creative, providential, and all-powerful God (Deut 32:6; 2 Sam 7:14; Mal 1:6; also Philo, *On the Cherubim* 27), and which, owing to Jesus' teaching on God's fatherhood, became a central feature of early Christian thought and prayer. It is stated in 1 Pet 1:2 that the choice of believers was made "according to God the Father's eternal plan or foreknowledge (*prognosis*)"; that is, it is the God of grace, the one who acts as loving parent or father who calls "out of darkness," who gives "new birth," who calls to a life of holiness (5:10; 2:9; 1:3, 15), and, before all time, predetermines the Christ-event (1:20). This choice is attributed to God precisely as father, the one who is called "the God and Father of our Lord Jesus Christ" (1:3) and the one whom believers invoke as father as well as judge (1:17). The one who chose is the one who cares for those who suffer (5:7) and will assist them in their time of difficulty (5:10).

The second part of the formula concerns the Spirit, and it is observed that the process of salvation or "making holy" (*hagiasmos*—see 1:15-16) is the Spirit's domain, from the activity of the prophets, to proclamation of the good news through the heavenly Spirit, to its abiding presence as source of hope (1:10-12; 4:14). By implication, the injunctions to live holy lives and to exhibit honorable and loving conduct (1:15, 22; 2:12) despite difficulties is made possible by the presence of the Spirit (4:14).

The final part of the triadic formula displays a more complex but ambiguous structure concerning Christ's role. Contrary to the frequent interpretation that the goal of this choice is "obedience to Jesus Christ" (see NRSV), it is preferable to view this complex formula as insisting that God made this choice "because of Jesus Christ's obedience and the sprinkling of his blood," an interpretation that explains the theme of obedience in christological terms as a parallel to the shedding or sprinkling of Christ's blood (on the themes of obedience and blood, see discussion of 1:14 and 19, respectively). Thus Jesus' role, indeed his obedience (for this theme see discussion of 1:14), is both soteriological (1:18-19; 2:24—use of sacrificial imagery; see Exod 24:3-8) and paradigmatic because believers, in following the lead of their model (2:21), are called to be "children of obedience," who are subject "to the truth" (1:14, 22). The triadic formula then expounds in a traditional way on the theme of election to prepare for the lengthy discussion (in this first major section) on the believers' new life and to prepare for the author's exhortation (in the following sections) regarding honorable behavior vis-à-vis insiders and outsiders and regarding Jesus as the model of suffering and consequent glory. The focus both here and later is the christological means used by God to call believers to eternal glory (5:10) and the model offered by Christ's innocent suffering (2:21-24). From the beginning the addressees of Asia Minor are reminded of their divine call, its socioreligious implications, and their vocation of obedient following in Christ's footsteps.

Greeting

(1:2b)

The author employs the traditional Christian greeting of "grace and peace," a greeting that is made explicit later in the letter. Beyond the wish that these be multiplied in the lives of the addressees, the author speaks of the themes of grace as a present and future gift from God and of peace as the result of God's salvific activity in Christ. Thus believers are recipients of God's grace in times of suffering (4:14; 5:6, 10), become stewards of this "manifold grace," and are promised grace when Jesus is revealed (1:10, 13; 3:7; 4:10; 5:5, 10, 12). Also, in their relations with outsiders and insiders they are to "seek peace and pursue it" (3:11), be of one mind, love one another, avoid revenge, make their defense with gentleness and reverence (3:8, 16; 4:8), and wish for peace within the community and with those outside (5:14b). So the author can bring the letter to a close by appealing to "the God of all grace" as the one who supports believers in their suffering (5:10) and to Christ as the model of peace, the one whose life is the pattern for Christian existence (2:21; 5:14b) both in relating to the members of the community and in dealing honorably with outsiders.

The letter opening then serves several functions. The author is introduced in strategic terms, first as related to Rome and the community's challenge as regards Roman authority and culture and second as sent by Jesus the example of behavior in the midst of suffering (see also 5:1). The audience too is introduced in its paradoxical context as beloved or chosen by God and so as foreigners or strangers scattered throughout the Roman provinces. Beyond this the opening prepares for the author's discussion of Christian existence as resulting from divine choice and gift and made possible through the Spirit and Christ's obedient suffering. The final wish for abundant grace and peace sets the tone for the optimism of the entire letter as the author prepares to exhort the communities as regards their internal and external problems as they live their lives as residents within a Roman context and as strangers in a pagan society (2:11).

Suggested Readings

Agnew, F. H. "1 Peter 1:2—An Alternative Translation." *CBQ* 45 (1983) 68-73.

Brown, R. E. et al, eds. *Peter in the New Testament.* Minneapolis: Augsburg, 1973.

Brox, N. "Tendenz und Pseudepigraphie im ersten Petrusbrief." *Kairos* 20 (1978) 11-20.

Dalton, W. J. "The First Epistle of Peter" in *NJBC,* 903-908.

Doty, W. G. *Letters in Primitive Christianity.* Philadelphia: Fortress, 1973.

Elliott, J. H. *I-II Peter/Jude* (with R. A. Martin. *James*). Minneapolis: Augsburg, 1982, 53-116.

__________. "Peter, Silvanus, and Mark in 1 Peter and Acts" in *Wort in der Zeit: Neutestamentlichen Studien.* Eds., Haubeck, H. & Bachmann, M. Leiden: Brill, 1980, 250-67.

Feldmeier, R. *Die Christen als Fremde. Die Metapher der Fremde in der antiken Welt, im Urchristentum und im 1. Petrusbrief.* Tübingen: Mohr-Siebeck, 1992.

Fitzmyer, J. A. "Introduction to the New Testament Epistles" in *NJBC,* 768-71.

Furnish, V. P. "Elect Sojourners in Christ: An Approach to the Theology of 1 Peter." *PSTJ* 28 (1975) 1-11.

White, J. L. "New Testament Epistolary Literature in the Framework of Ancient Epistolography." *ANRW* 25.2 (1984) 1730-56.

Through Mercy,
Chosen To Be God's People

(1 Peter 1:3–2:10)

Between the letter opening (1:1-2) and closing (5:12-14) one discerns three relatively unified blocks of material, the first (1:3–2:10), in standard epistolary fashion, introduced by a formal "blessing" addressed to God as father of "our Lord Jesus Christ" and the second and third (2:11–4:11 and 4:12–5:11) clearly marked off by the author's only two uses of "beloved" (*agapetoi*) in speaking to the addressees (2:11; 4:12) and by concluding doxologies (4:11; 5:11). This first section of 1 Peter establishes the foundation of the author's lengthy paraenetic discussion and introduces a series of related blocks of material that constitute a coherent whole. Evidence for such conclusions are of both a literary and a thematic nature.

In the first case there is a clear sign of unity in the author's literary use of themes in the construction of the whole. As the letter begins by emphasizing the theme of election in the opening ("chosen"), so it underscores it further at the beginning and ending of this large block of material by insisting in 1:3 that God's choice was made out of "mercy" and concluding in 2:10 that those who had not attained mercy had now received God's mercy. Such an inclusio unifies the foundational themes of this first block and underscores the character of the new life given the addressees. Indeed this inclusio involves the supporting themes of gift (choice in v. 1), living hope, and life from death in 1:3 and of call/choice and passage from darkness to the marvelous light in 2:9. Finally it also stresses the corresponding nature of new life or birth in 1:3 to that of becoming God's people in 2:10. One might also note the "obedience" of Jesus in 1:2 and the "disobedience" of some in 2:8.

Also, in structural terms one might note the author's efforts to unify the various blocks of this introductory section. Each of these is introduced by an overt reference to the believers' new life, thereby allowing the author to discourse on foundational issues as prologue to a treatment of the communities' situation. The first block (1:3-12) speaks of God granting Christians "a new birth" through the Christ-event, a life that provides "a living hope" (1:3) and so a basis for introducing the communities' "trials" (v. 6), their resolution in view of the Lord's return (vv. 5, 7, 9), and a first mention of the important double theme of Christ's suffering and his "consequent glory" (v. 11). The second section (1:13-25), in a more complex fashion, begins and ends on the theme of new life. After a hortatory statement relating to behavior in view of Jesus' return (v. 13), the author addresses the readers as "children of obedience" whose conversion means not only rejection of the past ("the desires that you formerly had in ignorance"—v. 14) but also requires a life of holiness (like God's—v. 15) and reverent fear (like Christ's—v. 17f). The section ends by reiterating the theme of obedience and new birth (v. 22) through the proclamation of the good news. The third block (2:1-10), also following a hortatory statement concerning behavior to be avoided, calls the readers "newborn infants" who are to seek Christ as spiritual food that provides growth (vv. 2-3) and as the living cornerstone of the divine edifice that is God's house and people (vv. 4f). The first major part of 1 Peter then focuses on the theme of new life, which God as father has bestowed upon those who were "called out of darkness into his marvelous light" (2:9). It is a life made possible by God's mercy and achieved through the Christ-event, that is, the death and resurrection that will provide a further basis, as suffering and glory, for the author's exhortation to the community on how and why to encounter the challenge presented by interaction with non-Christian neighbors.

A final structural issue should be addressed at this juncture. In contrast to the previous observations regarding the unity of 1:3–2:10, it has been proposed instead that, following more closely the epistolary analysis of Pauline documents, one should view 1:3f as a thanksgiving/blessing and 1:13f as the body opening of 1 Peter. Despite the fact that the usual transitional and formulaic devices for the body opening are lacking—such as requests, expressions of joy, and so on—other considerations are offered, for example, the imperative of v. 13 ("set your hope completely"), its inferential conjunction ("therefore"), and the function of the passage as indicating the principal occasion of the letter, to insist that 1:13 marks the beginning of the body of the letter. In effect this is hardly convincing for several reasons. The author's frequent use of participial and imperative constructions to introduce exhortation begins already at 1:6 and 8 (see commentary below). Further, the occasion of the letter is more properly introduced in 1:6 where the author speaks of "suffering various trials" and in 1:3f where the theme of hope is introduced as a foundation for the author's extensive exhortation. Further, such analysis overlooks the structural features that unify 1:3–2:10, whether the inclusio that binds the block of material or repeated allusions to the theme of new life, which provides the foundation for the author's insistence that the Christian communities are "God's people." 1 Peter is undoubtedly a letter but a letter whose form and function are very distant from that of the familiar papyrus letters, distant even from the Pauline letters that combine private and official characteristics. Instead 1 Peter is a circular letter whose author assumes the official persona of Peter and writes a public, general document to address a widespread socioreligious problem that the churches of Asia Minor found particularly vexing. The thematic division of the document into three major sections not only follows the letter's literary clues but also supports the document's exhortatory function.

Suggested Readings

Chevallier, M. A. "1 Pierre 1:1–2:10: structure littéraire et conséquences exégétiques." *RHPR* 55 (1971) 129-42.

Combrini, H. J. B. "The Structure of 1 Peter." *Neot* 9 (1980) 34-63.

Dalton, W. J. *Christ's Proclamation to the Spirits: A Study of 1 Peter 3:18–4:6.* Rome: PIB, 1989.

Goppelt, L. *A Commentary on 1 Peter.* Grand Rapids: Eerdmans, 1993.

Manns, F. "La théologie de la nouvelle naissance dans la première lettre de Pierre." *SBFLA* 45 (1995) 107-41.

Martin, T. W. *Metaphor and Composition in 1 Peter.* Atlanta: Scholars, 1990.

Michaels, J. R. *1 Peter.* Waco TX: Word Books, 1988.

Talbert, C. H. "Once Again: The Plan of 1 Peter" in *PFP*, 141-51.

Blessing: New Birth, Joy, Salvation
(1:3-12)

The first block of material (1:3–2:10) is introduced not by a thanksgiving but by a blessing formula ("blessed be the God . . . ") that, in epistolary fashion, offers praise or thanks to God for the blessings conferred on the Christian communities (3-5) but soon introduces both the addressees' situation and a first example of the author's paraenetic injunctions (vv. 6f). Thus, prior to discussion of the section's three components (3-5, 6-9, 10-12), it will be necessary to examine its form, structure, and function.

In place of the traditional thanksgiving form (see Paul's letters) to initiate correspondence with the addressees and to introduce some of the letter's themes, 1 Peter presents a *berakah* or blessing form. This formula would have been familiar to the author whether from the LXX version of the Jewish Scriptures, intertestamental writings, or early Christian tradition. While this blessing formula is regularly employed in direct address in contemporary

Jewish liturgy ("blessed are you, Lord God . . . "), its third-person form is consistent in the OT in contexts of prayer, whether by Abraham's servant (Gen 24:27—"Blessed be the Lord, the God of my lord Abraham . . . "), by Solomon (1 Kgs 8:15; see also Ps 72:18), or Ezra (7:27). The third-person formula continues to be used in intertestamental Jewish literature (*Pss Sol* 6:6; 1 QM 14:4; see also Luke 1:68f), where one finds an example of epistolary usage (2 Macc 1:17) similar to those of 2 Cor 1:3f and Eph 1:3f.

The blessing formula introduces, as in 2 Corinthians and Ephesians, what is traditionally a letter's health or thanksgiving period, the latter of which addresses the blessings received from God and foreannounces the themes of the letter, whether, as in 1 Peter 1, death and resurrection as suffering and glory (1:3, 6-7, 11), birth or new life (1:3, 14, 23; 2:2), or heavenly blessing or reward (1:4, 5, 7, 9, 12). While all three NT epistolary uses of the blessing formula begin by praising God for the blessings conferred on all believers (use of first person plural), 1 Peter 1:3 is unique for its immediate attention to the addressees and their concerns in v. 4 ("kept in heaven for you"). In this way 1 Peter is closer to the concerns of the Pauline thanksgiving (1 Thess 1:2-5; Phil 1:3-6), which focuses immediately on the addressees. Thus the Petrine letter is unusual both in choosing a blessing formula to dwell on the Christian's new life and unrelentingly and immediately in addressing the community's present difficulties, a fact that has a bearing on the structure of this first block of material.

It has often been remarked, somewhat inaccurately, that 1:3-12 comprises a single complex sentence that is extended by means of relative constructions at vv. 6 and 10. Instead these grammatical elements underscore a tripartite structure whose parts are loosely interrelated units: an anaphoric theological blessing that ends on the theme of future salvation (3-5), an exhortatory call for joy in the midst of suffering that also terminates with the concept of salvation but as a present reality (6-9), and finally a statement regarding this salvation as constituting God's plan in the past (prophets and angels) for the present ("doing these things as a service not for themselves but for you"—10-12). Each is introduced by formal grammatical structures:

v. 3	"Blessed be . . . , the one who . . . has given . . . "
v. 6	"for which/that reason" "rejoice . . . " (see v. 8: ". . . rejoice")
v. 10	"concerning which salvation . . . ."

The first unit (vv. 3-5) is introduced by the term *eulogetos* ("blessed be") and is extended not by the more frequent relative construction of OT usage ("God . . . who . . . "—1 Kgs 8:15, 56) but by a less frequent anaphoric construction used in some OT and intertestamental texts, as well as 2 Corinthians and Ephesians, namely, an articular participial construction ("blessed be the God . . . , the one who . . . has given us a new birth"—*ho . . . anagegnesas hemas*—1:3). The text is a declaration of God's salvific work through the Christ-event, a work that provides hope and promises an inheritance to a community that is now protected in view of present and future salvation. A carefully formulated Christian blessing provides the foundation for the author's following exhortation.

The second unit (vv. 6-9) refers back to the blessing ("for that/which reason") and insists that the communities of Asia Minor should rejoice. The verbal form could be a present tense or an imperative. There are good reasons to read it (see also v. 8) as an imperative (see discussion below). Verse 6 introduces the concept of rejoicing as the Christian reaction to God's blessing, but also leads the author, in a lengthy parenthesis, to speak more directly of the community's "trials" as a "test by fire" of its faith in view of Jesus' return, but a faith nonetheless that focuses both on the future and the present. This last note allows the author to return to the theme of joy (by repeating the verb "rejoice" in v. 8) and to dwell on the present, expected reaction of the community in light of faith as a foretaste of "assured salvation" (see v. 5).

The third unit (vv. 10-12) refers back explicitly ("concerning which/this salvation") to the theme of salvation, which has been of concern from the outset, whether a future or a present reality that relates to God's choice and gift. While insisting that the community's salvation has its origin in God's plan (prophetic activity and heavenly origin) and has cosmic ramifications as well (angelic concerns), the author notes two points: first, the key to this mysterious reality, into which the prophets inquired or angels longed to look, is the Christ-event as paradigm of suffering and glory (v. 11); and second, this divine concern and benefaction (grace) has the audience as its focus ("the grace meant for you"—10, "doing these things as a service not for themselves but for you," "announced to you," and "brought you good news"—v. 12).

The three units then show the progression of the author's thought from the concepts of hope and salvation implied in that of new life (vv. 3-5) to the community's lived response in the midst of its trials (vv. 6-9) to a return to the concept of salvation as it relates to the addressees' situation and to Jesus as the model of suffering and glory (vv. 10-12). From beginning to end the section focuses on the problem of the addressees.

Living Hope, Heavenly Inheritance,
Protection-Salvation (1:3-5)

This first unit introduces the concept of new life and the consequences this has for believers. Thus it contains two clusters of ideas: one concerning God's salvific work and the other relating to the author's threefold attempt (by means of three *eis* phrases in vv. 3-5) to explain the outcome of the believers' new life.

(1:3a) God's Salvific Work. The first cluster of ideas concerns the theological basis of Christian life: God, out of great mercy and through the Christ-event, gives believers ("us") new life. This combination of ideas is of great importance for it speaks of God's loving, compassionate nature according to Jewish tradition, of the early Christian belief in the christological agency of God's salvific activity, and of the believer's affiliation to a new people, a new family —namely, a new birth as children of God. Each concept merits some attention for the light it sheds on the thought of 1:3-5.

Structurally, this first cluster of themes forms part of the blessing formula (see earlier), wherein God is offered praise in relation to two interesting titles: "the God and Father of our Lord Jesus Christ" and "the one who, by his great mercy, has given us a new birth." Already in the previous verse the author has characterized God as the father who, from all eternity, has chosen the addressees thereby establishing a special bond, a theme that will be developed at greater length in 2:4f. In this case 1 Peter describes God no longer as the God of Israel but, with Gentile addressees in mind, as the one who bears a special relationship to Christ (see also 2 Cor 1:3; Eph 1:3), as the one who ultimately became known through him (1:21). Relying on the Jesus tradition (see Mark 1:15; 14:36), 1 Peter describes God as the lord, master, and loving parent of the one Christians acknowledge as God's messiah and their lord (3:15). Indeed the author here insists that the believer's path to God both in terms of revelation and access (1:21; 3:18) is through the Christian's lord. It is through him that they know of God's beneficent love.

The second title, meant as a commentary on the first, introduces the themes of mercy and new life. The concept of God's "great mercy" (*eleos*) is seemingly related to Israel's sense of its God as gracious, merciful, and compassionate or "abounding in steadfast love" (Exod 34:6). Indeed such a concept was readily associated with the covenant, as one finds in this Qumran prayer: "Blessed be the God of Israel, who keeps mercy toward his covenant, and the appointed times of salvation with the people he has delivered" (1 QM 14:4). In this prayer the focus is on fidelity to the original choice of a loving God, but that of 1 Peter 1:3 addresses the gracious choice of God who "calls [the believer] out of darkness into his marvelous light" (2:9) for, as the author insists, there is now mercy where originally there was none (v. 10). For the Christian as well as for the Jewish writer the divine choice results in the creation of "God's own people" (2:9-10); but, while for the latter the choice relates to God's gracious activity in the exodus and covenant, for the former it is made possible through the agency (*dia*) of the Christ-event, that is, "through the resurrection of Jesus Christ from the dead" (1:3; see also 1:1-2 ["chosen . . . because of . . . the sprinkling of Jesus Christ's blood"], 18-19, 21; 5:10).

In addition, the concept of new life has been puzzling for scholars both as to its background and its meaning in 1 Peter. The verb *anagennao* ("give new life or birth to") is extremely rare (only 1 Pet 1:3, 23 in the NT), though related concepts exist in a variety of contexts: the eschatological notion of "new creation" (Isa 65:17; *2 Bar* 32:6; Rev 21:11), the theme of spiritual birth or rebirth in conversion or baptism (John 3:3,7; Titus 3:5-7), divine adoption of devotees (Ps 2:7; Gal 4:4-7; Rom 8:14-15), and also the Essene concept of a transformed life in a new, covenant community (1QH 3.19-23). It is probably the last mentioned that is at the root of 1 Peter's concept of new life because, like the members of the Qumran community, Gentile Christian believers have, in conversion, renounced their former way of life (1:14, 18; 2:1; 4:1-4), have been purified and dedicated to a life of holiness (1:14-16, 22), and in invoking God as father (1:17) have become God's household (2:5; 4:17), people (2:9-10), and chosen race (2:9). In effect examination of the new-life passages in chapters 1 and 2 confirm the notion that 1 Peter intends by this theme to describe the new Christian way of life. Thus believers appeal to God as loving progenitor who is father both of Jesus Christ and of believers (1:3, 17, 23). Also, as "children of obedience" they are to be like their obedient brother and "redeemer" (for they were chosen "because of or through his obedience"—1:1-2) in renouncing their former way of life for a life of holiness (1:14-16; see also 1:23 and 2:2). Thus the first cluster of ideas focuses on the divine origin and cruciform nature of the believer's new life, a way of life that will both provoke and help to counter the challenge of being a Christian minority in a pagan society.

(1:3b-5) New Life and Its Consequences. The second cluster of ideas centers on the threefold statements regarding the consequences of this new life, each of which is introduced by an *eis* ("into or for") phrase, phrases that get progressively more complex in description (see below for a discussion of the third *eis* construction—v. 5b).

In the first place believers are said to be born anew "into a living hope." This concept of hope clearly orients the readers toward a future realization or fulfillment. The Christian's new life is directed toward and based on a future reality that the author describes in the following verses. Nonetheless, this hope involves the assurance of a salvific future made possible by God's raising of Jesus from the dead (1:3, 21). Undoubtedly, the author wishes to counteract current difficulties and to motivate current action by appealing to eschatological motivation. Why then the addition of the term *zosan* ("living")? The unique expression "living hope" is variously interpreted. While many appeal to Rom 5:5 ("hope does not disappoint us") to interpret this phrase or seek some contrast between Christian and non-Christian expectations (whether Jewish or pagan), it does not seem that such a contrast is intended because the author nowhere implies that the addressees possess a false notion of faith or hope (1:21). Instead the author, by use of the adjective, wishes to expand the meaning of hope (much as "living water" contrasts spring with nonflowing or cistern and not stagnant water: BAGD 337.4); hope essentially has a future focus but nonetheless, the author insists, has a present component because it impinges on present belief and practice (see discussion below of "living stones"—2:5).

The author in a second *eis* phrase goes on to qualify further the future character of this new life—since there is no conjunction between the two *eis* phrases, one should read "into a living hope, that is, into an inheritance." To emphasize its future nature, it is said that believers are born "into an imperishable, undefiled, and unfading inheritance" (v. 4). The term *kleronomia*, while frequently used in the LXX to designate inheritance or designated property (especially the land as Israel's promised inheritance), is chosen to extend the new life imagery, for believers are so described since they have become children of God and so heirs of God's blessing, eternal glory, or gift of life (3:7, 9; 5:11; see also various dominical sayings regarding inheritance, whether of eternal life or kingdom: Mark 10:17; Matt 19:29; 25:34; see also 1 Cor 15:50). It is particularly the term's eschatological rather than political nuance (i.e., contrast with the promised land) that is intended here, namely, its otherworldly, endtime character as reward for a godly life. In the words of Paul, "we are children of God, and if children, then heirs, heirs of God and joint heirs with Christ—if, in fact, we suffer with him so that we may also be glorified with him" (Rom 8:16-17). Moreover this future inheritance is described by a striking series of classical negative terms (use of *a*-privative) to underscore its eternal, otherworldly character. Employing terms that are often used to describe heavenly realities or eschatological reward (Wis 4:2; 6:12; 12:1; 1 Cor 9:25; *SibOr* 8:411), 1 Peter insists that this inheritance is threatened neither by death, evil, or time and therefore is reliable, worthy, and safe.

This heavenly reward is further characterized as "kept in the heavens for you," a phrase that recalls or depends upon various strands of apocalyptic and early Christian tradition. In several intertestamental apocalyptic texts one hears of a heavenly reward hidden or preserved in heaven for the holy one, whether "the portion of the righteous" (*1 En* 48:7) or a paradisiac kingdom or city soon to be revealed (*4 Ezra* 7:26; *2 Bar* 4:2-6). The first of these is particularly interesting since it also speaks of a "son of man" or "chosen one" being concealed in God's presence and of the holy ones receiving salvation in his name when he is revealed (*1 En* 48:6-7). Additionally one is reminded of dominical sayings from the Q tradition concerning a reward kept in heaven (Matt 5:12; Luke 6:23) or a treasure preserved and also kept safe in heaven (Matt 6:19-20; Luke 12:33). Finally the author's use of the perfect passive participle (*teteremenen*) describes not only the inheritance's origin in God's plan and its bestowal at the end of the process (see vv. 5 and 7) but also its present reality in the life of believers, a concept that recalls the Paulinist concern for the divine mystery that is both "hidden . . . and now revealed" (Col 1:26; Eph 3:9; also Rom 16:25). Thus this new life promises the believer an inheritance whose future is abundantly safeguarded and whose present existence already has a bearing on Christian life; it is prepared "for you," the addressees.

It is this actualizing note that leads the author to introduce later in v. 5 a third *eis* phrase to describe not only the consequences of divine protection but also of this new, divine life, a consequence that focuses structurally, once again, on the believer. Ever conscious of the readers' situation, the author underscores the purpose or goal of the future reward as focused on them and as having a parallel effect because not only is this inheritance reserved for them, but also they are guarded in view of this reward. Already the author anticipates the following discussion of the community's socioreligious problems, though there is mention only of the divine protection at this point. Interestingly, there is a concerted effort to emphasize further God's role in this matter, for the participles, "kept" and "protected," both are divine passives. Similarly the first is qualified by "in the heavens," a circumlocution for God or the heavenly realm, and the second is modified by the phrase "by the power of God." Thus, to stress the reliability of the God of grace's call to "eternal glory through Christ" (5:10; also 1:7), the author emphasizes God's role both as the one who initiates the salvific process and who presently safeguards the righteous. As a final statement on the addressees' status 1 Peter insists that God accomplishes this "through faith" (*dia pisteos*), a phrase that presumably means Christian commitment and way of life (BAGD 663.2d) but a commitment that will be tested and rewarded (see also 1:7, 9, 21; 5:9).

It is at this point that the author restates, in a third *eis* phrase, the goal of the believers' new life. Indeed they are divinely protected in view of or "for salvation," a concept that complements the previously-stated goals of new life: hope and inheritance. Like the latter, salvation, in its fullest, eschatological sense, is essentially a future that both provides hope in the present and looks to the future attainment of the promised inheritance. As a future, end-time reality it addresses particularly the gift or blessings of divine glory, light, life, or presence (1:7; 2:9; 3:7, 9, 18; 5:10) along with escape from eschatological judgment (2:12; 4:5, 17). But its context in v. 5 and particular usage in 1 Peter calls for some comment. The term "salvation" is modified both by an adjective and by an infinitive phrase, the two of which are traditionally translated: "for a salvation ready to be revealed in the last time" (NRSV). On the one hand, it is assumed, without much textual support, that *hetoimos* acts as an adverb and introduces an infinitive of purpose (BAGD 316.1); however, the term modifies the noun and therefore focuses on the present nature of this future reality (LSJ 704) and should be rendered "a certain, ready, or already prepared salvation" (see REB, NJB). With this adjective (a similar phenomenon occurs in the first *eis* phrase: "a living hope"), the author wishes to extend the range of the term by emphasizing its present existence and bearing upon Christian behavior. The infinitive modifier, on the other hand, stresses the future nature of salvation since it will be revealed in its fullness only at the endtime (use of *kairos* rather than *chronos* as in 1:20). Once again, future concepts are shown to have a significant impact on the present and so prepare for the author's treatment of the community's current difficulties. Finally there will be occasion below to discuss more generally the author's notions of salvation (1:9) and of revelation (1:7).

Glorious Joy in the Midst of Suffering (1:6-9)

A second unit (1:6-9) addresses the audience's situation and the response expected of those who believe. So already at this early stage the author mentions in concrete terms the problem confronting the community, "suffering various trials," and seeks to elicit a response in keeping with the new life discussed earlier. The mention of these difficulties, however, is brief, and the author returns to the concept of faith noted earlier in v. 5, namely, the believer's way of life, which involves testing (v. 7), trust rather than sight (v. 8), and perseverance (v. 9).

(1:6a) Joy as Response. Overall discussion of 1:6-9 discloses a number of problems to the interpreter: the antecedent of the transitional, opening phrase; the form and tense of the principal verbs; and, in relation to this, the nature of the joy and salvation noted in this passage. Some interpret the relative expression *en ho* (lit.: "in which or whom") as referring to the immediately preceding phrase ("in the last time") and so either read the following verb as a future (on weak textual evidence) or insist that it has an implied future sense ("at which time" or "then you will rejoice"). The entire passage then would have eschatological joy in view to counter present difficulties; such an interpretation would affect the reading of v. 8 as well. Others, preferably, see the relative expression as referring back to vv. 3-5 ("for which or that reason"—see v. 4; BDF 219 [3]) and so interpret the following verb as insisting that joy is a present reality despite current difficulties (true also of v. 8). Also one must consider the form of the verb *allaliasthe* and note that it could be read as an indicative or an imperative; the same is true of the verb in v. 8, despite minor evidence of scribal activity. While most translators and commentators opt for the former, there are a number of reasons to question such a conclusion and to choose the latter. There is something incongruous in insisting, both in vv. 6 and 8, that the community is in fact a paragon of joy in the midst of suffering when it seems that the author's goal is the exhortation to such a reaction among the addressees. Indeed the only other use of such terminology in 1 Peter confirms our choice of the imperative, because there too the audience is exhorted: "insofar as you are sharing the suffering of Christ, rejoice" (4:13). There too 1 Peter employs the present rather than the usual aorist imperative.

Also, it is often noted that such an exhortation would be both premature so early in a letter and disruptive in its present context. First, one assumes too much in thinking that later paraenetic letters should follow Pauline epistolary patterns. Not only does the blessing section of 1 Peter form a unit with subsequent passages (see earlier discussion of the inclusio and new-life theme), but it also uncharacteristically and graphically introduces the community's problems (vv. 6-7) and, in a manner reminiscent of Jas 1:2 and 5f, wastes no time in exhorting the audience to live according to its new commitment.

Second, the claim that imperatives would disrupt what is assumed to be the author's thought pattern calls for some structural observations. The twofold use of the verb "rejoice" (in identical form) offers what is probably the key to the author's composition of vv. 6-9. Having introduced the theme of rejoicing in v. 6, the author indulges in a long digression on the community's difficulties as a test of its faith and in v. 8b returns to the initial theme of rejoicing by repeating the original injunction. The focus of the passage then is on the theme of joy that should be characteristic of the believer's new life despite, and even because of, present trials.

The passage then begins in v. 6 by exhorting (use of imperative) the addressees to rejoice in light of God's gift of new life. There is a clear shift at this point from considerations of past divine benefaction (new life through Christ's resurrection from the dead) and its promise of future reward (hope, inheritance, salvation) to a focus on the present. Just as the proper reaction to divine election and benefaction is that of giving thanks or blessing God as giver, so the proper attitude of the believer is that of a joyful life.

(1:6b-8a) The Community's Situation. Before explicitating the theme of rejoicing, however, the author is led immediately to address, in a long parenthetical statement, the paradoxical character of the hearers' situation but returns at the end of the passage (v. 8b) and later in the letter (4:13) to the christological content and nature of the theme of Christian joy. This digression concerning the community's situation is occasioned by the paradoxical exhortation to rejoice because, while God's gift of new life and its eschatological promise readily call for a joyful reaction on the part of the recipients, there comes to mind immediately the crisis that has occasioned the writing of the letter. The problem is described simply at this point as "suffering various trials or temptations." Even though the author returns explicitly to the topic of Christian suffering (2:19f; 3:14f; 4:12f; 5:9-10) and provides further hints regarding the problems the communities of Asia Minor are encountering (see introduction above), several observations should be made at this point concerning the author's statement.

First, while the expression "various trials or temptations" can be characterized as vague, it can also be described as intentionally all inclusive (see also "same kinds of suffering" in 5:9) because seemingly the situation of the Christians of the area involved a wide range of issues, from slander (2:12; 3:16) to public accusations and abuse (3:9, 15-16).

Second, the sense of *peirasmos*, which means both "trial" and "temptation or enticement" (BAGD 640:1 & 2), is determined in this instance by what follows in v. 7; namely, it refers to "tests or trials" of one's faith (also 4:12; note Jas 1:2). The concept of "temptation or enticement" hinted at here is put off until 5:8 where the author will discuss Satan's role as adversary. In addition the term "suffer" (*lypeo*; see 2:19) is a synonym of the more widely used *pascho* (and its noun) to designate both the sufferings of Christ and of the community (1:11; 2:19-21; 5:9).

Third, two problems of translation arise in v. 6: the meaning of *arti* followed by an aorist participle and the sense of the conditional clause *si deon*. The first cannot mean "now" as usually concluded. Rather, it means "just now" or "recently" since it is employed with an aorist verb (LSJ 249). The second expresses a simple condition and means not "if it is necessary" but "since it is necessary." Further, since the author uses an aorist verb, one must conclude that suffering is not a contingency but a recent occurrence. Thus the overall translation should be: "even though for a little while recently you have had to suffer."

Fourth, the term expressing necessity in v. 6 (*deon* from *dei*) underscores the Judeo-Christian concept of God's salvific plan and places innocent Christian suffering under that rubric (see also 3:17).

Finally the expression "for a little while" probably does not refer to the nearness of the end (see 4:7) but to temporary sociopolitical conditions that have increased tensions between Christians and their non-Christian neighbors (see introduction and comments on 5:10).

In v. 7, rather than describe or respond to the communities' trials, the author dwells on the purpose of these, thereby justifying the choice of the term *peirasmos* interpreted as "trial" rather than "temptation." These difficulties have been permitted as an examination of the genuineness of the community's commitment or new life. Innocent suffering is viewed by the author as God's way of testing, and by implication of purifying or perfecting, the believers' faith. Interestingly, with an eye to the community's situation, the author focuses not so much on faith as on a commitment that has survived the test of fire; it is not faith but its genuineness that is "more precious than gold." The author wishes to underscore, at this point, not the gift of faith but the believer's perseverance when faced with difficult times. This genuineness then is forcefully described by the use of smelting imagery to contrast alloy-free but perishable metal with genuine faith that promises an eschatological reward. Both gold and faith require submission to purifying fire; the latter, however, is more precious since it is imperishable and will redound to "praise, glory, and honor when Jesus Christ is revealed" (for similar proverbial uses of smelting imagery, see Plato, *Republic* 336E, 413D-E, 503A; Jer 9:7; Mal 3:2-3; Wis 3:5-6; Ps 12:6; Prov 17:3; Sir 2:5; 1 Cor 3:10-14; Rev 3:18).

First Peter argues then that divinely appointed suffering purifies one's faith, which in turn is rewarded by ("found to result in") or has as its goal a threefold divine gift (see Rom 2:7-10 for a similar threefold reward). The first gift is "praise" as divine, final approval or recognition of one whose faith has been tested (also 1 Cor 4:5; see comments on 2:14). The second gift is the important theme of "glory" here seen as the eschatological sharing of God's presence (3:18) and nature by those whose faith has endured; this glory, nonetheless, also belongs to Christ who received it from God (1:21) and who bestows it upon the righteous (5:4). The third gift is the "honor or esteem" given to believers based on the position they have achieved by their faithful adherence to Christ the honored or precious stone (2:4—see discussion also of 2:7). It is obvious in this instance that the focus is on future, endtime gifts in view of present trials.

Mention of these endtime gifts leads the author to stress further their eschatological character and function by noting that this will occur "when Jesus Christ is revealed" (the preposition in the phrase *en apokalypsei* has a temporal, eschatological meaning rather than an instrumental nuance: "by means of"—see also 1:13; 4;13). On the one hand, recalling the apocalyptic language and imagery of v. 5b ("a salvation . . . to be revealed in the last time"), the author again appeals to the final manifestation of the messiah to insist that these divine gifts are the objects of hope and depend on perseverance. On the other hand, there is also an insistence that these are rewards given by the returning lord to the righteous. Employing endtime military or judicial imagery, the author presents the reader a further reason why present trials are a crucible or cleansing fire for a genuine faith.

The transition between vv. 7 and 8 is usually obscured in translation because the grammatical and thematic relationship between the two is not easily preserved. In the first instance the author employs the ubiquitous relative clause ("whom . . . you love") to extend the sentence structure (see vv. 8b, 10, 12a, b, c); there then follows a brief discussion of Jesus' present role. In the second instance the theme of v. 8 is suggested by the author's choice of the noun "revelation" (*apocalypsis*), rather than "coming or return" of Jesus to describe the endtime. Such a choice presumes the author's belief that Jesus is present within the community, though invisible currently, and that the endtime event will be a clearer manifestation of his presence. Thus v. 8 dwells upon the profound, paradoxical role of Jesus in the believer's new life.

Verse 8 then offers double statements concerning Jesus that should lead to expressions of joy or rejoicing. The first reads: "though you have never seen him (on textual problem, see *TCGNT* 687), you love him." Clearly past and present activities are contrasted, a fact that led earlier scholars to conclude that the former referred to an author's eyewitness knowledge of Jesus (see 5:1). Instead the author is addressing the situation of all believers who accept Jesus as the risen one who has returned to the Father. The second part of the statement is unusual in speaking of "loving Christ" rather than God. Scholars routinely refer to kindred, eschatological passages from James (1:12;

2:5) and Paul (1 Cor 2:9) to suggest that allusions to divine love would either have influenced the language of 1 Peter or that love and faith terminology would have soon become interchangeable for God and Jesus (as happens in later Christian texts: *1 Clement* 34:8; *2 Clement* 11:7; 14:5; *Martyrdom of Polycarp* 2:3). Rather, this unusual language seems to be an independent formulation by 1 Peter of the faith commitment (see also 1 Cor 16:22 for a similar concept) expressed as personal loyalty (and later as imitation: 2:21) to the Lord Jesus, and through this devotion to him to "come to believe in God, the one who [both] raised him from the dead and gave him glory" and promises the same to those who "love him" (1:21).

The second statement rephrases in a slightly different way and further clarifies the believer's relation to the absent Jesus. The author states: "though you do not now observe him, but still believe in him, rejoice." In a starkly parallel fashion the author contrasts past conversion and its first, enduring love with the anomalous present where faith, still without sight, is a reality that must issue in rejoicing—the point of departure in v. 6 for the author's long parenthesis on the community's situation. Thus, despite Jesus' current absence, no less than when he was proclaimed by the traveling missionaries (1:12, 23-25), commitment to him continues to be a reality as should the joy of discovery and devotion.

(1:8b-9) Joy Once Again as Response. Returning then to the original exhortation that the reality of divinely-given new life and its promise should illicit joy, the author qualifies this by stating that the addressees are to "rejoice with indescribable and glorious joy." Seemingly, the two descriptive terms have been chosen to underscore first the inability of language to express the paradoxical character of this joy and second its anticipation of or participation in future glory. This joy is indescribable because it occurs in the midst of or despite suffering and trials but already anticipates the glory promised when Jesus is revealed at the end (v. 7). An additional reason is given for this joy in v. 9, namely, that believers are already receiving or experiencing "the salvation of [their] souls" "as an outcome of [their] faith" (BAGD 442). Interestingly, this new reason contrasts and complements that given earlier. While it is promised in v. 7 that "the genuineness of . . . faith" will lead to future rewards and so furnishes the basis for joy, so now in v. 9 the author insists that the believer is already receiving in the present the result of this commitment. This result, described in v. 5 as a future reality, is presented in v. 9 as involving the present and expressed to the addressees as "the salvation of (their) souls or lives." Salvation in this instance refers to that part of the salvific process that began with the purification of believers' "lives by their obedience to the truth" (1:22), a reality into which one can grow (2:2). Also, the term, often translated as "soul" (*psyche*), refers here to the whole person or self (see 1:22; 2:11; also Mark 8:36-37), which has been transformed by a new birth.

In this second section (1:6-9), therefore, the audience is called upon to rejoice for three basic reasons. The first exhortation to rejoice is given following the author's extended statement concerning God's great gift of new life and its manifold, future and present, consequences (hope, inheritance, and salvation). The proper reaction (v. 6) of the believer to this divine gift of new life is a life of joy. Another reason for rejoicing is in fact introduced when the author notes that joy is the proper reaction to divine benefaction despite suffering, since these trials, in God's plan, confirm the genuineness of the sufferer's faith and prepare for an eschatological reward (vv. 6-7). This theme of joy in suffering is again addressed in 4:12-16 (see also Acts 5:41) and greatly amplified under the rubric of the exemplary character of Christ's suffering (2:21-24). Still another reason for the exhortation to joy is that the Christian's commitment already has a salvific effect on the life of believers who are called in the present to live a life of holiness (1:15) according to God's will (4:2) and who are protected while awaiting Christ's final manifestation (1:5; 5:10).

Salvation as Present and Future Reality (1:10-12)

The third unit (1:10-12) extends discussion of the theme of salvation, which is earlier characterized as a future reality or promised blessing that establishes hope and guarantees protection and as a process that has already begun in a life of joy, purity and holiness. Thus, while the first and second units (vv. 3-5, 6-9) dwell upon the future and present character of salvation, respectively, the third takes as its point of departure and focus the theme's setting in salvation history. To stress further the importance of this theme for the addressees, the author dwells upon its prophetic past and present fulfillment, that is, mysterious grace as the subject of prophetic activity and good news as related to "the sufferings destined for Christ and the glory to accompany these."

The entire unit presents difficulties to the interpreter owing to its unusual combination of themes, whether the role of prophetic activity, its seeming concern with endtime prediction, the meaning of "Spirit of Christ," and the relationship of these to good news, grace, angels, and salvation. Without referring to any specific prophets or OT texts, the author ventures to connect the theme of salvation to prophetic activity. The prophets are said, as in OT and contemporary Judaism, to be under the influence of the Spirit (Isa 61:1; Ezek 3:12; Zech 7:12; Sir 48:12-14), particularly in their concern for future salvation (Joel 2:28-32 [= Acts 2:17-21]; *1 En* 91:1). As a parallel to this theme, later in the unit those who announce the good news are also said to be under the influence of the Spirit "sent from heaven" (v. 12; often in Acts) and to be concerned about the same message. In the first case the message is described as "the grace meant for you," in the second as the "things . . . now . . . announced to you," and both as having to do with Christ's sufferings and glory. Further, with much emphasis the author notes that the prophets "made careful search and inquiry" and repeats that they "inquired about" the time of fulfillment. Also repeatedly the author insists that this revelation concerned not the prophets (nor "us") but "you," the audience. Last of all, two odd concepts also make their appearance in this compact statement regarding salvation, namely, that the Spirit that dwelt within the prophets was Christ's Spirit and that angels also are making inquiries.

A closer look at contemporary Jewish literature and other NT traditions shows that the ideas of 1 Peter are not new. First, one might consider the theme of prophetic inquiry about the end. While the NRSV speaks of the object of inquiry as "the person or time," it is best with most translators and commentators to view the Greek expression as meaning "the time and circumstances" (lit.: "which or what sort of time") since the issue is the time and not the person involved. Further, it is not unusual to have prophetic figures and communities inquiring about the time of the end, whether an end to the desolation of Jerusalem and the woes of its wise ones (Dan 12:6), the time of the end (1 QpHab 7:1; 1 Thess 5:1; 2 Thess 2:1-2), or the signs of the times (there is a focus here on inquiry: "when will this be"—Mark 13:4 or "how long and when will these things be"—*4 Ezra* 4:33 and often; see also *2 Bar* 14:1f).

Secondly one should note that the theme of revelation for a later generation is also well known. It has often been remarked that 1 Peter is unusual in stressing that the prophetic revelation (received and given) was not for the benefit of the messengers who are here said to know that it was meant for a later generation. On the contrary, in apocalyptic literature one routinely hears that heavenly revelation is for the end-time generation, whether written down, sealed, and kept secret (Dan 12:9; also *4 Ezra* 14:45-48) or as final instructions (*T. Levi* 1:1-2; Mark 13; *2 Bar* 76-87). Also NT writers frequently speak of prophetic and other OT sayings as meant for Christian fulfillment (1 Cor 10:11; Acts 3:24) and even that OT figures longed to see this reality (Matt 13:17; Luke 10:24; John 8:56). Thus not only did these figures know about and yearn for the fulfillment of the revelation they were imparting, but also in many traditions the prophets or seers serve as inter-preters or receive the interpretation of their visions for the endtime generation (*1 En* 1:2; Dan 12:9; see notes below on "the Spirit of Christ" and the angels' relation to salvation).

Why then has the author of 1 Peter put together these somewhat unusual themes, and how does the ensuing unit function within the letter? Focusing on various components, scholars have reached a variety of interpre-tations for this passage, invariably seeing a sharp contrast drawn between the promise as personified in prophetic experience with its realization as grace or salvation in the Christian community. Either the prophets, along with the angels, are seen as past witnesses of God's gift of salvation or their work of inquiry and "testifying in advance" are subsumed in the "now" of the good news and its new life and eschatological promise.

While some of these concepts are no doubt presumed or hinted at by the author, they are not sufficiently related by scholars to the purpose for writing and the overall meaning of the passage. For example, it is frequently noted that the author's emphasis is on revelation for the church as opposed to the promise to Israel ("serving not themselves but you"—12). Such an interpre-tation fails to note that the author speaks not of "us" (Christians in general) but repeatedly of "you" (the addressees of Asia Minor—see also 5:9). The passage is not primarily about the community of salvation nor even about Christian hermeneutics (Christian reading of OT prophecy) but about the trials being suffered by the readers of the letter and the author's exhortation in the light of these.

(1:10-12) The Paradigm of Suffering and Glory. Overall analysis of the passage points in the same direction. A first issue to be resolved is the rela-tionship between three important terms employed in vv. 10-12: salvation, grace, and good news. Despite frequent claims that the three are synony-mous or nearly so, a structural and thematic reading of the verses indicates otherwise. The actual usage of the first two terms in v. 10 is instructive. While the second ("grace") is mentioned in passing to identify the principal function of the prophets, the first is the primary concern of the author who wishes to clarify what has been said earlier about "salvation" in vv. 5 and 9. Thus it is presumed, based on traditional Christian hermeneutics, that the prophets' role was to foreannounce or prophesy concerning God's salvific activity, here described as "the grace meant for you." Though "grace" repre-sents a wide-ranging concept for 1 Peter, describing a beneficent God (4:10; 5:10), and encompassing both present and future benefactions (1:13; 3:7;

5:5), it is here used to characterize the fulfillment of God's promise. This activity is presumed by the author who wishes to explain the paradoxical nature of salvation, particularly as a present reality as noted earlier in v. 9. The prophets' "careful search and inquiry" concerns not messianic promise but the nature of the salvation just referred to in the previous unit. The third term, the "good news" (v. 12), presumably reflecting traditional content (announcing the Christ-event—see 1:3, 21, 25; 4:17) and serving as a differently-focused synonym of "grace," is likewise mentioned in passing to describe the principal function of Christian missionaries, not the principal concern of the author. Again, of more central concern is the theme of "this salvation" as it relates in v. 11 to suffering and glory and in v. 12 to "the things announced" in that regard.

A second issue concerns the object of the prophets' inquiry. Granted that this search and inquiry have as their goal the elucidation of the concept of salvation previously noted, this new activity focuses on a second prophetic function, namely, their "testifying in advance concerning the sufferings destined for Christ and the glory to accompany these." Presumably this activity is different from the traditional function ascribed to the prophets and is further qualified as involving the Spirit of Christ and focused particularly on discerning "the time and circumstances" of this revelation. Three important points therefore should be underscored here for a proper reading of 1 Peter.

First, the prophets are assumed to perform two functions: the fore-announcing of messianic grace on the one hand and of the sufferings and glory of Christ on the other. The first function concerns the soteriological function of the Christ-event: the death and resurrection as expiatory, source of new life, and eschatological grace (1:2-3, 13, 18-19). The second function involves its paradigmatic function: suffering and glory as the model for believers undergoing severe trials (1:6; 2:21). The first concept underscores the letter's discussion of Christian beliefs and practice particularly in the first part of the letter (1:3–2:10), while the second concept relates to the author's strategy in addressing the readers' situation.

Second, the prophetic inquiry is said to focus on "the time and circumstances" for the fulfillment of this new revelation, namely, when and how the suffering and glory of Christ have a bearing on the Christian situation. The time element is immediately and forcefully addressed in the following verse where the prophets are said to render service to the addressees—not themselves—and that these matters "have now been announced" to them. The whole revelation concerns the "now" of the readers' situation in terms of suffering and glory. The second element, that of "circumstances," concerns both the type of suffering involved and the context and nature of the glory promised. The author speaks frequently of suffering but insists that Christ is a model only of innocent suffering (2:19-23) and that participation in these in the present will bring about a sharing in his glory when he is revealed (4:13). At the same time the element of glory has a bearing on the present, because the Spirit of glory rests now on the believer (4:14; see also 1:8; 4:11).

Finally the prophets are said to have "the Spirit of Christ within them." One might be tempted here to explain this phenomenon in christological terms (subjective genitive: "Christ's Spirit") as the activity of the preexistent one (see Rom 8:9; 1 Cor 10:4—see discussion also of 1 Pet 1:20), but a better option is to view this passage eschatologically as God's Spirit that speaks of hidden things to come, in this case about Christ (objective genitive: "Spirit [prophecing] about Christ").

A third issue of concern in vv. 10-12 is the proclamation made to the present generation and its relation both to the prophetic message and theme of salvation. As in the case of prophetic activity, that of the Christian messengers is also twofold. Their principal function, also expressed in passing, is clearly the bringing of the good news; their second function is the announcing or proclamation of "those things" foreannounced by the prophets for the benefit of the addressees, a message involving Christ's suffering and glory. It is clear from v. 12a that the second function of the Christian messengers ("those who brought . . . good news") was to announce what the prophets had predicted ("testified in advance") and been shown concerning "the time and circumstances" of Christ's suffering and glory: "to whom it was revealed that they were doing these things (*auta*) as a service not for themselves but for you, which things (*ha*) have now been announced to you through those who brought you good news by the Holy Spirit sent from heaven." First Peter therefore wishes to underscore and conjoin the paradigmatic message of the Jewish and Christian groups to emphasize that the continuity of the divine plan for Christ as promise and fulfillment is the basis for the Christian paradigm of the present, paradoxical reality of innocent suffering and "glorious joy" (1:8). Indeed the message that the prophets discerned regarding "the time and circumstances" of Christ's example was intended for the audience and was so announced to that audience by the Christian envoys.

In addition several other items reinforce and further develop the above interpretation. First, the connection between vv. 9 and 10 (the topic of both focuses on the notion of present salvation) and the links drawn between the prophetic and Christian messages (what was foreannounced is now proclaimed) indicate that vv. 10-12 have as their central concern the addressees' present situation seen in light of Christ's suffering and glory. Second, the author underscores the trustworthiness of this salvific message by insisting on the divine origin first of the prophetic activity ("it was revealed to them"—divine passive) and then that of the Christian messengers (they proclaimed these things "by the Holy Spirit sent from heaven"). Third, 1 Peter insists that the true interpretation ("time and circumstances") of suffering and glory was made clear by the Spirit of Christ, a statement that seemingly points to Christ as the paradigm of these realities in the Christian's life and that receives considerable treatment later in the letter. Interestingly, in v. 12 the author notes that this new message of salvation has "now been announced . . . through those who brought . . . good news." This last statement also implies that knowledge of this message of salvation is to be found in the good news, presumably also in the example left by Christ (2:21).

Finally a note is called for concerning the concluding statement of v. 12: "things into which angels long to look." By all accounts this is a puzzling statement whose background and meaning are debated. Some have suggested a negative meaning of the statement by appealing to the limitations of angelic power and knowledge (*1 En* 16:3; *2 En* 24:3; Mark 13:32) or by insisting that the verb "desire" requires a negative sense (see use of noun in 1:14; 2:11; 4:2, 3). Others, more plausibly, defend a less negative usage by relating the statement to the theme of the paradoxical superiority of the human over the angelic realm in soteriological terms, either by insisting that the Christ-event concerns humans rather than angels (Heb 2:16), who rejoice over human repentance (Luke 15:10), or that knowledge of God's wisdom comes to these otherworldly figures through the church (Eph 3:10). Still others view the statement in light of the desire of all creation, including angels, for eschatological fulfillment, particularly human subjection to God through faith in Christ (Rom 8:19; Rev 5:11-14). It is the last two that offer insight into the author's meaning. Seemingly, on the one hand, it is the greatness of God's salvific activity that elicits angelic admiration. Thus the author would wish to draw a parallel to the opening statement concerning God's great mercy in giving new birth (1:3). On the other hand, the theme of eschatological fulfillment would be supported by the author's interest in the themes of creation, cosmic subjection and judgment, and eternal glory (3:18-22; 4:5, 11, 17, 19; 5:4, 10); besides, the only other reference to angels speaks of them as subject to Christ at God's right hand (3:22). In all likelihood then the author draws the first unit to a close by using a statement that evokes both the grandeur of God's salvific activity and the deep yearning of creation for eternal glory in God's presence (3:18; 5:10).

Suggested Readings

Cothenet, E. "Le réalisme de l'espérance chrétienne selon 1 Pierre." *NTS* (1981) 564-72.

Dauzenberg, P. G. "*Soteria psychon* (1 Pt. 1:9)." *BZ* 8 (1964) 262-76.

de Villiers, J. L. "Joy in Suffering in 1 Peter." *Neot* 9 (1975) 64-86.

Duport-Roc, R. "Le jeu des prépositions en 1 Pierre 1,1-12: de l'espérance finale à la joie dans les épreuves présentes." *EstBib* 53 (1995) 201-12.

Kendall, D. W. "The Literary and Theological Function of 1 Peter 1:3-12" in *PFP*, 103-20.

Kilpatrick, G. D. "1 Peter 1:11: *tina e poion kairon*." *NovT* 28 (1986) 91-92.

Martin, T. W. "The Present Indicative in the Eschatological Statements of 1 Peter 1:6, 8." *JBL* 111 (1992) 307-312.

Miller, E. G. "Deliverance and Destiny: Salvation in First Peter." *Interp* 9 (1955) 413-25.

Neyrey, J. H. "First Peter and Converts." *TBT* 22 (1984) 13-18.

Parker, D. C. "The Eschatology of 1 Peter." *BTB* 24 (1994) 27-32.

Shutter. W. L. *Hermeneutic and Composition in 1 Peter.* Tübingen: Mohr-Siebeck, 1989.

Tite, P. L. *Compositional Transitions in 1 Peter: An Analysis of the Letter-Opening.* San Francisco: International Scholars Publications, 1997.

Conduct: Holiness, Faith, Love

(1:13-25)

The first block of 1 Peter (1:3–2:10), as noted earlier, consists of three sub-units, the second of which receives our attention in this chapter. The subunit itself seemingly also falls into three parts (vv. 13-16, 17-21, 22-25), each of which is marked by structural and thematic features. The passage is connected to the previous unit by an inferential conjunction ("therefore") and so offers the reader a series of hortatory statements (use of ingressive imperatives to "express the coming about of conduct which contrasts with prior conduct" BDF 337.1) related to the theme of new life and its consequences for Christian existence. Each unit alludes to the theme of new life, also referring explicitly to the believer's pre-conversion existence, and adopts a distinct hortatory style and tone:

Initial Participle
      having prepared (13)   so if/since you invoke*(17)   having purified (22)

Imperative
      set your hope   live in fea   love one another
      be holy yourselves**(15)

Following Participle
        not conforming (14)   knowing that (18)   having been born (23)
Themes:

  New Life
      like children of obedience invoke as father   born anew

  Pre-conversion Status
      former desires   futile ways   purification-flesh/grass

Two variations should be noted: The first, indicated by an asterisk, points to the author's use of a "factual *if* clause" in place of an aorist participle. The second, designated by a double asterisk, notes the presence of a second imperative in that subunit.

It is clear from this structural overview that the second subunit (1:13-25) differs considerably from the first (1:3-12), especially in its strikingly paraenetic character. While in the first the author, at one point (1:6, 8), exhorts the community to rejoice in light of God's gift of new life, in this second subunit the imperative, situated between lengthy participial constructions, dominates the discussion as the author offers advice for a life of holiness (based on hope), of reverent fear, and of mutual love. New life demands purification or rejection of the old (see thematic elements) as well as conduct worthy of the one who called (1:15), imitation of the one who ransomed (v. 18; also 2:21), and love of those "born anew . . . from . . . an imperishable source or sowing" (23).

Further, one could ostensibly view 1:13-21 as a larger unit consisting of two parts (vv. 13-16, 17-21), a unit delineated by references to hope in vv. 13 and 21. Note, however, that v. 25 also raises the idea of hope by insisting that "the word of the Lord," the source of new life, "endures forever." Nonetheless, the structural features noted above indicate successive paragraphs of related paraenesis. Furthermore each of these three units presumes the theme of obedience (v. 14—"like children of obedience"; v. 22—"your obedience to the truth"; and v. 17—"if/since you invoke [God] as father") to establish its advice to the community.

Hope and the Call to Holy Conduct (1:13-16)

This first subunit follows the pattern noted above. An initial participial construction is followed by an imperative, which is itself modified by a subsequent participial statement. From this there emerges a stress on eschatological grace as the motivation for present action along with a strengthening of commitment. Returning in v. 15 to the initial call for righteous action and drawing a contrast to the impious ways of pagan life (see also 4:1-3), the author appeals to divine conduct as the model for human action. Finally the entire unit is joined to what precedes by the conjunction "therefore" to underscore the strong relationship that exits between belief and action. The gift of new life as the result of a divine call must result in a life of moral activity with a proper motivation.

(1:13a) Preparation for Action. The discussion opens with a stark LXX idiom, "girding one's loins," an expression that seemingly describes a person's preparation for work, namely, the gathering and fastening of one's loose, flowing garment to facilitate activity. The idiom is used of prophets who prepare for their task (Jer 1:17), of the Israelites who hurriedly participate in the Passover ritual (Exod 12:11), of believers who await Jesus' return (Luke 12:35), or more generally of moral readiness (Eph 6:14). In the case of 1 Peter one could stress eschatological readiness (frequent mention of Jesus' revelation; see also 4:7 on the nearness of the end) or preparation for action. In effect the latter is the preference of translators and commentators who render the unwieldy "gird up the loins of your mind" as "prepare (or make ready) your mind for action" (BAGD 53). Such a conclusion is further confirmed by the author's use of a second participle (without a coordinating conjunction) to explain the idiom in question, "that is, being self-controlled or focused" (*nepho*; see also 4:7 and 5:8). Thus the first participle, in the aorist, underscores mental effort and commitment, while the second, in the present, indicates a state of mind or mental balance.

(1:13b-14) Motivation for Action. These initial participial constructions prepare for the author's exhortation concerning the focus of Christian action, which is expressed first in a positive, imperative statement (13b) and then is contrasted, by means of a negative participial construction, to the believer's former motivation (14b). In the first case the addressees are presented a teleological motive for Christian activity, or as 1 Peter insists: "set your hope completely on the grace to be brought to you at the revelation of Jesus Christ." Such an exhortation is stark to say the least and, when insufficient attention is given to its context, regularly leads to an overly eschatological or pilgrim interpretation of the entire document. In effect two important points should be considered: the exhortation's relation to the previous unit on new life and its function within its present context.

It is clear that the author relates this exhortation to several themes developed in 1:3-12, namely, "living hope" received with the gift of new life (v. 3), the inheritance kept in heaven (whether praise, glory, and honor or grace—

vv. 4, 7, 10), and the recurrent motif of final revelation (vv. 5, 7). In each case the theme, while mainly futuristic in orientation, bears a present connotation for the author. Hope is a "living" reality; grace, whether referring to divine benefactions or more specifically to glory, impinges on the present; and the theme of Jesus' final revelation, for 1 Peter, presupposes his invisible presence already within the community.

In terms of context it should be noted that the author moves from present preparation and focus (v. 13a) to future or teleological motivation (v. 13b), to rejection of past incentives (v. 14), and finally to a second exhortation involving present, holy conduct (v. 15). Thus the eschatological exhortation of v. 13b is meant to reinforce Christian commitment and action.

In a subsequent participial construction (v. 14b) the author contrasts Christian to pre-conversion motivation. It is presumed that the addressees prior to their reception of God's word were, in their ignorance, subject to "the desires of the flesh," that is, "by human desires but [not] by the will of God" (2:11; 4:2). Though formerly they, like their non-Christian neighbors, spent time "doing what the Gentiles want" (4:3), they should no longer "be conformed to the desires or excesses" (*epithymia*) that controlled their past behavior (see discussion of 2:11; 4:2-4; 5:8).

Two further issues require some attention in order to obtain a more satisfactory overview of vv. 13-16. The first concerns the meaning and function of the Semitic-like expression "like children of obedience" (v. 14a; see the contrasting phrase of Eph 2:2). Both terms relate directly to the document's message because they reintroduce themes already seen in the opening and blessing, themes that are developed at greater length later in the letter. The term "children" recalls the theme of new life and conjoins believers with Jesus as God's children (see 1:3a, 17). Further, the addition of the theme of "obedience" at this point extends the discussion in several directions. While this term points to the purification of baptism ("having purified your souls through obedience to the truth"—1:22), it also suggests the addressees' relation to the obedient Jesus (1:2) who entrusted himself to the Father (2:23) as ransom for sin (1:18-19; 2:24; 3:18) and left to believers an example of obedience (1:14, 22; 2:21; 4:13; note that unbelievers are characterized by their disobedience: 2:7-8; 3:1; also 3:20). Thus the expression "children of obedience" underscores the believer's relation to Jesus as one who awaits his revelation in glory (as the grace to be given—1:13; 4:13; 5:1) and one who also, like Jesus, has renounced human desires in obedience to God's will (1:2, 14b; 2:23; 4:2).

(1:15-16) Call to Holy Conduct. A second issue concerns the importance of the exhortation to holy conduct. This subunit is unusual in that it contains a second imperative and thus requires some explanation of its meaning and function in relation to the author's message. On the one hand, one could explain the author's paraenetic contrast between past and present behavior by appealing to the tradition employed by Paul in Rom 12:2 where addressees are also advised against conforming to worldly impulses and instead to seek a renewal of the mind that is able to discern God's will. Also, one might seek some justification for this pattern in the OT passage that dominates 1 Pet 1:15-16. Indeed Lev 18:1f prohibits the Israelites from adopting the way of life of their neighbors and then in 19:2 establishes divine holiness as the standard for its behavior.

On the other hand, the structure and message of the passage is determined by its principal theme. While the concept of holiness is prominent in these verses, it does not dominate the entire passage; rather, the theme of holy conduct is the focus. From the beginning the author's concern, though not employing the term "conduct," is that of Christian effort and deed. The imagery of v. 13 is seemingly that of focused effort that results in honorable deeds (1:17; 2:12), deeds, in more general terms, that will bring about judgment of both Gentiles and the household of God (4:5, 17). More particularly, the author in vv. 15-16 is concerned with the theme of conduct (*anastrophe*). The addressees are exhorted not to be holy but to be holy in their conduct, because believers have been made holy by the reception of the Spirit (1:2) and are now expected to manifest this divine quality in their behavior. Indeed Christian conduct is to be contrasted with pre-conversion or Gentile ways (1:18; also 1:13b; 4:3-4) and is characterized throughout the letter by various terms such as holiness, reverent fear, honor, purity, and goodness (1:15, 17; 2:12; 3:2, 16). It is the first of these (*hagios*) that is both used to describe God's people (2:5, 9) and serves as an umbrella term to characterize its conduct.

The author has chosen an interesting, even daring concept to describe this conduct. The notion of holiness in Semitic and Greek traditions relates rather to the domain of the gods and their cultus and in effect applies to those humans and cult objects that are set apart from the world. Thus the term is used in 1 Peter of the Holy Spirit ("sent from heaven"—1:12), of believers who are a holy priesthood or holy nation as God's possession (2:5 and 9—see Exod 19:6), but here, in a bold move, the author uses the term to describe the Christian's relationship to and behavior vis-à-vis the world. Rather than underscore separation from the world and its everyday concerns, the expression "holy conduct" encompasses these. In a manner similar to

Paul's exhortation to holiness (1 Thess 4:3-8), 1 Peter daringly applies the concept of holiness to the community's ethical concerns, specifically to its relationship to insiders and outsiders.

What then has led the author to stress the relationship between a holy God and holy conduct? One could perhaps appeal to the traditional view of holiness as relating to purity and reverent fear and therefore to view Christian conduct in 1 Peter as shaped by the concept of purity and religious fear for the divinity (1:17; 3:2) and eschatological judgment (2:12; 4:5). It seems better, however, to view 1:15a as providing the clue to resolve this issue. While some translations render the Greek in the following way, "as he who called you is holy" (so the NRSV) and underscore the theme of divine imitation ("be holy as God is holy"), it seems preferable to read the prepositional phrase so as to emphasize activity or behavior: "like the Holy One who called you" (NJB) and to draw a parallel with v. 15b: "be holy yourselves in all your conduct." God's activity vis-à-vis human beings is to call them to a life of holiness: to proclaim God's mighty acts (choice of a race and holy nation—2:9), to do right despite suffering (2:20-21; 3:9), to receive eternal glory and to glorify God (4:11; 5:10). The author insists that it is the holy one who calls to a life of holy conduct, an exhortation that is defended by a citation of Lev 19:2: "be holy because I am holy." Ultimately the concept of holiness, for 1 Peter, is the Christian's duty to do good (doing God's will—3:17; 4:2, 19) despite bad times, that the ungodly or evildoer might glorify God (2:11; 4:11), that the open-minded might be won over (3:2), and "that God might be glorified in all things through Jesus Christ" (4:11). It is precisely as the Holy One that God calls believers to a life of holy conduct during their "remaining time in the flesh" (4:2).

Reverence and Belief in God through Christ
(1:17-21)

This second subunit presents a similar structure to the first, though in place of an initial participial construction the author employs a factual, conditional clause ("if or since you invoke"), which is then followed by an imperative statement and a subsequent participial construction. Once again one encounters the theme of new life (children who invoke God as parent) and a clear reference to the addressees' pre-conversion status (futile conduct or ancestral ways). The overall passage addresses further the issue of Christian conduct as it relates to reverence to the divinity and in light of human redemption. The focus then is on reverence for and belief in the God who devised this plan with the addressees in mind (v. 21).

(1:17) Reverence for God as Father and Judge. The initial clause introduces the author's motive for the subsequent exhortation and, at the same time, provides a link with the preceding subunit concerning "children of obedience" who are exhorted to "holy conduct" by a holy God. Thus the theme of holiness, whether involving the imitation of a holy God or the requirements of "holy conduct," leads invariably to the eschatological concept of God as judge—a holy God must of necessity "judge justly" (2:23), that is, with impartiality and according to the conduct or work of each person. Such a concept of God is particularly stark. In the first place the audience is said to address in prayer a judge who is impartial; the term employed is related to the Semitic idiom "accept someone's face" to express "respect of person," an expression that gives rise to the present Hellenistic formation (*al prosopolemptos*) to express the desirability of objective judgment. This term is seemingly reflective of advice given to ancient judges ("not to acknowledge someone's face or person" in rendering a verdict—Deut 1:17), of Jesus' impartiality (Luke 20:21), of the standards of Christian behavior (Jas 2:1), and particularly of God's lack of favoritism (Acts 10:34; Rom 2:11; Eph 6:9; Col 3:25). In the second place the above expression is further underscored by the parallel statement that judgment is rendered "according to the deeds of each" (see the author's stress on deeds and judgment: 2:12, 23; 4:5, 17). Reference to such a judgment by such a God would then constitute a harsh warning to the community, a warning, some would insist, that is confirmed by the following exhortation to live "a life of fear."

Several considerations lead us in a different direction, namely the reference to God as "father" (for discussion of this theme, see 1:2a), the function and meaning of *phobos* ("fear"), and the "exilic" context of the behavior enjoined.

The initial reading of v. 17a reveals some tension between the ideas presented. How does one reconcile the contrast between the invocation of God as inexorable judge and as father? Seemingly the latter does not fit in the context since the proper attitude toward a demanding judge is one of fear or, as most commentators insist, the author reminds the readers that the God they invoke as father is also, judge of the living and the dead (4:5). Nonetheless, the Greek seems to require the opposite, namely that the impartial judge is invoked as father, and it is on this premise that the following exhortation is given.

The key to the proper interpretation of the verse is the author's use of the term *phobos*. On the one hand, following the well-known OT tradition of "fear of the Lord" (see Deut 10:20-21), 1 Peter insists that the proper attitude toward God is one of "reverent fear" (NRSV), an attitude that is proper to God, supersedes all other relationships (2:17), nullifies fear of human opponents (3:6, 14), and requires a life or conduct directed to God in reverence, gentleness, purity, and the doing of good (1:17; 2:18; 3:2, 6, 15). Thus the author returns to the theme of conduct and its relation to God. On the other hand, the author's linking of the theme of fear to that of God addressed as father seems to have been suggested by the previously-cited OT text (see 1:16), which continues: "You shall each revere (*phobeomai*) your mother and father" (Lev 19:3; see also v. 14). Thus 1 Peter insists that since one addresses the final judge as father, as did Jesus (see 1:3, 14 and Mark 14:36 and the Lord's Prayer), one is committed to a life of reverential fear toward one's divine parent.

The remainder of v. 17 is often rendered "during the time of your exile" (NRSV and others), even though the term employed is *paroikia* and not *parepidemos* as in 1:1. Since different terms are used and since both refer equally to the entire audience, one is led to expect a difference in meaning (see 2:11 for use of both roots in addressing the readers). While the meaning of the second is socioreligious (see discussion of 1:1 and the introduction), that of v. 17b is political. *Paroikia* refers to believers' status as "resident aliens" in the Roman empire who have social and political duties vis-à-vis their neighbors and government (see earlier discussion of *diaspora* at 1:1). In a political sense the life of believers is seen as a time (use of *chronos*; also in this sense in 4:2) of social and political activity, but, as indicated in the exhortation, this activity must have God as its ultimate direction ("reverent fear" must characterize this behavior). Believers are God's servants who must accept their God-given political responsibilities (2:13-17). Finally the just judge will evaluate even the political deeds of each (see 2:11 for further discussion of religious and political terminology).

(1:18-19) Redemption through the Christ-Event. The imperative of v. 17 is followed by the author's customary participial construction, in this case, to provide an added motive for the exhortation ("because you know that"), a motive that is both christological and soteriological in character. Indeed in these verses the author turns to the community's traditional Christ-centered soteriology as further motivation for Christian conduct (see already 1:2 for introduction of this theme). In thematic terms the focus is on the purchase price and in structural terms ("not . . . but") on the imperishable ("more precious than silver or gold"—18), salvific offering of Christ's blood (v. 19).

The precise meaning of the soteriological language of vv. 18-19 is debated owing to the author's peculiar combination of terms. Indeed the principal verb *lytroomai*, ranging in meaning from "release by payment of ransom," "deliver from slavery or bondage," or, in more religious terms, "redeem," is variously rendered so as to focus on the concepts of ransom, payment for freedom, or redemption. Interpretation is further complicated both by contemporary usage of the *lytron* word family and by the addition of sacrificial and passover terminology in v. 19.

Greek usage favors the sense of "buy back," "ransom," or "manumission," while in the LXX one encounters more readily the sense of "setting free" or "redemption" without mention of price. The latter is frequently the sense one finds in NT usage, though the meaning of "ransom" is clearly intended in early tradition but without the mention of price (Mark 10:45; Matt 20:28). Since, however, the concept of price is structurally prominent in 1 Peter ("not with perishable things like silver or gold . . . but with the priceless/precious blood"), it would seem that the meaning is that of manumission (use not of the genitive of price but the dative of instrument to indicate the means), a concept suggested by Greek usage, LXX theology, and other Petrine passages. In the first case the focus on price and use of *lytroomai* would have suggested to pagan readers the current custom of sacral manumission, a process whereby a slave acquired actual freedom by placing money in a god's treasury so as to be symbolically ransomed or purchased by that god. In OT terms and with LXX terminology, the author is inspired by the concept of divine liberation of Israel from slavery in Egypt or in exile (Exod 6:6; Deut 7:8; Isa 44:22-23). It is probably the influence of Isa 52:3 ("you were sold for nothing and will not be ransomed with silver") that suggests both the concept of slavery and manumission with the mention of price or ransom (see 2:22f for use of Isaiah 53). The author employs early Christian tradition to extend the OT concept: "not with silver or gold but with Christ's priceless blood." Finally the concept of manumission or deliverance from slavery is supported by the author's insistence that God has acquired "a chosen race . . . a holy nation" (2:9) and especially that believers, in religious terms, are "God's servants or slaves" and, in political terms, a "free people" (2:16; see also 1 Cor 7:22-24). Thus believers are liberated "from the futile ways or conduct inherited from [their] ancestors" (see 4:3-4, especially "forbidden idolatry") and are born to a new life of holy conduct. Indeed they have passed "out of darkness into [God's] marvelous light" (2:9).

The addition in v. 19 of sacrificial and passover terminology renders more complex the author's thought, for at the mention of "blood" as the means of buying back human slaves (see also 1 Cor 6:20; 7:23), the author is led to modify this term both by the adjective *timios* ("priceless or precious") and by the phrase "like that of a lamb without defect or blemish" or "unblemished and blameless." In the first case use of *timios* suggests a contrast with "silver and gold" (see 1:7) and so hints at the "priceless" worth of Christ's "blood"; however, its present context and the author's use of the related term *entimos* in 2:4, 6 point to divine approval: "precious [in God's sight]." Christ's blood as the means or the price of redemption from slavery (see Acts 20:28 and especially Heb 9:11-14) has become precious to God in its character as perfect sacrifice. Such a concept is suggested by a passage from Ps 115:15: "precious in the sight of the Lord is the death of his holy one." In the second case the author makes explicit use of the community's soteriological tradition to describe Christ's death as the sacrificial offering of the blood of a perfect cultic and moral victim. Christ is described in OT terms as a physically or cultically unblemished victim (see Exod 29:28; Lev 12:6; Num 6:14; also Heb 9:14) but one that is also "blameless" in moral terms (see 2:22). But especially it is the image of the lamb, whether of the sacrificial system (Num 28–29; cf. Heb 9:11f), of the passover tradition (Exod 12:5—1 Cor 5:7 and John 19:36; cf. Exod 12:46) or that of the suffering servant (Isaiah 53—John 1:29, 36; Acts 8:32), that brings home to Christian readers the christological, cruciform character of their new life. Christ is God's means for their release from slavery and will be presented as their model for conduct in the midst of suffering (see 2:21-22; 4:13).

(1:20) God's Redemptive Plan. The title "Christ" is separated from its noun "blood" and is placed at the end of v. 19 presumably to stress its messianic character (see already vv. 3 and 11) and especially to introduce the hymnic phrases of the following verse. Each of these phrases is introduced, in anaphoric style, by a passive participle that has Jesus as antecedent:

> destined before the foundation of the world
> manifested [revealed] at the end of the ages

While some scholars wish to see here an incarnational perspective whereby the first verb indicates preexistence and the second speaks of Jesus' appearance in human form, it is preferable to view this couplet as expressing the eschatological framework of the Christ-event, namely, its origin in the long-decided plan of God and its realization in the coming of Jesus in the final age. The verb *proginosko* underscores prior knowledge, plan, or choice and in its present context indicates the pretemporal origin of the Christ-event in God's mind or foreknowledge. Indeed this concept of the divine plan involves the choice of believers (1:2) and relates to the activity of the prophets in regard to Christ's suffering and glory (1:10-12). The second verb, *phaneroo*, speaks of making visible and operative the things predestined for Christ and the audience's salvation. Thus the first term marks the beginning (before creation) and the second the final period of God's salvific plan in christological and eschatological terms.

But why does the author introduce the theme at this point in the discussion? The answer is related to the writer's keen interest in the addressees' pre-conversion status. If mention of their former subservience to enslaving desires (1:14) prepared for the liberating theme of v. 18a, the description of the audience's pre-conversion status in v. 18b as "empty ancestral ways" would certainly have created some uneasiness in the minds of the Hellenistic Christian readers, for whom the principle of antiquity was a sure sign of the validity of one's ancestral traditions. Indeed early Christians will be concerned about this principle both when defending themselves against the newness of their doctrines and by employing it to combat Gnostic teachers (Origen, *Against Celsus* and Irenaeus, *Against Heresies*, respectively). In this particular context, lest some readers see the renunciation of ancient, ancestral customs for recent Christian belief as a negative argument, the author in v. 20 insists that God's plan for the messiah is even more ancient because it predates "the foundation of the world." Christian belief in this divine plan is more venerable than the futile customs it replaces and, returning to an earlier theme (see 1:12), the author insists that this plan was manifested and put into effect in these last days "for your sake."

(1:21) The Addressees' Belief in God through Christ. The author draws this second subunit to a close by dwelling on three important themes that have previously received attention and by relating these to faith and hope directed toward God.

The first theme involves a point stressed in 1:10 and 12 that prophetic revelation was meant for a future audience and, more specifically, for the addressees. Thus v. 20, concerning God's atemporal redemptive plan, is brought to a close by the striking statement that this divine activity was meant for the readers of 1 Peter ("for your sake") and leads into v. 21 by dwelling on their status as believers. Thus the addressees, seen as the holy community of the endtime, are characterized as the focus of God's salvific plan, a plan that had as its goal to make them believers in and servants of God (1:21; 2:15).

The second theme, Christ's agency in the salvific process, has been previously enunciated (1:2, 3), particularly in vv. 18-19, but is reemphasized in a twofold way in v. 21. First, believers are who they are "through him" (*di autou*). Second, God is described as the one "who raised him from the dead and gave him glory," thereby making possible salvation for the addressees.

The third theme, the author's theological focus, is striking in a number of ways and calls for some discussion. It is clear from earlier statements in chapter 1 that 1 Peter follows early Christian belief in stressing God's role as the one who foreordains both the Christ-event and the call of believers (1:1, 15, 20-21), as the one who requires obedience of Christ and of believers (1:2, 14), and as the all-powerful father and judge who protects, reveals, rewards, and requires a life of holiness (vv. 5, 7, 9, 13, 15-16). It is particularly striking that twice in v. 21 Christian activity is said to have God as its goal (*eis theon* in both instances). In the first case the activity is described by a term that is variously interpreted in a passive ("faithful or trustworthy") or active sense ("one who believes"). One could opt for the former and relate the expression to the more general theme of hope (1:3, 13, 21b—see use of passive meaning in 4:19 and 5:12); the meaning would be that the addressees of Asia Minor "have come to trust in God" (NRSV) in the midst of their trying circumstances. The active meaning, however, seems preferable in linguistic and contextual terms. Use of the preposition *eis* following *pistos* suggests "believe in" (see the parallel verbal usage in 1:8); also such was the understanding of copyists who replaced the adjective with the more familiar verb (P^{72}, S, and other manuscripts). Likewise the term *pistos* in the late NT is frequently used simply to designate one who believes (Acts 16:1, 15; 1 Tim 4:10; Titus 1:6). In contextual terms one must view the meaning of this expression in relation to the concluding statement of v. 21c: "so that your faith as well as hope are set on God." The author in vv. 18-21 is focused on the Christian's commitment to God through Christ (note the stress on the Christ-event in 21b) and so is able at the very end of the unit to insist that both faith as a commitment to God through the Christ-event and hope as the awaiting of Jesus' coming to bestow God's glory are focused on God as both judge and father. The faith of v. 21c refers back to the author's discussion of soteriology in vv. 18f, and hope looks back to the stress on holy activity in view of future grace in 13f.

(1:21b) A Final Note on Resurrection and Glory. In describing God in v. 21 the author applies an unusual construction that few persons fail to note. The terminology of the first part of the construction, "raise from the dead," though formulaic and traditional (Rom 4:24; 8:11; 10:9; Gal 1:1; 1 Thess 1:10), is unique for this author, while that of the second relates to the letter's consuming interest in the theme of glory (see discussion of 1:11). From this many interpreters have concluded that 1 Peter formulates in the second part a commentary on the resurrection formula to underscore the transcendent nature of Jesus' new life. Such a conclusion fails to note the peculiar literary character of the passage, which in effect seems to be a hymnic fragment:

a	the one who raised		that one gave	a'
b	him		to him	b'
c	from the dead	&	glory	c'

The two members are parallels structurally and thematically. Each is governed by a participle that modifies God, but the two are arranged in a chiastic structure wherein the parallel elements appear in reverse order (abc—c'b'a'). Thematically the two members involve Jesus' post-resurrection activity, the first in soteriological and the second in exaltation terminology. The first is formulaic, as noted earlier, and known especially from the Pauline corpus. The second, though less well attested, is discernible from numerous NT texts that speak of Jesus' resurrection from the dead in terms of glorification ("taken up in glory"—1 Tim 3:16; God glorifying Jesus—Acts 3:13,15; Jesus "entering into his glory"—Luke 24:26, 46; see John 17:22 and Rom 6:4) or heavenly enthronement and reception of glory (1 Pet 1:11; 3:22; 4:13).

First Peter has chosen a hymnic parallel that once referred to Jesus' resurrection not as a means to describe the new reality of post-resurrection life but to give further cohesion to the logic of the literary unit. By referring to the resurrection from the dead in the first part of the structure, 1 Peter underscores the soteriological character of Christian faith; and by expressing the theme of glory in the second part of the structure, the author stresses the importance of hope in the addressees' lives. In this way the author speaks of Jesus' resurrection from the dead as a backward reference to his salvific death as the price for freedom (1:18f) and speaks likewise of his reception of glory as a way of underscoring the document's motivational strategy: a holy life is possible and necessary in view of future glory. Finally 1 Peter concludes in 21c that both belief in Jesus' salvific death and resurrection and trust in the call and promise of glory are anchored in one's relationship to the God who raised Jesus from the dead, gave him glory, and thus reassures those who share in his sufferings that they, when reviled for the name of Christ, shall share similarly in divine glory (4:13; 5:10). Thus the author reassures the addressees that their faith and hope are set on their father and judge as they live in reverent fear as servants of God and members of the Roman state.

Mutual Love: Both Genuine and Constant (1:22-25)

Like the two previous subunits, the third one also presents an initial participial construction, followed by an imperative and a second participial statement. Once again one encounters the themes of new life (being born anew) and the addressees' pre-conversion status (implicit in the concepts of purification and withering flesh or grass). The focus of the passage is on the exhortation to mutual love, but first the author dwells on the addressees' conversion and finally, following the exhortation, on the character of this Christian obligation.

(1:22a) Conversion and Purification. The initial participle introduces the theme of purification seemingly without transition or connection with the previous passage. Scholars have proposed several explanations for the present order of themes, whether a traditional link between hope and purification as in 1 John 3:3 ("all who have this hope in him purify themselves") or a more general connection of this theme with the earlier concepts of redemption from and rejection of former conduct (1:14, 18-19). Further complicating the issue is the meaning of purification in this context: does it have a moral or cultic sense?

The answer to these queries lies in structural and thematic considerations. It should be noted again that the three subunits of this general section have a similar structure and that each of these prepares for its paraenetic injunction. In the first instance (v. 13f) LXX language (see Jer 1:17) concerning preparation for work introduces an exhortation to hope and holy conduct. In the second instance (v. 17f) the theme of divine invocation (God as father—see Jer 3:19) leads to an injunction to reverence before and belief in God, and thus the author is able to conclude: "so that your faith as well as hope are set on God" (v. 21). In the present instance (vv. 22f) a similar approach is adopted by the author. Borrowing a LXX phrase from Jer 6:16 ("you will find purification for your souls"; note that Matt 11:29 follows the Hebrew: "you will find rest for your souls"), the author introduces the theme of purification as a prelude to the injunction to mutual love. Thus the introduction of the theme of purification and its meaning in this verse are to be sought in the relationship between the two participial constructions ("purified" and "born anew") and the central injunction to mutual love.

Though the term *hagnizo* could and does bear a moral sense of separation from former evil ways (as in Jas 4:8: "purify your hearts"), it is more likely that the author's use of the perfect tense indicates that the term is used in a cultic sense ("cleanse with water"—LSJ 11) since the act is a past one that continues to affect the present. Additionally the parallel with the second participle ("born anew") suggests a similar meaning, namely, new life in baptism. Beyond this, the purification is said to have occurred "through or by means of obedience to the truth" and to involve the whole being ("your souls"—see 1:9; 2:11, 25; 3:20; 4:19). The first phrase presumably alludes to conversion whereby the term "obedience" underscores commitment and "truth" and, in contrast to pagan ways, expresses believers' adherence to the "living and enduring God" (cf. Rom 2:8). Such a conclusion is confirmed by the author's reference to the addressees as "children of obedience" (1:14) and of nonbelievers as those who "disobey the word" (2:8—use of *apeitho*; see also 3:1, 20; 4:17—"disobey the gospel of God"; similar language is used in Gal 5:7; Rom 10:16; and 2 Thess 1:8). Like Christ (1:2; 2:23), Christians are by definition obedient to the will of God and will be so in confronting unavoidable suffering (3:17). A final reason for insisting that purification here refers to baptism at the time of conversion is the author's language in describing the believer's responsibility to love others, namely, *philadelphia*, or love of one's new siblings. Baptism or ritual purification at the time of conversion incorporates believers into a new family whose members are "brothers and sisters" toward whom one has a responsibility of mutual love.

(1:22b) Exhortation to Genuine Mutual Love. After an initial participial statement the author, as is true of the previous two subunits, addresses paraenetic concerns in the form of an explicit imperative clause. It should also be noted that, as in the cases of the previous subunits, the initial participial construction prepares for the topic to be considered in the following injunction. In this particular case the author, before exhorting the addressees to love one another, insists that purification has "genuine mutual love" (*philadelphia*) in view. As noted earlier choice of the term seems to be motivated by the author's wish to stress the Christian's baptismal commitment to God and to life of holiness and love within the fellowship (see 2:17; 4:8).

Strangely enough the following imperative repeats these ideas in a rather explicit fashion, a fact that requires some explanation. In the first place 1 Peter insists that purification has as its goal:

    a   a love of fellow Christians
    b   that is genuine or sincere and then exhorts
         the addressees by way of conclusion: (therefore)
    b'   from the heart
    a'   love one another

The author then adds a final adverb to complete the exhortation (see discussion below). It is clear from this structure that the repetition is intentional, but it is also suggested that the variation in terminology deserves attention in discerning the author's message. On the one hand, while the love terminology can be applied interchangeably or in a complementary way in early Christian tradition (Rom 12:9-10; 1 Thess 4:9-10; 1 John 3:10-11), there is seemingly a distinction being made here. In the first instance believers have been admitted into the community of faith ("the brotherhood"—*adelphotes*: 2:17; 5:9) and must work out their commitment ("faith" in Pauline terms) in a demonstration of genuine love. The focus is on the commitment and its new familial relationships and responsibilities. In the second instance the focus is on the mutual character of the exchange, namely hospitality and mutual service by employing one's God-given talents (4:8-11). The second phrase complements the first term and reinforces the Christian's new socio-religious situation.

On the other hand, the author uses different terminology to describe the concept of love. In the first case the term is *anypokritos*, meaning "sincere or without dissimulation" and so focusing on the public or ecclesial character of the believer's responsibility. The second phrase "from the heart," employed in the paraenetic injunction, bears a similar meaning to the first but now stresses the inner motivation for such behavior that must proceed from the core of one's being and commitment (see discussion of 3:4 and a similar contrast in Rom 12:9-13).

The author's paraenetic injunction repeats the prior statement concerning the believer's commitment to "sincere love of fellow Christians" but adds particular emphasis on the mutual and radical character of this responsibility. In addition the author terminates this injunction with the important adverb *ektenos*, a term that is variously translated as emphasizing intensity ("zeal or fervor") or expressing a temporal concept ("constancy"). In the first instance the term would be a virtual synonym for "from the heart," seeming unduly repetitious. In the second instance the term would introduce a temporal concept that will then occupy the remainder of the passage. The author wishes to stress not the intensity of this love—that is already done by the terms "genuine" and "from the heart"—but its longevity, that is, the believer's perseverance in love until the Lord's return in glory (see 4:8 for similar use of the adjectival form of the term).

(1:23-25) New Birth. Taking a clue from the previous verse on new birth and the constancy of love, the author now turns to other characteristics of this new birth.

New Birth from Imperishable Procreation. Following the imperative the author introduces a second participial construction whose function seemingly is to defend the temporal character or constancy of the love commandment. The theme of new birth, discussed at several points earlier (1:3; see also vv. 14 and 17), is reintroduced to insist upon its imperishable source (*ek*) and therefore to defend its enduring character. Thus 1 Peter insists that the believer's new life derives from an imperishable (see 1:4,18; 3:4) *spora*, a term that means not "seed" as is often suggested but "sowing, procreation, or origin" (LSJ 1629). The author insists, and will repeat later, that the believer's new birth is of divine origin. In fact similar statements are made in 1:3 where God is said to have given the addressees a new birth and in vv. 14, 17 where the addressees call upon God as progenitor or father.

Means: through the Word or the Good News. At the end of v. 23 it is said that this new life is accomplished "through the word of God," a phrase that is further clarified at the end of the passage by insisting that "this word is the good news that was announced to you" (25b). For 1 Peter the expression "the word of God" is the equivalent of "word" used absolutely ("disobey the word"—2:8; 3:1) or "gospel of God" (4:17; also the verbal uses 1:12, 25; 4:6) and bears a traditional content, namely, the announcing of the Christ-event (1:3, 19, 21; 2:24). Also in a traditional vein the author insists that God's means (*dia*) for communicating new life was the word announced as "good news" for the addressees' benefit.

Source: the Living and Enduring God. There is debate whether the two participial adjectives modify word or God. Appeal is made to biblical tradition to defend either the first ("the living and enduring Word"—Heb 4:12; Matt 24:35) or the second ("the living and enduring God"—Dan 6:27). In the first case it is claimed that the author employs the OT concept of the creative divine word (Gen 1:3f; Ps 33:9; Isa 55:11) to portray God as acting in human lives by means of an active, life-giving, and permanent reality. The concept is further defended by appealing to a parallel concept in Heb 4:12 and to the subsequent statement of v. 25, itself a citation from Isa 40:8: "the word of the Lord endures forever." In the second case it is asserted that such an interpretation lays stress on word, whereas the author seems to focus on God as the source of new life and its enduring character in loving conduct. Besides, undue emphasis is placed on the scriptural citation concerning "the enduring word" rather than on the divine source both of new life and of the word through which life is communicated (see below for discussion of citation). In v. 23 then the author's focus, as it was in vv. 17-21, is on God who is both life-giving and enduring; vv. 24-25 direct the readers' attention to the temporal element, which the author has already emphasized by employing terms such as "constancy" and "enduring."

Scriptural Proof. The subunit ends with a relatively long, verbatim LXX citation (vv. 24-25), a citation whose form, meaning, and function pose questions for the modern reader. There are three differences between the Greek text of 1 Peter and that of Isa 40:6-8, differences that are minor but not insignificant. The former adds the term *hos*, thereby changing a metaphor into a simile ("all flesh is *like* grass"), and modifies the LXX "all human glory" to "all *its* [flesh] glory." These two changes are not due to variant LXX tradition but to the author's activity. The first insists not that "flesh" is lowly or empty but rather that, like grass, it is perishable; in other words, it will "wither." In the second case, rather than the LXX focus on the flesh as humanity ("human glory"), one encounters a shift back to the concept of "flesh" ("its glory") in a neutral sense of an earthly as opposed to a heavenly sphere, that is, "not as sinful and hostile to God, but simply as limited and provisional" (*TDNT* 7:126). The third difference, "word of the Lord" in place of the traditional "word of God" (following the Hebrew text), can be explained in two ways: either as due to redactional activity or to LXX tradition. In the first instance some insist that 1 Peter transforms the LXX text to facilitate a christological reading of the passage, a conclusion, they note, that is supported by 1 Pet 2:3 and 3:15 as well as the author's seemingly consistent christological usage of *kyrios* or lord. In the second instance there is sufficient manuscript evidence to suggest that such a LXX reading was known to the Christian author (especially from the Lucianic LXX tradition).

In light of the previous discussion, what can one then say about the meaning and function of the OT citation? On the one hand, the citation functions as a defense of the author's insistence that love must be constant. Having stressed earlier that Christian new life derives from an imperishable, enduring divine source, the author appeals to the Hebrew Scriptures to contrast this new life with earthly existence and to underscore its enduring character. Thus, by the addition of "like" to the LXX citation, the author is not saying that earthly existence ("all flesh") *is* lowly, empty, or sinful but that it *is like* grass in its ephemeral or perishable nature; its glory will wither, and its flower will fall. Over against this reality the author contrasts the divine, imperishable heavenly life that comes about through the word of God and that demands a genuine and constant love.

On the other hand, the citation raises questions about the meaning of the terms "word" and "lord" and about the relationship of v. 25b to the

Isaian citation. It is clear from v. 23 that "word" bears a theological sense, "the word of God." In v. 25a, however, employing the LXX *rhema* rather than *logos*, the meaning is not obvious, especially in the expression "the word of the Lord." While it is often maintained that "lord" in 1 Peter consistently refers to Christ, it is debatable that such a simple conclusion obtains in this letter, because the double reference to "lord" in 3:12 (= Ps 33:15-16) certainly refers to God as judge (see 2:23), and the uses of "lord" in 2:3 and 3:15 as here in 1:25 are borrowed from LXX passages (Ps 33:9; Isa 8:13; and Isa 40:8, respectively) and lead the author of 1 Peter to clarify contextually this OT usage. In the present case I would venture to suggest that "word of the Lord" is a parallel to "word of God" (v. 23), a conclusion that is supported by the author's usage elsewhere. Either "word" is used absolutely ("obey or disobey the word"—2:8; 3:1) or "good news" is God's ("disobey the gospel of God"—4:17) or is "sent from heaven" (1:12).

Two further considerations also suggest a theological reading. First, the contrast in the citation corresponds to and defends the earlier contrast between the perishable and imperishable origin of new life. All flesh is of earthly origin; it withers, falls, and so is perishable. On the other hand, the word is of heavenly origin; it endures and so is imperishable. The author's point in the second part of the citation is not that the word is eternal, but the implied logic is that "new life is *like* the divine, abiding word." Second, v. 25b sheds light on the meaning of the citation; the author adds, in midrashic fashion, a clarification of the previous OT statement: "that word," God's utterance, is precisely the good news come from heaven (see 1:12), the message about Christ's death/suffering and resurrection/glory (1:3, 10-11, 21).

Finally this section, like the previous ones (see 1:12 and 21), ends on a note of actualization: "the good news that was announced to *you*." The author's focus is on the addressees' situation and in this particular case on the constancy of the love that the members of the community owe one another (see 3:8; 4:8; and 5:5 where the author returns to this pressing issue).

Suggested Readings

Dalton, W. J. "So That Your Faith May Also Be Your Hope in God" in *Reconciliation and Hope: New Testament Essays on Atonement and Eschatology*. Ed., R. J. Banks. Grand Rapids: Eerdmans, 1974, 262-74.

Evang, M. " '*Ex kardias allelous agapesate ektenos*': Zum Verstandnis der Aufforderung und ihrer Begrundungen in 1 Petr 1, 22f." *ZNTW* 80 (1989) 111-23.

La Verdiere, E. A. "A Grammatical Ambiguity in 1 Pet. 2:12." *CBQ* 36 (1974) 89-94.

Manns, F. "La théologie de la nouvelle naissance dans la première lettre de Pierre." *SBFLA* 45 (1995) 107-41.

Osborne, R. P. "L'utilization des citations de l'Ancien Testament dans la première épître de Pierre." *RTL* 12 (1981) 64-77.

Schlosser, J. "Ancien testament et christologie dans la Prima Petri" in *Etudes*, 65-96.

Thurén, L. *The Rhetorical Strategy of 1 Peter. With Special Regard to Ambiguous Expressions.* Abo: Abo Academy, 1990.

van Unnik, W. C. "The Critique of Paganism in 1 Peter 1:18" in *Neotestamentica et Semitica: Studies.* Eds., E. E. Ellis and M. Wilcox. Edinburgh: T. & T. Clark, 1969, 129-42

Growth as God's People
(2:1-10)

This third subunit brings the letter's first major block of material (1:3–2:10) to a close and consists of three passages whose relationship is perhaps not as obvious to modern readers as it was to their intended audience. In stylistic terms the first passage consists of a paraenetic injunction whose connection to what precedes is expressed as a conclusion ("therefore") but whose relationship to the second passage is clear in grammatical terms (use of a relative construction; see also 1:10f) but less so in thematic terms. Finally the third unit draws a clear contrast between unbelievers who reject the precious stone and believers who constitute God's people. Thus it is readily conceded that vv. 4-10 consist primarily of interwoven OT citations and allusions that are engaged to describe the christological foundation and elect character of the Christian community but that the relationship between these and vv. 1-3 is less obvious. It is our intention therefore to examine the form and function of each section and to discern the role each plays in the author's paraenetic strategy.

An additional feature of the three sections under discussion, and a further clue to their function, is the appearance in each section of distinct result or purpose constructions. In the first case the addressees are exhorted to choose food that will "result in growth for salvation" (2:2); in the second they are to allow themselves to be formed into a house or priesthood "for the purpose of offering spiritual sacrifices acceptable to God" (v. 5); and in the third it is stated basically that believers are now a holy people "to make known the praises" of God (v. 9). It is around these central themes that the author organizes a series of insights on the community's elect character and responsibility toward "the one who called [them] out of darkness into his marvelous light" (v. 9b).

Divine Food for Growth into Salvation (2:1-3)

In structural terms this first section (vv. 1-3), as well as the second (vv. 4f), has much in common with the immediately preceding subunits: 1:13-16, 17-21, and 22-25, because its central paraenetic injunction is framed by two distinct subordinate constructions. The passage opens with an extended participial construction (as in 1:13, 22) and introduces an imperative clause that is further modified by a "factual *if* clause" (see 1:17, which opens in this fashion) in place of a second participial construct. Like the previous three subsections, it introduces the theme of new life ("newborn infants") and refers explicitly to the addressees' pre-conversion existence (they have rejected their former loyalties or vices—2:1; see also 4:3-4).

(2:1) Rejection of Human Desires. The subunit opens in a manner similar to 1:13. In both cases an inferential conjunction ("therefore"—*dio* and *oun*, respectively) draws a close connection between the paraenetic character of the new passage and the preceding doctrinal discussion, and in both cases a participial construction prepares for the following injunction. Interestingly, the author again employs a clothing image (see 1:13—"gird up the loins of your mind") to express the shedding of old garments, in this case the garments of human desire (the title of the section is suggested by the texts of 2:11 and 4:2). The verb *apotithemi* means literally the removal of clothes (see Acts 7:58) and here obviously reflects the paraenetic usage of contemporary moral philosophers and the tradition of the early church, whereby conversion is seen, on the one hand, as involving "the laying aside" of immoral attitudes and practices (described as works of darkness or given in a list of vices) and the assuming of new behavior or loyalty (described as "putting on the Lord Jesus Christ," receiving the salvific word or food, or as requiring loving behavior—see Rom 13:12-14; Eph 4:31-32; Jas 1:21). While one might insist that such language is more figurative than literal (meaning simply "rid oneself of"—NRSV; see Heb 12:1), one might counter that 1 Peter is fond of clothing imagery (see 1:13; 4:1; 5:5; also 3:21) and that the baptismal context of 2:1-3 and the early Christian practice of converts wearing white garments would support a more literal interpretation, a nuance that would not be lost on the addressees.

The author insists that the old garment of the converts' former lives involved immoral attitudes and practices. To describe this pre-conversion status, a list of vices is formulated, a list whose terms are commonly found in contemporary vice catalogues (see Rom 1:29-31; Gal 5:19-21; Col 3:5, 8; and *Barnabas* 20:1) but whose particular configuration and function merit attention. The list of vices consists of five terms; the first two are singular nouns and are each introduced by "all," and the other three are in the plural, only the last of which is preceded by "all." While one can appeal to the five-fold lists of Col 3:5, 8, 12 to suggest a traditional source for this list or point to the proverbial three ("all") as also indicating formulaic use of paraenetic material, it is more convincing to seek the meaning and function of this particular list in the author's configuration of the catalogue and role it plays in its context.

Despite the frequent tendency of commentators and translators to view the initial participle as having a present, imperative force and thus to interpret the vice list as an injunction focused on moral effort (see NRSV: "rid yourselves . . . of all"), it is preferable to insist on the verb's aorist form and to view the activity as related to the believer's past choice at conversion ("having divested yourselves of"). The vice list of 2:1 relates to the addressees' Gentile past, much as does Paul's vice catalogue in Rom 1:29-31, and their submission to the forces of darkness (see 2:9, 11; 4:2-4; 5:8-9). Converts have rejected "all dependence on evil and all use of deceit" (singular terms indicating domain and means—see 2:16 and 22) and the conduct that flows from these as "acts of insincerity, envy, and slander" (plural terms denoting specific acts). The threefold use of "all" to introduce the first two terms confirms, on the one hand, the generic character of the first two, singular nouns and, on the other hand, the qualification of the last term in the same way ("all slander") probably allows the author to underscore both the libelous nature of the community's situation (see discussion of 2:12; 3:16) and its duty to refrain from trading such abuses and insults (2:23; 3:15-16). One would do well therefore to paraphrase v. 1 as follows: "therefore having divested yourselves of all evil activity and its deceitful means, whether through acts of insincerity, envy or especially slander" and to see its function not as presenting a parallel, introductory exhortation but as introducing the following injunction concerning spiritual food.

(2:2a) Instinctive, Spiritual Desire. It is often remarked that one would expect to find a list of virtues in v. 2 in place of an injunction for pure food. It is traditional for moral writers to exhort audiences to refrain from given vices and to embrace a parallel list of virtues (Col 3:5f; Eph 4:31-32); such an expectation for 1 Peter is strengthened when one transforms the initial aorist participle into a present imperative. However, if one follows more correctly the past (aorist) character of the activity and relates this rejection to conversion, then one's expectations are different. In contrast to the rejection of Gentile loyalties and practices, one might expect the Christian, in more stark terms, "to have turned to the living and true God" (1 Thess 1:9), to "put on the Lord Jesus Christ" (Rom 13:14), or "welcome . . . the [salvific] word" (Jas 1:21). The image of food or "pure milk" in 1 Peter is employed to develop the themes of Christian commitment and growth in the context of new birth. Thus the rejection of the Gentile world, expressed in terms of divesting oneself of worldly loyalties and behavior (see discussion of 1:15), is subsumed under the rubric of birth and consequent growth and nourishment.

Like Newborn Infants. The new injunction is introduced by a striking phrase "like newborn infants." While the expression reintroduces the theme of new life, which figures prominently in chapter 1 (see vv. 3, 13, 17, 23), it none-theless adds a distinct note of recent birth. Since both terms stress this notion (lit.: "recently born babies") it has often been suggested either that the audience consists of new converts or that the author is employing a bap-tismal source for the composition of the letter. Such conclusions easily overlook the fact that the phrase functions as a simile; the addressees are not newborn babes but are to act like newborn babies who yearn for their mother's milk. Thus the phrase serves both to reiterate the theme of new life and to prepare for the following injunction.

New Loyalties and Instinctive Desire. So having set the tone for the new exhortation (a turning away from past desires), the author advises the audi-ence in v. 2 to "long for or desire" its proper nourishment in the manner of newborns that instinctively desire their mother's milk. In this regard two major points are being made. First, the author's choice of the verb *epipotheo* ("to long for or desire") indicates to the addressees that former desires of the flesh, which involved ignorant behavior, war against the soul, and conflict with God's will (use of *epithymia*; see 1:14; 2:11; 4:2, 3), have their parallel in the present as the result of new loyalties, which bring about new desires. LXX usage confirms such an interpretation because in the Psalms the righteous person is repeatedly said to "long for or yearn" for God's com-mandments, judgment, or salvation and especially to be in the presence of the Almighty (41:1; 61:10; 118:20, 131, 174). In 1 Peter there is a repeated stress on the innocent person's seeking after God's salvation, judgment, and presence (1:5, 9; 2:2, 11; 3:18; 4:5, 17; 5:10). Second, this new desire, like the old ones (4:3—"doing what the Gentiles want"), is presumed to be instinctive, because believers are to act like newborn babes in their desire for their mothers' milk. Here too an OT passage, using the same verb, expresses a similar idea: "as the hart longs greatly for the fountains of water, so my soul longs for you, O God; my soul has thirst for the living God; when shall I come and appear before God?" (Ps 41:1-2). Thus new loyalties (rejection of the realm of darkness or vice and commitment to that of light and virtue— see 2:1-2, 9, 11-12) suggest an equally natural desire for the fruits or nourishment of that realm.

Milk as Divine Kindness and Nourishment. The addressees are exhorted to "long for the pure, spiritual milk" (NRSV). Just as the preceding aorist participle is usually rendered as a present imperative and interpreted as exhorting the readers to avoid unholy behavior, described in a list of vices, so the following aorist imperative is usually seen as encouraging them to focus their attention and effort on what is presumed to be the figurative milk of the good news. Such an interpretation presupposes a number of conclusions to the issues raised by vv. 1-3. It is assumed that the exhortation of v. 2 parallels those of 1:13-25, namely, that they concern effort: work or conduct in hope, in reverent fear, and through acts of love—the new exhortation then would command greater appreciation of the life-giving, nourishing word. Also, this aorist imperative, like the previous ones, is usually interpreted as offering general directions to the community, that is, treated as a present imperative (see BDF 337 [2]). Further, the image of milk is seen as representing Christian sustenance (see 1 Cor 3:2; Heb 5:12-13) and its modifying adjectives (*adolos* and *logikos*) as insisting on its figurative and spiritual (or "word-like") character. Thus Jesus (or "the Lord" of v. 3 and its OT citation) becomes in effect the word, the milk, or content of this nourishment that the addressees are exhorted to desire with greater intensity with their spiritual growth in view. The goal of vv. 1-3 would then be the exhortation to the audience to long more strenuously for the genuine nourishment that God's word (1:23) affords.

A number of considerations lead me in a different direction in interpreting vv. 1-3. First, one should examine the image of milk. While one readily remembers NT passages that describe elementary instruction as milk as opposed to solid food (1 Cor 3:2; Heb 5:12-14), one should also consider contemporary usage where the theme represents divine love and kindness. In the first-century Christian *Odes of Solomon*, God the Father is presented in feminine fashion as providing for believers—this assistance is compared to "milk [which] flows from the woman who loves her children" (40:1). The Father is the source of the milk, and the Son and Spirit have a role to play in sharing this life-giving, holy milk (8:14; 19:2; 35:5). There is no doubt that in these passages the nourishment stands for God's mercy or love, as it does in 19:1: "a cup of milk was offered to me, and I drank it in the sweetness of the Lord's kindness" (see also 14:3 and the related imagery of 1QH 7:20-22; 9:35-36 from the Dead Sea Scrolls).

Second, the context in which the imagery is used also argues for this line of interpretation. The passage opens with an aorist participle that describes a past event (rejection of the past), to which the following injunction contrasts a present commitment to God and divine nourishment. The author's use of an aorist imperative indicates not an exhortation to a pattern of behavior or activity but to a "vivid and absolute" commitment to a new loyalty (for this type of "global aorist," see *BG*, 253) and source of dependence. In addition the adjective *adolos* indicates the "pure or unadulterated" milk or love of God for human creatures, and *logikos* underscores the "spiritual or heavenly" character and origin of this new care and assistance (see *T.Levi* 3:6).

Third, the thematic context of new life supports such an interpretation. It is clear that God as father gives believers a new birth (1:3) and as mother provides the newborn with the indispensable source of growth. If from 1:25 one must conclude that God gives nourishment through the word or good news, then from 2:2 one is led to suggest that this nourishment, expressed as "pure milk," refers to divine sustenance given to children by a parent who cares (5:7, 10).

(2:3) New Life and New Food. This first passage ends with a curious clause that is translated "if indeed you have tasted that the Lord is good." The conditional clause, like that of 1:17, indicates an "indicative of reality," "border(s) on causal 'since' " (BDF 372), and provides an added reason for the preceding exhortation concerning heavenly sustenance. The wording of the clause is borrowed from Ps 33:9—the author has modified the original imperative to an aorist indicative and has omitted a second verb ("and see") to underscore the vivid character of the food imagery. How does one interpret this statement?

On the one hand, the author's choice of theme and text owes both to traditional and personal reasons. It is clear from Hebrews and suggested by the *Odes of Solomon* that Psalm 33 and its themes were of interest to contemporary Christian thinkers. The former speaks of believers having been "enlightened" and having "tasted the heavenly gift" and "the goodness of the word of God" (6:4-5) and the latter that the righteous drink God's "holy milk," "live by it," and have enjoyed "the sweetness of the Lord's kindness" (8:14; 19:1). Psalm 33 also seems to have been a favorite of the author who not only cites at length from it in 3:10-12 (= vv. 12-16a) but also seemingly was attracted by many of its themes: blessing, sojourn, enlightenment, affliction, hope, fear of the Lord, and the humble in spirit (vv. 1, 4, 5, 8, 9, 18—see 1 Pet 1:3, 6, 17, 21; 2:9; 5:5, among other passages). Perhaps more important for the author of 1 Peter is the Psalmist's preoccupation with the suffering of the innocent or righteous and with the promise of divine protection and deliverance (see especially v. 19: "the afflictions of the righteous are many, but out of them all will the Lord deliver them").

On the other hand, the function of v. 3 merits some attention. In the first place, as has been noted above, the verse offers a strong reason why the addressees should rely wholeheartedly on their new sustenance. Indeed at conversion they were given a sweet taste of God's kindness; thus their participation in the Christ-event via the good news should further convince them that God's nourishment is pure and sweet. Second, v. 2 reinforces the passage's relation to 1:23 where a distinction is clearly made between heavenly or imperishable generation and the means employed. Here too the author clearly distinguishes between God's loving kindness and the christological medium by which it is dispensed. To this end the author has changed the focus of the verb from a general invitation to experience the Lord's goodness (in the Psalm) to a specific reference to the time when the addressees divested themselves of their past loyalties and turned to God when they accepted Jesus' invitation. This invitation is characterized as tasting the Lord's goodness, a theme that seemingly relates to the Jesus tradition that characterizes his yoke as pleasant (Matt 11:28-30) and therefore suggests a pleasant lord (as in Ps 33:9) who mediates God's mercy, goodness, and love (Titus 3:4-5) under the guise of heavenly milk. God has given new life and graciously presents new, heavenly food, a food that believers have already tasted in Jesus.

(2:2b) Growth into Salvation. Immediately following the exhortation to yearn for God's sweet sustenance, the author, using a *hina* clause, expresses the purpose of this nourishment: "in order that, by this means, you might grow (fully) into salvation." In considering the immediate thematic context (infants, milk, and growth), one would expect the goal of such nourishment to be spiritual maturation. Indeed such is the case in other similar NT passages where maturity is the goal of Christian growth (Eph 4:13; Heb 5:14; Jas 1:2-4). Indeed 1 Peter speaks of "growing into salvation." While the term *soteria* can refer to physical as well as religious well-being, its usage in 1 Pet 2:2b and the meaning of the passage generally requires some attention.

Interestingly the author emphasizes the means by which the growth will occur. While it is a process that requires human activity, it nonetheless has divine assistance as its impetus. Addition of *en auto* ("by it or by this means") therefore stresses once again the role of divine assistance. The author, by means of the verb "grow," focuses on the process that must occur, a process that involves human effort related to heavenly assistance or food. This human effort refers backward and forward to the author's paraenetic injunctions concerning holy conduct vis-à-vis both fellow believers and Gentile neighbors. Further complicating the issue is the author's use of an aorist verb, a point that is not frequently noted. Seemingly, such a construction adds a note of finality or fullness both to the process and goal involved. There is care then on the author's part to direct proper attention to the activity's goal.

Perhaps the most crucial clue to the author's meaning is found in the interpretation of the term *soteria* ("salvation"). Clearly for 1 Peter the term refers to a future reality that is "to be revealed in the last time" (1:5); that is, it will be fully enjoyed only at the endtime. However, already in v. 5 (by use of the qualifier "an already-prepared salvation") and especially in v. 9, the author insists that salvation is also a present reality that the believer has begun to enjoy. In fact the concept of salvation for 1 Peter is related both to the consummation when praise, glory, and honor are bestowed on the righteous (1:7) by the returning lord and to present divine protection of the addressees in the midst of trials and unjust treatment (1:5-6; 5:9-10). Finally the author's use of the term in 1:10-12 directs the reader's attention to the ultimate goal of such terminology, for salvation is said to be patterned on Christ's experience of suffering and glory. In the present believers are to grow (with divine assistance) through trials and gentle defense (1:6; 3:15-16) like those of the obedient Christ (1:2; 4:13) and so are to place their worries on a caring God (5:6-7). Thus, by means of divine protection, trusting in God, and with much effort (see 5:7-8), they are to grow in the present through lives of holiness so as to receive fully the salvation bestowed upon Christ and promised to obedient children. Just as the addressees' "faith and hope are set on God" (1:21), so are their growth in holy behavior and strength in adversity, which depend on divine nourishment.

Christ as God's Stone of Faith and Stumbling (2:4-8)

This second section bears some of the characteristics of the preceding units but also manifests a marked change in thematic focus and composition. As earlier, the unit opens with a participial construction followed by an imperative, but in place of the customary participial complement there follows a series of three OT citations whose connecting link is the term "stone" (*lithos*). Rather than the usual references to new life and the addressees' former existence, one finds a new ecclesiological focus. Indeed one also finds a clear shift from the personal food and growth imagery of 2:1-3 to that of social existence as God's spiritual edifice or holy people. While some, relying on this thematic shift, have posited a sharp break between vv. 3 and 4, it should be noted that, in grammatical terms, the relation between the two sections is indeed close (see 1:9 for a similar situation involving a relative construction). The connection between these sections focuses on the "lord" of the OT citation of v. 3, which the author, in midrashic fashion, wishes to identify as the Lord Jesus. As it is stated in v. 3 that God's means par excellence for giving spiritual sustenance is the experience ("tasting") of Jesus at conversion, so, in v. 4 through a change to building imagery, it is proposed that the means for becoming a member of God's people, seen as a spiritual house with Christ as cornerstone and believers as living stones, is precisely the acceptance of the Lord Jesus in baptism (or "coming to him" as God's "chosen, precious stone"). Thus this new section and the one following focus more particularly on ecclesiological issues, vv. 4-8 on Christ as God's stone of faith or stumbling and vv. 9-10 on the new people constituted out of God's mercy.

Few would deny that vv. 4-10 present a number of features that create difficulties for the interpreter, whether the role and source of the "stone" citations in vv. 6-8, the function of the "purpose constructions" of vv. 5 and 9, the relationship of the OT citations and allusions to the surrounding text, and finally the overall function and meaning of the passage. Several proposals have been made concerning the form and therefore interpretation of these verses.

In earlier scholarship it was customary to view the OT citations and allusions of vv. 6-10 as scriptural proofs of the ideas formulated in vv. 4-5. This was particularly noted since vv. 6f ("for it stands in scripture") seemingly confirmed such a conclusion and were presumed to derive from a hymnal or quotation source that was secondarily added to the main composition.

In more recent times it has been proposed that vv. 4-10 are a midrashic composition (similar to or under the influence of pesher-like materials by the Qumran community) to explicate the "stone" citation of Isa 28:16, a composition that is further developed by citing (Ps 118:22; Isa 8:14; and Hos 1:6f) or alluding to other OT passages (especially Exodus and Isaiah). The purpose of such a composition would have been to describe the Gentile Christian's relationship to Christ in Jewish terms as God's house, priesthood, and holy people.

Another proposal that merits attention here is the suggestion that the passage consists of two parallel sections: vv. 4-5a, which borrows terms from and comments on vv. 6-8 (the set of OT "stone" citations); and v. 5b, which anticipates vv. 9-10 (allusion to Exod 19:6). The composition therefore would consist of double allusions to OT passages to underscore the Christian community's character as God's new covenant community and household.

The major feature of these proposals seems to be their attempt to understand the relationship between the OT passages and the author's composition. More recent scholarship is correct in insisting that vv. 4-5 draw their terminology and themes from the OT passages, but one is hard pressed to see how v. 8 (about "the stumbling stone") fits into a midrash on Ps 118:22 or how vv. 4-5a prepare for that particular citation (Isa 8:14). Further, the alleged parallel between vv. 5b and 9-10 is not convincing (beyond the use of two terms); nor is the relation of vv. 9-10 to a supposed midrash on Ps 118:22. Finally and more important is the objection that these proposals do not sufficiently examine the structure of the composition and the role the citations and allusions play in the overall passage. Several clues suggest a different approach: the centrality of the exhortation in v. 5a and its accompanying participial construction ("to come to" Christ) and purpose for becoming a "spiritual house" and "holy priesthood," the relationship of Christ and believers as stones to the "stone" citations, and the important statement of v. 7a that divides vv. 4-8 neatly into positive and negative statements about believers and unbelievers (vv. 9-10 return to a positive discussion of those who believe).

(2:4-7a) In and Through Christ the Stone. Clearly vv. 4-5 borrow from the community's scriptural tradition. For example, the themes of "chosen, precious stone" and "building/rejection" are taken from Isa 28:16 and Ps 118:22, respectively. Seemingly, this new composition is the result of meditation or preaching on the community's messianic texts. These are, however, not the central elements of the new composition but instead are incorporated in the author's vision of the believer's relation to Christ and their sacrificial activity vis-à-vis "the living and enduring God."

The message of vv. 4-5 therefore must be detected from the passage's structure. The unit, as earlier passages, opens with a participial construction whose function is to extend (beyond v. 3) the discussion of the believer's relation to the Lord Jesus and by its change of tense (from the usual aorist to the present) to stress the author's concern about the addressees' need to focus on community concerns. As the Christian is said in v. 3 to have experienced the Lord at conversion, so in v. 4 the author explains this event, using building imagery, as an ongoing event of approaching the same Lord and participating with him in the construction process. Through the use of "stone" imagery from the community's store of messianic texts the author insists, as is done in the gospel tradition (Mark 12:10f and parallels; see also Acts 4:11), that it is the resurrected one ("living stone") who after his crucifixion ("rejected by mortals"—also borrowed from the "stone" citations) becomes God's "chosen, precious stone" in the building process (use of terms from Isa 28:16). As Christ was eternally destined and now manifested in God's plan for the addressees (1:20), so here he is said to have been the "precious and chosen cornerstone" for the present construction of God's house. The participial construction therefore creates the setting and underscores the christological basis for the following exhortation about God's holy edifice.

In formulating the crucial exhortation, 1 Peter draws an interesting parallel between Christ "the living stone" and the audience, which is addressed as "living stones." Two important points are being made here. On the one hand, by comparing believers to Christ and by qualifying each explicitly as "living" stones, the author reintroduces the theme of new life and reiterates what was said in 1:3, namely, that new birth was made possible through Christ's resurrection. It is as "living stones" that believers are to be associated with the "living cornerstone." On the other hand, the theme of imitation, which becomes a major point later in the letter (see especially 2:21f), is introduced rather explicitly. Christians are to become part of God's edifice precisely as "living stones" in the manner of their lord who is the "living stone or cornerstone." Earlier hints concerning imitation, or at least comparison between Jesus and believers, are found in 1:2-3 and 14 where both are qualified as obedient children of the Father. The theme of imitation will climax in the author's insistence that the addressees, in living a holy, new life as God's people, are to be like Christ in confronting innocent suffering and abuse.

In structural terms the key to the author's message is found in the exhortation of v. 5, where the readers are told: "allow yourselves likewise to be built into a 'spiritual' house, that is, into a holy priesthood . . . " (see below for remainder of exhortation). Once again a present tense rather than the usual aorist is employed to stress the author's interest less in eschatology than in ecclesiology. The building terminology, already suggested by the "stone" metaphor, is borrowed from Ps 118:22 but applied to God as the builder (divine passive rather than middle voice) of a new house whose cornerstone is Christ and whose building blocks include believers (see addition of *kai autoi*—"yourselves likewise"). The product of this building process is described as an *oikos pneumatikos* (literally, "a spiritual house"), a phrase that is immediately followed by *eis hierateuma hagion* (literally: "for a holy priesthood"). The meaning and relationship between these expression have been variously interpreted. On the one hand, the standard translation is as follows:

"built into a spiritual house to be a holy priesthood" (NRSV). Such a translation opts for the usual meaning *oikos* as an edifice (or "temple") and interprets the following phrase as appositional; that is, believers are both an edifice and a priestly group. On the other hand, it has been suggested that, rather than positing an awkward change in imagery from a building to a group of people, one should read *oikos* as designating "God's household" (see 4:17). Instead, taking into consideration the entire injunction, I am led to disagree with the second and to modify the first slightly. The building and stone terminology in the first part of the statement suggests an edifice and not a group of people as the basic image (stones are built into an edifice). Also, the following reference to priesthood and the ensuing purpose construction concerning sacrifice argue in the same direction. Additionally the expression *eis hierateuma hagion* should be translated in a more literal fashion: "for a holy priesthood." At this point the author will not identify this group but will return to this issue in v. 9 where a list of images will be joined to that of priesthood to describe God's people. At this stage 1 Peter is more interested in the social image of many stones forming one unified whole, which has as one of its goals an interest in divine worship.

The injunction reaches a climax by stating a new paraenetic goal: "the (ultimate) offering of spiritual sacrifices acceptable to God through (or for the sake of) Jesus Christ." The peculiar language of the entire injunction, however, calls for some scrutiny. Twice the author uses the term *pneumatikos*, once with "house" and once with "sacrifices." Besides the building terminology, there is a decided emphasis on terms related to sacrifice or worship. In addition the offering of sacrifice is what a priesthood is expected to do. So, why the seemingly tautalogous emphasis on a "*holy* priesthood" or "*spiritual* sacrifices *acceptable* to God?" From the outset it is clear that the author wishes, by means of the injunction and its purpose construction, both to emphasize the social nature of the new movement (many stones are built with Christ into one house) and to insist on the Christian duty toward God expressed in sacrificial terms (a priestly offering to the Almighty).

To this basic statement are added a number of modifiers that seemingly allow the author to reiterate important themes and further clarify the letter's purpose. The insistence on "a *spiritual* house" and "a *holy* priesthood" reiterates what was said in 1:2 concerning the Spirit's sanctifying role and in 1:15-16 concerning the holy conduct related to the believer's new life. The new house is to be the locus of the Spirit's work, and the priestly activity is to emanate from a life of holiness (see 1:17). Further, the author's designation of the sacrifices as "spiritual" and "acceptable to God" signals an important aspect of the letter's message. For 1 Peter, as for Paul (Rom 12:1-2) and the author of Hebrews (13:15-16), who employ similar language, sacrifice is no longer the presentation of physical offerings but, in the words of the latter, the offering of one's words, doing good, and sharing what one has—"such sacrifices are pleasing to God" (on the notion of "spiritual sacrifice" in late Judaism, see *TDNT* 3:183-87). It is in this sense that much of the paraenesis of 1 Peter is to be understood: namely, holy or reverent conduct, genuine love, and honorable deeds that are pleasing to God (1:15, 17, 22; 2:12). Finally these offerings are said to please God *dia Iesou Christou*, a phrase that seems to indicate reason—"for the sake of Jesus Christ" (BAGD 181.II.1)—rather than agency (see 1:21 or 4:11). In this manner the author indicates to the addressees that their activity, particularly their trials, "have God's approval" (2:20) because they are sharing God's suffering (4:13)—these sacrifices are welcomed by God because Christ, in experiencing them, was obedient to God's will (1:2, 11; 2:21). This crucial injunction then addresses the community's situation by reminding it that its holy behavior as a believing community has Christ as model and so is pleasing to God.

Following the important injunction of vv. 4-5, the author presents a scriptural justification by citing Isa 28:16 verbatim and by insisting, in conclusion, that God's precious stone is the believer's most precious possession. Applying a standard citation formula ("as it is stated in Scripture"), 1 Peter offers biblical confirmation (see use of *dioti* for citations also in 1:16, 24) for the preceding exhortation to unity. The quotation is the first of three "stone" passages that had messianic currency in the early tradition; thus the same text is cited in Rom 9:33 in a form that partially disagrees with the Septuagint. On the one hand, both Paul and 1 Peter read: *tithemi en Sion* ("I am setting up in Zion") in place of LXX *ego embalo eis ta themelia Sion* ("I am laying as foundations of Sion"). On the other hand, while Paul conflates a phrase from Isa 8:14 with this passage (see later citation in v. 8), 1 Peter cites more faithfully the central part of the verse to read: "a chosen, precious cornerstone," omitting only an adjective with possible ransom nuances ("costly or precious"—*polyteles*; see 3:4) and a second reference to foundations. The resulting citation allows the author to reiterate the theme of divine initiative and choice of a suitable soteriological agent (1:20-21), to restate Christ's role in ecclesiological terms (already suggested by the expression "a living stone"), and finally to dwell on human reception of this "chosen, precious" instrument.

Obviously, the citation has provided some of the terminology of v. 4 (stone, chosen, precious) and serves to give biblical confirmation to its themes, but it also renders more explicit the building imagery (use of "cornerstone") and introduces the principal theme of the remainder of the passage (vv. 7-8), namely, the acceptance or rejection of God's chosen instrument under the rubric of the "living stone." As one detects a shift in v. 4 from christology to ecclesiology, so one discerns a similar movement in the citation where stone and building terminology gives way to belief and its consequences: "whoever believes in him (or it) will not be put to shame." This negative expression of vindication of those who believe both suggests the following development concerning believers and unbelievers and gives us a clue concerning the author's use of OT texts. One discerns an obvious thematic connection with another scriptural passage (Ps 33:5—"put to shame"), which has already featured prominently in the author's composition (see 2:3-4 and its relation to Ps 33:5, 8) and is cited at length in 3:10-12 (= 33:12-16a). The composition of 1 Peter clearly shows the influence of and meditation on a variety of favorite OT texts.

In a compound sentence that draws an important conclusion and introduces an extended discussion of nonbelief as rejection of "the living stone," the author draws attention once more to the basis for Christian behavior, the choice or refusal of God's chose one. In a brief concise statement a conclusion is drawn and underscored: "you then who believe possess something precious." This statement has been variously interpreted as focusing on Jesus as precious, on the term *time* as referring to endtime vindication or present honor, or preferably on the believer's commitment to Jesus as the cornerstone of God's "spiritual house."

(2:7b-8) To Nonbelievers: A Stone of Stumbling and Shame. The division of the text at this point indicates not grammatical but thematic units because the author immediately contrasts the addressees to non-believers who are poignantly characterized by means of two further traditional "stone" citations. The first of these recites verbatim Ps 118:22. This text is used in the Synoptic tradition to describe Jewish rejection of Jesus (Mark 12:10 and parallels; see also Acts 4:11) and is employed in 1 Peter in a similarly negative way but to characterize all nonbelievers ("rejection by mortals"—2:4). While from this text one could argue for parallel houses or constructions (Christian and Gentile), one suspects that 1 Peter, like other NT writers, employs the proverbial "stone" text of Ps 118:22 to address the paradoxical claim that God uses a seemingly unworthy instrument, in this case a cast-off stone, as the centerpiece ("head of the corner" or "cornerstone") of a new construct. It is not the unbelievers, as such, who gain 1 Peter's attention but the unbelievers as the antithesis of the chosen, believing community. The unbelievers, the author insists—in a manner to reassure a suffering audience—will be put to shame or disabused (see 3:16) and hopefully will finally glorify God in light of the addressees' holy conduct (2:12). Additionally the author is not interested in developing a theory of parallel sacred and secular houses or kingdoms but rather in helping the addressees who as "servants of God" are being motivated to live up to their responsibilities as wards (even as "resident aliens" or *paroikoi*) of the Roman state. This "stone" citation then addresses the reality of the community's suffering and maltreatment in christological terms. They, like Christ their lord (3:15) and model (2:21), are encountering rejection and are promised that the very act of being rejected for Christ's sake (4:16) constitutes them "living stones" of a spiritual house.

A second "stone" passage, drawn from Isa 8:14, follows in 2:8. In effect the text is not so much a quotation as a borrowing from a verse of Isaiah two parallel phrases to describe God's chosen agent of salvation as a source of calamity to those who reject him. Three of the four terms are identical to the received version of the LXX while the final word *ptoma* is replaced by the synonymous noun *skandalos* ("that causes stumbling or falling"). Since the same situation arises in Rom 9:33 and since later Greek translators of the Hebrew (Aquila, Symmachus, and Theodotion) render Isa 8:14 with this term, we suggest that these two Christian writers had a variant Greek text at their disposal. In the case of 1 Peter these OT phrases are employed in conjunction with the citation of Ps 118:22: first, to underscore the conscious rejection of Christ by unbelievers and their consequent nonassociation with him as members of a spiritual house and, second, to point out that, as a result of rejection, he (as a stone) has become for them a cause of further calamity or stumbling, as the punishing initiative of God in the lives of the unrighteous (e.g., 1 Kgs 22:23; Ps 80:12; Ezek 14:9; Rom 1:24f; 11:25; Mark 4:11-12; 2 Thess 2:11-12).

Finally the author brings the passage to a conclusion by reiterating the theme of stumbling (use again of the OT term) and by relating this reality first to the preaching of the good news and then to God's overall plan. First, they have disobeyed the word (see 3:1) or were not obedient to the truth (1:22; also v. 14), and so their refusal is punished by further calamity; they are indeed "put to shame" (2:6; 3:16). Second, 1 Peter wishes by a double use of *tithemi* (once with God as subject and once employing a "divine passive"—vv. 6 and 8b) to present the twofold results of the divine plan: God's choice or setting of the precious stone is destined to have a salvific effect for believers on the one hand, but on the other the stone is destined to be the means of the ruin of those who reject its role. Those who disobey therefore invariably stumble on or are shamed by the stone that was meant for their honor.

A Holy People to Make Known God's Praises   (2:9-10)

This third section brings the first major part of 1 Peter to a close on the note on which it began, namely, God's mercy in giving new life or, here in vv. 9-10, in forming a new people. The subject of this new section is sharply contrasted with what precedes: "but you (on the other hand)." As the previous verses and their OT citations had focused on the status of nonbelievers, so now the author underscores the basic difference, already expressed as a stark contrast in v. 7a, between those who reject the "cornerstone" and those who are joined to this stone to form "a spiritual house." Thus this new section directs the addressees' attention to the communal nature of that new structure and to the privileges and responsibilities expected of those whom God has called.

(2:9a) The Community's Titles of Honor. The author begins by applying to the Christian community a series of OT titles that dwell on its social character. These four titles ("chosen race," "royal priesthood," "holy nation," and "people that is his possession") are clearly drawn from two OT passages: the first and last from Isa 43:20-21 and the second and third from Exod 19:6. Seemingly, the double titles from Exodus have been incorporated verbatim into the author's more extended use of the passage from Isaiah that speaks of God's providential care for Israel: "to give drink to my chosen race, my people which I have acquired (or preserved) to declare my praises" (43:20-21). I dare say that meditation on this passage has suggested not only some specific titles for the Christian community but also both the earlier reference to God's bestowal of liquid nourishment to believers ("pure, spiritual milk"— 2:2) and the subsequent statement later in v. 9 of believers' duty vis-à-vis the God who called them.

Interestingly, the first three titles refer back to themes already treated while the fourth points forward to the discussion of vv. 9b-10. Clearly the first title underscores the theme of "choice" or divine election, which permeates the letter (see especially 1:1 and 5:13) and which becomes a virtual title for God as "the one who calls" (1:15; 2:9, 21; 3:9; 5:10). The second title refers back to the priestly reference of 2:5 and the addressees' duty of worship and holy conduct vis-à-vis their God and Father, a theme that is developed further later in the verse. The third of these titles focuses on the question of holy conduct proposed as a divine imperative (1:15-16), both as a duty toward God (1:17) and toward believers and nonbelievers (1:22; 2:12). Each of the nouns (race, priesthood, nation, and people) stresses the social, communal character of the addressees' new life as God's people and, cumulatively, these express the movement's complex, open relation toward contemporary society.

It has been proposed that the second expression *basileion_hierateuma* be read not as a single ("royal priesthood") but as a double title ("a kingly house, a body of priests"). Besides the fact that each title consists of a double construction (a noun and a modifier), it should be stressed that each derives from the LXX and that its meaning should be sought in relation to its source. This expression and the one that follows in Exod 19:6 act as a parallel pair to describe Israel's relation to its neighbors in terms of its covenantal relationship to God. Here too 1 Peter adopts religious and political terms to describe a community's responsibilities toward a society and its king or emperor who are subject to God but whose subjects nonetheless are God's servants (2:13, 16-17).

(2:9b) Responsibilities and Exhortation. Following upon a series of titles that stress the community's common origin in God's call, its politico-religious role in society, and its common culture as a result of its holy conduct, the community is described as God's special possession. This fourth title is interesting as it sheds light on the believer's responsibility, a theme expressed as a purpose clause: "that you might make known (or proclaim) the praises of" God; it is of interest also since its formulation is closely related to its OT source. Isa 43:21 states that God has acquired (*peripoieo*—for the NT form, see Mal 3:17) a people "to relate or describe my praises" (*tas aretas mou diegeisthai*). The text of 1 Peter has suggested varying translations and generated debate concerning the meaning of the purpose clause.

On the one hand, it has been suggested that the purpose clause envisions missionary activity on the part of the community. Such a conclusion is based on the assumption that the purpose constructions of 2:5 and 9 are parallel mission statements, that the verb *exangello* envisions public proclamation, and that the noun *aretai* refers to God's miraculous or mighty deeds. The text then would be translated: "proclaim the mighty acts of" (NRSV). On the other hand, it is objected that the parallel between vv. 5 and 9 is exaggerated, that the verb *exangello* never refers to preaching or mission in the LXX but rather that this verb and its object noun fit more satisfactorily a liturgical context. Thus one should translate: "sing the praises of God" (NJB) in worship.

I would insist that neither option is satisfactory since some of the arguments advanced are either not convincing or questionable and since neither really captures the author's intention. In the first place it is doubtful that *exangello* in its few LXX uses always refers to activity directed to God in worship and never suggests public proclamation. Instead this verb along with other cognates and especially *diegeomai* (the verb used in Isa 43:21) are used as synonyms in parallel constructions to "declare, tell, proclaim, make known the praises" of God or exemplary believers. While some uses may suggest prayers of praise (Pss 9:14; 72:28; 78:13), others clearly address the issue of making praise, works, or wisdom known to others, whether in deed or speech. Thus Sir 44:15 employs the following couplet in praise of ancient believers:

> the people will tell of their wisdom (*diegeomai*),
> and the community will make known their praise (*exangello*)

(see similar parallels in Sir 18:4; 39:10; Isa 42:12). Besides, one should note that a Hellenistic reader would have understood *exangello* as indicating a public vocal statement (LSJ 580). Second, it does not seem that mission or proclamation is the author's intention; in fact the term *arete* refers probably to "glory or praise" rather than to miraculous power (BAGD 106.2). Indeed the author is interested less in mission than in speech and activity, which allows or forces nonbelievers and evildoers to "glorify God" eventually (2:12) or at least to understand the hope that motivates Christian behavior (3:15-16). Third, the attention paid to vv. 5 and 9 as parallels should be extended also to 2:2 because in all three passages the author concludes paraenetic or exhortatory claims by stating a purpose or goal. In v. 2 believers are exhorted to yearn for divine kindness or nourishment that they might do the deeds and express the defense of the salvation that already is theirs and is yet to be fulfilled (1:5, 9). In v. 5 the members of God's spiritual house are to present to God their honorable deeds as spiritual sacrifices that share in Christ's suffering (2:12; 4:13). In v. 9, then, Christians as God's special possession (namely, as "a chosen race, a royal priesthood, a holy nation") have as their task, in their lives and in their speech, the relating or revealing of God's praises. The author's goal ultimately is the exhortation to and defense of Christian behavior, even suffering, as "honorable deeds" in the eyes of outsiders (2:12) or as loving service toward insiders (1:22; 3:1f, 8; 4:8).

(2:9c) God's Call. The one who is the object of the believer's praise is fittingly designated as "the one who called [them]." The theme of election permeates the letter and here refers back to the addressees as "a chosen race," namely, as those whose new life begins in God's choice and whose ultimate goal is the glorification or praise of the one who called. The author at this point adds a note concerning the divine call, which has been variously interpreted: "called . . . out of darkness into (or "to"—*eis*) his marvelous light." Clearly the call "out of darkness" refers to the community's pre-conversion days when ignorance, emptiness, drunkenness, and idolatry reigned in their lives (1:14, 18; 4:3). It is less clear, however, whether "the marvelous light" has already dawned or is yet to come. Does the author suggest a call to an eschatological state or the possession of a present reality? The choice is a difficult one. On the one hand, the letter's frequent treatment of salvation, reward, glorious joy, and the reception of the inheritance and glory argue for the former, namely, a call "to" eschatological light or glory. On the other hand, contemporary authors make frequent use of darkness and light terminology to describe conversion, especially from paganism (note *Joseph and Aseneth* 15:12; 1 QH 4:5f; Rom 2:19; Acts 26:18; see also 1 Thess 5:4-5).

Two considerations lead me to opt for the second interpretation. First, the author characterizes the light by the term "wonderful or marvelous" (*thaumastos*), a term that seemingly derives from Ps 118:23. There the word describes human reaction to God's choice of the rejected stone (see citation in 2:7; also Mark 12:11 and Matt 21:42). Such usage suggests a present not a future activity. More importantly the immediate context, namely, the contrast between "once and now" of v. 10, seems to demand such a meaning: past darkness and present light. Nonetheless, it is quite possible that, like the themes of salvation and glory (see discussion of 1:8-9; 4:14; and 5:10), light is meant to suggest further that eschatological realities are anticipated in the believer's new life and holy conduct.

(2:10) God's People. Picking up the earlier contrast between the periods of darkness and light and underscoring further the important theme of divine choice and beneficence (see titles of v. 9, nourishment of 2:2, and new life through mercy in 1:3f), the author draws material once again from the OT to formulate a concluding statement concerning the addressees' status as God's people, a statement that reinserts, in a stark way, the theme of mercy with which the first part of the letter began. Drawing from Hos 1:6, 9-10 and especially 2:25 the building blocks of v. 10, 1 Peter addresses the issue once more of Christian converts being constituted into a spiritual community, in this case "God's people." Focusing on the theme of election, the author insists that God chose disparate people living in darkness, a state exemplified by the titles Hosea gave his children to designate lack of divine favor ("no-people" and "lacking in mercy"), and has through mercy constituted these individuals into a special "people." As Gentiles the addressees did not seemingly form part of God's plan, but now out of divine mercy or compassion they have become God's special possession.

Thus the author draws the first part of the letter to a close on the note on which it began, namely, that the addressees are God's children, for through compassion or mercy God has given them new life. Once they were not a people, but now through divine choice they have become God's chosen people, built, with Jesus their brother, into a spiritual house whose duty is to glorify their loving parent through honorable deeds as citizens or wards of a state that challenges its conduct or "demands . . . an accounting of the hope" that motivates this conduct (3:15). With such a foundation in mind, a communal life made possible by God's mercy and achieved through Jesus Christ's obedient suffering, the author will proceed in the following section to exhort the addressees on how and why to encounter both the challenge presented by interaction with non-Christian neighbors and the demands of mutual love within God's house.

Suggested Readings

Achetemeier, P. J. "Newborn Babes and Living Stones: Literal and Figurative in 1 Peter" in *To Touch the Text: Biblical and Related Studies*. Eds., M. P. Horgan and P. J. Kobelski. New York: Crossroad, 1989, 207-36.

___________. *1 Peter*. Minneapolis: Fortress, 1996.

Best, E. "1 Peter II. 4-10—A Reconsideration." *NovT* 11 (1969) 270-93.

Elliott, J. H. *The Elect and the Holy: An Exegetical Examination of 1 Peter 2:4-10 and the Phrase "basileion hierateuma".* Leiden: Brill, 1966.

Francis, J. " 'Like Newborn Babes'—The Image of the Child in 1 Peter 2:2-3" in *Studia Biblica*. Ed., E. A. Livingstone. Sheffield: JSOT, 1980, 3:111-17.

Hill, D. "To Offer Spiritual Sacrifices . . . ' (1 Peter 2:5): Liturgical Formulations and Christian Paraenesis in 1 Peter." *JSNT* 16 (1982) 45-63.

Manns, F. "'La maison ou réside l'esprit." 1 P 2,5 et son arrière-plan juif." *SBFLA* 34 (1984) 207-24.

Osborne, R. P. "L'utilization des citations de l'Ancien Testament dans la première épître de Pierre." *RTL* 12 (1981) 64-77.

Prigent, P. "1 Pierre 2, 4-10." *RHPR* 72 (1992) 53-60.

Sandevoir, P. "Un royaume de prêtres?" in *Etudes*, 219-29.

Schlosser, J. "Ancien testament et christologie dans la Prima Petri" in *Etudes*, 65-96.

Schutter, W. L. *Hermeneutic and Composition in 1 Peter*. Tübingen: Mohr-Siebeck, 1989.

Snodgrass, K. R. "1 Peter II.1-10: Its Formation and Literary Affinities." *NTS* 24 (1977) 97-106.

Thurén, L. *The Rhetorical Strategy of 1 Peter. With Sprcial Regard to Ambiguous Expressions*. Abo: Abo Academy, 1990.

Vanhoye, A. "La foi qui construit l'église. 1 P. 2:4-9." *AS* 26 (1973) 12-17.

Exhortation for Resident Aliens and Religious Exiles

(1 Peter 2:11–4:11)

The letter's second major block, the other two being 1:3–2:10 and 4:12–5:11, is explicitly introduced by direct address: "beloved" (see also 4:12) and is distinctly brought to a close by a formal doxology: "To whom belongs glory and dominion forever and ever. Amen" (see similar situation at 5:11). Further the block opens with the theme of Christian relations toward outsiders with divine, eschatological glorification in view (2:12) and closes on that of relations among believers with divine, eschatological glorification once more in view (4:11).

This extended block of material, on the one hand, addresses the community's situation both as regards its relationship to certain groups of outsiders and as regards its treatment by these same outsiders. On the other hand, the problems of various members as well as those of the community are likewise given some attention. While few question the paraenetic character of this long section, most scholars find the overall structure and train of thought difficult to discern. It is clear that 2:18–3:7 either constitutes or resembles a domestic or household code like those found in Col 3:18–4:1 and Eph 5:21–6:10f (see related material in the Pastorals: 1 Tim 2:8-15; 5:1-2; 6:1-2; Titus 2:1-10; 3:1) and that it is introduced (2:11-17) and concluded (3:8-9) by general material similar to that of Eph 5:21 and 6:10f (see below for further discussion of these codes). Thus scholars readily see 2:11–3:12 as a literary unit—some insist that it constitutes a major literary block since, like the previous one (1:3–2:10), it is brought to a climax by an extended OT citation (3:10-12). Nonetheless, one should note that citations more frequently bring shorter units to a close: 1:13-16, 22-25; 2:4-8; 4:12-19; and 5:1-5).

In more general terms one could envision the remainder of the letter as a structural address to all Christians in 2:11-17, to specific groups in 2:18–3:7, to all believers once again in 3:8–4:19, to groups once more in 5:1-5a, and finally to all Christians again in 5:5b-11. What one really derives from such observations, however, are the simple facts that the present block and the one that follows (4:12–5:11) are addressed to the entire audience and that each of these blocks has a unit that addresses specific groups: 2:18–3:7 and 5:1-5, respectively. Thus more careful structural and thematic analysis is required to discern the author's train of thought and message.

It is here proposed that 2:11–4:11 consists of a fairly coherent whole, offering three related subsections of diverse length. The first consists of an extended duty code (2:13–3:7), which is introduced by addressing the community's relation to outsiders (2:11-12) and which is brought to a conclusion ("finally" to indicate the ending not the beginning of a subunit) by lending attention to the members' mutual concerns (3:8-9). The unit itself is rounded off by a long OT citation to lend paraenetic support to the community's need to do good in the face of abuse (use of Ps 33:13-17). Each unit of the code addresses particular individuals, though that addressed to "servants or members of the household" offers the author an opportunity to develop the major theme of innocent suffering as imitation of Christ (2:21-15).

The second subsection (3:13–4:6), seemingly, is a lengthy passage whose unity is often called into question, particularly as concerns the author's train of thought in 3:17 and 18f and in 3:22 and 4:1f. In effect the entire section consists of three subunits: 3:13-17 regarding the community's suffering and need for holy conduct, vv. 18-22 presenting an extended hymnic statement of Christ's saving activity, and 4:1-6 offering further exhortation in view of Gentile behavior. Examination of other parts of 1 Peter offers the reader a clue in discerning the author's method of composition, for a similar pattern occurs in 1:6-9 and 2:18–3:1. In the first case the author is led to digress, at the mention of rejoicing, on the paradoxical suffering of the community but nonetheless returns in v. 8 to the theme of rejoicing. In the second case advice to household members who suffer unjustly is the occasion for another digression concerning Christ as the model of innocent suffering—the author returns in 3:1 to the code structure being followed. In 3:13-17, 1 Peter addresses the community's innocent suffering and in v. 18 begins a presentation of Christ as the model once more of unjust abuse; but this new train of thought suggests more extensively not only the paradigmatic but also the soteriological role of Christ's suffering (see 1:18-20). Thus in vv. 18-22 the author digresses at length on the community's traditional concept of Christ's salvific activity. Following this digression 4:1 repeats the initial terms of 3:18: "Christ . . . suffered." 4:1-6 then continues the train of thought interrupted earlier and offers further exhortation to the addressees concerning Christian-

Gentile relations, all the while relying on the strong soteriological statement made in 3:18-22.

The third subsection (4:7-11) offers a brief eschatological exhortation to the community concerning mutual relations. Similar themes have already appeared in 1:22 and 3:8-9. Finally this third section has a parallel function to the closing (5:6-11) of the next major block, which also culminates in a formal doxology. The three subsections of this block therefore address the major issues of concern to the author and audience, namely, Christian relations with outsiders and the proper motivation and context for confronting unjust treatment and slander. As in the other divisions of the letter, one discerns here from the document's clues the author's exhortatory purpose and strategy. In structural terms it should be noted that the first subsection, 2:11-3:12, serves as an excellent introduction to the entire block. Specifically, 2:12, with its focus on honorable behavior in the face of slander, announces the themes of 3:13f with its insistence on a clear conscience and good behavior in the face once more of slander (v. 16); and 3:8, on mutual love, prepares explicitly for the beautiful passage on ideal community life (4:7-11). In structural and thematic terms, therefore, 2:11–4:11 is a unified and focused block of material addressed to the readers' situation.

Suggested Readings

Achtemeier, P. J. *1 Peter*. Minneapolis: Fortress, 1996.

Balch, D. L. "Early Christian Criticism of Patriarchal Authority: 1 Peter 2:11-3:12." *USQR* 39 (1984) 161-73.

Combrini, H. J. B. "The Structure of 1 Peter." *Neot* 9 (1980) 34-63.

Dalton, W. J. *Christ's Proclamation to the Spirits: A Study of 1 Peter 3:18-4:6*. Rome: PIB, 1989.

Goppelt, L. *A Commentary on 1 Peter*. Grand Rapids: Eerdmans, 1993.

Martin, T. W. *Metaphor and Composition in 1 Peter*. Atlanta: Scholars, 1990.

Michaels, J. R. *1 Peter*. Waco: Word Books, 1988.

Talbert, C. H. "Once Again: The Plan of 1 Peter" in *PFP*, 141-51.

Honorable Conduct: Duty Code
(2:11–3:12)

The second major block of 1 Peter, 2:11–4:11, is well known, particularly what is usually designated as its household or domestic code, 2:11–3:12. Seemingly, the central part of this passage offers advice to slaves, wives, and husbands (2:18f; 3:1f, 7) or, it will be argued below, to the Christian members more generally, then to the women, and, briefly, to the men of the household. The closest analogue to such exhortations is found in the household codes of Colossians and Ephesians. Owing to these similarities and obvious differences (namely, the introductory injunction concerning civil authorities and the concluding advice to the community regarding mutual relations—2:13-17 and 3:8-9, respectively), there is much debate concerning the form, structure, and function of the entire passage. Does one stress the similarities or differences between 1 Peter and other codes in attempting to discern the author's purpose? Does the choice of groups for whom particular advice is reserved indicate particularly vexing problems within the community, or does this choice present opportunities for the author apologetically to discuss relations with outsiders or to encourage outward-directed activity? Additionally, in considering the content and structure of this passage, should one view it as a type of household code or more generally label it a duty code? Does this unusual code have as its goal cultural accommodation with Greco-Roman society or social cohesion of the community as a religious household? Finally how do the various segments of the code relate to the author's purpose for writing?

On the one hand, one can approach the study of this passage from the vantage point of the standard household code and view its function, in a similar fashion, as concerned with household management. In structural terms such a code usually addresses three pairs of related persons: wives and husbands, children and parents, and slaves and masters. In paraenetic terms the code is interested in the proper relation of the first member of the pair to the second: duty of wives to husbands, children to parents, and slaves to masters. Presumably the function of such literary structures would be either the proper management of the household for the general good of society or, in Christian terms, either to correlate the thinking of believers to that of pagan neighbors or to set up a parallel domestic structure for God's household. In the case of 1 Peter the author's use of a modified household code would indicate either a concern about relations with outsiders (whether defense of Christian behavior as consistent with Roman mores or even the exhortation to civic responsibility—focus on women or on civil authority) or a focus on self-defense against slander and on inner cohesion (adherence to God's household rather than that of the Roman state).

Such a perspective presumes that use of the household code with its primary function as providing standards for household management determines the message of 1 Pet 2:12f. Several factors render such an approach suspect from the start. If 1 Peter wishes to use the household code as a model either to foster inner cohesion or to ease external friction regarding Christian conduct, it is strange that much of the content and structure of the code is omitted. Indeed only one pair remains intact (wives and husbands or women and men); one disappears entirely; and of the third there remains only an injunction addressed to "household" slaves. This hardly seems conducive to the development of parallel household imagery for Christian relations and even less to provide a schema for the behavior of its members. Further the addition of parallel injunctions regarding attention to social exterior and religious interior structures (at the beginning and ending of the passage) point in a different direction for an adequate solution. Indeed the introductory verses (2:11-12) provide the crucial setting in the community's life for the interpretation of the entire passage.

On the other hand, one can approach the issue from the perspective of the well-known Hellenistic teaching on duty that was developed by Stoic and later moral philosophers, as derived from the human being as a free moral agent with social responsibilities. It is particularly clear from Epictetus that humans are "a fragment or part of God" (*Discourses* 2.8.11) and are bound to imitate the free, beneficent, and faithful deity (2.14.13) who, through rational activity or philosophy, frees human agents (4.7.16-17) from pain and fear and teaches them to maintain "both [their] natural and . . . acquired relationships, those namely of son, father, brother, citizen, husband, wife, neighbor, fellow-traveller, ruler, and subject" (2.14.8; see 3.2.4; 4.6.26). Duty thereby results from the freedom that allows a clear vision of what should be, expressed either in a traditional household format, as advising "how a husband should conduct himself toward his wife, or how a father should bring up his children, or how a master should rule his slaves" (Seneca, *Moral Epistles* 94.1) or more generally as stating the "necessary laws" of duty between classes: seniors and juniors, rulers and subjects, benefactors and receivers of benefits, masters and slaves, and parents and children (Philo, *Decalogue* 165-67) or the duty of certain relational categories: the human being, the citizen, the child, and the brother or sibling (Epictetus, *Discourses* 2.10.1-9).

In light of the above discussion one understands more readily the household format of contrasting pairs employed by Colossians and Ephesians and the loosely formulated duty code favored by 1 Peter and presupposed in the Pastoral Epistles. Indeed both the form and themes of the former are clarified by such comparison, because 1 Peter presumes, in the manner of Stoic philosophers, that believers, as servants of God, are free people who nonetheless have responsibilities (doing good and not using "freedom as a pretext for evil"—2:16). This freedom liberates them from human fears (3:6, 14) and challenges the threat of pain and persecution (see especially Christ as the model of innocent suffering—2:21-24). In addition this freedom allows believers to have a clear vision of what should be or, in 1 Peter's terms, what has "God's approval" or is "God's will" (2:20; 4:2; see also 2:15; 3:4, 17; 4:19). Christian duty is seen under two important headings: social-political and socioreligious responsibility. It is no accident that the passage begins by addressing the audience both as *paroikoi* ("resident aliens") and *parepidemoi* ("religious exiles"). They retain their natural relationships with their pagan neighbors as members of the Roman Empire (so their duty to government and emperor [2:13-17] and neighbors [*passim*]) and have acquired new relationships (the community is called an *adelphotes* or "brotherhood"—2:17; 5:9), relationships that call for ethical discernment and responsibility in one's relations with non-Christian neighbors and fellow believers.

In dealing in overall terms with the code of 1 Peter, one might offer observations, following Epictetus' comments, in two important areas. First, employing Epictetus' list of "natural and acquired relationships," one might see how 1 Peter, in the code and throughout the letter, is interested in these various relationships, those of "son or child, father or parent, brother or family association, citizen, husband or wife, neighbor, fellow-traveller, and ruler and subject" (*Discourses* 2.14.8). Clearly the first two relationships (child and parent) are extensively developed in the theme of new life, which believers have received from God as father. Furthermore the themes of brotherhood and fellow-traveler appear as acquired relationships that both constitute believers as a social unit (fellowship or brotherhood, spiritual house, God's people) and designate believers as "religious exiles or wanderers" (see discussion of 1:1). The remaining relationships find their place in the author's code, whether this involves the believer's role as citizen in relation to governing authorities, to the basic relations between ruler and ruled, and men and women. It has often been observed that Colossians and Ephesians begin with relations within the Christian family and work outward to include those of the workplace and that 1 Peter begins, much like Epictetus' list, from external, political relations and focuses on gender issues as they relate to the household. Perhaps the best insight into the author's purpose is found in the order of this entire passage and its treatment of specific themes:

(2:11-12)	Introduction to Code
(2:13-17)	Social and Civic Duty
(2:18-25)	Duty of Household Members
(3:1-6)	Duty of Women
(3:7)	Duty of Men
(3:8-12)	Conclusion

The order of the units seems to be dictated by the author's desire both to address the community's relations with its pagan neighbors (based on duty to "every human creature") and to underscore how Christian duty is affected in internal and external terms (as members of Christian and non-Christian households). Believers are addressed both as responsible citizens and members of God's house.

Second, another important introductory observation concerns the very nature of duty and the author's conception of this. Again making use of the observations of Epictetus (*Discourses* 2.10) in his chapter on discerning human duty, one notes that his discussion revolves around the four following relational categories: duty as a human being, as a citizen, as a child or son, and as a brother or sibling. It is striking how 1 Peter insists that human freedom and choice lead to the following complex exhortation: "honor everyone; love the family of believers [brotherhood]; fear God; honor the emperor" (2:17). Seemingly the author envisions Christian duty toward other humans, fellow believers, "the God and Father" of all, and the emperor as personification of the political order (see further discussion below). The author's code then borrows from current Hellenistic moral teaching and incorporates traditional Jewish and Christian paraenesis to address the community's most pressing needs as it faces pressures from outside, and inside (see discussion of 3:7 and 5:1-5), which threaten its inner unity, tranquility, and resolve.

Finally one should note the following structural considerations. The introductory unit underscores the positive and negative factors involved in the discussion of duty by beginning and closing with direct address: "as resident aliens and religious exiles" and "as evildoers." The second section opens with an aorist imperative (*hypotasso*), which is extended in the succeeding units by participial phrases reiterating the original injunction by using the same verb (2:18; 3:1) or other relational terms (3:7, 8-9). Further, after the exhortation to all believers in 2:13-17, the author addresses various groups directly and concludes by speaking again to "all" (3:8). Finally it should be noted that the author brings the middle sections to a similar conclusion by having recourse to a closing simile, each introduced by *hos*: "like free people" (2:16), "like sheep" (2:25), "like Sarah" (3:6), and "like co-heirs" (3:7).

Suggested Readings

Achtemeier, P. J. *1 Peter*. Minneapolis: Fortress, 1996, 172-227.
Balch, D. L. *"Let Wives Be Submissive": The Domestic Code in 1 Peter*. Chico: Scholars, 1981.

__________. "Hellenization/Acculturation in 1 Peter" in *PFP*, 79-101.

Elliott, J. H. "1 Peter, Its Situation and Strategy: A Discussion with David Balch" in *PFP*, 61-78.

Goppelt, L. "The Station Code Tradition" in *A Commentary on 1 Peter*. Grand Rapids: Eerdmans, 1993, 162-79.

Prostmeier, F. R. *Handlungsmodelle im ersten Petrusbrief.* Würzburg: Echter, 1990.

Introduction to Code (2:11-12)

A first short unit addresses the entire community and provides a context for the subsequent duty code. The exhortation concerns Christian conduct, which has both a civic and an ecclesial component. These two features are underscored thematically and structurally.

In structural terms one notes the beginning of a new section (see also 4:12). Not only does the author begin by addressing the audience by the term "beloved" (it is used as an initial vocative also in 1 and 3 John and Jude 3) but also by giving the stark exhortation "I urge you" (*parakaleo*). Owing to the use of the latter it has been proposed that 1 Peter is here employing a *parakaleo* formula to introduce a major paraenetic section. Such a formula, which occurs occasionally elsewhere in the NT (see Rom 12:1-2; 15:30-32; 1 Thess 4:1-2, 10b-12, among others), consists of a reference to the audience (usually direct address) following this verb of exhortation, an optional preposition modifier, and an exhortation expressed in an infinitive construction or *hina* clause. In the present case direct address precedes the verb "exhort or urge," there is no prepositional phrase, and it is assumed that the author employs a subsequent infinitive construction. However, more careful analysis suggests a different, more satisfactory option. The verb following *parakaleo* should probably be read as an imperative (*apechesthe* with P⁷² A C L and other manuscripts) rather than as an infinitive (*apechestai* with most mss)— note that an imperative is used at 5:1 in a similar construction. These considerations along with several others suggest a structure for 2:11-12 that is more consistent with the style of 1 Peter and will offer several clues for the interpretation of the passage and for discerning its function vis-à-vis the following code.

The resulting structure for this passage is consistent with what is proposed for 1:13f, 17f, 22f; 2:1f, 4f, namely, a threefold construct usually consisting of an initial participial statement, followed by an imperative, and further developed by a subsequent participial construction. In the present case the usual opening construction is replaced by "beloved, I urge you . . ." and is followed, in typical fashion, by imperative and participial constructions. For our purpose it is important to insist, here as in the other passages noted, that the imperative or injunction is the central element and that the preceding and succeeding constructions play a role relative to it. They either present the context of or offer a reason for the exhortation. Thus the meaning of the passage must be sought by relating the components to one another.

(2:11) Initial Negative Exhortation. The themes of the first component are noteworthy. The community is addressed as "beloved" (*agapetoi*—see also 4:12), a term and its cognates (1:22; 2:17; 3:8; 4:8) that repeatedly underscore the principal feature of Christian fellowship, namely, mutual love and divine condescension or election (1:1, 3). Additionally the author begins the section by using the verb *parakaleo* ("urge, exhort, or encourage") to introduce first a duty code involving relations principally with outsiders, again in 5:1 to urge amicable relations between members of the community, and finally in 5:12 to characterize the entire document as a letter of exhortation or encouragement. After having discoursed on the reality of Christian new life and having exhorted believers to appropriate "holy conduct" as God's people, the author by means of this verb turns formally to the section of the letter that addresses concrete problems involving nonbelievers, apparently the crisis issue that leads the author to compose the letter.

From the outset the addressees are characterized as both "resident aliens and religious sojourners or exiles." First Peter is not addressing two displaced, social groups (permanent and temporary residents) but rather characterizes all the letter's audience by the terms *paroikoi* and *parepidemoi*. They are, on the one hand, members of Roman society with civic and humanistic duties and, on the other, God's elect living among nonbelievers and bearing the burden of marginal rights, ostracism, and verbal abuse. The two terms, already employed in 1:1 and 17 (see discussion), underscore the dual character of Christian conduct, namely, believers' natural relationship to society and the duties this involves and their acquired relationships involving responsibilities toward God, fellow believers, and Gentile neighbors. The first term focuses on the audience's political status and responsibilities (as less-than-full participants but having civic duties nonetheless), whereas the second term focuses on the addressees' status as members of God's elect, holy house, scattered among nonbelievers (with consequent problems caused by these new relationships). It is with these dual considerations that the author introduces both the following injunction and lengthy duty code.

What then is the source of this striking politico-religious terminology, particularly the unusual combination of *paroikos* and *parepidemos*? Beyond the fact that such terminology was common in contemporary Greek culture, one only has to look to Jewish tradition as source, because there Abraham offers the two terms to describe his (politcal and religious) status in Palestine (Gen 23:4) and pious Jews describe themselves thus in prayer to God (Ps 38/39:12). On the one hand, the second term focuses on the Christian's elect status, that is, as religious sojourner (see discussion of 1:1); on the other hand, the first of the pair emphasizes the believer's political context and responsibilities (see discussion of 1:17 and duty codes below).

The second component consists of a straightforward injunction whose structural context and meaning are clarified by a comparison with 1:13-14. In the latter an introductory paraenetic construction (double participial construct encouraging action) introduces a positive injunction and a subsequent, parallel negative statement (imperative and participial construction, respectively). Thus in 1:13f the "setting of one's hope on grace" is interpreted in an antithetical parallel in v. 14 as the rejection of one's "former desires." In 2:11-12 an initial exhortation ("I urge") introduces another imperative, which is followed by a parallel participial statement. In this case the former expresses a stark negative injunction and the following participial construction expresses an antithetical, positive statement.

Interpretation of the second component, however, is not an easy matter, since its terminology lends itself to a variety of options. Employing traditional paraenetic language ("abstain or keep yourselves away from"—1 Thess 4:3; 5:22; Acts 15:20, 29; 1 Tim 4:3), 1 Peter draws a sharp contrast between a dark or negative past and a positive, honorable present. The difficulty does not lie principally in the interpretation of this first element (though some would translate the verb as "resist or do not give in to"—presumably under the influence of the later verb: "wage war against") but rather in discerning the following one, namely, what the injunction warns against: *ton sarkikon epithymion* (lit.: "fleshly desires"). Recent translation of this phrase and its interpretation in 1 Peter reflect a range of anthropological and interpretive presuppositions. Does the noun *epithymia* represent a positive (neutral) or negative reality ("impulse, desire, passion, lust"), especially as modified by the adjective *sarkikos* ("natural, bodily, worldly, carnal, sinful")? Thus one could propose a positive ("natural or bodily impulses"), a tendentious ("carnal or worldly lusts" or "passions of the flesh"), or an evil sense ("sinful desire or lusts"). The problem is compounded by the following relative clause, which states that these "desires" are at "war with the soul or deeper self" (see 1:9 for discussion of "soul"). The several major interpretive alternatives are not particularly satisfying; one would insist either that natural, good impulses are naturally in conflict with the higher or religious self (a paradoxical anthropology), that human impulses are the antithesis of spiritual or heavenly loyalties (influence of a Paulinist view), or that the human level is basically corrupt and must be rejected (a corrupt nature concept).

Careful analysis of the author's use of the terminology in question and further consideration of the second part of the injunction yields a different interpretation. In the first place *epithymia* (and its verb—1:12) in 1 Peter seems to represent a neutral (Stoic) meaning such as "desire or impulse," which usually or often leads to excess or false loyalties—this seems to be the meaning in both 1:14 and 4:2-4 (on the concept of false loyalty, see discussions of 4:3 and 5:8). In the second place the adjective, related to the noun *sarx* or "flesh," represents not the Pauline antithesis between flesh and spirit but rather the natural, good world that nonetheless is subject to death and false loyalty (see 1:24; 3:18, 21; 4:1-2, 4, 6; 5:8). Third, the following relative clause, which scholars interpret as modifying absolutely the preceding "desires" ("*which* wage war"), is introduced not by *hos* but by *hostis* (the only case in 1 Peter) and so suggests a causal nuance ("inasmuch as"—see *BG* 215). Thus the entire injunction should read: "abstain from natural impulses in as much as they [in their excesses] wage war against the soul." There emerges from a study of 1 Peter an anthropology that sees human desires as good but as limited, often leading to excess, and needing constant discipline on the part of believers who live and work in a world of ignorance and darkness (1:14; 2:9). Some of these "human desires or impulses" (see also 4:2) work against or "do battle against" the soul (for the conflict between the world of the flesh and that of God's will as expressed in military imagery, see 2 Cor 10:3; 1 Thess 5:8) and must be resisted. By implication and as introduction to the duty code, the author suggests that all is not negative in Greco-Roman culture. Believers must resist those elements that "wage war against the soul" (see also resistance of the satanic opponent in 5:8-9); nonetheless, they still have the duty to "honor everyone . . . [and] . . . honor the emperor" (2:17).

(2:12) Parallel Positive Exhortation. The third, final component presents a positive antithesis to the injunction as further motivation for the community as it faces its critical situation in the guise of increased slander. The new component appears in the form of a participial construction and acts as a counterpart to the previous negative statement. Both the terminology and style of v. 12 indicate that the conduct about which the author speaks is not only holy, reverent behavior but also deeds that are meant to be seen as honorable or beautiful. Indeed on other occasions 1 Peter speaks of Christian behavior as doing good (use of *agathos* and *agathopoieo*—2:14-15, 20; 3:6, 11, 13, 17) but here twice employs the synonym *kalos* to insist that Christian behavior be both good and publicly acknowledged as such, specifically that it be deemed "beautiful or honorable" in the eyes of Gentile neighbors. Two other points underscore this conclusion. The position of the adjective *kalos* at the end of the long participial construction, separated considerably from its noun, indicates that the emphasis and motivation for the following *hina* clause is precisely its honorable or public character ("making your conduct . . . so honorable, that . . . "). Also, later in the verse the author, employing a verb that stresses the visible or public character of an event (*epopteuo*—see also 3:2), insists that pagan neighbors are to "observe [their] honorable or visible deeds."

Again there is an emphasis on Christian behavior (see 1:15, 18; 3:1-2, 16), but in this case the focus is on its public setting in a Gentile context. Here and in 4:3 the author employs a Jewish, LXX term (*ta ethne*— "the nations") for non-Jews to apply to non-Christians (see also Matt 5:47; 6:7). It is in this context also that the author inserts the first explicit reference to the community's critical situation. Good behavior is to be the public antidote or weapon of believers against Gentile slander. The author expresses the theme succinctly: "though they malign or slander you as evildoers." The term used here and in 3:16 (see also 2:1 for the noun; also Jas 4:11 and 2 Cor 12:20) is *katalaleo* ("speak against or slander"), a term that speaks volumes concerning the addressees' situation. It addresses not persecution but verbal abuse, presumably misrepresentation of Christian beliefs, customs, and motivation (see 3:15).

How precisely, however, are we able to discern the community's situation? Two important terms here provide some information. The first (*katalaleo*), while having the technical meaning of "slander or malign," implying false accusation, also suggests a range of possibilities, from malicious gossip to defamation of character to evil reports and formal, legal prosecution viewed as unjust. The term can also refer to public ridicule (see LSJ 897). The second term (*kakopoieo*—"do evil") seems to presume the opposite of what Hellenists would consider as everyone's duty as a person and citizen. Presumably, the accusation that the pagan population leveled against the Christians of Asia Minor is not that of being "a murderer, a thief, a criminal (*kakopoios*), or even a mischief maker" (4:15). Instead this accusation of "evildoing" involves Greco-Roman customs and responsibilities that Christian behavior called into question, challenged, rejected, or neglected; these issues 1 Peter addresses in the ensuing code and the remainder of the letter. If certain addressees or even the community itself are taking an adversarial position against civic duties or are disclaiming responsibilities toward Greco-Roman structures, 1 Peter is quick to address both Christian duty and

Gentile perception of Christian behavior. Whether believers were wrongly accused of neglecting their civic responsibilities (e.g., participating in public service, office, or army—Origen, *Against Celsus*), of "being haters of the human race," or of belonging to a "pernicious superstition" (Tacitus, *Annals* 15.44), the accusations were nonetheless taken seriously by the author of 1 Peter who addresses both perceived and actual problems.

Ultimately, the author insists that, in this Christian-Gentile exchange and possible confrontation, the goal is God's glory in the form of Gentile obedience to the father and judge of all. The ultimate weapon in this exchange is to be "the good and honorable behavior or deeds" of those so accused, deeds that are publicly viewed by the accusers and thus bring about a change of mind and heart (see 3:1 for a concrete example of this principle). Believers are to give a gentle and reverent defense of their conduct (3:15-16a) and even to shame their opponents by their innocence (3:16b). But ultimately it is the paradox of innocent suffering that, as in the case of Christ (2:21f), will bring about a public, eschatological acknowledgment of the God of mercy.

This public acknowledgment is expressed as "glorifying God on the day of visitation." Both expressions merit some attention. The first (*doxazo ton theon*) relates to one of the most important themes of the letter: Christ's suffering and glory. God's glory (4:11; 5:10), which is bestowed on Christ as vindication for his paradigmatic suffering (1:11; 4:13; 5:1) and atoning death (1:18, 21) and which is promised as eschatological reward for innocent suffering (1:7; 5:4), already plays a role in or impinges on the life of believers who are to exhibit "glorious joy" (1:8) and on whom the "Spirit of glory rests" already (4:14). There remains, however, the expression that concerns us: "to give glory to or glorify God." Considering the term's Hellenistic and LXX context, one must probably view it as meaning "extol, hold in honor, or acknowledge" (see LSJ 444; also Exod 15:1-2). Indeed Paul's text in Rom 1:21 captures the term's deeper nuance: "to honor God as God." Thus believers, whether as the result of genuine community affection or innocent suffering, are to acknowledge God's supremacy (4:11) or merciful will (3:17; 4:16). So in 2:12 it is the author's wish (use of subjunctive) that the community's adversaries might, in light of their Christian neighbors' holy and honorable conduct, acknowledge God as a merciful father and judge and as faithful creator.

This brings us to the second expression "on the day of visitation" and leads us to inquire about its meaning in this particular context. This familiar LXX idiom is used for a divine intervention that can be viewed in ominous terms as a day of judgment or punishment (Isa 10:3; Jer 10:15; Wis 14:11) or in a less threatening way as a time of reward or rejoicing (Gen 50:24f; Wis 3:7; also Luke 19:44). While it is possible that 1 Peter intends the former (it is the time of judgment for "the living and the dead" and for the righteous and the ungodly—4:5, 17-18; see NRSV: "when he comes to judge"), it is more likely that a less ominous sense forms part of the author's strategy. The final day (1:5; 4:7) is to be one of revelation, joy, glory, and journey to God's presence (1:7, 13; 3:18; 4:13; 5:1, 4, 10). Clearly such is promised to believers, particularly those who persevere in their innocent suffering, but it is also part of the author's strategy that innocent suffering testifies both to one's obedience to God's will (like Christ) and assists in healing the wounds of others (also following Christ's lead; see 2:20-24). The good behavior of believers is meant, in God's plan, to lead unbelievers to acknowledge God's sovereignty (2:12; 4:11) and thus to experience God's visitation as a gracious event.

It should also be noted that, although the ending phrase of v. 12 ("on the day of visitation") has an unmistakable eschatological sense (see discussions also of 1:5, 7, 17; 4:13; 5:1, 4), the entire verse need not be read in an apocalyptic sense. First Peter probably expresses the wish that opponents not only glorify God at the eschaton but also that they, as enlightened neighbors (seeing good works and being convinced by gentle defense: 2:12; 3:16), be among those who glorify God in the last time. An optimistic, missionary reading is possible and probable.

A final brief note should be made regarding the striking similarity between 1 Pet 2:12b and Matt 5:16: "in the same way, let your light shine before others, so that they may see your good works and give glory to your Father in heaven." From a linguistic point of view, there is no doubt that the authors draw from the same tradition but it is also evident that each has a different goal in mind. In the case of Matthew the objective is the missionary outlook and activity of the community, while in 1 Peter the perspective is that of God's plan and its eschatological fulfillment—Christian "good works" on the religious level are also to be "honorable deeds" on the political level, behavior that is to lead even Gentiles to "accept the authority" of the "faithful creator" (4:19) that "God may be glorified in all things through Jesus Christ" (4:11).

Suggested Readings

Brox, N. *Der erste Petrusbrief.* Zurich: Benziger, 1979.
Elliott, J. H. *A Home for the Homeless: A Sociological Exegesis of 1 Peter, Its Situation and Strategy.* Philadelphia: Fortress, 1981.

Feldmeier, R. *Die Christen als Fremde: Die Metapher der Fremde in der antiken Welt, im Urchristentum und im 1. Petrusbrief.* Tübingen: Mohr-Siebeck, 1992.

Giese, H. "Lebenszeugnis in der Fremde. Zum Verhalten der Christen in der paganen Gesellschaft (1 Petr 2,11-17)." *SNTU* 23 (1998) 113-52.

Meeks, W. A. *The Moral World of the First Christians.* Philadelphia: Westminster, 1986.

Pilch, J. J. " 'Visiting Strangers' and 'Resident Aliens.' " *TBT* 29 (1991) 357-61.

Van Unnik, W. C. "The Teaching of Good Works in 1 Peter." *NTS* 1 (1954) 92-110.

Social and Civic Duty (2:13-17)

Interestingly, in approaching a series of case studies on the subject of duties as these relate to honorable behavior, the author begins not with members of the household but with relations with outsiders, particularly persons who represent civic structures. Indeed the first code unit does not deal with parties regularly treated in household codes, whether wives and husbands, children and parents, or slaves and masters, but rather focuses on human responsibility; namely, the passage begins by addressing duty to "every human creature" (v. 13—see comments below) and ends by exhorting the community to "honor everyone" (v. 17). Additionally the passage opens by insisting on duty toward "the emperor as supreme" and closes by exhorting the community to "honor (also) the emperor." Thus vv. 13-17 form a succinct unit.

Further this first code segment presents a number of challenges to the reader. In it one finds the clues to its function both in relation to the immediately preceding injunction (2:11-12) and as providing the structural and thematic key to the following segments of the lengthy code. Moreover there are a number of interpretive issues that have created some debate. In the first case the author addresses both negative and positive points made in the introduction, namely, abstaining from aspects of Roman culture that are considered destructive for Christian living and conducting oneself in a way that Gentiles also consider honorable. While avoiding idolatrous behavior that might be linked to acceptance of the emperor as an incarnation of the gods or of government officials as sponsors or servants of religio-cultural activity, the author insists that government officials as human creatures on the one hand and as servants of the political structure and order on the other are to receive their requisite honor. Thus the "forbidden idolatry" of the Gentiles, along with other excesses of "human desires" (4:3-4; see also 1:14; 2:1), are to be avoided; but these human agents are not to be demonized, because they are creatures who deserve honor and civic agents who serve the common good. A major feature of the code, therefore, is 1 Peter's intention to address what is to be avoided as un-Christian and what is nonetheless to be fostered as agreeable to and honorable in the eyes of non-Christian neighbors.

In the second case vv. 13-17 are crucial for understanding the remainder of the duty code. In structural terms it should be noted that only v. 13 provides an imperative for the various segments of the code, because each succeeding unit, like additional examples or cases, is introduced by an initial participial construction (2:18; 3:1, 7, 8-9), which is to be interpreted as a continuation of the original injunction. Thus 2:13 serves as a structural introduction to the succeeding code units. This conclusion is further indicated by the fact that in v. 13 there appears for the first time the verb *hypotasso*, a term that is then engaged to begin the next segments on household members and women (see discussion of 3:7 and 8-9 for consideration of their duty terminology). So one must conclude that 2:13 provides both a thematic and structural introduction to the lengthy duty code.

Finally, vv. 13-17 present a number of exegetical challenges whose solutions influence the overall interpretation of the unit. First, the duty code is dominated by the verb *hypotasso* whose meaning is variously given as: "be subject, obedient, submissive to," "accept the authority of," or even "defer to." The first option is by far the most frequently chosen since the verb is often applied in contexts that suggest the subordination of one group to another (e.g.: slaves to masters, wives to husbands, etc.) and since the codes of Colossians and Ephesians employ *hypakouo* ("obey or be subject to") as a synonym. Such an option, however, causes problems for cases where subordination is not seemingly the issue, for example, mutual relations within the community (5:5; 1 Cor 16:16; Eph 5:21) or association with other humans (2:13—see below). The second option ("accept the authority of") recognizes the issue as one of relationship but also opts for some type of subordination or obedience; in this case 2:13 still presents problems, as does the relationship of the passages on men and community relations (3:7 and 8-9, respectively) to the initial injunction of 2:13. The third option takes seriously what 1 Peter says in 2:16 concerning freedom and so suggests that the meaning is voluntary submission (something commanded in the name of the Lord). A better option, I believe, is to examine more carefully the term's linguistic history and early Christian usage. Clearly the root *tasso* and its cognates suggest order and organization (LSJ 1759-60). Indeed Paul in Rom 13:1-7 employs this root four times in his discussion of Christian relations to political structures. It is particularly enlightening that the Hellenistic verb *hypotasso* is used not only to describe relations that involve subordination but also others that suggest voluntary acceptance of ("subject oneself to") some-one's authority and especially a person's relationship to those in authority, to organizational structures, and to others generally (*TDNT* 8:39-45). From such study one is led to conclude that the verb in question is concerned with organization and a person's relationship to that organization and its mem-bers. Thus its meaning would be "recognize one's association with, relationship to, or duty toward" (LSJ 1897), a sense that includes subordina-tion as well as non-subordinate relationships and their duties. First Peter is interested in a range of relationships and their various duties toward the individuals and groups involved.

Second, the expression *pase anthropine ktisei,* that toward which one should "be submissive" or "discharge one's duty," is understood in three dif-ferent ways: "to every human institution or authority," "to every human creature," and "to every authority ordained for human beings," the last option being a variant of the first but suggesting, under Pauline influence (Rom 13:1), that the political structure is of divine origin. Since the Greek text of 1 Peter does not seem to suggest or support the last option, the dis-cussion therefore centers on the first two. The obvious, literal meaning of the phrase in question is the second choice given above, because the term *ktisis* regularly, both in Classical and LXX Greek, means "creation, created thing, or creature." Many modern scholars, however, sensing a thematic and contex-tual problem have sought a different solution, particularly since the noun also is used in Greek for the founding of a city and since the terms "all human . . ." in 1 Pet 2:13 would seem redundant. This solution (first option) nonetheless is unsatisfactory since its meaning is derived *ad sensum* rather than from linguistic usage. In defense therefore of the second option it should be noted that the author speaks in vv. 13-14 of persons not institu-tions, that the reference in v. 13 to "all human persons" forms an inclusio with "honor everyone" in v. 17, and that a modified interpretation of the verb *hypotasso* (not "submit" but "recognize your duty toward every human creature") eliminates the perceived contextual problem—one should note that the ancient Syriac and Vulgate versions read the text in a similar fashion.

A third crucial issue concerns the identity of "the lord" in the opening statement ("for the Lord's sake"—*dia ton kyrion*) and the function it plays in the first injunction and in the author's concept of duty generally. At first blush one might be tempted, in the context of the creation motif just noted, to view the absolute use of *ho kyrios* as referring to God as creator (see 1:20; 4:19) and to insist further on the theological character of the author's parae-nesis. However, most scholars insist that *kyrios* in 1 Peter usually indicates the risen lord (see discussion of 1:3, 25). Besides, in light of the author's injunction in 3:15 to "sanctify Christ as lord," one might suggest that an issue at stake in the community's thinking and relations with Gentile neighbors was the nature of Christ's lordship as it related to that of the emperor and even to that of the celestial powers of Hellenistic belief (3:22; see also Col 1:15; 2:15). A christological motif is likewise of importance in the following segment of the duty code. Such was indeed my original choice, but further study of the remaining segments of the duty code suggest once more the theological option. This is especially true if one considers the injunction in 2:18 to do one's duty toward superiors "in deep reverence (to God)" and in v. 19 to remain faithful to one's duty even when faced with unjust suffering when this is done "in full consciousness of God" (see also the expressions "in the same way" of 3:1 and 7 and "inherit a blessing" of 3:8). Thus "for the Lord's sake" in 2:13 provides the ultimate reason why Christians have a duty toward other humans. Such a conclusion is reinforced by v. 16, which provides the basis for their obligation to honor all people, namely, that they are "God's slaves or creation." So the expression "for the Lord's sake" in v. 13, serving as the foundation for duty toward all human creatures, forms an inclusio with the statement in v. 17 that, because they are "God's servants" (v. 16), Christians are to "honor everyone."

(2:13-14) Social and Civic Duty. With these introductory considerations in mind, it is now possible to address the author's overall meaning in 2:13-17. First, we look at the initial injunction. The opening imperative can be described as the superscript for the following segments of the code where the author employs an initial participial construction (2:18; 3:1, 7, 8-9) to extend the impact of the initial injunction. The author begins the initial exhortation by advising the addressees to "recognize their duty toward all human creatures," for as fellow humans (rational creatures according to Epictetus), they can lay a claim to honor and respect.

The author adds as motivation: "for the Lord's sake," a phrase that could allude to Christ's death for all the unrighteous (3:18; also 2:24), but most likely underscores what vv. 16-17 will develop; namely, that as "God's servants" or creatures, believers have duties or owe respect to all fellow human creatures. One suspects here a less-than-honorable treatment of Gentile ways and persons (see especially 4:3-4), a fact that prompts the author to remind believers of their humanistic duties, duties that extend to the emperor and other government officials. As humans first and secondly as guardians of social and cosmic order, they are owed honor and respect. In a manner similar to Paul's exhortation to the Romans (13:1-7), 1 Peter recognizes the role of government and insists that the addressees perform their civic duty in a manner compatible with their Christian beliefs. The emperor as head and officials as agents of organized rule have as duty in their turn the responsibility of order as deterrent to evil and a promotion (public approval) of good conduct for the common good.

(2:15) The Role of Good Conduct. Next we turn to the author's sharp rejoinder to what may have seemed a naive treatment of government activity. If in the best of all possible worlds, government authorities pursue and punish evildoers and lavish praise and benefactions on those who do good for their fellow citizens, then why the suffering of those who do good? Such a possible objection leads the author to make an additional reference to the community's critical situation. The response, however, is not an attack on traditional theories of government (see Prov 24:21; Wis 6:1-4; Dan 2:37f; Rom 13:1-7) but rather a reaffirmation of this view by insisting both on their civic duty as Christians and on God's plan vis-à-vis their present difficulties. Verse 15 is a partial restatement of v. 12 in which the addressees are advised to pursue even more resolutely their goal as good citizens: the doing of good or the performing of their civic duties. Implied in this statement is the warning not to neglect their duties and not to merit the accusation of being "mischief makers" (see 4:15). But the performing of one's duty has an added purpose for believers, since by that means God's will or purpose is achieved (see also 3:17 and 4:19). God engages their good conduct to counteract the opponents' slanderous, or at least accusatory, speech. Interestingly, the use of the verb "silence" (*phimoo*) further emphasizes the verbal and social rather than physical (persecution) character of the community's troubles.

Additionally the qualification of the opponents as "ignorant, foolish (senseless) people" underscores an uneasy yet optimistic relationship between Christian and Gentile neighbors. Indeed the good, or at least civil, relationship between the two is said to be hindered by "ignorance" or lack of knowledge (see 1:14 for a description of the pre-conversion state) and by a lack of understanding (*aphron*—"non-understanding" rather than "silly or foolish"). On the one hand, the terminology reflects a willingness to explain such behavior as due to a lack of acquaintance with Christian beliefs and practice. On the other hand, these terms, along with the addition of *anthropos* ("humans or mortals"—see also 2:4), also suggest a malevolent opposition (see 5:8 for its satanic nuances). Thus there is hope that an accounting can lessen the tensions between neighbors (3:15-16) and even more that holy behavior will make believers more socially and politically acceptable in the eyes of the doers both of good and of evil (3:17). Finally it should be noted that the author may have in mind the Jewish concept that "the fool" (Ps 52:1) is one who denies God in every-day life both in failing to do good and in pursuing abominable behavior (4:3-4).

(2:16-17) Duty as God's Servants. After a brief parenthesis on the role of good conduct, the author returns to the concept of duty, emphasizing that the basis of Christian duty is freedom and the knowledge that this freedom brings. Like the Stoics, 1 Peter holds that true obligation comes not from servile fear but from freedom that allows knowledge of reality—in gaining freedom, believers learn that they are "God's servants or creations." With this vision of reality they should understand their relationships to other mortals, to their fellow believers, to their creator, and also to the emperor and the state he rules. These duties conform to what Epictetus (*Discourses* 2.10.1-9; 14.8) holds as the principal duties of the enlightened human being. Also for 1 Peter, mortals and mortal institutions are owed honor or respect. To their fellow believers they owe mutual affection and assistance, and to God they owe thanks and reverence ("fear or awe"—see also Rom 1:21).

Also, it should be noted briefly that, in v. 16, at the mention of freedom the author sharply reminds the addressees that they are not to abuse their liberation as "a cover or pretext for evil behavior" or for ignoring their duties. Surely 1 Peter is not simply responding to slanderous accusations but is addressing also the novel and careless behavior and attitudes of many converts, which caused suspicion and ill-will among Gentile neighbors. Ultimately it is the freeing concept of being God's servants or creatures that forms the basis both for a good sense of moral and civic duty and for optimism in dealing with social and political problems.

Finally 1 Peter's choice of the themes of "honor, love, fear, and honor" as encapsulating the believer's fourfold duty needs some explanation. In the first place it should be noted that only the first of these, "honor all mortals," is an aorist and thus reiterates structurally the initial injunction of v. 13. In thematic terms also it can be considered a restatement of that injunction for the verb *timao* ("honor") here refers to the recognition of status and rights of others (also Rom 13:7). Like the verb *hypotasso*, it advocates recognition of relationships—in the case of the latter in terms of duty and of the former in terms of dignity or recognition of proper status. Thus the first injunction includes all humans (also v. 13)—opponents and enemies included. Choice of the term "honor," which in biblical literature also expresses duty to God and parents (Job 34:19; Exod 20:12), is instructive for understanding 1 Peter's anthropology and politics, for the author presents as the basis for duty respect for the status of all. Recognition of humans as "servants of God" and thus free to understand human relationships leads to recognition of their true position and rights. Choice then of the remaining terms (as present imperatives) adds further specificity and emphasis on the subject of duty: mutual love as the byword for Christian fellowship; reverence and awe for God as parent, creator, and judge ("servants of"—contrast Prov 24:21 where one is enjoined to fear both God and the king); and honor or recognition of the emperor's political role ("as supreme" but also as human creature). Verse 17 then restates the Christian's duty to all human creatures (see v. 13), advocates their political and religious goals (state and community), and insists on absolute dependence on God only.

Suggested Readings

Bammel, E. "The Commands of 1 Peter 2:17." *NTS* 11 (1964-65) 279-81.

Elliott, J. H. "Disgraced Yet Graced: The Gospel according to 1 Peter in the Key of Honor and Shame." *BTB* 25 (1995) 166-78.

Giese, H. "Lebenszeugnis in der Fremde. Zum Verhalten der Christen in der paganen Gesellschaft (1 Petr 2,11-17)." *SNTU* 23 (1998) 113-52.

Goldstein, H. "Die politischen Paranese in 1 Petr und Rom 13." *BibLeb* 14 (1973) 88-104.

Kamlah, E. "*Hypotassesthai* in den neutestamentlichen 'Haustafeln'" in *Verborum Veritas*. Eds., O. Böcher and K. Haacker. Wuppertal: Brockhaus, 1970, 237-43.

Légasse, S. "La soumission aux autorités d'après 1 Pierre 2.13-17: version spécifique d'une parénèse traditionelle." *NTS* 34 (1988) 378-96.

Lugo Rodriguez, R. "El verbo *hypotassein* y la parenesis social de 1 Pe 2,11-17." *EM* 9 (1991) 57-90.

Sleeper, C. F. "Political Responsibility According to 1 Peter." *NovT* 10 (1968) 270-86.

Snyder, S. "1 Peter 2:17: A Reconsideration." *FNT* 4 (1991) 211-15.

Duty of Household Members (2:18-25)

This new segment of the code addresses household matters, particularly the relationship between persons of inferior and superior authority. Indeed the very structure of the household is predicated on such relationships, and the author focuses attention on the possible difficulties or suffering that is the lot of the inferior. It is in this way that 1 Peter introduces most directly the major theme of innocent suffering (see explicit references also in 2:12 and 15), yet without ignoring the requisite duty that inferior has toward superior. Once again the verb *hypotasso* is employed to underscore the recognition of duty even in unpleasant circumstances. At the same time the introduction of the theme of innocent suffering as meeting God's approval leads naturally to the presentation of Christ as the model of such suffering.

If one theme, almost without effort, leads thematically to another, such development causes structural awkwardness. Indeed one can simply divide the segment into two parts: vv. 18-20 on unjust suffering in the context of household relationships and vv. 21-25 as consisting of an excursus on Christ's suffering or death as having paradigmatic and soteriological functions. Thematically it is clear that the two sections are related by the concern for innocent suffering, but it is also evident that the household concerns of the first part disappear in vv. 21-25. In other cases where 1 Peter digresses significantly, there is some effort to return in compositional terms to the original train of thought (1:6-8; 3:18-4:1; see also 1:13f, 18f, 21), though in this instance a return in 3:1 to the code structure is a step in that direction. Also indicating that vv. 21f are an excursus is the fact that it is introduced by the same terms as 3:18: "for Christ also" (*hoti kai Christos*). I conclude from the above that discussion of Christian suffering within traditional social structures has led the author, at some length, to address this issue in christological terms and thus to present Christ's innocent suffering as the model for inescapable, unmerited abuse, as well as God's soteriological instrument.

(2:18-20) Duty and Suffering of Household Members. The first part pursues the duty code structure by speaking directly to community members (direct address), by reiterating the basic principle of duty but, while presuming the force of the original injunction (imperative of v. 13), gives the new exhortation as a case study of Christian duty and so employs a participial construction. Believers are addressed precisely in their roles as members of the household. The term employed is *oiketes,* a term that means "belonging to the household" but that is traditionally rendered "servant or slave." Since 1 Peter speaks of the relationship between these persons and others called *despotes* ("master of the house, lord, owner"), it is assumed that the household pair of "slave/master" is intended, even if Col 3:22; 4:1 and Eph 6:5, 9 employ *doulos* and *kyrios* for this pair. This disparity is variously explained. Scholars routinely presume that these terms are used as synonyms (see the questionable reference to Prov 22:7) and suggest that 1 Peter is reluctant to employ the traditional terms of the household code, owing to the religious overtones of each (see 2:16 and 13—"slaves of God" and "for the Lord's sake," respectively; similar concerns are expressed for the Paulinist writers even in their use of these terms). While such an explanation may account for the avoidance of the terms in question, it does not address the choice of terms—why speak specifically of "household slaves" and their "owners"? Are household slaves as a social group a major concern for the communities of Asia Minor? Or are we dealing here more specifically with household relationships: inferior to superior or members of the household and those with authority over them? See also the discussion of terminology for the community code: presbyter/elders and younger members (5:1-5). In effect vv. 18f deal not specifically with slaves, nor even slave owners, but with Christians, more generally as members of households. What is presented as the reality or even the ideal for the *oiketes* or those belonging to the household (innocent suffering, lack of deceit in speech, abstention from retaliation, etc.) is predicated of all believers (see especially 3:8-12), who are also called "servants or slaves (*douloi*) of God" (2:16).

It is my conclusion here that 1 Peter is addressing the audience generally as members of households (including women and men later) and their duties within established social structures toward their superiors (*despotes*). In effect the household becomes the paradigm for establishing social relationships and duty but also the context for dealing with problems that may arise within those structures. Inferior members (in terms of authority) are exhorted to recognize their traditional duties toward their taskmasters or owners regardless of circumstances. These circumstances themselves ("not only to the good and gentle but also to the harsh") are expressed in a general, schematic way to underscore the principle of duty in its structural context and thereby to address more succinctly the problem of innocent suffering.

Once again (see discussion of v. 13) the author adds a seemingly innocent phrase to qualify the believer's duty as a member of the household—this is to be done "in all fear or reverence" (*en panti phobo*). While one could view the awe or reverence as owing to human masters, one should instead consider the phrase as providing an added motivation for doing one's duty toward superiors, namely, "out of deep, divine reverence" (see discussion of 1:17 and 2:17 where "fear or reverence" is proper in one's relation to God and not the emperor). Verse 18 therefore repeats the motivation for duty toward others as expressed earlier in 2:13 and 16-17.

In vv. 19-20, 1 Peter presents an interesting restatement of the issue of unjust suffering in the context of doing one's duty. Having stated clearly and without exception the householder's duty toward those in authority (v. 18), 1 Peter, in a complex structure consisting of two positive and one negative composite clauses, insists repeatedly that innocent suffering has God's approval. Clearly vv. 19-20 form a unit whose structure and repetitive elements call attention to the community's "fiery ordeal" (4:12) or trials that are testing the genuineness of their faith (1:6-7). The unit begins and ends with the curious expression: *touto . . . charis,* a phrase that is best rendered "such is commendable" or "merits favor"—the occurrence at the end adds *para theo*: "in the eyes of God" (i.e., "this merits God's favor or grace"). Verse 19 expresses in a positive way the general principle of unjust suffering ("if someone undergoes pains"—see also 1:6) as being commendable, if this is borne *dia syneidesin theou*. The principal noun *syneidesis* is a technical term for the conscience or moral awareness (see 3:16, 21 and generally in the NT) but here, owing to its linguistic ("of God") and thematic context, probably bears the general lexical sense of "awareness or full consciousness of God" (BAGD 786.1) and serves as a parallel or explication of the earlier phrase "out of deep, divine reverence" (v. 18). Thus v. 19 restates the exhortation of duty but focuses more particularly on the problem of unjust treatment at the hands of someone in a superior position.

Verse 20 restates this crucial issue by insisting first on what it does not involve (a good report for bearing merited beating or punishment—see 4:14-16) and then by restating more succinctly both believers' duty toward superiors ("doing good") and their patient endurance of suffering that might result from such a situation. This type of suffering, while unsought, has God's approval and merits divine favor (see also 3:17). The repetitive character of vv. 18-20 and the progressive statement of the issue of innocent suffering (as related to duty, as involving a possible case, and as focused on the addressees' situation—vv. 18, 19, and 20 respectively) draw the reader's attention to the critical nature of this problem in the lives of the believers of Asia Minor, who are both "citizens or resident aliens" of the Roman state (with consequent civic and social duties) and members of God's people or "religious sojourners or exiles" (with God's pleasure in view).

(2:21-25) Christ as the Model of Innocent Suffering. The second part of the pericope on the "duty of household members" consists of a long excursus on Christ's innocent suffering and its bearing on the addressees' current situation. Though no longer interested seemingly in the household relationship of inferior to superior, the author nonetheless takes pains to express the close thematic connection between the two sections, either by employing the connective *gar* ("for") or by referring back explicitly to the theme of innocent suffering ("to this or to the above"—*touto* recalls structurally the crucial theme of vv. 19-20). Further it is particularly the term *pascho* ("suffering"— vv. 19, 20, 21, 23) that interconnects the two parts of the pericope. Also, a close connection is made between the suffering of Christ and that of believers as owing to God's call (*kaleo*) to a life of holy conduct in imitation of Christ's giving of himself in view of promised, eternal glory (1:15; 2:9; 3:9; 5:10). Finally this christological excursus, like that of 3:18-22, is explicitly joined to the first part of the pericope by the expression "because Christ also (suffered)," thereby drawing a connection with earlier discussion of the theme of suffering.

Verses 21-25 present a number of features that challenge the modern reader. The anaphoric structure (repeated used of relative clauses modifying "Christ") and use of traditional themes have suggested to some the use by 1 Peter of an early hymn to Christ, a text that would have been considerably expanded to accommodate the author's interest in Christ as the paradigm of innocent suffering. Thus an original statement about Christ's death or suffering (see discussion of Greek text below) would have been expanded in v. 21 by insisting on imitation of Christ and by the addition of v. 23 to stress the innocence of Jesus' ordeal. However, another striking feature of this passage, its close relation to Isa 53:4-12, has led others to view the composition as owing to 1 Peter's direct use of Isaiah 53 or indirect dependence on early Christian tradition to formulate a much-needed paraenesis on Christian suffering. For many reasons scholarly opinion has tended to favor the latter. While other passages in 1 Peter can convincingly be ascribed to early hymnic resources (1:20, 21; 3:18, 22), vv. 21-25 seem more convincingly to be the product of the author's use of the OT passage, under the influence of early tradition, to dwell on Christ's suffering as the paradigm for Christian suffering despite honorable, responsible conduct. Also, another feature of this passage continues to intrigue readers, namely, the coherence of vv. 24 and 25 with the rest of this code segment. How does v. 24 with its emphasis on the soteriological function of Christ's suffering relate to the author's obvious preference for its paradigmatic function? Also how does v. 25 relate to the author's overall paraenetic message?

Various structural proposals have been made to explain both the composition and message of vv. 21-25. On the one hand, one could view this passage as a midrashic composition based on Isaiah 53 to address first the Christian response to or duty in light of the Christ-event (vv. 21-23) and then to underscore the basis of the believer's salvific experience (vv. 24-25). Such a suggestion helps in coming to grips with the author's paraenetic message. On the other hand, it has been proposed that these verses present a chiastic structure (a: salvific death in v. 21b, b: exemplary suffering in v. 21c, b': Christ as example in vv. 22-23, and a': Christ as Savior in vv. 24-25), whereby the soteriological and paradigmatic functions of the Christ-event are carefully related for the readers' benefit, though with special emphasis on the latter.

Perhaps the key to understanding the author's composition of vv. 21-25, as well as the weakness of the above proposals, is to be found in the analysis of v. 21b: *hoti kai Christos epathen* [or *apethanen*] *hyper hymon* ("because Christ also suffered [or died] for you). The first reading ("suffered") is to be preferred from a textual, contextual, and compositional point of view. Use of *pascho* is both strongly supported by the ms tradition (majority and major mss—note that the important witness of Sinaiticus is diminished by its preference for "died" also in 3:18 and 4:1) and by 1 Peter's preference for the theme of suffering (use of this verb twelve times). Further, if one is correct in rejecting the questionable reading of "died" for 2:21 and 3:18, then the verb *apothenesko* is nowhere used by the author. Finally compositional considerations explain both the origin of the unique phrase *pascho hyper* ("suffer for") and the abundant scribal activity in 2:21; 3:18; and 4:1. It is suggested that 1 Peter begins with the traditional confessional formula "Christ died for . . ." (Rom 5:5, 8; 14:15; 1 Cor 15:3; 2 Cor 5:15) but as a concession to the audience's situation opts for the theme of suffering rather than dying, thereby creating a new idiom: "suffer for." Indeed the author, while greatly concerned with the soteriological function of Christ's passion as the basis for Christian faith (1:2, 3, 18f; also 2:24), is interested in presenting it as the paradigm not of martyrdom but of innocent suffering. Thus the term *pascho* becomes for 1 Peter a means of presenting the addressees' troubles as "sharing the sufferings of Christ" (4:13) not in a soteriological but in a paradigmatic fashion. While it is suggested that Christ himself shared in their suffering (use of *kai*: "Christ *also* suffered"), it is clearly emphasized that his suffering had an exemplary function. Therefore the scribal activity in 2:21; 3:18; and 4:1 should be explained as the attempt of copyists to transform the rare "suffer for" to the more frequent, and seemingly synonymous, "died for."

In light of the above, it is also suggested that v. 21 provides the key to understanding 1 Peter's rhetorical strategy concerning innocent suffering. Verses 18-20 present the structural context of the believer's life, namely, that of political, social, and religious duty, on the one hand, and that of unmerited suffering within the established structures, on the other hand. Once it is established that the suffering in question is not the result of irresponsibility but rather of temporary (1:6; 5:10), misguided activity on the part of outsiders and unsympathetic, uncomprehending superiors, it is affirmed that such suffering has God's approval, because, first, the addressees are doing their duty "out of deep, divine reverence" and, second, that in the divine call to come to Christ (2:4) they are provided the paradigm (vv. 21f) for addressing Christian living, even in its harshest trials.

Verse 21 not only draws an explicit connection between the addressees' suffering and that of Christ but also insists that such suffering is part of God's plan for the audience (see 1:12), for Christ's suffering was meant to provide a pattern (*hypogrammos*) for their lives. The second part of the verse therefore becomes an explanation of "suffering *for you*," that is, literally "to leave you an example or model to follow." Christ's suffering then provides the ultimate paradigmatic motivation since the believer accepts that Christ's innocent suffering received God's approval and vindication in glory and so leaves "footsteps" for the readers to follow. They are to act like Christ or follow in his footsteps; they are to be true to the shaping pattern of his life and behavior if they are to share with Christ in God's glory (5:10).

Having insisted on the paradigmatic function of Christ's suffering ("for you," "leaving . . . an example," and "follow . . . in his footsteps") and having employed general, if picturesque language to describe this model, the author in a series of parallel relative clauses describes in more concrete language Christ's behavior in the face of suffering—1 Peter's focus now is on "*suffering for you*." Imitating the anaphoric style of early christological hymns (Col 1:14-20; 1 Tim 3:16), the author presents three successive *hos* ("the one who") clauses to discourse on Christ's suffering as it relates to the audience's situation. Verse 22, introduced by the relative pronoun "who," is drawn verbatim from Isa 53:9b—only the initial "iniquity" (*anomia*) of the LXX is replaced by "sin" (*harmatia*). This modification could reflect the author's anticipation of the term twice in v. 24 (itself a borrowing from Isa 53:4) to draw a further connection between the paradigmatic and salvific functions of the Christ-event, but more probably the author wishes by the use of this noun to present Jesus as the antithesis of the inferior who "does wrong and is beaten" for it (v. 20 employs the verb *hamartano*). This verse therefore applies the parallel statements of Isaiah to insist on Jesus' innocence and so to describe further the pattern required for Christian behavior in the face of unjust suffering. Finally there is in this verse a particular note on the doing of good ("not doing wrong or committing sin") as in 2:12, 14 and on the verbal nature of the abuses (see discussion of 2:12; 3:15-16; and 4:14).

Verse 23 continues the anaphoric use of relative clauses modifying Christ. In this case 1 Peter constructs an intricate series of antithetical parallels to describe Christ's paradigmatic behavior in the face of unjust treatment. Showing familiarity with the passion tradition, the author constructs a double parallel on the theme of retaliation. In the face of "verbal abuse" or slander (*loidoreo*—see John 9:28; Acts 23:4), during the trial and death scenes Jesus was silent (Mark 14:61; see chapters 14 and 15 generally) or "did not return the abuse" of the mocking crowds and soldiers (see the exhortation of 3:9). Additionally, when faced with suffering, Christ did not invoke divine judgment as a response (here *apeileo* means "to threaten" with retributive justice) as is common in early Jewish and Christian literature (Deut 32:35; 4 Macc 9:9; 10:11; 2 Thess 1:6; Rev 18).

Following two statements of what Christ did not do ("return abuse" or "threaten"), 1 Peter counters with a positive alternative, a statement that nonetheless is not easy to interpret. In 23c the author states, "instead he handed [. . .] over to the one who judges justly"; unstated is the object of the verb *paradidomi*. Many scholars propose a reflexive object ("he handed himself over" or "put his trust") and understand the statement as related to 4:19 where suffering believers are exhorted to "entrust their souls to a faithful creator" and perhaps to the theme of Jesus' obedience (1:2). Others suggest "his cause" or "judgment" as likely implied objects. All the same, the context seems to imply that Christ gave over to God the issue of dealing with his enemies ("he handed these [or the judgment of these] over" to God). While such an option might imply that the author's main concern is that sure and severe judgment be left to God as just judge, it seems more plausible that 1 Peter again reveals an optimistic attitude toward nonbelieving opponents, who, it is hoped that on seeing the honorable deeds and unmerited suffering of believers (here: Christ himself), "might glorify God on the day of visitation" (2:12). The focus therefore would not be on Christ or believers "putting their trust" in God but rather on their doing their duty, even to the point of suffering, and entrusting the outcome, as regards their nonbelieving opponents, to a "faithful creator" and God of mercy (1:3; 4:19) who is able to bring a non-people "out of darkness into his marvelous light" (2:9-10).

Verse 24, while continuing the anaphoric use of the relative pronoun *hos* ("the one who"), turns in a seemingly abrupt way to soteriological considerations. What precisely has brought about this shift in theme is hard to determine, though several suggestions are usually made. (1) 1 Peter returns more directly to Isaiah 53 and so to the community's traditional use of the Servant's vicarious suffering. Indeed the beginning and concluding portions of v. 24 are taken verbatim from that OT passage. (2) The author's use of *paradidomi* in v. 23 (as well as its use in Isa 53:6, 12) might have suggested its traditional, redemptive use (see Rom 4:25; 1 Cor 11:23; Gal 2:20). (3) Having commented in vv. 21c on "for you" and in vv. 22-23 at length on "suffering," the author returns to the more basic explanation of "suffered or died *for you*." Jesus' passion has a paradigmatic function for the addressees, but the behavior required and the life expected of all believers are related to the passion's soteriological role. Perhaps owing to all of these factors, 1 Peter turns to this topic by constructing from Isa 53:4 and 12 the memorable Servant-like statement, he "himself bore our sins," and by insisting on its cruciform character: "in his body on the cross." While the term *anaphero* could suggest a sacrificial act on Christ's part (see 2:5; also the priesthood imagery of 2:9), namely that he "brought our sins . . . to the cross" (BAGD 63.2—see instead 63.3), it is preferable here to see, via the influence of Isa 53:11-12, the meaning that he "bore or took away our sins" as one who bears innocently our sinful burden (see also Heb 9:28). The instrument of this atonement or removing of sins and its consequences is Christ's crucified body, a point emphasized by use of *autos* (he "himself") and "body and cross." The last two terms underscore, on the one hand, the physical reality of redemption and life in the world and, on the other, the stark reality of Jesus' innocent suffering by a method reserved for criminals or evildoers (*xylon*: "wood or gallows"—see Deut 21:22-23; Gal 3:13; Acts 5:30).

By means of a result clause (introduced by *hoti*: "so that") the author expresses the role of Christ's vicarious death, first in a negative and then in a positive statement. In terms reminiscent of Paul's statement in Rom 6:11-12 ("dead to sin and alive to God"), but from a different perspective, 1 Peter addresses believers' renunciation of the past, defined as "separation from sins," and their turning to God, described as "living for righteousness or doing what is right." The author's terminology forms a striking contrast with Pauline usage; 1 Peter's concern here is with the activity that distinguishes the pre- and post-conversion status of believers. It is not the renunciation of natural impulses per se that is envisioned but "of those (impulses) which wage war against the soul" (2:11), those acts that one must classify as "sins." The contrary of these sinful acts is a life of righteousness or of doing good (see also 3:14). First Peter then has borrowed the language of Isaiah 53 to express Christ's saving activity in a traditional way but then in a subsequent construction applies this theme to the community's situation. The addressees, as a result of Christ's saving activity, must "have no part of sinful deeds"; instead they are to lead lives of holy conduct according to the pattern established by Christ (1:15; 2:21).

The entire passage is brought to a conclusion (vv. 24c-25) by a final anaphoric use of the relative pronoun (*hou*: "by whose [wound]"). Once again 1 Peter has recourse to Isaiah 53 to express another aspect of Christ's saving activity, which in turn is also applied to the community's situation. Verse 24c, a verbatim citation of Isa 53:5 (with a change from first to second person plural), addresses once again the salvific character of Christ's activity: healing by means of his suffering or wounding. The remainder of the passage (v. 25) presents an interesting assortment of images: "wandering sheep" (borrowed from Isa 53:6) that return to Christ, seen as shepherd and guardian.

Clearly this final verse is intended as an explanation of why the healing was necessary and what its effect is in the lives of the addressees.

Such an interplay of themes was made possible by early Christian tradition, which made use of these in a variety of contexts. The theme of healing, which is used to characterize the salvific meaning of Christ's suffering, would certainly be understood by the readers as referring to conversion—such usage would be familiar from the Synoptic tradition (Mark 2:17; Luke 4:23). The description of the audience's pre-conversion status as resembling "stray sheep" draws from both Jewish and Christian tradition, which often viewed the people of Israel as lost, stray, or without a shepherd (Isa 53:6; Ezek 35:5-6; Matt 10:6; Mark 6:34). The term *epistrepho* in early Christian tradition acquired the sense of conversion or more literally "turning to God" (1 Thess 1:9) and, in its use of Isa 6:10 (Mark 4:12; Matt 13:14; Acts 28:27; and John 12:38-40), the tradition easily associated the themes of "turning or returning" and "healing." Already in the Synoptic and later tradition there are hints of Jesus being viewed as the shepherd in charge or in search of stray sheep (Mark 14:27-28; Acts 20:28; John 10:11f; Rev 17:17; see also Luke 15:1-7).

First Peter does not offer a direct clue for interpreting the theme of healing. While some insist that the term refers back to the concept of sin alluded to in v. 24a and b (thus the healing of the illness of sin by vicarious suffering) and so connect v. 24c with the preceding relative clause (NRSV), it is preferable to postulate two relative clauses addressing different aspects of Christ's soteriological activity. In v. 24a-b one finds "the taking away of sins" explained immediately after by a dependent clause regarding sin and righteousness. In similar fashion in vv. 24c-25 one encounters another relative clause regarding "healing by [Christ's] wound" explained by a *gar* clause on stray sheep reunited with their shepherd. Borrowing a clue from Isaiah, who connects healing and the straying of sheep, 1 Peter seems to insist on a theme noted earlier, namely, that the readers who were once "not-a-people" (2:10) or individuals "wandering like sheep" have become God's people by "being brought back to the shepherd and guardian of [their] souls" or being (see 1:9). Seemingly by their conversion or return to God's salvific agent the addressees have now been healed (Isa 6:10 and NT usage) or ransomed from their sordid past (1:18). Indeed the God of grace has called them to eternal glory in Christ (5:10) and now, by their return from their ignorant past to the chief shepherd's protection and guidance, they have received a foretaste of the "Lord's goodness" (2:3). The healing then is the believer's return to God's good graces. While awaiting Jesus' return in glory (4:13; 5:4, 10) to be led to God's presence (3:18), believers have ceased to be "wandering sheep" and have become the Lord's herd or flock (5:2-4) and receive his protection.

Thus while the imagery of "wounding and healing" addresses the soteriological character of the Christ-event, v. 25 relates these themes to the community's situation as "religious exiles" who nonetheless find their unity and protection in Christ their "shepherd and guardian" (on these last two themes, see 5:2-3 and 1:5; 3:14-15; 5:10).

Members of the household, therefore, have duties toward their superiors, duties that must be exercised in full awareness of God's will, because believers have been called to model their lives on Christ's example—even in suffering. This innocent suffering of Christ that brought about forgiveness and healing has God's approval as does that of believers who "follow in his footsteps." Also, though they may be "religious exiles" living among their pagan neighbors, they are nonetheless a distinct flock united and led by its shepherd (and Christian stewards and elders—4:10; 5:1-4) and protected in view of the day of visitation.

Suggested Readings

Bechtler, S. R. *Following in His Steps. Suffering, Community, and Christology in 1 Peter*. Atlanta: Scholars, 1998.

Carrez, M. "L'esclavage dans la Première Epître de Pierre" in *Etudes*, 207-17.

Elliott, J. H. "Backward and Forward 'In His Steps': Following Jesus from Rome to Raymond and Beyond. The Tradition, Redaction, and Reception of 1 Peter 2:18-25" in *Discipleship in the New Testament*. Ed., F. F. Segovia. Philadelphia: Fortress, 1985, 184-209.

Osborne, T. P. "Guidelines for Christian Suffering: A Source-Critical and Theological Study of 1 Peter 2.21-25." *Bib* 64 (1983) 381-408.

Philipps, K. *Kirche in der Gesellschaft nach dem 1. Petrusbrief.* Gütersloh: Gerd Mohn, 1976.

Prostmeier, F. R. *Handlungsmodelle im ersten Petrusbrief.* Würzburg: Echter, 1990.

Richard, E. "The Functional Christology of First Peter" in *PFP*, 121-39.

Duty of Women (3:1-6)

This new section of the code and the following (3:7) focus on the central members of the household, usually classified as "wives and husbands" but here more generally identified as "women and men." Many scholars assume that 1 Peter, though not retaining the "slave/master" pair in tact (see 2:18f) and eliminating that of "child/parent" of the traditional household code (see Col 3:8–4:1; Eph 5:22–6:9), here addresses first the Christian wife and then, briefly, the Christian husband. Such a conclusion leaves many unanswered questions, not the least being why the exclusive attention to Christian wives in pagan households as opposed to the treatment that Christian husbands bestow on the "weaker" female sex. Such emphasis as well as the peculiarity of some of the terminology and themes have led to much debate concerning the author's purpose, the situation being addressed, and the nature of the texts themselves.

It is therefore suggested that 3:1-6 is addressed not specifically to Christian wives whose husbands are nonbelievers but more generally to Christian women, with some attention given to those who live in pagan households. Careful examination of the pericope's terminology along with its focus confirm such a conclusion and assist greatly in resolving the debated issues noted above. The extended advice given to Christian women falls into three grammatical and thematic units: vv. 1-2 on duty toward non-Christian men of the household, vv. 3-4 on feminine behavior that is pleasing to God, and vv. 5-6 on OT models for such behavior.

(3:1-2) Duty Toward Non-Christian Men of the Household. In a manner similar to 2:18f this first section introduces the duty code structure by speaking directly to the community members involved (direct address), by insisting on the principle of duty, and by reiterating here also the imperative of 2:13 by means of a participial construction, which presents a new case study—women are to recognize their responsibilities "by doing their duty vis-à-vis the men of the household" (use again of the verb *hypotasso*). It is at this point that one must examine closely the special character of the author's terminology. The opening term *homoios*, "likewise, in the same way," is variously interpreted depending on how one views the previous passage (slaves or household members) and the verb *hypotasso*. Are wives, or women more generally, "to be submissive, subordinate, or obedient" to their husbands, or men of the household, in the manner of slaves to their masters or owners? It is suggested that the term refers to the motivation for household members' basic duty (women in this instance—see also 3:7 and 5:5). Just as all believers (2:13f) and all members of the household (v. 18f) are exhorted to display good behavior "out of reverent fear" or as "being fully conscious of God," so women in question are to approach their duty in the same manner (see further discussion of the phrase "by reverent fear" in v. 2 below).

Also of interest is the author's manner of characterizing the addressees and the object of their attention as *gynaikes* and *andres* respectively, terms that generally designate "women and men" but often also "wives and husbands." While the first of these terms could ostensibly designate "wives" (twice in v. 1), its use in v. 5 to refer to the "holy women" of Israel and its relation to the second term seem to require the meaning "women." It is particularly the author's use of the seemingly redundant phrase *tois idiois andrasin,* literally: "toward your own men," which indicates that the subject is not simply "wives" (see Col 3:18-19; Eph 5:25) but men more generally of the household. The same expression will again be used in v. 5 where the subject, seemingly, concerns "holy women" and "their duty toward the men" of the family. The admonition to women then to "do [their] duty toward the men of the household" presumes contemporary familial and social structures whereby women, in the various stages of their lives (as daughters, wives, or dependent widows) or their social status vis-à-vis the household (as slaves, freedwomen, or clients) find themselves invariably linked to established male figures to whom they are duty-bound. Christian women, like their pagan counterparts, have duties within the household, and it is the author's advice that they live up to these responsibilities—however much these vary according to locale, status, and area of life. They are to live responsibly according to their situation in the household, a situation that is defined in relation to male and female roles—this is done with an eye to problems that community members are encountering.

While the opening of the pericope (v. 1a) addresses the duties of Christian women as these relate to their gender roles and positions within the household, immediately, as in 2:18, the text introduces a problem case, namely, the relationship of Christian women to men of the household who are not Christian. This worst-case example is introduced by requisite legal terminology: "so that, even if some do not . . . they may be." (One should note the conditional particle *ei,* the indefinite plural *tines,* and the stark use of the future indicative after *hina*—see BDF 369.2). Clearly the advise is given to all Christian women, even those who are associated in households with men who "do not obey the word." Indeed those who are not Christian presented special problems for Christian women; specifically, in Roman households women, and wives in particular, were expected to adopt the gods of the paterfamilias (Plutarch, *Moralia* 140D). Thus they are to do their duty toward the men of the household (the remainder of the pericope will address that issue), even those who are non-Christians and so have different religious and social expectations. So, the *hina* clause provides an added reason for insisting on the women's responsibilities.

In view of the previous discussion, several further points should be made regarding vv. 1-2. First, it is assumed that obligations of duty apply even in cases where men of the household are not believers, because in such circumstances an added motive exists for positing exemplary conduct. This motive, like that for all believers (2:12), is a missionary outreach to Gentiles, in this case nonbelieving members of the household, that they might be moved or persuaded by the conduct or honorable deeds of the Christian women (see also 1 Cor 7:12-16). Indeed this particular passage helps to sway the balance in deciding that in 2:12 the author envisions not only eschatological but also missionary results from Christian example. Also in the present case the verb "win over" (*kerdaino*) underscores the author's missionary perspective (see 1 Cor 9:19-23; Matt 18:15). Additionally the expression "do not obey the word" (see also 2:8 and 4:17) clearly designates nonbelievers. It has been suggested, with some plausibility, that such terminology, especially in light of 2:8, may indicate men who have rejected the Christian message and may even be overtly hostile to Christian members, the vulnerable ones being the Christian women of their households.

Second, the theme of public Christian conduct, noted earlier in 1:13, 15, 17; 2:12, again takes center stage. The author employs the term "conduct" twice, stresses its public, observable character (as in 2:12), and, by means of a play on the term *logos* ("word"), notes that "obedience to the word" will come about "without a word" or through exemplary activity. First Peter's insistence on "wordless witness" in this case owes perhaps to a wish to avoid either retaliatory exchange of insults (2:12; 3:16) or the appearance of being "busybodies or mischief makers" (see 4:15). For non-Christian men who were probably already acquainted with the Christian "word" or message, what was needed was not further apologetics but rather the example of Christian practice, particularly the chaste lives of gentle women (choice of *hagnos*, meaning "pure" in place of *hagios* or "holy"). Also, one might suggest that this advice to the women is meant to parallel the example of Christ, who in his silent dignity "did not return abuse" (2:23).

Further, in discussing this feminine conduct, the author employs an intriguing descriptive expression: *ten en phobo hagnen anastrophen hymon.* The extended object is usually translated "your pure and reverent conduct," as though 1 Peter had used two adjectives to describe the women's allegedly traditional behavior vis-à-vis the men of the household. In view, however, of the author's use of the *phobos* ("fear or reverence") word family throughout the letter (see 2:17; 3:16), particularly the expression *en phobo* (1:17; 2:18), and the grammatical construction of the expression in question (the prepositional phrase seemingly modifies the adjective "pure"), it seems best to render the entire construction as follows: "observing your conduct made pure by reverent fear." Once again holy conduct and Christian duty would be described as motivated by one's relationship to God—women, indeed all Christians, must direct their lives to God in reverence (1:17), for it is such motivation that renders their conduct pure in the sight of God, fellow believers, and Gentile neighbors.

Finally we might insist that the advice of 3:1f is addressed to Christian women generally, particularly as members of the household. In v. 1b a rather troublesome example is offered, probably because such a situation presented egregious cases of innocent suffering. Christian women were not in this case to conform to Roman mores by adopting the gods of the household, but like Christ were to suffer responsibly and in silence, with the hope that their noble conduct might bring about obedience to the word.

(3:3-4) Feminine Behavior That Is Pleasing to God. The following verses present an extended contrast between negative (v. 3) and positive feminine behavior (v. 4), the author's attempt to describe what "doing one's duty toward men of the household" means. The grammar and terminology of the lengthy period, however, present a challenge for the modern reader who finds it difficult to grasp the overall meaning and function of the passage. It is generally assumed that there is a distinct parallel between the two clauses, so that the "external adornment" of v. 3 corresponds to the "hidden person or self" of the following verse. Such a view, however, seems counterindicated both by the grammar of the construction and its thematic context, since there is a surprising shift away from "adornment" in the second clause to a focus on the "inner person" (the parallel subject) instead. Further such a view would demand a parallel between external decorative activity (in v. 3 concerning hair, jewelry, and clothing) and the inner core of the person (with its various attributes in v. 4). Besides, how does either the activity of the first verse (seen as adornment) and the authentic being of the second (with no reference to activity) relate to the prior discussion of duty and conduct? Also, from such a perspective it is difficult to see how the proper adornment of "the holy women of old" (v. 5a), the acknowledgment of their duty toward "their own men" (v. 5b), and the obedient activity of Sarah (v. 6a) relate to the author's purpose and message to Christian women.

Several clues are given in vv. 3-4 to support a different view, one that relates these two verses with what precedes and follows, and that focuses on internal and external activity as examples of feminine conduct. The following translation indicates some of the particulars:

> Let not such adornment be an external one,
>> whether the plaiting of hair and the wearing of gold jewelry
>> or the putting on of garments;
> instead, let the hidden person of the heart (adorn you)
>> with the imperishability [or an imperishable activity]
>>> of a gentle and quiet spirit;
> such (adornment) is very luxurious [or precious] in God's sight.

The first clue to be examined is the author's use of a relative possessive rather than a regular possessive pronoun (*hon* in place of *hymon*: "whose" rather than "your") to introduce v. 3. Such usage indicates a close grammatical connection with the previous verse, in fact indicating that "your conduct" of v. 2 is now being presented as "adornment" in v. 3. The translation "such adornment" attempts to indicate the author's point that "pure conduct" must not be confused with external cosmetic or stylish beauty aids. Second, 1 Peter's use of a paraphrastic construction (the imperative of the verb "to be" with a noun introducing several activities) allows a focus on external action (one could translate with the NRSV: "do not adorn yourselves outwardly") and prepares for the second clause in v. 4. Third, one must take a clue from the previous verbal construction to understand the point being made in the second clause, which in effect has no apparent verb. While most scholars suggest that a subject and verb be supplied and that the nominative serve as a predicate nominative ("let it [adornment] be the hidden person . . . "), it is preferable to view the earlier verbal construction as doing double duty: "instead let the hidden person . . . adorn you." Fourth, the prepositional phrase *en to aphtharto*, whose grammatical character is debated (*IBNTG* 57, 79), would be interpreted in a traditional way (e.g., "clothe or adorn with"— BAGD 259.4b) and the neuter adjective would indicate either an "abstract [concept] . . . with dependent genitive" ("the imperishability of a gentle and quiet spirit") or "a particular definite thing or act" ("an imperishable deed or activity"—see BDF 263.1-2). Finally the conclusion of v. 4 (*ho estin enopion tou theou_polyteles*) deserves some attention. With most scholars we agree that the initial relative pronoun ("which") must be seen as referring to the preceding positive statement. It must also be pointed out that, whereas 1 Peter usually employs *timios* or a related term to speak of someone or something as being "precious or valuable" (1:7, 19; 2:4, 6), the adjective *polyteles* instead is used. While it is a synonym of the former word group (see *polytimos* in 1:7), it nonetheless has the nuance of indicating something "luxurious or lavish." The choice is hardly fortuitous, for 1 Peter wishes to say that such ornamentation or adornment, representing honorable behavior, is the type of luxury that God finds pleasing in a Christian woman.

The adornment imagery of v. 3 is chosen as being appropriate for the discussion of proper feminine behavior. While scholars, in commenting on the threefold feminine ornamentation of this passage, routinely cite Greco-Roman authors on the excesses and dangers of such finery (Plutarch, *Moralia* 141e; Juvenal, *Satires* 6:457-65; see also *T. Reuben* 5:1-5), presumably in light of their contrastive interpretation of v. 4, it seems preferable to see here a choice of imagery that allows a contrast between Gentile and Christian behavior, done in a picturesque, feminine mode. Seizing on what is traditionally described as feminine preoccupation with physical beauty and luxury, and demanded by social mores (the construction of intricate hair-dos and the love for opulent decoration and dress), 1 Peter does not seem to condemn these or even to suggest possible dangers or excesses (see 4:3-4 for the author's knowledge of this). Instead, taking a clue from 2:11, I suggest that the author would view these as natural tendencies and would oppose them only to the extent that they "wage war against the soul."

First Peter's approach in v. 4 to the issue of proper feminine behavior might best be seen against the background of current Hellenistic thought. While some writers saw feminine luxury as an excess or danger to be avoided, others exhorted women to aspire to prudence, dignity, and good behavior as befitting honorable women. Such behavior and virtue, it would appear, was what men desired and expected of a good woman (see Epictetus, *Encheiridion* 40). Presumably, 1 Tim 2:9-10 would subscribe to the above, adding that good works are "proper for women who profess reverence for God." First Peter offers a different perspective, one based on the anthropological model of the showy, external and the hidden, inner person. No doubt 2 Cor 4:16-18 offers a similar anthropological structure; there Paul contrasts the transient, outer nature and the unseen, eternal being. While Paul focuses on the outer and inner being as such, 1 Peter addresses the activity or conduct deriving from each. 1 Peter insists that the conduct of a Christian woman must not be the product of the exterior being, here described as beautifying oneself, but that one should seek instead the adornment provided by "the hidden person of the heart" (the heart represents the deepest, sincere part of one's being and for the Christian, the recesses of a purified soul —1:22; also 3:15). Interestingly, the adornment is no longer particularly feminine in its description. Like all believers, women are to seek good works that persist, the imperishable or eternal product of the inner, purified being.

Finally "the imperishable activity" or "pure conduct" in question is further qualified by two important statements. First, the activity is said to derive from "a gentle and quiet spirit or disposition" (on *pneuma* as meaning "state of mind or disposition"; see also 1 Cor 4:21—BAGD 675.3c). While some interpreters in the past have readily pointed to these qualities as owing to the author's concern for feminine behavior, more careful analysis shows that neither gentleness ("humility"—*praus*) nor silence ("guietness"—*hesychios*), in this context are particularly feminine in quality or intent. In effect all Christians are to be gentle (see related term in 3:16; also the synonym from the *tapeinos* word family: 3:8; 5:5-6) in their dealings with each other and with outsiders. Thus the behavior of Christian women has much in common with that of other believers. As regards silence it is clear that the author refers back to v. 1 where women are said, in a play on words, to win over to "the word" the unbelieving men of the household "without a word." It should be pointed out that Hellenistic writers often advised people in adverse conditions to meet slander or verbal abuse with quietness or with kindness (Musonius, *Orations* 10, 16; Plutarch, *How to Profit by One's Enemies* 90d-f). In the case of 1 Peter the terms "gentle" and "quiet" are selected with care, the first to correspond to the context of verbal abuse and misunderstanding (avoid reciprocal insults: 3:9) and the second as a means to bring men of the household, knowledgeable of Christian preaching, to "obey the gospel of God." Second, as noted earlier, 1 Peter speaks of such conduct as being most acceptable in God's sight and chooses a term that relates this concept to the adornment imagery used earlier—the adornment (conduct) that results from such motivation is far more "luxurious" (in place of "precious") than beauty aids in God's sight.

(3:5-6) Old Testament Models of Feminine Behavior. The paraenesis for Christian women is brought to an end by an extended appeal to the behavior of ancient Jewish women as the models and particularly to that of the renown Sarah as their progenitor in ideal feminine behavior. First Peter's treatment of these examples is done in two stages.

First, the holy women of Israel's ancestors serve as models of behavior for Christian wives (v. 5). What has been described in the previous verse as the activity of "the inner person" or the ideal adornment of the wife is said precisely to be the way "the holy women" of Israel conducted or adorned themselves. What is being presented to Christian women as ideal finds a precedent in the lives of these Israelite women who are described as leading holy lives because they placed their hope in God. The emulation of the conduct of these ancient women is more than following their virtuous example; this conduct is characterized as holy and based on hope in God like that advocated for Christian believers more generally (see 2:13-16, 21). The means and standard for such behavior was the doing of one's duty toward one's husband (see v. 1).

Second, 1 Peter follows the example of contemporary moralists in offering material illustrative of the behavior in question, whether silence when faced with verbal abuse or gentle rebuke to counter slander or misunderstanding (see earlier references to Musonius and Plutarch)—a similar use of OT traditions appears in 1 Tim 2:8-15 where reference is made to the example of Adam and Eve. In the case of 1 Peter the general example of the holy women of old is rendered more specific by appealing to the case of

Abraham's wife Sarah (v. 6). Interestingly, her behavior is characterized by two expressions: she "obeyed (*hypakouo*) Abraham" by "calling him lord or master (*kyrios*)."

The background for these characterizations is found in biblical and household traditions. The example given is clearly related to Gen 18:1-15, the Oak of Mamre episode, particularly v. 12, the only occasion where Sarah speaks of her husband as *kyrios*. Gone is the original context of Sarah's amusing protest that she cannot have a son: "my lord is old"; in its place one finds the concept of Abraham's lordship as head of the household. While later Jewish tradition sought, in its interpretation of this passage, to make Sarah an agent of domestic peace (*Midrash Rabbah* to Lev 9:9), 1 Peter, employing this same passage, wishes to present her as the ideal woman who treated her husband as master of the household. Likewise, to describe Sarah's relationship to or activity toward her husband, the author employs the verb *hypakouo*, a term that usually expresses the subservient relationship of child to parent or slave to master in household codes (Col 3:20, 22; Eph 6:1, 5) or in general usage (*T. Judah* 1:4; *T.Gad* 8:3; Josephus, *JA* 13.275; Rom 6:16). Its use here is problematic, because while the noun (*hypakoe*) is employed to express Christ's acceptance of God's will for him (1:2) or the believer's conversion described as commitment to the Father or as acceptance of the truth (1:14—see Acts 6:7; Rom 10:16; 2 Thess 1:8), the verb appears only here in what is seemingly an unusual construction. In effect it rarely describes a wife's relation to her husband and, in the few cases known to me of such usage, one should probably argue not for the meaning "to obey or be subject to" but "to show respect for one deserving greater honor." The latter meaning derives from the male's presumed physical and mental superiority and his consequent role, in the marriage relationship, as a guide for the "weaker sex" (see discussion below of 3:7). Thus "the good wife does not act in a superior way toward her husband but with deference" (Philemo the Comedian, *Fragments* 132), accepts his guidance in the household context (Josephus, *Against Apion* 2:201) and defers to him to maintain his benevolence (*PLondon* 5.1711.35).

From the above discussion I conclude that 1 Peter has chosen the term *hypakouo* in place of *hypotasso* in this case to describe the woman's duty toward her husband more specifically in household terms as acknowledging the husband's role as head or lord of the household and as deserving deference and greater honor (see 3:7 once more). It is in this sense that 1 Peter sees Sarah's use of the term *kyrios* as recognizing Abraham's higher position and greater honor (see BAGD 459.1b), even in the trying circumstances portrayed in Genesis 12 and 20 (the Israelite couple in Egypt and Gerar as "brother and sister"), where she obeys her husband despite his unjust treatment of her. Thus Sarah was a model woman compared to Abraham, for by regularly calling him "lord" (present tense) she acknowledged his position as head of the household and conferred upon him the requisite respect and honor (aorist to express a complexive or overall sense—BDF 318, 332).

In a concluding statement (v. 6b) 1 Peter applies the example of Sarah, and by implication that of the other holy women, to the Christian women among the addressees—they have become her children. The choice of terminology and its application, however, have led to some discussion concerning the author's meaning. For example: what type of relationship does the term *teknon* imply? When do contemporary women become Sarah's daughters? And what relationship does this image have to the two concluding present participles? It is sometimes suggested that since, in early Christian tradition, Abraham is often presented as the father of believers (Luke 19:9; John 8:39; Rom 4:11-12; Gal 3:7; Heb 2:16), 1 Peter would be joining other writers who speak of both Sarah and Abraham as the spiritual progenitors of believers (Isa 51:2; Rom 9:9; Gal 4:23-30; Heb 11:11). Thus Sarah would be the spiritual mother of Christian women. Such a conclusion, however, raises questions about the interpretation of the remainder of the text. If the aorist "you have become" refers to conversion, then how should one interpret this in relation to the women's present activity? It is preferable to view the "child" imagery of v. 6 in terms of the principal theme of the pericope, namely, ideal feminine conduct. Christian women have become Sarah's children because her behavior has become the model of theirs. One might best explain the sequence of tenses as a "proleptic aorist" ("you have already become her children"), which anticipates or regards as fulfilled the conditions of the immediately following verbal statements interpreted as conditional participles ("by doing . . ." or "since you have already done . . ."—see *BG* 257). The issue is not that good behavior or works have transformed responsible women into holy women but rather that pure Christian conduct makes these women the children of Sarah, the model wife or woman.

The final participial constructions focus on two particular aspects of recommended behavior. In the first case the author reiterates a basic theme of honorable behavior, namely, "the doing of good" (as opposed to "the doing of evil"—2:12, 14-15, 20; 3:17; 4:15), including public deeds that nonbelieving men or observant Gentile neighbors would view as good or noble (see discussion of 2:12). The second participle introduces the concept of fear, a theme that is certainly pertinent for the situation but one that does not at first blush seem to derive from the story of Sarah. A closer look, however, at the conclusion of the OT episode reveals a clue for understanding both the author's composition and meaning. Immediately after Sarah calls Abraham "lord," there follow the "Lord" God's severe reprimand and a final statement regarding Sarah's doubt-inspired laughter and fear. From this statement 1 Peter probably concludes that Sarah's doubt had been caused by her past fear (use of aorist in LXX—Gen 18:15) and that she was no longer subject to intimidation. To formulate this theme the author borrows a phrase from Prov 3:25: "to fear alarm or intimidation" (see other contacts with this OT book in 4:8, 17 and 5:5, particularly the extended citation of Prov 3:34 in the last mentioned). Like Sarah, and like other believers (see 3:14 for a similar formulation based on Isa 8:12), Christian women are not to be subject to human fears (*phobeomai*) in hostile or trying situations but "in reverence" (use of *en phobo*; see 1:17; 2:18; 3:2) to "entrust themselves to a faithful creator, while continuing to do good" (4:19).

Suggested Readings

Balch, D. L. *"Let Wives Be Submissive": The Domestic Code in 1 Peter*. Chico: Scholars, 1981, 95-105.

Brox, N. "'Sara zum Beispiel . . .' Israel im ersten Petrusbrief." In *Kontinuität und Einheit*. Eds., P. G. Müller & W. Stegner. Freiburg: Herder, 1981, 484-93.

Daube, D. "*Kerdaino* as a Missionary Term." *HTR* 40 (1947) 102-20.

Kiley, M. "Like Sara: The Tale of Terror Behind 1 Peter 3:6." *JBL* 106 (1987) 689-92.

Manns, F. "Sara, modèle de la femme obéissante: étude de l'arrièreplan juif de 1 Pierre 3,5-6." *BibOr* 26 (1984) 65-73.

Schlosser, J. "1 Pierre 3, 5b-6." *Bib* 64 (1983) 409-10.

Scholer, D. M. "Woman's Adornment: Some Historical and Hermeneutical Observations on the New Testament Passages 1 Tim 2:9-10, 1 Pet 3:3-4." *Daughters of Sarah* 6 (1980) 3-6.

Duty of Men (3:7)

The advice to Christian men forms an important but uneven pair with that given to women. Its briefness probably is due to the fact that when husbands converted to the Jesus movement, it would have been expected, following the dynamics of the household, that women, particularly their wives, would adopt the new religious movement. Thus the exhortation is given to Christian men and, in contrast to that given to women, deals with issues of concern to a Christian household. The principal concern of this section of the code, however, continues to be the basic duty of family members as related to their specific position within that household.

This section of the code, like the previous two (2:18f; 3:1f), begins by speaking directly to the community members involved (direct address), again insists on the principle of duty, though with a shift in terminology, and once more reiterates the imperative of 2:13 by use of a participial construction that offers a new case study—men are to face up to their duty by the way they "live together [with women members of the household]." In effect 1 Peter, after having addressed directly the men within the community and having referred back to previous exhortation (the expression "in the same way" will be discussed below), approaches this group and its responsibilities in a threefold series of statements: two extended participial constructions, which approach the issue of duty from anthropological-social and from religious perspectives, and a concluding purpose clause, which provides an ecclesial rationale for the exhortation.

From the beginning it is clear by the use of the first participle, as is true in 2:18 and 3:1, that the author prolongs the force of the initial imperative of 2:13 ("recognize your relationship or duty to") and provides an additional case, namely, that of men vis-à-vis the women of the household. The specific duty of the former, however, is expressed not by the verb *hypotasso*, a term that underscores duty in terms of status or position (see earlier: 2:13, 18; 3:1, 5), but by terminology in the following three statements that stresses a mutual relationship between men and women. The first participle (*synoikeo*) emphasizes precisely this interdependent relationship; the man's responsibility is defined by the very nature of the household (including marriage) context: "cohabitation" with women in a family relationship. The first statement, however, pursues the realities of this social institution in light of the anthropological insights of the time, making use of traditional formulas to express what moderns would classify as male presuppositions. It was readily accepted in the thinking of the Hellenistic world, from the time of Plato (*Republic* 5.455D, E; 457A; *Laws* 781A) that women were inferior to men in physical, intellectual, and moral terms. Such a situation is reflected both by the terminology and exhortation of this first statement.

Men are to begin their assessment of the situation by remembering that women are members of "the female sex" (use of the neuter of *gynaikeios* to underscore the feminine gender) and that they are thereby recognized as "the weaker vessel" of the human pair. In the case of the latter the term *skeuos* points to both men and women as human creations that serve either as instruments of beneficent or evil powers or as receptacles or vessels (see *TDNT* 7.360-62 for general discussion). It is the latter—the human as receptacle of various powers or gifts (see 2 Cor 4:7; Rom 9:21f; 1 Thess 4:4) —that points here to women, as well as men, as vessels containing a variety of abilities but, in the case of the woman, having weaker or more limited powers (in accordance with contemporary anthropology). So it is in light of these considerations that 1 Peter insists that cohabitation be "in accordance with (see BAGD 407.2.5) [the males' superior] knowledge" (*kata gnosin*); the woman needs the guidance or direction of the man's intellect. Thus the first statement of the advice to Christian men takes as its starting point the presupposition of its culture (the woman's weaker ability) and advises that proper cohabitation requires the man to provide for these limitations either by providing intellectual guidance in moral matters or by giving due consideration of physical weakness in the face of the harsh realities of a society so dependent on physical labor. The concept then of mutuality in this case relies on male and female as being human vessels or creatures and on the responsibility of the former as the "stronger vessel" to assist the latter in its role as household or marriage partner.

First Peter's second statement addresses a different principle of motivation, one that might more properly be called religious. While in the first exhortation men are advised that they owe their women counterparts assistance, owing to their mutual status as interdependent human creatures, so the second suggests that their common, eschatological goal requires the men to "assign (equal) honor" to the women. The terminology of the statement, "fellow-heirs" and "as also" (or "since they also"—*hos kai*), suggests a sharing of equal honor between household members or spouses (even the term *aponemo* would suggest the "rendering of honor that is due"). Indeed this "inheritance," which is "kept in the heavens" (1:4) and described as "the grace which consists of eternal life" (*charitos zoes*—3:7; see also 1:3; 4:6; also 3:18), acts starkly as the absolute equalizer between men and women, husbands and wives. This is especially so since for 1 Peter the eschatological reality, described as "the grace that Jesus Christ brings" (1:13) or as "present hope" and "assured inheritance," requires "indescribable and glorious joy" because it is already being received as the outcome of faith (1:3-9).

The exhortation to Christian men ends on the intriguing note that the above is necessary "so that [their] prayer may not be hindered." Such a rationale for the exhortation is difficult for the modern reader to grasp since the letter provides few clues for its interpretation. It is hard to know what the term *egkopto* entails, whether lack of seriousness and discipline on the part of the household members or spouses (hinderance—see 4:7) or extended delay in performing the activities of one's communal life (see 4:3-4). Since 1 Peter addresses formally the topic of prayer elsewhere only at 4:7f, it is probably safe to assume that the thematic context of that passage provides insight for the interpretation of this one. It is presumably the holy conduct of the household members that is at stake: their mutual life, their hospitality, and their stewardship in employing God's manifold gifts. Husbands and wives, like other believers, indeed all members of the household, must prepare themselves for action and live reverently (1:13, 17). Indeed the advice to Christian men begins by insisting that they are to act "likewise or in the same way" as women and members of the household generally, that is, with reverence (see 1:17; 2:18; 3:2, 15) "that God may be glorified in all things through Jesus Christ" (4:11). Prayer then for 1 Peter, as in the Christian tradition more generally (Matt 5:23-24; Mark 11:25; 1 Cor 11:33-34; Jas 4:3), is intimately related to one's honorable behavior toward others. Finally the author's exhortation ends by insisting that the prayers of both men and women ("your" refers not only to men but also to all members) and therefore their life of holiness are made possible by a proper attention to mutual honor and love.

The last point raises an interesting issue concerning 1 Peter's paraenesis as addressed to Christian men. While in the household codes of Colossians and Ephesians (3:19 and 5:25, respectively) husbands are admonished to love their wives, in 1 Peter men instead are exhorted to bestow honor on women, the honor due everyone (2:13, 17) and, by the reference to common prayer, they are reminded of the mutual love that believers are to have for one another (1:22; 4:7-8). Seemingly, for 1 Peter mutual honor precedes and is the basis for mutual love in the household and the marriage relationship.

Conclusion (3:8-12)

The code is brought fittingly to a close ("finally") by returning to general advice addressed to the entire community ("all of you"). In addition this section of the code reiterates the earlier exhortation to recognize one's duty (2:13) by use once more of participial constructions that focus first on behavior within the community (v. 8) and then on behavior involving outsiders (v. 9). There then follows in vv. 10-12 an extended, nearly-verbatim citation of Ps 33:13-17a, a passage that is seemingly chosen to conclude the duty code by reiterating some of its principal themes and to introduce the following issue of suffering and vindication. Discussion of this passage then falls easily into two parts: vv. 8-9 on ideal Christian behavior and vv. 10-12 on scriptural justification for such conduct.

(3:8-9) Ideal Christian Behavior. In two successive statements 1 Peter encapsulates what is to be expected of the believers of Asia Minor. In the first statement (v. 8) the addressees are given in a list of five unusual adjectives a profile of ideal community conduct, while in the second statement (v. 9) they are presented with Jesus' nonretaliatory behavior (see also 1:23) and advice in the face of insult or abuse. Clearly the themes of these two verses derive from early Christian paraenesis, especially those of oneness of mind (Rom 15:5; Phil 2:2; also Acts 4:32), mutual affection (Rom 12:10; 1 Thess 4:9; Heb 13:1; 2 Pet 1:7), humility (Eph 4:2; Phil 2:3; Jas 4:6), and non-retaliation (Matt 5:44; Luke 6:28; 1 Thess 5:15; also 1 Cor 4:12). Even the concepts and terminology of sympathy (Heb 4:15; 10:34; 1 Cor 12:26), compassion (Col 3:12; Eph 4:32; Phil 2:1), and blessing in the face of insult (1 Cor 4:12; Luke 6:28; Matt 5:44) are well documented in early Christian texts. It is Rom 12:10, 14-17, however, that offer the most striking parallel. In those verses Paul is concerned with these same themes and employs similar terminology to that of 1 Peter. All the same, the order of the themes and the difference in terminology argue for independent use of early paraenetic materials by the two authors, even allowing for the possible use of the former by the latter. It is clearly in the instances where the two are closest in terminology that 1 Peter shows the greatest interest in those particular themes and terms, whether *philadelphia* or "mutual affection" (1:22; see also 2:17; 4:8), nonretaliation (2:23), or humble-mindedness (5:5-6).

While the predominant use of participles in this section of Romans and the extensive character of its paraenesis for community life have suggested to some scholars the use by Paul of a primitive Christian source, it is readily agreed that the text of 1 Peter is fundamentally different. The author has drawn from the community's general store of tradition first a concise list of well-known concepts concerning relations with fellow believers and then has formulated from this same tradition an extended but more familiar (see Rom 12:17; 1 Thess 5:15; see also 1 Pet 2:23) antithetical statement concerning treatment of outsiders. The list of v. 8 is decidedly Hellenistic in terminology; most of these occur only here in the NT and not at all in the LXX (contrast with the very different fivefold list of Col 3:12).

The series in 1 Peter focuses on proper mind-set, beginning with "oneness of mind" and ending with "humble mindedness," thereby stressing the goal of unity and peace on the one hand (see vv. 10-12; also 2:5, 9 and the code generally) and the proper relation of creatures to fellow creatures and to God on the other (see 5:5-6). These two crucial virtues form an inclusio around the three affective qualities of holy conduct: sympathy, love, and compassion, the first and last of these laying stress on the essential, mutual affection of believers toward one another. Not surprisingly, the central virtue of the list is that of *philadelphia*, the virtue that renders creatures most like their loving parent who is a "faithful creator" and merciful progenitor of new life (1:3; 4:19). An interesting parallel to 1 Peter's list, which both insists on the relationship between the unity of believers and humility (see discussion of 5:5) and on the primacy of mutual love, is a striking contemporary text from Qumran: "all should work in real unity, true humility, mutual concern, and correct thinking toward their fellows in the community of holiness and as children of the eternal fellowship" (1 QS 2:24). Finally it should be said of v. 8 that the virtues 1 Peter describes to encapsulate the ideals of Christian behavior do not of themselves exclude conduct vis-à-vis outsiders. While some of these ideals underscore ecclesial unity and interrelationship, each prepares for the meekness or humility that God approves as the basis of human interaction, christological imitation, and divine emulation (1:15-17; 2:21-23; 5:5-6).

In v. 9, 1 Peter returns to more traditional terminology to address the believer's relationship to outsiders, particularly in light of the addressees' situation. The concept of nonretaliation is expressed in a traditional fashion and expanded to recall the believer's christological model. Thus the believer is not to "repay evil for evil" nor, like Christ, to "return abuse or insult" (2:23). Choice of the terms "evil" and "insult" (*loidoria*) point on the one hand to the author's use of a traditional formula to characterize perceptions of Christian behavior ("evildoers"—see discussion of 2:12) and on the other underscores the verbal and social nature of Gentile mistreatment of believers.

In antithetical fashion the author holds up not Jesus' example of silence when faced with violence but his advice to "bless those who curse" them (Luke 6:28; see also Matt 5:44). Presumably one could insist, in literal fashion, that 1 Peter advises "speaking well" of those who level insults; however, the expectation of "inheriting a blessing" favors the above interpretation. Finally the author returns to the theme of the glory promised to innocent sufferers by insisting that God called believers to a new inheritance, preserved in heaven (1:4), a blessing that can only be described as God's "eternal glory in Christ" (5:10).

(3:10-12) Scriptural Justification. The second section of the concluding pericope is an extended citation of Ps 33:13-17a. The differences between the text of 1 Peter and the Psalm are minor, indicating not a different textual tradition but a community's meditative use of a LXX passage to meet its religious needs. Thus the modifications in the introductory verse ("the one who") and of the successive imperatives in vv. 10b-11 indicate general paraenetic use and application of the biblical text to a new context. Interestingly, in this way the author reinforces the imperatives of the LXX text to underscore the initial, structurally-central imperative of the duty code in 2:13.

An important question to resolve in interpreting 1 Peter's reading of the Psalm is whether the language of life, good days, and peace refers to an eschatological future or to a this-worldly reality. It seems clear enough that the Psalmist envisions a life of blessing in this world for the righteous, but how does the Christian writer read this passage? Many assume that the ending of v. 9: "the inheritance of a blessing"—read as an eschatological reality—governs the interpretation of the following citation. Thus life and good days would refer to entrance into glory on the day of visitation for the righteous, while there would be punishment for "those who do evil" when "the time has come for judgment." Such an interpretation, however, fails to see that the blessing of v. 9 acts as eschatological motivation for present behavior, that is, blessing rather than insulting one's enemy.

Instead it is preferable to view vv. 10-12 as the author's insistence that life, good days, and peace are made possible in the present as the result of new life and honorable or holy behavior. Verse 10a focuses on the author's optimistic expectations that a *modus vivendi* is possible between believers and nonbelievers. In this part of the verse the author sets up the desired goal ("let those who desire . . . "—the plural is employed, with the NRSV, to avoid awkward gender forms) and then in 10b begins in a series of third-person imperatives to suggest how to achieve that goal. In the language of the Psalmist 1 Peter reiterates the principle of nonretaliation (see 2:23; 3:9a). This passage further underscores the author's insistence on the verbal or social nature of the situation ("tongue from evil" and "lip from speaking deceit") as well as the need to avoid (or to cease) retaliatory evil or deceitful speech (2:1, 22). Beyond this, v. 11a repeats the oft-heard exhortation of "avoiding evil and doing good" as the standard for honorable behavior and as God's means for winning over hostile nonbelievers (see 2:12; 3:1-2). Verse 11b provides the author with a key statement for the letter's paraenesis: "let them seek peace and pursue it." The quest for peace, for eschatological peace (1:2 and 5:14b), is also a pursuit of harmony or concord with one's non-Christian neighbors—life and good days in the view of the Psalmist and of 1 Peter are synonymous with the peace, which the Christians of Asia Minor should seek to establish in their neighborhoods. No doubt, 1 Peter agreed with Paul's advice to the Roman community: "if it is possible, as far as it depends on you, live peaceably with all" (Rom 12:18).

The citation from Psalm 33 is brought to an end in an interesting fashion. Verse 12a-b fittingly cites the Psalmist's assurance that the Lord God looks favorably on the righteous and listens to their prayer (for protection and prayer, see 1:5 and 4:7). First Peter could have ended the citation at this point but selects the beginning of the following verse of the Psalm to reassure believers less sanguine about the possibility of good days or peace that God both abhors evil and holds evildoers accountable. The statement serves on the one hand as a warning that Christians not act in retaliation as evildoers and on the other as a promise of vindication. This last point, however, is tempered by 1 Peter's choice to end the citation without citing the Psalmist's conclusion: "to destroy a memorial of them from the earth" (Ps 33:17b). Once again one notes the author's reluctance to deal severely with the community's antagonists; it is hoped that the good relations between Christians and non-Christians are possible and that honorable behavior on the part of the former will foster peace and perhaps enlightenment. Finally the author's choice to cite v. 17a of the Psalm (also its beginning and ending), no doubt, points to its function as conclusion to the duty code (duty and so harmony in a Greco-Roman setting) and as introduction to the following passage on Christian vindication.

Suggested Readings

Balch, D. L. "Early Christian Criticism of Patriarchal Authority: 1 Peter 2:11-3:12." *USQR* 39 (1984) 161-73.

__________. "Household Codes" in *Greco-Roman Literature and the New Testament: Selected Forms and Genres.* Ed., D. E. Aune. Atlanta: Scholars, 1988, 25-50.

Lecomte, P. "Aimer la vie: 1 Pierre 3/10 (Psaume 34/13)." *ETR* 56 (1981) 288-93.

Lohse, E. "Parenesis and Kerygma in 1 Peter" in *PFP*, 37-59.

Osborne, R. P. "L'utilization des citations de l'Ancien Testament dans la première épître de Pierre." *RTL* 12 (1981) 64-77.

Piper, J. "Hope as the Motivation of Love: 1 Peter 3:9-12." *NTS* 26 (1980) 212-31.

Prostmeier, F. R. *Handlungsmodelle im ersten Petrusbrief.* Würzburg: Echter, 1990.

Schlosser, J. "Ancien Testament des citations dans la Prima Petri" in *Etudes,* 65-96.

Senior, D. "The Conduct of Christians in the World (2:11-3:12)." *RE* 79 (1982) 427-38.

Soteriological and Paradigmatic Role of Suffering
(3:13-4:6)

This section of 1 Peter is a complicated and difficult one on several counts. Not only is it hard to discern the overall topic of the section, but also it is a challenge to follow the author's train of thought, especially between vv. 13-17 and 18f. Additionally the christological and eschatological material of vv. 18-22 (also 4:6) present further problems in terms of source and interpretation. Finally the language and terminology of the section are particularly taxing to the modern reader.

A cursory look at the subtitles given to these various pericopes or the entire passage by translators and scholars as well as their proposed divisions indicate a certain malaise at discerning the author's overall message. Perhaps the best way to broach this subject is to recognize the three natural parts of the passage, 3:13-17, 18-22; 4:1-6 and to seek their interrelationship in the author's style and thematic interest.

First, it seems clear that the theme of suffering connects all three paragraphs. Not only does the term *pascho* ("suffer") occur repeatedly (3:14, 17, 18; 4:1, 1), but also in the first section it is related to Christian maltreatment (3:13, 16), in the second to Christ's death and post-death activity, and in the third to the new life brought about by Christ's death (4:2, 3, 6). Thus in thematic terms 1 Peter, I suggest, is concerned both with the soteriological and paradigmatic function of suffering.

Second, the disjointedness of the section relates to the author's stylistic peculiarities. Seemingly in 3:18 1 Peter begins a statement concerning Christ's suffering, launches into a lengthy discussion of the soteriological role of Christ's suffering and death, and only at 4:1 returns, by repeating the terminology of 3:18, to the original discussion. Similar developments occur in 1:6-8 and 2:21f. In the case of 1:6 the exhortation to rejoice is followed by an extended statement of the believer's precarious situation but is resumed in v. 8 by the repeated exhortation to rejoice. In the case of 2:21 a discussion of innocent suffering brings about an extended statement on Christ's suffering as a paradigmatic and soteriological reality—interestingly both 2:21 and 3:18 are introduced by the phrase "because Christ also suffered" (note that the excursus of 1:6b-8a also involves the theme of suffering). Rather than returning to the concept of Christ's suffering in this second case, 1 Peter in 3:1 resumes the original code structure of the overall exhortation begun in 2:11. Thus 3:13–4:6 should be viewed structurally as an extended treatment of Christian suffering that is interrupted by an excursus on Christ's suffering, death, and post-death activity, a passage that consists in thematic terms of an extended discussion of Christian suffering both as it is grounded in the saving effectiveness of Christ's own suffering and salvific journey to God and as it reflects on Christian life and behavior according to the divine will.

Innocent Suffering But Gentle Defense (3:13-17)

Following the extended duty code or lengthy exhortation addressed to the community concerning its responsibilities toward members and outsiders, the author turns more specifically to an issue raised earlier (2:12, 15, 19-23; 3:9), namely, the suffering experienced by the righteous. This first unit (vv.

13-17) follows logically upon the concerns of the code, particularly its concluding OT citation—one should note the repeated use of the roots *kakos*, *agathos*, and *dikaios* ("evil, good, holy," respectively) and the theme of zealous pursuit of holy conduct. Thus the author begins by insisting that all who do their duty need not fear maltreatment at the hands of authorities or conscientious neighbors (see 2:12, 13-15) but asserts, with an eye toward the community's situation, that "suffering for doing good" is a source of blessing. With this introduction 1 Peter begins a discussion of innocent suffering and proceeds to address the believer's response to such treatment. This first pericope falls into three grammatical and thematic units: vv. 13-14a on the blessedness of innocent suffering, 14b-16 on the believer's desired response to such treatment, and v. 17, by way of conclusion, on the blessedness once more of suffering for doing good. In structural terms the first and third parts underscore the importance of the exhortation given in the second concerning proper Christian response to Gentile maltreatment.

(3:13-14a) The Blessedness of Innocent Suffering. First Peter begins the discussion with an impressive compound-complex sentence, whose meaning has been variously discerned. It is readily pointed out that there is a seeming contradiction between v. 13, which assures believers protection from harm, and v. 14, which concedes that they are suffering all the same. Similarly the verbs of the two conditional clauses present difficulties; the first, though an aorist, is usually rendered as a present tense ("you are"). The second, a rare optative, is hesitantly treated as a hypothetical conditional ("should you suffer"; see also v. 17). Also, the idioms "zealous for good" (*tou agathou zelotai*) and "suffer for righteousness" (*pascho dia dikaiosynen*) are sometimes interpreted in relation to Zealot and Pauline influence, respectively. Finally the function that the beatitude of v. 14 plays in the author's message is debated: is this blessedness a present reality, or is it future in character in the manner of the beatitude of Matt 5:10? Answers to these questions or solutions offered to the problems raised have led to a variety of proposals for the composition of the letter, for the understanding of the community's situation, and for the interpretation of this passage and the letter more generally.

Once again the clues for the interpretation of this passage are to be found in the author's stylistic tendencies and thematic interests. Indeed the structure of 2:19-20, on innocent suffering as bearing God's approval, confirms 1 Peter's complex use of parallel conditional sentences here also to underscore this same theme, as an introduction to the issue of proper Christian response (vv. 15f). In both cases one encounters well-constructed parallel conditional statements, first a general principle or claim and then a particular focus on the theme of innocent suffering. While the structure of 2:19-20 is more complex, that of 3:13-14 is more succinct and its message more focused:

13	now who will maltreat you,	a
	if/since you became jealous for good (activity)?	b
14	however,	
	even if you should suffer for (doing) what is right,	b'
	you are (still) blessed.	a'

In structural terms the parallel "if" clauses or protases (focused on "doing good") provide the related assurances for the opening and concluding statements (*a* and *a'*). Interpretation of the passage must take these observations into consideration.

Examination of these verses in light of the author's thematic interests bears out the above comments. Verse 13 begins with the term *kai* ("now, so" —see BDF 442.2), as does 1:17, to draw a conclusion from what precedes. The addressees are assured that, owing to God's protective gaze (2:12) and the believer's conscientious attention to duty as honorable conduct (code generally and especially 2:14 on governors who punish wrongdoers and protect doers of good), they will not suffer maltreatment (*kakoo*). The statement is expressed as a rhetorical question ("who will maltreat you") whose answer is a self-evident: "no one." The remainder of the statement takes the form of a conditional, factual clause (use of aorist): "since you became zealous for doing good." At conversion the addressees committed themselves to the pursuit of honorable deeds. In effect the expression "zealous for good" is 1 Peter's formulation of the traditional moral quest, whether the Psalmist's "desire for life" or "the doing of good" (see citation of Ps 33:13-15 at 3:10-11), the Pastor's "zealous for good deeds" (Titus 2:14), or the common Greek phrase "zealous for virtue or goodness" (*arete*: Isocrates, *Epistles* 4B or Philo, *On Virtues* 175). Verse 13 then is a rhetorical statement of principle: Christians, dedicated as they are to honorable activity (2:12) and to holy, righteous conduct (1:15-17), have both political and divine assurance that no harm will come to them, for governors have as their duty "the praise of those who do right" (2:14) and "the eyes of the Lord are on the righteous" (3:12).

It is in light of this last statement that we turn to an analysis of v. 14 and its seeming contradiction. Indeed the verse does state that members of the audience are suffering or may suffer for doing what is right. What then is the author's meaning in v. 14, and how does this relate to what is expressed in v. 13? Several proposals have been made to resolve the tension between the two

verses. A common suggestion is to see the term "maltreat" in v. 13 as referring to inner harm (and so appeal to Isa 50:9) or as a reality that threatens
Christian faith. One could then translate "who will really harm you?"
Another option is to focus on v. 14 and to view the term *pascho* along with
the optative (also in v. 17) as meaning "suffer death"—in this way v. 14
would not contradict the earlier statement. Another solution envisions the
second statement as an exception to the general rule just stated. While
defending v. 13 as a restatement of 1 Peter's conviction that, in God's plan,
good necessarily follows good (2:12, 15; 3:1-2, 9; see also Matt 5:16; Luke
12:7) or as a principle of reassurance (as explained above), these scholars
maintain either that 1 Peter notes the exception of those who suffer "for
righteousness' sake" (or as Christians—see 4:16) or more generally that the
principle of political and divine protection is valid, though some are suffering despite their devotedness to what is right. Both would insist that 1 Peter
wishes to underscore the blessedness of those who are suffering.

Several observations should be made as regarding these proposals. It is
not convincing in linguistic and contextual terms to insist either that *kakoo*
means anything but "maltreat" in relation to the repeated use of *pascho* in the
sense of "being maltreated or suffer" or that the latter in two instances (3:14,
17) should mean "suffer death" rather than its usual meaning of "suffer" in 1
Peter. The last suggestion agrees more fully with what I see as the structure
and function of these two verses. As noted earlier, v. 13 is to be seen as a
statement of assurance of protection (or blessedness—see further below);
namely, that as "resident aliens" who are devoted to doing good (2:14) and as
"religious exiles" who live their lives reverently in the sight of a merciful Lord
(1:17; 2:10; 3:12), believers will suffer no harm. Drawing from the parallel
features of v. 14 one should view it both as a commentary on the general
statement of v. 13 and as an application of its principle to those who "are suffering for doing what is right." Verse 14 is introduced by *alla*, a term that
here contrasts the two clauses, "taking back or limiting [the] preceding
statement" (BAGD 38.2). Such a conclusion is further indicated by the subsequent *ei kai*: "however, even if." Thus the parallel "if" clause also speaks of
"doing what is right" (synonymous for "good activity" in v. 13) but "takes
back" what is earlier stated, namely, that some "are suffering." The author's
use of the optative would support such a reading. Though some scholars suggest that 1 Peter employs the optative here out of consideration for the
addressees' suffering and thus handles a painful issue with some delicacy,
such an interpretation is hardly acceptable in grammatical terms for use of an
optative in a conditional clause regularly indicates a lesser degree of actuality
(*IBNTG*, 150). While earlier scholars have appealed to such usage to bolster

a partition theory for the letter (an earlier document wherein persecution is a distant possibility and a later one wherein it is raging: 1:3–4:11 and 4:12–5:11, respectively), such is not the case for references to suffering generally—it is a present reality throughout 1 Peter. Nonetheless, the optative has a particular function within the intricate conditional construction of vv. 13-14. The first verse enunciates the principle or ideal of political reality: praise or protection for those who do good (also 2:14). The second verse expresses an exception to this general rule not as a fatalistic vision of the future but as a remote possibility for most honorable and righteous people, though hopefully a short-lived reality (1:6; 5:10) for some in the communities of Asia Minor and in other parts of the church (5:9), who are suffering as a result of their Christian commitment (4:16). The optative expresses this concept as a theoretic exception (*BG*, 323) to make a further point, namely, that the blessing of protection implied in v. 13 for the righteous is promised nonetheless to those who suffer despite or because of their love for what is right (on the term *dikaiosyne* see 2:24).

Based on the previous discussion one can draw the following conclusions regarding vv. 13-14a, especially 1 Peter's use of the optative within this complex structure. (1) First Peter insists that even though some in the community suffer as Christians, seemingly in contradiction of the very principle of divine and political protection for the righteous, they are "still blessed." (2) Rather than express immediately the reason for this claim, the author focuses on exhortation to those suffering abuse but will return to the issue of blessing in the present for the righteous sufferer in 4:14. (3) The addressees have already been introduced in 1:5 to the concept of divine protection (see also 5:10) and so will more readily understand and accept the author's point. (4) This passage adds further insight on the author's position on suffering and Christian optimism. Suffering as a Christian, 1 Peter insists, is not the ideal for the believer. Instead, suffering for doing what is right, if it is God's will (v. 17), is a distinct possibility (so use of optative) for all believers who are promised the blessing of divine protection. Implied in the author's claim is that innocent suffering is a difficulty for the community that may yet be resolved through honorable behavior (2:12).

(3:14b-16) Proper Response to Mistreatment. Having reintroduced the topic of innocent suffering, but as a painful exception to the principle of political protection, 1 Peter, after briefly underscoring the assurance of divine protection or blessedness, turns to the believer's response to such treatment. In stylistic terms this passage offers three initial imperative clauses supplemented by an extended construction, consisting of adjectival, adverbial, and participial phrases, and terminates in a complex result clause. The imperatives form a contrasting group of two negative statements and a positive exhortation drawn freely from Isa 8:12-13. The first two imperatives act as an introduction to the central paraenetic statement of 15a, which is itself explicated by a series of modifiers involving proper Christian defense in the face of opposition. The style of 3:14b-16 then is reminiscent of that encountered in 1:13f; in place of an initial participle one finds here a double imperative followed by the central exhortation (an imperative), and an extended participial construction (on vv. 15f-16 see below).

Essentially, the three imperative constructions of vv. 14b and 15a are taken verbatim from Isa 8:12-13, whose text has been adapted to a new literary context. Thus 1 Peter has simplified the negative adverbs of the initial imperatives, has modified the *autou* of the first into *auton* ("afraid of them" —one might argue for a different text type), and has underscored the contrast between the negative and positive imperatives (addition of a second *de*: "not . . . nor . . . but"). Lastly, the central or positive imperative has been modified in two ways. First, rather than "sanctify the Lord himself," the text of 1 Peter reads "sanctify the Lord Christ" or "Christ as Lord." Second, the expression "in your hearts" is added to the exhortation. Such modifications again confirm 1 Peter's meditative, homiletic use of favorite OT passages to formulate advice to the beleaguered communities of Asia Minor (see 2:8 for use of Isa 8:14).

The initial advice, expressed in two negative imperatives borrowed from the OT text, focuses on the concept of fear. The text of the first of these, owing to its Semitic cast, literally: "do not fear their fear," is interpreted in two ways, whether one views "their" as a subjective genitive ("do not fear what they fear") or as an objective genitive ("do not be afraid of them"). While both are possible grammatically, the latter seems preferable in contextual terms (*IBNTG*, 40), because the object of fear is not seemingly pagan religion and customs but rather pagan opponents themselves who malign or demand a response. Additionally the second imperative confirms this interpretation by dwelling on the topic of intimidation. Thus the negative imperative clauses prepare the readers for the author's positive exhortation that follows. Interestingly, the quaintness of the LXX text lends a scriptural tone and authority to the author's advice.

In v. 15 the author, still engaging the text of Isaiah, turns to the positive (use of *de* or "but" as a contrasting particle) part of the exhortation. Use of the text of Isaiah to express the central element of the paraenesis requires of 1 Peter both a modification of the OT text and an extensive commentary on what such activity means on the believer's part. The textual modifications noted earlier involve the christological transformation of the Isaian statement; it is no longer "the Lord" God who is "sanctified" but God's agent "the Christ" whose lordship is acknowledged. The LXX verb employed, *hagiazo*, clearly does not mean "to make holy or consecrate" but, in the context of acknowledging Christ as Lord, it refers to the reverence afforded him as God's salvific agent. Thus believers, having committed themselves in conversion to God through Christ, are exhorted to conquer their human fears by bold acknowledgment, at the core of their being or "in (their) hearts" (see discussion of 1:22; 3:4), of Christ's lordship and holiness. So the first element of the author's discussion of proper Christian response to adverse treatment by the pagan population is to insist, employing the LXX terms of Isaiah, on the believer's faith commitment in christological, personal terms.

But just as believers are called by a holy God to express their new life outwardly in holy conduct (1:15-16), so are they expected to express their interior commitment to and reverence for Christ by an exterior defense of their new loyalties—what is in the heart must be expressed by the mouth as defense (see also Rom 10:9-10). So v. 15b begins a lengthy, second segment of the discussion, namely, the public defense of Christian belief or expectations, the manner of this apology, and its effect on those who are the cause of Christian suffering.

The apology itself (*apologia*) is presented in straight-forward terms as the means by which believers publicly acknowledge Christ as their lord. The statement is introduced by a nominative plural adjective that functions, as in 3:8, in an implied participial relationship with the preceding imperative: "acknowledge Christ as Lord . . . by always (being) ready." To explain the background of such Christian apology one could appeal to the Jesus tradition, particularly the Lukan version, that addresses the themes of human fear and formal defense before civil and religious authorities (12:4, 11). It is clear from Lukan terminology that the setting is legal; the situation of 1 Peter is more ambiguous. While the expressions *apologia* and *aiteo logon* can bear a formal, legal interpretation (legal "defense" and "demand an accounting," respectively—see BAGD 26, 96), they can also suggest less formal verbal and social conflict (see 1 Cor 3:9; Plato, *Politics* 285D). The other terms also point in this direction, particularly "always," "anyone," and "ready." First Peter does not seem to have occasional or unusual litigation in mind (though not excluding this—the formal prosecution of the second-century Pliny-Trajan correspondence is far too late for consideration here) but rather the everyday social exchange between suspicious neighbors. These terms, particularly the last (see discussion of "ready" at 1:5 and 4:5), point to a Christian stance vis-à-vis society that might best be described as defensive or apologetic on the one hand and as missionary witness on the other (see 2:11-12). The believer's everyday stance is a willingness and readiness to explain or give an accounting of Christian beliefs and praxis, here described as "the hope that is in you."

In view of the above, how then are we to interpret the defense that believers are to make, and what is to be its focus? On the one hand, the author's choice of terminology, which stresses verbal exchange and reasoned response, underscores a positive approach toward Roman neighbors, which is open both to missionary goals and peaceful coexistence. The defense that is to be made presumably is an explanation, on request, of what Christians stand for and why they act the way they do. The focus on oral terminology suggests that the author is confident that reason will succeed "in silencing the ignorance of the foolish" (2:15). No doubt the author intends, within the limits of honorable behavior (see below), for believers to answer in kind, namely, to respond to lack of information and to rectify misinformation. On the other hand, the apology or defense is not a philosophical disquisition on Christian faith (formal apologetics will develop in later centuries) but an explanation of present conduct that is centered on a future promise. Interestingly, 1 Peter speaks of "hope" rather than faith to describe Christian belief. The reader has been led to expect such usage from the author's discussions earlier of hope (see 1:3, 13, 21; 3:5). Indeed for 1 Peter faith is the acceptance of and perseverance in the pattern of hope, which Christ's death and resurrection made possible and which his journey established as model for Christian living. The focus of 1 Peter is to address Christian behavior both as the source of pagan misunderstanding and as the means itself of social tolerance and religious enlightenment.

This apology, while responding to misinformation or, at least, while addressing every manner of inquiry, must not succumb to retaliatory speech or exchange of abuse. Instead it must be done "with gentleness and reverence," virtues whose exact meaning and application, however, are questionable. Are these attitudes directed toward God or toward Gentile neighbors? A variety of responses have been given: both address human questioners; both point to God; or the first involves the neighbors and the second looks toward God. The terms themselves provide no clues; these must be sought in the author's limited usage. In the first place the term *phobos* is regularly used by 1 Peter to describe human reverence for God as opposed to honor, which is owed to all human creatures (2:17; see also discussion of 1:17; 2:18; and 3:2). Thus a life lived in reverence or fear before God is to affect one's relationship to others, an attitude that will be developed further in the following statement on conscience and judgment. As regards the second term, *prautes*, there are fewer data on which to base a conclusion, namely, the cognate term of 3:4 and the synonymous theme of *tapeinos* or humility developed in 3:8 and 5:5-6. In each case one is under the impression that 1 Peter's concern is that of the relationship of humans as creatures to fellow creatures, whether of believers to one another or to outsiders. In the present case choice of the term "gentleness" draws attention to the context of verbal abuse and misunderstanding and underscores the author's non-confrontational, apologetic strategy. The limits of honorable and holy behavior, therefore, involve both honor or respect for opponents and fear or reverence for God as merciful father and faithful creator.

Finally 1 Peter turns to the effect that such apologetics should have on those who are unwitting opponents of the community and who are the cause of Christian suffering. Before turning directly to this theme, however, 1 Peter again stresses the innocent character of this suffering: only with "a clear or good conscience" does the believer's example have its desired effect (see 4:15-16). The term *syneidesis* here and in v. 21 is employed in its technical sense of moral awareness (see discussion of 2:19) and underscores the innocence—not just punishment—of those who are suffering.

Employing a construction similar to that encountered at 2:12 and repeating its theme of verbal abuse or slander (*katalaleo*), 1 Peter dwells further, in passing, on the nature of the maltreatment encountered by believers. Those who are accused of "speaking ill" (see discussion of 2:12) of the addressees are said to "insult or treat with spite (their) good conduct in Christ." Interestingly, it is not the believers who are made the object of this scorn but their conduct. In this way the author is able to focus, as in 2:12 by the use of the term "honorable," on the claim that Christian behavior, if examined honestly, is both good in Christian terms and honorable in the eyes of pagan neighbors—the apology is meant gently to clarify misunderstanding or silence ignorance. Also the expression *en Christo*, often used by Paul, is employed for the first time by 1 Peter (see also 5:10, 14). While the expression in this instance is virtually a synonym for "as Christians" (see 4:16), one senses here as well as in the other uses of the expression a sense of incorporation or belonging to Christ put at the service of the author's strategy, particularly as this relates to the themes of suffering and glory. In 3:16 the addressees are portrayed as imitating Christ through innocent suffering, in 5:10 as sharing in his glory, and in 5:14 as belonging to Christ as lord, shepherd, and guardian (2:25; 3:15), while walking in his footsteps (2:21).

The effect finally of those who oppose Christian behavior is described in OT terms: "that (they . . .) might finally be put to shame or disabused." Use of the aorist subjunctive points to the author's hope of an eminent cessation of such opposition, and citation once more of Isa 28:16 (see 2:6) suggests again a positive outcome in view of innocent Christian behavior. While one could dwell on the term *kataischyno* ("be put to shame") as indicating eschatological judgment or condemnation (see 2:7-8; 4:18), one is probably more justified in interpreting the term in light of the author's optimism that nonbelievers will recognize "good behavior in Christ" as conduct that has Christ as its foundation stone (2:6 and Isa 28:16). In the OT the term, in a positive sense, stresses the righteous' dependence upon God as foundation (Ps 21:6) and, in a negative sense, suggests either a change of mind on the wayward's part (Jer 2:36) or shameful condemnation (Jer 6:15). In the present case 1 Peter exhorts the addressees to conduct that is anchored on Christ the cornerstone so that these opponents might be disabused of their ignorance and glorify God. Seemingly, 1 Peter is less interested in the punishment of the opponents and more in proper strategy to counter pagan opposition. Christian defense, like honorable conduct, has peaceful coexistence and divine lordship in view.

(3:17) The Blessedness of Innocent Suffering. This first section is brought to an end by means of a pithy statement that returns to the point of departure, namely, the blessedness of innocent suffering. Interpretation of this verse has raised a number of issues. (1) It is regularly noted that the passage is a virtual repetition of 2:20 as well as a restatement of 3:13-14. Furthermore the form of the verse has often been likened to a maxim or proverb, similar to that attributed to Socrates by Plato (*Gorgias* 508C: "it is worse to do wrong . . . than to be wronged"). Verse 17 then would be a more general application of the advice given earlier to household members (2:20). (2) Instead it has been suggested by others that the verse is a proverb related to the themes of suffering and judgment. Suffering indeed is an ambivalent reality, and the righteous may have to suffer now, but just judgment insists that doers of evil will suffer in the hereafter. Thus v. 17 would focus on eschatological vindication. (3) It is preferable, however, to view v. 17 in relation to its function in the passage. While it is a restatement of 2:20 (and an anticipation of 4:15-16), it has as its function the insistence that such innocent suffering is a blessing if it is God's will. Suffering is not supposed to be the lot of the good citizen and righteous believer, but, if despite gentle defense God should will such suffering, it is a blessing (see 4;14), because that is the example left by Christ for believers (2:21). Again, 1 Peter's concern is not the punishment of evildoers but exhortation to those concerned about innocent suffering. Important in this regard is the author's use of the optative: "if the will of God should so decree"—inescapable (divinely willed) suffering is blessed, according to 1 Peter, not fatalistic acceptance or provocation of opposition (on the "will of God"—see 2:15). Therefore, in this section 1 Peter insists that political and religious protection is a blessing cherished by all doers of good (3:13) but, should suffering be God's will despite gentle dialogue, innocent sufferers continue to be blessed because of Christ's suffering (3:18f) and "because the spirit of glory . . . rests" on those who follow Christ's footsteps (2:21; 4:14).

The Saving Effectiveness of Christ's Suffering and Journey (3:18-22)

A new section begins with v. 18; clearly the author begins this long excursus by reiterating the theme of suffering but immediately, in offering a reason why (*hoti*—"because or for") innocent suffering is nonetheless a blessing, dwells more directly on Christ's salvific role, namely, his suffering "for sins once for all" and, more at length, his post-resurrection activity. Thus v. 18 begins by offering the term "suffer" for Christ's action and ends by speaking more traditionally of Christ's "death" instead. There is a clear shift from the community's critical situation to a consideration once more of its soteriological beliefs. While earlier 1 Peter had addressed Christ's death in terms of ransom as the basis for belief in God (see 1:18-21) and Christ's innocent suffering as salvific, paradigmatic, and a source of reconciliation with one's "shepherd and guardian" (2:21-25), the present passage focuses on Christ's resurrection, consequent salvific activity, and exaltation at God's right hand. In effect this entire section might best be described as Christ's heavenly journey as the source of salvation (v. 21) and means of divine union (v. 18).

Before examining the passage in some detail, we are led to discuss two important issues: (1) resources and (2) the spirits, Noah, and Christ's salvific journey.

Resources. There has been much discussion concerning the sources employed by 1 Peter to compose this section, owing to its formulaic language and unusual themes. In the past scholars have proposed finding in 1 Peter a generous use of early hymnic material, particularly 1:20; 2:21-24; and 3:18-22, the parts of the letter that are readily recognized as special christological sections. While there has been much reluctance to viewing the second passage as relying on such material, there has been more openness to viewing the third, sometimes in conjunction with the first, as representing or borrowing from an early christological hymn. Indeed the anaphoric style of 1:20, that is, the use of two participial phrases that have Jesus as antecedent, is usually underscored as hymnic and so sometimes associated with 3:18f as forming a continuous hymn. At first blush the couplet seems to indicate a preexistence christology; however, a closer look reveals not an incarnational but eschatological perspective that focuses on God's overall design (see comments earlier). Instead, with most scholars, we direct our attention and efforts to 3:18-22. There has been much variety even in this instance in proposed reconstructions of the alleged hymnic material. Some begin with v. 18a concerning Christ's "death for sins" and his leading of believers to God. Others focus instead on the anaphoric "death in the flesh" and "life in the spirit" formulas of 18b as indicating the core section of the hymn. A few scholars see the "preaching to the spirits" as also belonging to the hymnic source. Finally most propose all or part of v. 22, regarding Christ's enthronement and victory over the heavenly powers, as derived from hymnic materials.

Such analyses demonstrate the difficulty and conjectural nature of source reconstruction. In effect 1 Peter seems to have combined several types of material: a credal formula in 18a that has been modified from "died for sins" to "suffered for sins" (see Rom 6:10; 1 Cor 15:3); hymnic material in vv. 18b, perhaps 19, and 22; and contemporary hermeneutical material by which to associate the rebellious spirits and the story of Noah to Christian baptism (vv. 20-21) and Christ's lordship (v. 22). A variety of stylistic features confirm the extensive redaction of 1 Peter in combining these various traditions, whether the use of *hoti kai Christos . . . hina* ("for Christ also . . . because") of v. 18 as in 2:21, the joining of parallel pairs by *men . . . de* in v. 18b as in 1:20, the extensive use of relative constructions in vv. 19-22 to connect diverse themes (see 1:6f), and such resumptive techniques as the repetition of "Christ" in vv. 18 and 21, of *poreutheis* ("having gone") in vv. 19 and 21, and the extensive use of participial phrases throughout. These familiar stylistic features argue against the extensive use of a continuous hymnic source, although one is able to isolate the following as likely fragments:

> put to death in the flesh
> made alive in the spirit (18)
> having gone to the spirits in (their) domain (19)
> who is at the right hand of God
> having gone to heaven
> where angels, authorities, and powers recognize their duty to him (22)

Presumably 1 Peter is relying on the anaphoric use of the participles in vv. 18, 19, and 22 to present various stages in Jesus' salvific journey and to add other traditional themes associated with his post-resurrection activity, namely, his subjection of the cosmic powers, his ascension to the heavenly realm, and his enthronement at God's right hand (see Rom 8:34; 1 Cor 15:24-28; Phil 2:9-11; 3:21; Col 1:16; 2:15; 1 Tim 3:16).

The Spirits, Noah, and Christ's Salvific Journey. From the earliest centuries there has been a debate about the identity of the "spirits" of 3:19, of their relation to the Noah story, and the function played by the theme of baptism in this long excursus on Christ's salvific role. The discussion centers on whether the *pneumata* ("spirits") of v. 19 refer to human spirits or to supernatural or angelic powers.

Since the time of Augustine until recently the traditional interpretation of the Western Church has been the former, namely, Christ's preaching to Noah's sinful contemporaries and, in general, his descent into the underworld to free its imprisoned spirits. In addition, recent scholars who defend this position note, on the one hand, that Christ's preaching is germane to the situation of redeemable humans and not to that of the doomed angels or spirits of the Genesis and Enoch stories (see below) and, on the other, that even the perverse and seemingly doomed flood generation is offered salvation through Christ by a merciful God. Also, "the proclamation of the gospel even to the dead" of v. 6 is seen as confirmation of this interpretation. In this view Christ is seen as descending to the underworld to proclaim liberation to the spirits of the notorious flood generation before his ascension into heaven.

Many recent scholars question this view and have returned to the interpretation accepted in the first Christian centuries, namely, that the "spirits" in question refer to supernatural beings whose story is developed first in Gen 6:1-4 and then extensively in Enoch literature. In this later Jewish tradition the misbehavior of the "sons of God" with the "daughters of men" is interpreted both as an angelic rebellion and as the proliferation of sin on earth. So the angelic "sons of God" or watchers become responsible for human corruption and provoke the flood as divine punishment on sinful humanity. It is suggested therefore that 1 Peter presumes the story of Enoch's heavenly travels to encounter the rebellious spirits imprisoned in the second heaven (*1 En* 6-16; *2 En* 7:1-3; 18:3-6) as the pattern for Christ's travel through the heavens as a journey of proclamation to and subjugation of the spirits prior to his enthronement at God's right hand.

While credible defense of both options can be found in recent scholarly literature, it is my belief that the second option provides a more satisfactory hermeneutical background for the reading of the text. It is particularly the author's use of the term "spirits" (for angelic rather than human creatures), the relationship between these figures and Noah in Enoch tradition, and the integration of these into Christ's salvific journey that point to this option. These reasons will be examined further in the following commentary.

(3:18) Christ's Salvific Role. This new excursus is introduced in a stylistic and thematic manner similar to that of 2:21 ("for Christ also . . . suffered . . . so that"). Whereas in the first instance the theme of divine call leads to a discussion of the paradigmatic function of Christ's innocent suffering, in this case the theme of divinely-willed innocent suffering brings about an extended exposition of the soteriological function of his passion. From the outset the textual integrity and formulation of the statement call for some comment. Though the reading "suffered for sins" (use of *pascho*) is less well attested than "died for sins" (*apothnesko*), it is nonetheless preferable since the latter verb is nowhere else employed in 1 Peter, since the former appears so frequently and is so central to the author's message and strategy, and since the soteriological theme itself ("for sins") would have led to much scribal activity (*TCGNT* 692-93). This point leads us therefore to a discussion of the statement's formulation. Starting presumably from a traditional formula, such as "Christ died for (our) sins" (see Rom 6:10; 1 Cor 15:3—see also Gal 1:4), 1 Peter constructs a unique but familiar-sounding statement to draw a closer connection between the community's situation and Christ's sacrificial act. Adding to the expression's soteriological character is the insistence, as in Rom 6:10 and Heb 7:27; 9:12; 10:10, that this sacrifice is efficacious in having overcome the sinful divide that separated God and humanity. Clearly the expression "suffered for sins" is 1 Peter's subtle way of suggesting that innocent sufferers are indeed "sharing Christ's suffering," not as co-redeemers (see Col 1:24) but as travelers who walk in his footsteps (2:21).

In a parenthetical remark 1 Peter insists both on Christ's innocence (reiterating the theme of v. 17) and on the soteriological character of his suffering: he is "the just one" who suffered or died "on behalf of the unjust." The expression, the contrasting use of *dikaios* and *adikos*, is a striking one since in its classical (see Aristotle, *Nichomachean Ethics* 5.2; Xenophon, *Memorabilia* 4.4.13) and NT usages (Matt 5:45; Acts 24:15) the terms compare good and evil persons or more specifically doers of good as opposed to doers of evil. Indeed 1 Peter's use of the *dikaios* word family would indicate the same (see especially 3:12). Instead the thematic context, probably under the influence of Isa 53:11 (see 2:24 for citation of this OT verse), demands that one see in these terms a soteriological rather than an ethical sense: the righteous servant suffers and dies on behalf or in place of the ungodly (*asebes* in Pauline terms, though see 1 Cor 6:1, 9). The shift from vv. 17 to 18 is a striking and complex one, for 1 Peter continues to use terms appropriate to the community's situation. Gradually, however, the author infuses them with soteriological nuances; Christ's suffering becomes an atoning death, and the term unrighteousness takes on the meaning of godlessness or violating God's law (see *TDNT* 1:151)—Christ the innocent, righteous agent bears the sins of unrighteous humanity.

Following the above soteriological remark 1 Peter expresses succinctly the teleological purpose of Christ's atoning suffering: "so that he might bring you to God (or into God's presence)." Clearly the statement addresses the theme of access to God; however, scholars interpret this passage in a variety of ways, either as something already achieved and thus presently operative or as an eschatological goal that provides present assurance. In grammatical terms the evidence is ambiguous; while one could insist that use of the aorist points to a past event, it is equally possible that the aorist is to be interpreted as punctiliar to indicate a process or journey that will be completed at the eschaton.

One might find clues, however, in two areas. Other final clauses in 2:21, 24 and 4:6 point neither to a past activity nor explicitly to a future event but rather to a present reality ("walking in footsteps," "living for righteousness," or "living in the spirit," respectively). In each case 1 Peter focuses on present Christian conduct. More importantly we might look at the term employed: *prosago*. In Pauline literature the noun *prosagoge* is employed to describe the believer's "access" to God (Rom 5:2; Eph 2:18; 3:12). While some have suggested that the term could indicate the introduction of Gentile converts to the one God, more properly it is suggested that such access for 1 Peter would have a cultic or sacrificial sense (as in Exod 29:10; see the Vulgate's translation of this passage: "that he might offer us to God") or offer a priestly nuance (as in Exod 29:4; Lev 18:24)—in both cases see the terminology of 1 Pet 2:4, 9. Additionally the verb can indicate the admission of someone before magistrates or law court (Exod 21:6; Acts 16:20) or before the king (Xenophon, *Cyropaedia* 1.3.8). Though one might want to opt for the concept of divine access, as suggested above, perhaps in a Pauline sense one suspects that the context demands a different choice. Either one could suggest that Christ leads the believer to judgment (see 4:5, 17-18) or, more probably, that 1 Peter is developing in a more precise manner a journey motif as part of the letter's message and strategy. The goal of Christ's salvific activity is the presentation of believers to the God of glory. Christ has come and gone (a motif developed immediately after), acts as guide (footsteps), and will return in glory to "bring [believers] to God." The meaning then of *prosago* fits into 1 Peter's strategy both in providing hope for a suffering audience and a christological model for Christian existence.

Verse 18 ends by reiterating the basic tenets of Christian belief: "death in the flesh" and "life in the spirit," a contrast that refers not to body and soul but to two modes of existence. In the first case life according to the flesh characterizes human existence and Christ's salvific death, while in the second the reference is made to Christ's new mode of life as risen Lord; such a distinction is also made in other hymnic materials (see 1 Tim 3:16; Rom 1:3-4). Indeed 1 Peter will return to this terminology and theme in 4:6. By citing this hymnic fragment, in a loose relation to what precedes, the author is able to focus once again on Christ's activity. In this instance the *men . . . de* contrast allows a restatement of Christ's salvific death as the precondition of his resurrection, which now becomes the focus of the remainder of the passage, for it is the activity of the risen Lord that takes center stage in the following verses.

(3:19-21) Christ's Heavenly Journey. Though these verses have received considerable attention from scholars (see earlier), at this point I will focus on an interpretation of the passage that identifies the spirits as rebellious angels and their descendants and that finds its hermeneutical key in the theme of Christ's heavenly journey. The opening of the verse presents problems, because its Greek text, *en ho*, literally "in or through which," is variously interpreted: as a relative pronoun having a temporal or causal sense ("on which occasion" or "thus"), as a direct reference to the term "spirits" ("in which"), or in more general terms as a reference to Christ's resurrected state ("in which state or mode of existence"). The last mentioned meets the least resistance in grammatical and thematic terms (whether the author's use of the dative or the meaning of "spirit"). Seemingly, it is the author's intention to insist that this activity was carried out precisely by the risen Lord now "alive in the spirit."

From the outset 1 Peter introduces the journey motif. Interestingly, nothing is said about the direction or goal of Christ's travel: "having gone." While many interpreters assume that the author intends a descent to the underworld prior to Jesus' resurrection, it is more appropriate to the thematic context and the author's style to connect this participle with the identical term in v. 22 where Christ is said to be at God's right hand: "having gone to heaven." In this way 1 Peter introduces the beginning of Christ's heavenly journey and resumes the theme at the end of the passage by characterizing this activity as terminating in Christ's heavenly ascension. It is not a question of two journeys, one to Hades and another to heaven, but rather an extended description of Christ's post-death activity as a triumphant, salvific journey to God (see Phil 2:9-11; 1 Tim 3:16).

The first event mentioned on this journey is Christ's activity among the spirits. Each part of the statement demands some attention, whether the identity of the spirits, the nature of Christ's activity among them, or the place where these reside. In each case also the terminology is intriguing.

Christ's audience is said to consist of "spirits," a term that regularly refers to supernatural beings, but that in certain contexts and with qualifying phrases can also refer to humans. In this instance we conclude that 1 Peter is speaking of the "sons of God," later identified as angels or watchers, who rebelled against God and introduced moral corruption on earth (see Gen 6:1-2; *1 Enoch* 6-16), activity that is explicitly linked to the deluge and the revelation to Lamech's son, Noah (*1 En* 10:1-3). According to this early Enoch tradition these rebellious beings are bound and cast into an earthly dungeon where they will be kept for judgment day when they will be cast into an eternal prison (10:4-5, 12-13; 14:4—see Jude 6; Rev 20:1-3). Later tradition, however, locates the prison dwelling of these rebellious beings in the second heaven (*2 En* 7:1-3; 18:3-6; see already *1 En* 18:15-19:1; 21:10). It should be noted, nonetheless, that the offspring of these beings, also called evil spirits, will dwell on the earth and inside the earth (15:8-10) and will pursue their immoral activity there until the consummation of the world.

Christ, like Enoch, is said to encounter these spiritual beings. Whereas the latter, after interceding for them, is made to proclaim their condemnation, Christ's activity is expressed by the verb *kerysso,* a term that usually means "preach" but that has the basic sense "proclaim" (BAGD 431). Does Christ preach redemption to Noah's unrepentant contemporaries or proclaim judgment against the rebellious angels? In light of v. 22 and the traditional lore concerning Christ's lordship over the cosmic powers (see earlier), it is more likely that he proclaims (only use of *kerysso* in 1 Peter) God's cosmic victory. However, why the anticipation of cosmic victory at this point, unless 1 Peter in v. 19 intends to underscore Christ's invasion of Satan's earthly domain? Instead v. 19 envisions Christ's proclamation to the evil spirits or descendants of the rebellious angels, a theme similar to Jesus' claim in Mark 3:22-27 that Satan's kingdom or house is being plundered. The risen Christ is victorious over the spirits of this world or, at least, has liberated believers from their domination.

The above conclusion presumes the discussion of the spirits' abode, described by 1 Peter as a *phylake.* The term is regularly translated as "prison" and presumed to be the earthly or heavenly locale where demonic spirits are kept. If I am correct in viewing the spirits as evil spirits that are now preying upon believers or Satan's minions that seek to devour the addressees (1 Pet 5:8-9), then one must not view them as being in prison. The root *phylasso* means "to watch, protect, or guard" and so is employed for those who "guard or protect" a domain or figuratively and defensively to describe one's final refuge (*TDNT* 9:242-44). In the first case Zeus' palace is said to have guards to prevent unlawful access (Plato, *Protagoras* 321d; see Gen 3:25 where cherubim guard the entrance to the garden). In like manner evil spirits would be seen as the guards to prevent entrance into Satan's kingdom. In the second case the demons of the endtime are said to find a final refuge in crumbling Babylon, which is described as their "dwelling (and) haunt or refuge." In the same way evil spirits would have found a dwelling on earth, a refuge from their heavenly home. Like Babylon, earth has become the last refuge and domain of the fallen angels and their descendants. It should be noted that the same tradition calls the latter "the armies of Azaz'el," "the messengers of Satan leading astray those who dwell on the earth" (*1 En* 54:5-6). Christ's victory then has threatened this domain and robbed it of its power and dominion. For further discussion of the relation between the spirits of v. 19 and the cosmic powers of v. 22, see commentary below.

Mention of the evil spirits in v. 19 leads in the following verse to a description of their offense as a prelude to the story of Noah and its relation to Christian baptism. While the offence of the rebellious angels and of their descendants ("in former times") is characterized in Enoch as producing all manner of corruption on the earth, in 1 Peter it is described as "disobedience," a term employed to designate rejection of the gospel (2:8; 3:1; 4:17). Several interesting facts should be noted here. Only in this case is the verb *apeitheo* employed without an object. Also, the positive form of this root is never used but is seemingly replaced by the positive synonym *hypakoe* (1:2, 14, 22; also 3:6). Clearly the theme of obedience is a central one for 1 Peter whether in describing Christ's salvific role (1:2), the believer's acceptance of God's call (1:14), and the exhortation to holy conduct (1:22), particularly as submission to God's will. By contrast, those who do not believe are described as disobedient to God's call. First Peter's use here of the term *apeitho* in an absolute way points backward to the original offense of the rebellious spirits and forward to an obedient Noah whose activity brought salvation to some and foreshadowed Christian baptism as a means of salvation to many. The former are described thus to Enoch: "they are evil rebels against the Lord, who did not listen to the voice of the Lord [another version reads: 'who did not obey the Lord's commandments'] but consulted their own will" (*2 En* 7:3 and A). Thus their fault and that of their descendants for 1 Peter was disobedience, a disregard of God's will that brought about corruption on the earth as well as punishment. In contrast the latter is one who obeyed the Lord's command to build an ark for the salvation of the few (see *1 En* 10:2, 3 and often) and leads in Christian terms to another, greater story concerning salvation involving water (v. 21).

The story of Noah, with a surprising number of details, is brought into the author's discussion for a number of reasons. Not only is this story repeatedly associated in Enoch and related tradition to that of the rebellious angels (see also *T.Naphtali* 3:5; *Jubilees* 5), but also it provides a convincing situational and salvific link between "former times" and the present ("now"—vv. 20-21) when rampant disobedience is countered by God's gracious offer of salvation. Indeed in the Jesus tradition, according to the Q source, a close connection is also drawn between Noah and the endtime: "as it was in the days of Noah, so will it be in the days of the Son of Man" (Luke 17:26; also Matt 24:37). Presuming this close, typological connection, 1 Peter appeals to this ancient story to address the community's situation and God's salvific intervention in their lives.

The days of Noah are said to be a time when God's patience is sorely tested. However, rather than stress the original story's allusion to God's impatience and resolve to punish the rebellious spirits and humanity (Gen 6:3, 5-7; also *T.Naphtali* 3:5), 1 Peter chooses to emphasize divine "patience or forbearance" (see *1 En* 60:5-6), a time when rampant disobedience was countered by the simple, obedient event of the building of the ark as a means of safety or salvation for a remnant among the Israelites. Though there is an implied statement of judgment concerning Noah's contemporaries, it is God's eagerness to save and the means of safety that receive attention. By employing the verb *apekdechomai* 1 Peter emphasizes God's desire to save: "gladly or anxiously waited." It is the ark and the water of the deluge that are the means chosen to bring the remnant to safety. Some would give *dia hydatos* a local sense ("through or out of the water") and so suggest, in light of later rabbinic tradition, that Noah passed through knee-high water to reach the ark (see 1 Cor 10:1-2). Such a reading would make the ark the means of safety, a conclusion that is made impossible by the following reference to baptism. *Dia* then has an instrumental sense: "by means of water." Interestingly, the author notes the detail that "a few, that is, eight persons" (*psyche* indicates the whole person; see 1:9, 22f) are saved. While the number is derived from the original account and is traditional (Gen 7:13; *SibOr* 1:280-81; 2 Pet 2:5—resurrection symbolism is probably not intended), 1 Peter's insistence on the small number is probably significant. Most scholars suggest here that the author, under the influence of the Jesus tradition (Matt

7:14; 22:14; etc), draws a stark parallel between the Israelite remnant and the presumed small number of people responding to the Christian message. One might suggest instead that 1 Peter on the one hand stresses God's great eagerness for salvation even of the few and on the other leaves open the possibility (judgment is in the future—see 4:17-18) that the Gentile population will respond to the divine call through the witness of their righteous Christian neighbors.

The story of Noah leads, with some grammatical awkwardness, to a discussion in v. 21 of Christian baptism. The old story about salvation obtained by means of water becomes the prototype for God's new initiative among the addressees. While some suggest here the use of baptismal tradition or more particularly of a homily to account for the letter's imagery and terminology, it is more plausible to credit the author with creative use of the Noah tradition to suggest present salvific activity as a result of Christ's heavenly journey (note the present tense: "baptism . . . now saves you"). Mention of Christ's victorious activity within the spirit world leads, via an extended excursus on Noah and baptism, to a discussion of the present effects of his death and resurrection. It is particularly the provocative expression, "baptism now saves you," which leads the author into further soteriological considerations. Having suggested a parallel between the flood and baptismal waters and having attributed a salvific role to each, 1 Peter is led to clarify the sense in which the latter saves. Thus the remainder of v. 21 in the form of a parenthetical explanation, consisting of contrasting negative and positive statements ("not . . . but"), insists on what baptism signifies.

Both the structural components and the thematic context provide clues for the interpretation of 1 Peter's concept of baptism as a salvific activity. A first reading of the parenthetical explanation would lead one to expect "not only is baptism a washing . . . but it is also a pledge . . . ." Instead the author says: "it is not . . . but it is . . . ." In light of this, the negative statement, literally: baptism is "not a removal of dirt from the flesh," merits careful attention. While the application of water is a physical act of washing, it is nonetheless a symbolic one that may represent ritual or bodily purification or the renunciation of moral evil. Whether this "removal of dirt" alludes to the rite of circumcision (comparison is made with the language of Col 2:11; 3:8-9) or, preferably, to renunciation of moral defilement (see 1:22), in neither case would this external washing be a saving activity. Spiritual cleansing is meant to accompany or even to give meaning to the washing symbolism of baptism, but it is not 1 Peter's concept of baptism itself.

The thematic context provides background for the positive statement. Just as in former times the disobedience of the many and the righteousness of the few were involved in the outcome of the Noah story (v. 20), so in the present is the process of salvation related to human commitment. The author insists that baptism saves "in as much as it is a pledge to God from a clear conscience." The term rendered "pledge" (*eperotema*) has the basic meaning "question or request" but acquired in popular Hellenistic usage (BAGD 285.2) a contractual sense, which it seems to have in this instance. Thus baptism represents a commitment to God on a person's part (as a counterpart to disobedience in v. 20). This pledge is made "out of (rather than "for") a pure conscience" or heart (see discussion of *syneidesis* at 2:19 and 3:16); that is, believers, through baptism, commit themselves to God with full awareness and conviction.

Just as the parenthetical discussion of baptism, in an attempt to explain its salvific though not automatic character, has treated gingerly the theme of subjective salvation (namely the human response to divine initiative), so the remainder of the verse returns more firmly to the traditional concept of objective soteriology by stating that "baptism saves . . . through the resurrection of Jesus Christ." In a manner similar to 1:3 and employing virtually the same terms 1 Peter insists both that new life is now given believers and that they participate in salvation in the present through the Christ-event. In the first case new life is contrasted with the mention of "resurrection *from the dead*" and in the present case, respecting the thematic context of the heavenly journey, salvation is said to be made possible by Jesus' resurrection and heavenly enthronement. Salvation, which is both a present and future concept for 1 Peter (see discussion of 1:9-10), is here seen in its present effects in the lives of believers as a result of Christ's post-death activity. Christian commitment or pledge to God becomes the channel for the risen Lord to exert transforming power in the daily lives of the addressees and protection from the powers that threaten them (see v. 22).

(3:22) Christ's Heavenly Abode. Mention of "Jesus Christ" at the end of v. 21 brings the author back, grammatically and structurally, to the theme of Christ's heavenly journey. Through the use of hymnic material that is joined by a familiar relative pronoun and that shows traces of anaphoric style and enthronement themes, 1 Peter expresses in graphic and triumphant terms the heavenly destination of Christ's journey to God.

The first of the three statements of v. 22, "who is at God's right hand," is identical to Paul's phraseology in Rom 8:34 but reflects early Christian tradition (Mark 14:62 par; Acts 5:31; 7:54-55; Eph 1:20; Col 3:1; Heb 1:3; 8:1; 12:2), which ultimately depends on Ps 109:1: "sit at my right hand" (see Mark 12:36 par; Acts 2:34; Heb 10:12). This theme, borrowed from ancient royal ideology (see Mark 10:37), was employed by the early church to indicate Christ's exaltation in relation to God and eschatological domination in relation to the entire cosmos, a concept to be developed later in the verse. In this way royal dignity and divine authority were claimed for Christ and, in the case of 1 Peter, provided a further basis for the community's confidence.

The second statement, "having gone to or entered heaven," reiterates the theme of journey noted in v. 19 and underscores Christ's heavenly abode where the believer's inheritance is likewise kept (1:4). Indeed it is from this vantage point that Christ will return with the crown of glory (5:4) to summon the righteous and bring them to God (3:18).

The final phrase, "once the angels, authorities, and powers have recognized their duty to him," focuses on another aspect of Christ's enthronement, namely, his cosmic lordship. This theme is widespread and traditional, though its formulation varies according to the OT resources employed. Thus one finds the image of the "bowing of the knee" in dependence on Isa 45:23 (Phil 2:10; for other uses, see Rom 11:4; 14:11), of enemies becoming "a footstool for the feet" as related to Ps 109:1 (Acts 2:35; Heb 1:13; 10:13; see also Mark 12:36 par), or of the submission "of all things under foot," phraseology borrowed from Ps 8:7 (1 Cor 15:27; Eph 1:22). The last mentioned involves the verb *hypotasso* used with subjugation terminology: "to put or place under his feet." Scholars therefore assume that the verb by itself suggests subjugation (see Rom 13:1, 5). While Paul employs this verb repeatedly in 1 Cor 15:24-28 seemingly to insist on Christ's cosmic, victorious role, it is done under the influence of Ps 8:7, which is in fact cited in v. 27. It is suggested then that the verb underscores proper relationship even for Paul (see discussion of 2:13), and that it is the context that qualifies its special nuance. Of particular interest to us is 1 Peter's use of the verb without subjugation terminology presumably to insist that the cosmic powers, which once were disobedient (3:20), have now recognized their duty to Christ the Lord and are now obedient subjects (v. 22 resumes the proclamation theme of v. 19).

Finally the list of spirits (angels, authorities, and powers) matches but does not duplicate other NT lists (1 Cor 15:24; Eph 1:21; 3:10; 6:12; Col 2:10, 15; though see Rom 8:38)—1 Peter wishes to include the totality of supernatural beings dwelling in the heavenly region. Seemingly, the author brings Christ's journey to a fitting conclusion by insisting that heavenly order has been reestablished. Jesus is now lord of heaven where he awaits the day of visitation. In apocalyptic terms 1 Peter, like Col 2:10-15 and Eph 1:20-22, sees Christ's victory over the heavenly spirits as already achieved (contrary to other traditions; see 1 Cor 15:24-28 and Heb 2:5-9) but also realizes that his lordship is yet to be achieved among nonbelievers and is threatened by hostile neighbors and demonic opponents (3:15; 5:8-9). The heavenly battle has been won, but the earthly struggle continues as a fiery, general ordeal or as an enticement away from commitment to God (4:3-4, 12; 5:8-9). Thus Christ's victorious journey to God and enthronement are the believer's assurance that he will return as a willing shepherd with the crown of glory (5:4).

Exhortation to Live According to God's Will (4:1-6)

After a long excursus on Christ's post-death activity, a new section begins rather abruptly, it would seem. In reality, the author repeats the theme and terminology of 3:18, the starting point of the long christological excursus, and thus returns to the issue of the community's vilification at the hands of Gentile neighbors. After having counseled a gentle defense in the face of maltreatment and having underscored Christ's salvific activity, 1 Peter focuses once again on good conduct (see 3:16) as constituting Christian life according to God's will. The focus of this section is clearly the believer's new life (note the focus on "living" in vv. 2, 3, and 6—use of three different verbs) as contrasted, in general terms, to human desires (v. 2) and life according to the flesh (v. 6) and, in concrete terms, to Gentile dissipation (v. 3).

In structural and thematic terms the passage falls into three sections. The first, vv. 1-2, introduced by the conjunction *oun* ("therefore"), employs Christ's suffering as the basis for an appeal to a life, which means a break with the past (see already 1:14; 2:11). Within this context 1 Peter speaks of the problematic issue of suffering or death and its relation to sin. The second section, vv. 3-5, connected by the conjunction *gar* ("for"), addresses the audience's life as Gentiles, the reaction of their former co-religionists to their conversion, and the reassurance of divine judgment on both the living and the dead. The third segment, v. 6, also introduced by *gar*, acts as a final note ("this is why") on the issue of believers who have passed away before Christ's return (see also 1 Thess 4:13-18), a problem suggested by the final words of v. 5: "to judge the living and the dead." Thematically, then, 1 Peter returns to an issue hinted at in v. 2: life during "the remaining time in the flesh." It is in this context that one must discuss the identity of the dead who have been evangelized.

(4:1-2) A Break with the Past. Following an extended christological excursus, 1 Peter returns to the theme of innocent suffering. Just as 3:18 had shifted this terminology from the believer to Christ ("Christ also suffered") and had led to a lengthy soteriological discussion ("put to death in the flesh"), so 4:1 cites the earlier terms and themes ("Christ suffered in the flesh"—for an analysis of the textual problems, see *TCGNT*, 694) to address once more the community's situation. Again the term "suffering" is chosen in place of "dying" (see 2:21, 23; 3:18; 5:1) in deference to the addressees' situation, but to retain a soteriological nuance 1 Peter creates a new expression: "suffer in the flesh," an expression that is patterned on 3:18 ("put to death in the flesh") and that, in like manner, leads the reader to expect a contrast between "death or suffering in the flesh" and "life (in the spirit)"—see vv. 2, 6. Thus the opening clause of v. 1 sets the christological basis for the following exhortation.

It is clear from the above structural and thematic overview and from the author's return to the imperative form that this new subsection is strikingly different from what precedes. After a long excursus on the community's soteriological beliefs, the latter resumes its earlier paraenetic concerns; the addressees are exhorted: "on your part arm yourselves with the same insight." The imperative, in a manner similar to 1:13f, reintroduces the themes of concerted effort as well as new life and its demands of purification or rejection of earlier conduct.

We turn therefore to the paraenetic statement. The phrase *kai hymeis*, which is generally rendered "arm *yourselves also* . . . ," requires instead, because of the word order, a contrast with what precedes: just as Christ did, "you on your part." In this way 1 Peter insists on the theme of imitation as in 2:22-24 where, as here, Christ's suffering to abolish sin requires on the part of believers that they likewise avoid sin and live for righteousness. For the exhortation 1 Peter employs the term *hoplizomai*, which could be rendered "prepare yourselves" (the verb is usually used for the preparation of meals, drinks, self) or, more literally, "arm yourselves" (its meaning would be indicated by accompanying military terminology: arms, ships, soldiers). While the second interpretation is the unanimous choice of scholars, this preference is based on Pauline usage and the alleged affinity of baptismal tradition for moral armament imagery (Rom 6:13; 10:4; 1 Thess 5:8; Eph 6:10-17; see *TDNT* 5:298-300). On the one hand, the author's seeming nonconfrontational approach to Gentile maltreatment (gentle defense: 3:16) might indicate nonmilitary imagery. On the other hand, the mixture of concrete with abstract, mental imagery as in 1:13 and the use of military imagery in 2:11 ("desires of the flesh that wage war against the soul") in a similar context lead me also to opt for the latter. First Peter employs the term *ennoia* as object, a term that might suggest "resolve" but more likely underscores "insight or understanding." In effect the term is chosen to underscore further the link between 4:1 and 3:18f. In their battle against human desires, believers are to adopt as armor "the same or very understanding," which has just been described in the excursus on "Christ's suffering in the flesh."

There follows immediately at the end of v. 1 a *hoti* clause whose meaning and function are debated. While some view the clause as providing the reason for the injunction ("for or because"), others see it as offering its contents ("namely or that"). In addition most consider the clause as a parenthetical remark whose function somehow explains what the "insight or understanding" should be. More problematic is the author's statement that "the one who has suffered in the flesh has done with sin." Most scholars, on theological grounds, insist that Christ cannot be the one intended, directly or indirectly, since the statement would imply that he once was subject to sin. In light of this, most commentators have opted to explain the clause, despite grammatical uneasiness (use of aorist and perfect tenses), as a general principle regarding the salvific value of suffering ("whoever has suffered. . ."). Finally a wide range of suggestions have been made to explain the apparent relationship between suffering or death and the cessation or conquering of sin. Appealing to various strands of Jewish and early Christian thought, particularly Paul in Rom 6:7 ("for whoever has died is freed from sin"), suffering has been seen as a source of purification or atonement, as a disciplined battle against desire and sin, as a synonym for atoning martyrdom, or in Pauline terms as baptismal death to sin with Christ.

Convincing objections are raised against the above suggestions, particularly the Pauline and atoning interpretations. Foreign to the thought of 1 Peter are both the concepts of death to sin through baptism and of suffering as a purification of one's life from sin. More attention is now paid to the thought of 1 Peter and the passage's immediate context. In grammatical and stylistic terms the *hoti* clause must be seen as a parenthetical statement that explains the term "understanding" (*ennoia*) and whose subject ("the one who") has "Christ" as antecedent. Indeed the expression "the one who has suffered in the flesh" is a repetition of the initial statement of v. 1 ("since Christ has suffered in the flesh") and explains what the Christian's new insight or understanding should be, because without further clarification the reader might assume that suffering or even martyrdom is to be the determining factor of the believer's perspective. Thus the *hoti* clause explains parenthetically the meaning of *ennoia* (the conjunction should be rendered: "that is"), which itself flows from Christ's salvific suffering or death as expressed in 4:1 and 3:18f, particularly the latter's insistence that "Christ . . . suffered for sins once for all," an activity that made possible "life in the spirit" for Christ and for those who are saved through baptism as the conscience's fundamental pledge to God (3:19, 21; see 4:2).

The major difficulty in such an interpretation is resolving the author's statement (citing Isa 53:9) that Christ "committed no sin" (2:22) with the ending of the *hoti* clause, which implies the cessation of sin on the subject's part. The term employed by 1 Peter is *pauo*, a verb whose form as a middle or passive means either "to cease" or "be free." Since most scholars presume a general subject ("whoever") they render the term as "finish, break from, renounce, or be freed from" to express the renunciation of or separation from a past life of sin. However, if one assumes that Christ is the subject of the clause, one could view *pauo* as indicating his freedom from the power of sin, death, and suffering or more generally as expressing the termination of Christ's dealings with sin. The first option is less appealing since 1 Peter, in contrast to Paul, does not view sin as an evil power or domain but rather as evil activity (usually "sins") under the power of "human desires" or "desires of the flesh" (see 2:11 and 4:2). The second option is more in keeping with 1 Peter's insistence that "Christ suffered for sins once for all" (2:18), though he himself was sinless (2:22), and that, as a result of his bearing human sins on the cross, believers are now to be "free from sins" (2:24). Thus Christ, the one who has already suffered in the flesh, is now finished dealing with or is through with sin once and for all. This is the insight that believers are to adopt in imitation of Christ himself. They too are to have no dealings with sin.

In v. 2 the author returns to the basic structure of the sentence, namely, an imperative statement supplemented by a final, infinitive construction introduced by *eis to* ("so as to"). The exhortation is aimed at the lives of the addressees, lives described as "the remaining time in the flesh." Interestingly, the term "flesh" (*sarx*) is employed both for the sphere of Christ's salvific death (and rejection of sin) and for the arena of Christian lives (and their battle against those human desires "that wage war against the soul"—see also 2:11). The flesh then characterizes human existence as a neutral, limited sphere (see discussion of 1:24) that can be governed either "by human desires [or] by the will of God." It is in this sphere that deliverance in both objective (Christ-event) and subjective terms (human response) occurs, for as Christ bore away sins in the flesh so must believers live their lives in the flesh. Beyond this 1 Peter insists that, like Christ, believers must no longer be subject to "human desires" that may lead to sin (see v. 3 following), but rather like Christ, who is through with sin, they are to act ("live out their lives"— *bioo*) according to "God's will."

Verse 2 then gives further clues for understanding 1 Peter's anthropology (see discussion of 2:11). Human beings, while redeemed or healed in the sphere of the flesh by Christ's suffering, remain nonetheless in that sphere where they are to conduct their lives according to new standards or under a different impulse. The old impulses are characterized as "human desires" (*anthropon epithymiai*), the new as "God's will" (*thelema theou*). In the first case both terms deserve attention. The Greek *epithymia*, as in 2:11, means not sinful but natural impulse or desire that often leads to excess. While in the earlier text 1 Peter qualifies this desire as being "of the flesh," to address the believer's ethical battle "in the flesh," in this case the synonymous term *anthropos* is employed to underscore a different nuance. Both terms here represent two-sphere thinking; flesh in contrast to spirit to speak of death and life in their respective spheres and the human or mortal in contrast to the divine to emphasize the source of ethical motivation. Natural desires or impulses influenced by human limitations, weakness, and false loyalty (see vv. 3-4 and 5:8-9 for examples of such activity) are no longer to provide the impetus for Christian behavior. Instead believers are to spend the remainder of their lives in the world or flesh under a new impulse, "God's will." The expression is not explained at this point (elsewhere it is employed to address innocent suffering—2:15; 3:17; 4:19), but 1 Peter has repeatedly made clear what God wishes or wills (the expression is a parallel to the following "what Gentiles want") in terms of Christian conduct. The author's long series of exhortations have made clear to the reader what God desires: eschatological hope, holy, God-like conduct (1:13-17), lives of reverent fear (1:17), mutual love (1:22), honorable or good deeds, avoiding evil, and even bearing innocent suffering (2:11f, 21; 3:17); but especially God's will addresses the believer's duty to all human creatures, both in religious and political terms, and insists on absolute dependence on God (2:17)—even resistance of the satanic opponent (5:8-9). The believer's post-conversion life continues in the flesh but acquires an otherworldly motivation or impetus.

(4:3-5) Right Conduct among Unbelievers. A new section begins in v. 3 that shows a close thematic relation with what precedes. The conjunction indicates that this passage serves as an explanation of the previous statement concerning "human desires." Additionally the first verse focuses on behavior that results from such motivation, described as "what the Gentiles want or like to do." Beyond this, 1 Peter indicates the type of reaction that results from nonconformity to standard social and religious customs. This passage, therefore, treats three important issues: the addressees' conduct before their conversion (v. 3), the hostile response of Gentile neighbors to these new loyalties (v. 4), and the author's assurance that just judgment will prevail in the end (v. 5).

In contrast to the addressees' "remaining time in the flesh" the author speaks of another period, in the past (v. 3), when they acted under the impulse of "human desires." This pre-conversion period is interestingly described as the time when the addressees behaved like Gentiles. The difficult phraseology of the verse, "enough time has passed for (your) doing what the Gentiles want," has led most scholars to view the passage as an ironic understatement about lost or excessive time spent in immoral pursuits, thereby emphasizing the urgency of the "remaining time" (see also 4:7). One suspects, however, that by means of this terminology 1 Peter is making an oblique reference to the *makrothymia* or "patience of God" (see 3:20), which has graciously tolerated the believers' former behavior but now urgently requires a life of holiness in conformity with God's will.

This past existence or "what the Gentiles want" is described in terms of a traditional vice list; the audience, like other Gentiles, is said formerly to have "lived in licentiousness, (unbridled) passion, drunkenness, orgies, carousing, and forbidden idolatry." The list of six items is interesting in terms of source and function. On the one hand, the terms rarely appear in the LXX; at the same time the series does not match any known vice list. At best one or two of these terms are found in other NT lists (Mark 7:21-22; Rom 13:13; 1 Cor 10:14; 2 Cor 12:20-21; Gal 5:19-21; Col 3:5; Titus 3:3; also in Dead Sea Scrolls lists); two are found only here in the NT (drunkenness and carousing). Nonetheless, these various terms are employed in a negative sense or as vices in current Hellenistic literature, particularly those that refer to lack of temperance. Thus all are found in some NT or contemporary Hellenistic vice list. On the other hand, the combination and focus of this particular list seems to be due to the author of 1 Peter, who has organized the terms into a threefold pattern: the first two addressing sexual or licentious behavior, the third, fourth, and fifth aiming at intemperate conduct; and the last seemingly dwelling on the cause for such dissipation (see also the REB). One might render the entire list as follows:

> having lived
> in licentiousness and unbridled passion,
> in drunkenness, orgies, and carousing,
> ultimately in forbidden idolatry.

The function then of this list, as deduced from its structure and from the author's thematic interests, is to draw a further, close connection between ethical and theological concerns.

The above conclusion concerning the function of the vice list is confirmed by two further considerations. Not only does 1 Peter's use of *epithymia* ("desire"), both as a comprehensive term in v. 2 and as a specific vice in v. 3, confirm the use or influence of a catalogue of vices, but it also underscores the importance of the former (Gentile behavior as governed by human desires or impulse) in interpreting the latter (vices as excesses of dissipation resulting from a disregard or disobedience of God's will). Ethical or holy behavior is directly related to setting one's faith and hope in God (1:14-16, 21). The last vice is curiously qualified by the term *athemitos* meaning "lawless, wanton, or forbidden" idolatry. Though admitting that idolatry of itself would be reprehensible in Jewish and Christian terms, scholars nonetheless routinely opt for the meaning "wanton" in this context as emphasizing the author's insistence that such behavior would be repugnant to God. Since this is the only reference in 1 Peter to idolatry, it is hard to accept the claim that it is a central theme requiring such emphasis. Instead one should probably view the entire expression in relation to the theme of disobedience. While most uses of the terms *apeitheo* ("disobey"—2:8; 3:1; 4:17) and *hypakoe* ("obedience"—1:14, 22) relate to human reaction to the Christ-event, two passages, once with each term, have a bearing on the present issue. The spirits, in their rebellion against God, are said to be "disobedient" (3:20; see also discussion of 5:8-9), while Christ, in contrast to other humans, is presented as the obedient one (1:2). Idolatry, as in Paul, is both the refusal to honor God and the "exchange of the glory of the immortal God for images" (Rom 1:21, 23). At the same time this disobedience leads to ignorance, futility, foolishness, and excesses (1:14, 18; 2:15; 4:3-4). Thus one should read "forbidden idolatry" as 1 Peter's suggestion that disobedience of God's law (whether as creator or revealer) is at the basis of human sin, a situation remedied by Christ's obedience and requiring human submission. Gentile misconduct then flows from this idolatry.

In v. 4, 1 Peter focuses more directly on the reaction of Gentile neighbors to the addressees' new way of life. The peculiar, vivid terminology of the verse underscores the urgency of the situation and provides important clues to the nature of the problem. In changing abruptly from a description of the audience's pre-conversion behavior to the neighbors' perplexity at the changes involved, the author clearly indicates, though in polemical terms, the socioreligious nature of the believers' suffering as Christians. Prior to their conversion believers had participated fully in the socioreligious culture of the Roman cities. Being members of society then, as now, meant unquestioned involvement in that society's life, customs, and beliefs. The author's use of the term "surprise" (*xenizo*—see also 4:12) describes not the newness of Christian mores but rather their nonparticipation in or renunciation of the dominant culture. Employing negative terms the author speaks of unquestioned adherence to Roman culture ("rushing with them") as a thing of the past for believers and so a source of perplexity and animosity on the part of the Gentile population.

Gentile conduct is again described in interesting terms as "an outpouring or excess of dissipation or godlessness." The first term *anachysis* stresses 1 Peter's sense of sin as unbridled passion, that is, uncontrolled or excessive urges. The second term *asotia*, while indicating extreme corruption nonetheless, hints at the lack of salvation or godlessness. What Gentile Roman neighbors hold as the height of culture, the author of 1 Peter characterizes as unbridled passion lacking divine direction. In this divergence of views lies the core of the conflict between the Christian community and its Gentile neighbors. Estrangement from the dominant culture, probably aggravated by impolitic behavior, provided the basis for ostracism and vilification of Christian converts. In fact v. 4 ends by stating that perplexed Gentiles end up "vilifying" (*blasphemeo* here has a secular meaning: "slander or speak ill of"—see also Luke 23:39) nonconformist members of their society. In this verse 1 Peter clearly places the blame for the conflict on cultural and religious expectations; believers refuse to join their neighbors in their former socioreligious activity and so there results social ostracism and verbal abuse. It is in light of this basic problem that one must evaluate the author's multi-faceted strategy in dealing with the communities' maltreatment and suffering.

Indeed v. 5 addresses immediately one facet of the author's approach. The audience is assured that those who "demand an account of them" (3:16) and especially who "vilify" them will themselves be called upon to "render an account" (*apodidomi logon*) to the supreme judge. Thus defense is the believer's concern, but judgment is an eschatological issue to be left in the hands of God (see also 2:23), who is ominously described as "ready to judge" (see 4:7, which speaks of the end as being near). Scholars are divided concerning the identity of the judge: is it Christ or God since both are given this task in the NT? On the one hand, use of the traditional phrase "judge the living and the dead" would suggest the former option since it is employed about Christ in its other NT usages (Acts 10:42; 2 Tim 4:1). On the other hand, for 1 Peter it is God who is elsewhere characterized as judge (1:17; 2:23); we therefore opt for the latter. In paraenetic terms then the author is able to remind the readers that the one who calls and gives new birth (1:3, 15), who raised Jesus from the dead and gave him glory (1:21) is the same who will be the universal judge of all, both "the living and the dead." Seemingly, the author's exhortation ends by dwelling on the urgency of Christian perseverance, on vindication, and on reversal of roles.

(4:6) Life in the Spirit Even for the Dead. A final verse is added that, in stylistic terms ("for this is why"), sounds like an afterthought. But it is also a passage whose meaning has been much debated. It is particularly the preaching to the dead that has caused the difficulty. Who are these "dead," and how does this theme fit into the author's discussion? Three basic views have been proposed in this regard, views that must be examined at least briefly before a discussion of the overall passage.

First, the dead are assumed to be the disobedient spirits of 3:19 or those who dwell in the abode of the dead (either the righteous or all those deceased). Such an interpretation presumes the concept of Christ's descent to the underworld to proclaim universal salvation or victory. Second, some scholars suggest that the term *nekroi* here refers to the "spiritually" dead. Third, the dead are identified as Christians who died prior to the Lord's coming. Convincing objections can be raised against the first two views. It is hard to see how either fits into the author's discussion. Besides, universal salvation offered to the disobedient or unknowing dead is both a strange concept and one that does not offer consolation to an audience suffering at the hands of the disobedient. Additionally the term *nekros* means physical death in v. 5 and could hardly change so radically in meaning in the following verse.

It is the third option that is most convincing. While some have suggested that the expression "proclamation even to the dead" seems to imply preaching to those who are already dead (see the first and second options), it is more plausible that this particular term is employed to draw an obvious connection with the idiom "the living and the dead" of v. 5 and here means simply: "those who have since died." First Peter then is speaking of Christians who have already died. The obvious place to acquire background for this passage is Paul's discussion of a similar topic in 1 Thess 4:13-18. Members of the Thessalonian community are concerned about the fate of those among them who have died before Christ's coming. The issue seemingly is the advantage the living would have over those who have already died. The community's question leads Paul to reassure them that both the living and the dead (after being raised) will accompany the risen Lord on his heavenly journey. There will be no disadvantage; all believers will meet the risen Lord together. In 1 Peter also the issue of believers who have passed away is brought up, not seemingly as a concern of the community but rather as an opportunity for the writer both to show that God is judge of the dead (see v. 5) and to discourse on the meaning of death and life in Christian terms. The preceding verse as well as the remainder of v. 6 confirm such an interpretation.

It is striking that in discussing Gentile behavior (vv. 3f) 1 Peter stresses the theme of life, though condemning its dissipation and idolatry, and only speaks of future judgment. In a similar way the exhortation to believers also emphasizes "living the remaining time in the flesh . . . according to God's will." Thus the repeated focus on life, even judging the living, while appealing to a Hellenistic audience (believers also "desire to see good days"—3:10), would nonetheless have suggested the test-case of "the faithful dead." The remainder of v. 6 addresses precisely the issue of death in the flesh as contrasted to life in the spirit.

Before offering further observations regarding v. 6, it should be noted that its concluding *hina* clause with its contrasting (*men . . . de*) and stylistically parallel statements has been the object of much discussion and varying interpretation. In effect three items are contrasted:

judge/condemn	vs.	live
in the eyes of/as mortals	vs.	in the eyes of/with the life of God
according to the flesh	vs.	according to the spirit.

It is particularly the first statement that offers difficulty. Much depends on how one renders the verb *krino*, whether as "judge or condemn," and how one envisions the agency of the passive verb (who judges or condemns?). Some scholars take their clue from v. 5 and interpret the first statement as addressing eschatological judgment. Others view the passage, in light of the letter's situation, as referring to persecution or martyrdom on the part of Gentile oppressors. In considering more closely the context of "the faithful departed" and the contrast between "death in the flesh" and "life in the spirit," a third, more satisfactory interpretation has emerged and is reflected in the following translation:

> so that,
> though they be condemned (to death) as mortals
>   according to the flesh,
> they might live with God's life
>   according to the spirit.

Such an interpretation does justice to the terminology employed and to the parallel structure of the two statements and also fits well in the overall thematic context.

One should probably interpret v. 6 in a two-step approach. The basic structure and theme of the verse correspond to a fundamental Christian belief, which might be expressed as follows: " . . . there was proclamation of the gospel . . . so that . . . [believers] might live with God's life according to the spirit." The second statement of the parallel employs traditional terms such as the verb *sozo* to describe eternal life and the expression "according to the flesh" to connect the believer's resurrected state to that of the risen Lord (3:18). Only the expression *kata theon* (lit.: "according to God") is not traditional, though it is used in the Pauline corpus to mean "according to God's will or standard" or "in God's eyes" (Rom 8:27; 2 Cor 7:9-11) and "in God's image" (Eph 4:24). It is the latter that leads us in the right direction, because contextually the text, "created according to God," means "created according to God's image." In like manner, and in parallel with the preceding *kata anthropous*, the present passage, "live according to God," gives the sense of "live with God's life." Proclamation then has as its goal "eternal life in the domain of the spirit."

When one adds to the above structure the further element of the ones to whom proclamation is made ("the dead or the faithful departed"), then one sees how the first statement of the parallel structure fits in. The issue is not the judgment of these believers but their death (meaning of *krino*). Also the contrast calls for present death "according to the flesh" and the promise of future life "according to the spirit." It is at this point that one should consider the parallel: "according to mortals" and "according to God." In the first case mortals, being of the flesh, are like "grass that withers" (1:24); death is their common lot. In effect believers who pass away are, like all humans, condemned to physical death. In the second case it is no longer "new birth into a present or living hope" (1:3) that is at issue but the sharing of God's life or glory (5:10; also 3:18). First Peter, like the author of Wisdom (3:1-4), believes that though the death or departure of righteous believers may be deemed a disaster by nonbelievers, these faithful departed are at peace and look forward to eternal life or immortality. Thus God is the judge of both the living and the dead, both of whom are judged according to their lives of righteousness.

3:13–4:6 then begins and ends on the blessedness of those who are "zealous for good," whether they suffer innocently or have died living according to God's will. In the final analysis the good news of the Christ-event was preached so that all "might live with God's life" following their "remaining time in the flesh." In the meantime the addressees should know that suffering, which in Christ's life was instrumental in the salvation of humanity, now serves, if it is God's will, a paradigmatic (whether cleansing or missionary) function, for following in Christ's footsteps one will ultimately be brought into God's presence to receive, like Christ, the crown of glory (2:21; 3:18; 5:4).

Suggested Readings

Achtememier, P. J. "The Suffering and Triumphant Christ" in *1 Peter*. Minneapolis: Fortress, 1996, 239-74.

Brox, N. *Der erste Petrusbrief.* Zurich: Benziger, 1979.

Bultmann, R. "Bekenntnis und Liedfragmente im 1. Petrusbrief." *ConBNT* 11 (1947) 1-14.

Dalton, W. J. *Christ's Proclamation to the Spirits: A Study of 1 Peter 3:18–4:6.* Rome: PIB, 1989.

Goppelt, L. "Christ's Hades Proclamation in the Context of the History of Religion" in *A Commentary on 1 Peter*. Grand Rapids: Eerdmans, 1993, 260-63.

Lewis, J. *A Study of the Interpretation of Noah and the Flood in Jewish and Christian Literature*. Leiden: Brill, 1968.

Lohse, E. "Parenesis and Kerygma in 1 Peter" in *PFP*, 35-59.

Michaels, J. R. "Eschatology in 1 Peter iii.17." *NTS* 13 (1966-67) 394-401.Perrot, C. "La descente aux enfers et la prédication aux morts" in *Etudes*, 231-46.

Reicke, B. *The Disobedient Spirits and Christian Baptism: A Study of 1 Pet. 3:19 and Its Context*. Copenhagen: E. Munksgaard, 1946.

Schutter, W. L. *Hermeneutic and Composition in 1 Peter*. Tübingen: Mohr-Siebeck, 1989.

Shimada, K. "The Christological Creedal Formula in 1 Peter 3,18-22— Reconsidered." *Creedal* 5 (1979) 154-76.

Community Exhortation in View of the End
(4:7-11)

This short subunit brings the second major block of material in 1 Peter (2:11–4:11) to a sharp close with a brief exhortation to the community and a formal doxology. In the past scholars have pointed to similarities between this passage and the remaining section of the letter, particularly the community exhortation in 5:1-5 and the second doxology in 5:11, to support a composite theory for the overall composition, namely, an earlier document prior to persecution and a later addition focused on ongoing suffering. A careful look at 1 Peter shows, however, that these various factors argue not for a composite theory but rather for a unified composition that addresses many facets of the community's situation (see introduction). In fact 4:7-11 follows closely upon the preceding discussion concerning pre- and post-conversion behavior. Thus having exhorted believers to conduct according to God's will while addressing Gentile behavior (4:1f), 1 Peter now returns to their "remaining time in the flesh" by pointing to the eminent parousia or "end of all things" (4:7). In this case the focus is on community life and treatment of other believers.

In structural terms the passage consists of an introductory temporal statement and a double imperative clause (v. 7), which is complemented by three successive, complex participial constructions (vv. 8-10). The author further develops the exhortation by addressing community activity under the basic categories of speech and action ("if anyone speaks . . . if anyone serves . . .") and brings the paraenesis to a conclusion with a wish for divine glorification and a formal doxology (v. 11). In thematic terms the author focuses on the community's behavior as compared to that of other believers, exhorting them to genuine mutual love and service (see also 1:22; 2:17). The passage then becomes an explicitation of what was said in 2:17 regarding mutual love within the Christian fellowship. Ultimately, prayerful conduct within the community has the same goal as gentle relations to outsiders (3:16) or all human creatures (2:13, 17), namely, "that God may be glorified" (2:12; 4:11).

Prayer and Eschatological Motivation (4:7)

The discussion on community conduct is prefaced by a temporal statement that, in most translations, appears far too abruptly but that, in the Greek text, is introduced by the postpositive conjunction *de* ("now" or "now that"). By means of this particle 1 Peter draws a closer connection with what precedes concerning the believer's "remaining time in the flesh" (4:2). In this case, employing terminology from the Jesus tradition (*engizo*: "be near or at hand"—Mark 1:15 par; Luke 21:31) and influenced by paraenetic interest in the theme of the imminent end (employing the same or other terminology: Phil 4:4-5; Rom 13:11-14; Heb 10:25; Jas 5:7-8; also 1 Thess 5:1-2), 1 Peter reiterates the urgency expressed earlier in 3:20 and 4:2-3 in terms of God's patience and mercy.

At this point one might ask whether the expression "the end of all things" is employed primarily as a synonym for "the day of visitation" (2:12), of Jesus' final revelation (1:7, 13; 4:13), or for "the eschaton" (1:5) or beyond that whether the author intends to make a further statement about what is perishable and imperishable. Earlier in the text 1 Peter underscores the imperishable character of the believer's heavenly inheritance as opposed to the perishable nature of earthly things such as gold or silver (1:4, 7, 18). Also new life is said to derive from imperishable generation (1:23). The domain of the flesh, however, will wither like grass (1:24), its time limited (4:2). Indeed the flesh is subject to the sentence of death (4:6). There is here also an emphatic reference to the transience of the world of the flesh as opposed to the imperishable and eternal sphere of the spirit. Reference to the proximate "end of all things" serves then to underscore the importance of hope in the lives of believers (see 1:13, 17; 3:15). Also it prepares for the sober-minded advice that follows. Finally the author subscribes to the traditional, early Christian belief that the end was near, a belief that persisted throughout the first century (Rom 13:11-12; Heb 10:25; Jas 5:8; see 2 Pet 3:4f).

Having underscored the seriousness of the believer's situation and the importance of a life governed by hope, 1 Peter returns to the consequences ("therefore"—*oun*) the latter has for the community's life. The author's exhortation centers around two crucial themes: *sophroneo* ("sound or sober-mindedness") and *nepho* ("mental balance or self-control"). The latter also appears in 1:13 and 5:8 in significant paraenetic contexts, while the former occurs only here. However, the concept of "mind-set" (*phren*) plays a crucial part in the author's discussion of the community's life (3:8); indeed 4:7-11 might be considered a commentary on 3:8, where proper mind-set is essentially defined as involving mutual love along with sympathy and compassion (see also 5:5b). In the present passage the author dwells at greater length on community responsibility and activity. Proper mind-set in this case is defined not in terms of unity and peace as in 3:8 but, with the addition of "mental balance," as moderation of one's desires (see comments on "desires" in 1:14; 2:11; and 4:2-3), being wise or sober in one's judgment (see discussion of 5:6-8), or evaluating one's situation in light of eschatological considerations on the one hand and as alert, self-controlled, and balanced in the midst of foolish ignorance, warring desires, evil forces, and false loyalties on the other hand (1:14; 2:12, 15; 4:2; 5:8).

Interestingly, such a mind-set, prepared and focused for loving activity (see 1:13), is said to have "prayer" (*proseuche*—see also 3:7) in view. Clearly prayer, for 1 Peter, is closely related to such activity, for failure to treat one's spouse with honor can be a hindrance to prayer (3:7). No doubt, prayer in this letter also involves various modes of address to God, such as intercession and petition (1:17; 3:12), but primarily it involves the believer's relationship to God. Believers are to live God-centered lives, that is, in reverent fear (1:17; 2:17; see also 2:18; 3:2). Their faith and hope are to be set in God

(1:13, 21; 3:5) whom they address as father, judge, and creator. Thus a life dedicated to fostering this reverent relationship to God is simply a sober, focused mind-set that envisions this new life as the offering of spiritual sacrifices and praise (2:5, 9) to the Lord of all.

Love and Hospitality as Manifold Grace of God (4:8-10)

Immediately following the imperatives of v. 7b, the author qualifies the required mind-set and discipline, which foster a life of prayer, by a series of two complex participial and one straightforward adjectival constructions: "having . . . , [being] hospitable, . . . serving . . . ." Each of these introduces a different facet of community life that has as its goal the glorification of God through prayer—vv. 7b on prayer addressed to God and 11b on divine glorification form an inclusio, thereby underscoring the God-centered character of the believers' new life of mutual love and service.

The first participial construction (v. 8), dealing with mutual love, is introduced by an expression ("above all") that underscores its traditional priority for Christian living (see Mark 12:30-33 par; 1 Cor 12:31f). The exhortation to love one another, and the theme more generally of affection are frequent and crucial for 1 Peter. In 1:22 the author touches on some of the themes here presented. Christian purification has precisely "genuine mutual love" as its goal. Further this love is said to have a public or ecclesial character and an eschatological context (see discussion of "genuine and constant"). In 2:17 believers are exhorted to a relationship of love toward other believers, a relationship that is based on and presupposes honor for all. Thus their mind-set is to be one of mutual love (3:8), and their conduct is to be governed by activity that benefits others in view of the Lord's return—in effect the term *ektenes* should here also be rendered "constant" as in 1:22. While the motivation for mutual love in the latter is attributed to new birth, here it is said that "love covers a multitude of sins," an enigmatic Christian maxim (see also Jas 5:20; *1 Clement* 49:5; *2 Clement* 16:4) that ultimately depends on the Hebrew, not LXX, version of Prov 10:12 and other biblical phraseology (for "multitude of sins," see Ezek 28:17-18; Sir 5:6). Furthermore the meaning of this maxim in the author's discussion is unclear, whether one considers the meaning of "cover" (which usually signifies "forgiveness" in the OT—see Ps 32:1) or the one whose sins are affected (the one who loves or the one who is loved). The term *kalypto* can hardly have a soteriological sense here but must have a general meaning, such as "remove from sight or cover over" (BAGD 401.2a). Also, from the context and from the maxim's use in Jas 5:20, we suggest that the author is speaking of the sins of the one who loves. Thus we conclude that 1 Peter's meaning is paraenetic in character, namely, that the loving actions of one who is less than perfect makes that person far more acceptable to others within the community. Love hides many imperfections and generates loving action in return.

The second construction (v. 9) is an adjectival one and presumes an unexpressed copula "being." The entire verse acts as a parallel to the statement on mutual love, on the one hand presenting "hospitality" (*philoxenos*) as an example par excellence of *agape* and on the other demanding that it be done with cheerfulness or "without complaining." Alluding to a tradition that was a distinct feature of Greek culture (Homer, *Odysseus* 14.45f; Ovid, *Metamorphosis* 8.610f) and a popular motif of the Jesus and paraenetic tradition (Mark 2:15f; 14:4f; Rom 12:9-13; Heb 13:1f), 1 Peter focuses on the motivation and manner of community living. While many stress the missionary aspect of this motif (even good works have a missionary objective —see 2;12), it is particularly the new familial relationships that are here underscored by love of the brotherhood or household of faith (see 2:17; 5:9). Hospitality and respect are encouraged toward all human beings but here, by repetition of "toward one another" and the insistence on cheerfulness (see 1:6, 8), 1 Peter is emphasizing the counterpart to alienation and ostracism. Conversion may have brought about a rupture of former relationships, but it has also provided a new family of believers, which requires hospitable interchange among its members. At the same time the author acknowledges the challenge of such social exchange (within and among house churches) and prepares for later discussion of community relations and functions (vv. 10-11; 5:1-5).

A third, more complex participial construction (v. 10) now focuses on *charismata* or use of one's gifts, once more, for the mutual benefit of the community. The structure of the verse leads the reader to concentrate on its central theme: divine gifts for the service of God's people. Indeed the verse introduces first the notion of gift (a: "as each has received a gift"), then addresses its use (b: "serving each other with it"), and returns to responsible use of the gift (a': "like good stewards of God's manifold grace"). Insisting, in a manner reminiscent of Paul (1 Cor 12:1f), that gifts are received and not self-generated, the author returns at the end of the verse to the theme of responsible use of God's many blessings. To describe the latter theme 1 Peter employs an important expression: *kaloi oikonomoi*, a phrase that is usually rendered "good stewards or managers." The first term, in light of its twofold use in 2:12, probably stresses its visible (ecclesial) or honorable character. The second term recalls earlier images of the community as God's house or household (see 2:5, 18; also 4:17). Thus its members have been given gifts that are precisely for the social and religious good of the community.

Two topics in v. 10 call for further attention: 1 Peter's conception of grace or gift and of Christian service. The term *charis* or grace is employed eight times in 1 Peter (see 2:19, 20 for a special use of the term) to denote divine, present, and future benefactions (1:2, 13; 3:7; 5:5) or more specifically to describe a beneficent God. In the present case the term signifies the divine source of the gifts received by believers, for indeed God is "the God of all grace" (5:10) and determines what each receives from this "manifold or rich" treasury (see Rom 12:6 for a similar association of grace and gift). The theme of service is here expressed by the verb *diakoneo*, a term already employed in 1:12 to describe the prophets' role vis-à-vis the Christian community. In this instance the term focuses on the passage's overriding concern: mutual love and assistance. It is no accident that each of the three successive participial constructions contains a prepositional phrase regarding mutual concern ("for one another"). In v. 10 the author stresses even further the mutual character of service, for believers are to employ their God-given gifts ("serve each other with it") in the manner God intended. Gifts are given for this reason, and believers as members of the household are to show themselves as honorable stewards of God's beneficence. The theme of service will reappear in the following verse.

Glory to God in Speech and Service (4:11)

In grammatical terms v. 11 marks a change in the development of the author's thought. The series of complementary constructions (modifying the exhortation of v. 7) has come to an end, and a new statement concerning preaching and service precedes a purpose clause about divine glorification and a formulaic doxology. Rather abruptly, it would seem, 1 Peter is here presenting two fundamental examples of ecclesial service or of divine gifts. This rudimentary list, however, has little in common with other NT lists (e.g., Rom 12:6-8; 1 Cor 12:7-11; also Eph 4:11). Besides, the generic terms employed hardly qualify as types of service, especially since the author repeats the term *diakoneo* from the previous verse for one of these activities. The issue then is the relationship of v. 11 to what precedes and the function it plays in the author's paraenesis. Perhaps the best way to approach this verse is to view it structurally as a counterpart to v. 7. In v. 11, 1 Peter addresses the entirety of Christian activity as it has a bearing on the believer's relationship to God, prayers in v. 7, and divine glorification in v. 11. Such a conclusion will best be understood as the three units of the verse are examined.

The initial double "if" construction provides not examples of gifts or service but instead summarizes all community activity into the basic components of word and deed. While some commentators, under the influence of Acts 6:1-6, propose to see here an ecclesial division of functions (ministries of the word and of charitable activities), it seems best to view the two statements in their entirety (speaking/God's oracles and serving/God's strength) as a parallel exhortation to v. 7. On the one hand, all Christian speech should strive (an implied imperative: "let it be as") to be prophetic; that is, believers should employ speech to interpret present events in light of God's revelation or will ("as one who delivers God's oracles"—see 2 Cor 2:17). Christian speech, whether teaching, preaching, exhortation, or gentle defense, should be undertaken with prayer in view. On the other hand, all activity (earlier described as being oriented to service of one another) should draw upon the strength that God provides in abundance (*choregeo*). The concept of divine strength, though here expressed by the unique term *ischys*, is implied in passages that speak of reception of divine gifts and growth into salvation (1:9; 2:2, 5; 4:14; 5:10). The double "if" construction therefore addresses the entirety of Christian activity from God's perspective (double emphasis: "like God's oracles" and "with God's strength"), whether speech as honorable and not malevolent utterance (2;12; 3;16) or loving service of others as drawing strength, in the midst of suffering, from new birth of imperishable generation (1:22-23). Both the audience's new ecclesial context and its current socioreligious situation are thereby addressed.

The goal of this God-centered activity is expressed succinctly in the following *hina* clause: "so that God may be glorified in all things through Jesus Christ." Clearly this statement reiterates what was said earlier in 2:12 but here adds global and christological nuances. The expression "in all things" reinforces the interpretation given earlier concerning the global import of "speaking and serving," and the reference to Christ reminds the readers not only that they are suffering ultimately "for the name of Christ" (4:14) but also and especially that earthly glorification of God comes about by human acceptance of God's messiah as Lord (3:15).

First Peter ends the passage and indeed the second major section of the letter by appending (use of a relative pronoun) a formulaic doxology. It is debated whether it is addressed to God or to Christ. Though the immediate personal name ("Jesus Christ") could be considered the logical antecedent, a credible case could be made for either option. Ultimately, it is the God-centered character of the passage as well as the formulaic use of "through

Jesus Christ," which leads me to view the doxology as referring to God. Additionally, the nearly identical statement of 5:11 adds support to this conclusion. First Peter brings the exhortation to an emotional ending by reaffirming God's glorious or radiant being (*doxa*) and eternal dominion (*kratos*) as faithful creator, judge, and parent. The first term "glory" is clearly of great importance to the author's strategy in insisting that believers who share Christ's sufferings will also share in the glory to which God has called them (4:13; 5:10). The second term, which is far less frequent in doxologies, is employed presumably to allow the author to remind suffering believers that power or dominion (see also 5:11) belongs to the God whom they invoke as both father and judge (1:17) and who will deliver them in their time of need (5:10-11). The term *amen* serves to affirm the author and audience's faith and hope in the "God of all grace" (5:10).

Suggested Readings

Best, E. *1 Peter*. Grand Rapids: Eerdmans, 1982.

Hiebert, D. E. "Living in the Light of Christ's Return: An Exposition of 1 Peter 4:7-11." *BS* 139:555 (1982) 243-54.

Kline, L. "Ethics for the Endtime: An Exegesis of 1 Pt. 4:7-11." *RQ* 7 (1963) 113-23.

Parker, D. C. "The Eschatology of 1 Peter." *BTB* 24 (1994) 27-32.

Senior, D. *1 and 2 Peter*. Wilmington DE: Glazier, 1980.

Spicq, C. "Prière, charité, justice . . . et fin des temps (1 Pet 4:7-11)." *AS* 50 (1966) 15-29.

Final Considerations and Renewed Exhortation

(1 Peter 4:12–5:11)

The letter's third major block, like the second (2:11–4:11), is introduced by addressing the readers directly ("beloved") and by resuming the rapid pace of the earlier paraenesis. Like the second section it is also brought to a close by a formal doxology ("to him belongs dominion forever. Amen"—5:11). In contrast to the previous block, which deals at length with Christian relations toward outsiders, this one focuses on community concerns, whether sharing Christ's sufferings (4:12), addressing community responsibilities (5:2, 5), or offering the believers of Asia Minor some closing advice (5:6f). This final block, therefore, with its introductory expression of direct address and concluding doxology, both forms a parallel structure to the central section (2:11–4:11) and consists of a fairly coherent whole. Thus, the block opens by speaking of believers sharing Christ's sufferings (4:13) and closes by alluding to the universal sufferings of Christians (5:9)—there is additional concern about suffering in 4:15, 19 and 5:10 as well as 5:1. Also adding to the sense of coherence that the author wishes to convey is the opening statement in 4:12 that the believers of Asia Minor are surprised at their sufferings as though they are things "unheard of" and the closing reassurance that "the same kinds of sufferings" are being endured by believers in other parts of the Roman world (5:9).

This final section consists of three relatively distinct but interrelated subunits. The first of these (4:12-19) addresses once more the issue of innocent suffering, no longer in terms of possibly abusive contexts (2:18f; 3:2) or public situations requiring Christian defense (3:13f), but more specifically and at length in relation to the themes of suffering and glory (see discussion of 1:11). In effect this section refers back to a number of earlier statements about suffering "various trials" and about rejoicing (1:6-8), about blessedness in suffering (3:14), about future glory (1:7) that nonetheless impinges on the present (4:14; see also 1:9f), and about doing good, suffering unjustly, and submitting to final judgment (2:11-12, 19; 3:12). In this section, therefore,

1 Peter addresses in a more focused way the community's critical situation along with present and future motivation for coping with these difficulties.

The second subunit (5:1-5) presents what might be classified as a community duty code addressing elder and younger members. One would not be wrong in viewing this shorter passage as a parallel to the earlier, lengthy duty code of 2:11–3:12, since both are introduced by the paraenetic expression "I exhort you" and make extensive use of relationship terminology (especially *hypotasso*—see 2:13f and 5:5). In the present case 1 Peter addresses what ostensibly are authority situations in a decidedly nonauthoritarian way— elders are not to "lord it over" their flocks but rather to act as models. The author's strategy seemingly is dictated less by the need of addressing structural, ecclesial issues than by the concept of service demonstrated by the chief shepherd and emulated by older members on behalf of those severely tested and the promise of the unfading crown of glory that Christ will confer. All therefore are exhorted, via an OT citation (Prov 3:34), to a mind-set that is divinely pleasing, that is, humility or awareness of one's role as a creature or child of God and fellow servant vis-à-vis other believers.

The final unit (5:6-11) develops the theme of humility and stresses vigilance and trust in "the God of all grace." In a way this section is a commentary on the earlier citation from Proverbs (see 5:5b) and an affirmation of the author's already stated paraenetic exhortation: "so then, let those who suffer according to God's will entrust their being to a faithful creator, while doing good" (4:19). God will protect and provide strength to those (world-wide—5:9) who recognize their role vis-à-vis all creatures, who exhibit love for fellow believers, live in reverent fear of their father and judge, and insist on showing respect to the emperor (2:17), while acknowledging God's eternal dominion (5:11).

From beginning to end therefore the author is conscious of the community's critical situation of being, in social and political terms, resident aliens and, in religious terms, exiles among their Roman neighbors. At the same time 1 Peter misses few opportunities to motivate the believers of Asia Minor to "cast their cares on" a merciful God.

Suggested Readings

Achtemeier, P. J. *1 Peter*. Minneapolis: Fortress, 1996.

Dalton, W. J. *Christ's Proclamation to the Spirits: A Study of 1 Peter 3:18-4:6*. Rome: PIB, 1989.

Goppelt, L. *A Commentary on 1 Peter*. Grand Rapids: Eerdmans, 1993.

Martin, T. W. *Metaphor and Composition in 1 Peter*. Atlanta: Scholars, 1990.

Michaels, J. R. *1 Peter*. Waco TX: Word Books, 1988.

Talbert, C. H. "Once Again: The Plan of 1 Peter" in *PFP*, 141-51.

Sharing Christ's Sufferings
(4:12-19)

At first the title given to this subunit may seem limiting since 1 Peter from the outset states that the addressees are now sharing Christ's suffering so that they might also share in his glory (v. 13). Thus the unit would be a full explicitation of the author's twofold theme of suffering and glory. However, a closer look at the entire unit reveals what many scholars of the past have discerned as an urgent treatment of the problem of suffering. Indeed the author chooses provocative terminology ("surprise," "fiery ordeal," and "something unheard of") to describe a situation that is now qualified as current. These are some of the factors that in the past led many scholars to posit a different context for this section of 1 Peter, even leading some to view earlier uses of conditional constructions ("if you endure . . . " or "if you do suffer . . . "—2:19-20 and 3:14, respectively) as indicating possible suffering and the present tense in 4:12-13 as underscoring an actual occurrence. Instead, what one encounters in this passage is a discussion not of individual situations that might occur to certain Christians but, in language similar to 1:6-9, of the overall situation of innocent suffering. As in the earlier passage the author is also concerned with the themes of testing and present joy in view of eschatological glory; in both cases suffering is a present reality.

What then is the focus of this passage and what does it contribute to the author's message and strategy? How in other words should the unit be read? Several proposals have been made for understanding its themes and emphasis. The passage might be seen as having two points of emphasis: vv. 12-16 as focusing on suffering as grace (whether joy, blessedness, or glorification of God) and vv. 17-19 as viewing suffering as the anticipation of judgment. The author's goal then is the presentation of suffering as a Christian necessity and the development of a theology of suffering. It has also been suggested that a series of injunctions (vv. 15-16) have been framed by introductory and concluding statements of assurance (vv. 12-14 and 17-19, respectively). The author's focus then would be on the consolation that eschatological glory and future judgment bring to those experiencing the fiery ordeal.

In each case structural indicators are overlooked in the quest for thematic development. Both ignore the series of "if" constructions in vv. 14, 16, 17b, and 18 and surprisingly suggest a break between vv. 16 and 17a, which in fact are related as principal and subordinate clauses. It is here proposed that the passage is comprised of three interrelated grammatical units: vv. 12-13 consist of an introductory injunction and contrasting modifiers, vv. 14-17a offer parallel "if" constructions that conclude on a note of judgment, and vv. 17b-19 present another set of parallel "if" constructions and an extended paraenetic conclusion. Each unit presents related motives (eschatological and present glory as well as trust in the judgment of "a faithful creator") for the addressees to persevere under the trying circumstances of their fiery ordeal.

The major theme therefore of this section is that of "sharing Christ's sufferings," for the author's concern is the present, painful situation of the addressees and helping them to cope. They are promised that as they share in Christ's sufferings so will they share in his glory (vv. 12-13). They are also assured that they possess already the spirit of glory (God's Spirit) and so must glorify God through Christ (vv. 14-17a). And finally, in view of final judgment they must persist in doing good despite the suffering they encounter (vv. 17b-19).

Sharing in Christ's Suffering and Glory (4:12-13)

Like the second major block of material, this one also opens with a striking term of endearment "beloved" (*agapetoi*); in both cases the author addresses the community's painful situation. In the first instance the setting is maltreatment in the context of Christian-Gentile relations (2:11-12); in vv. 12-13 the issue presumably is the community's extreme frustration when faced with these problems. From the beginning the addressees are exhorted: "do not be surprised or astonished" (*me xenizesthe*), a phrase that suggests a high level of anxiety and resentment on the part of some within the community. The same term is employed earlier in 4:4 to express the Gentile populace's perplexity and indeed animosity at the converts' renunciation of Roman beliefs and customs. Here also there is a hint of perplexity (see further below) though perhaps not of animosity (though see references to non-retaliation: 2:23; 3:1, 9, 16). Instead, believers are exhorted not to be ashamed (v. 16). The element of surprise is further qualified by use of the same root *xenos*: "as though something unheard of (or strange) were happening to you." The newness of neighborly animosity and the deep resentment of cultural differences and even its rejection must have been difficult issues to deal with on the part even of enthusiastic converts. At this point the author does not confront directly the fallacy of believing that these sufferings are new or unheard of (note the repeated use of "you" and the contrast with "throughout the world" in 5:9). Instead there is an indirect answer given to this question in the following verse by reference to Christ's paradigmatic suffering.

The community's difficulties are described as a "fiery ordeal . . . to test" believers. Again, there is only a hint here concerning "temptation" (see discussion earlier of *peirasmos* at 1:6)—1 Peter will return to this theme at 5:8. While many focus on this fiery terminology to suggest persecution, official or not, as the cause of the community's problems, it should be noted that the expression describes not the difficulties themselves, and probably not endtime conflagration, but the purpose that suffering serves in God's plan. In both cases smelting imagery is employed to speak of present purification in view of eschatological reward. Thus the fire terminology refers to the testing rather than to the events that cause difficulty.

In contrast ("but"—*alla*) to the initial, negative injunction not to be surprised (perhaps also not to be intimidated—see 3:14), 1 Peter exhorts the addressees in positive terms to rejoice instead since they are sharers of Christ's sufferings. As in 1:6-9 there is here also a fervent exhortation to rejoice in the midst of suffering. While in the former the motivation for such joy is described as eschatological "praise, glory, and honor" (1:7), in the present case the author develops explicitly not only the paradigmatic theme of suffering (2:21) but also, in an appended *hina* clause ("so that"), that of glory. Verse 13, more than any other passage in 1 Peter, makes clear the paradigmatic function of this twofold theme. Suffering (not death) and glory (not resurrection) have been chosen for this purpose; again it should be noted that the traditional themes are frequently invoked in soteriological contexts. In the graphic terms suggested by 1 Peter, namely, that of journey, footsteps, and final, earthly revelation to award a crown of glory to believers and to bring them to God (see 2:21; 3:18f; 5:4), one can envision Christ's journey as the schema for Christian life and, in its present Petrine formulation, as a model for consolation to a suffering community. Christ's journey, encompassing his suffering in the flesh on the one hand and his enthronement in glory on the other, becomes the paradigm for Christians, who like their lord, are suffering innocently and, by following in his footsteps, can look forward to his return to confer upon them the crown of glory and to take them into God's presence.

The structural elements of v. 13 underscore the important link that 1 Peter posits between innocent suffering and consequent glory and, in this passage, between joy in the midst of suffering and indescribable joy when Christ's glory is revealed. Indeed the first half of the verse connects current suffering with the exhortation to rejoice in the present, while the second half (or *hina* clause) links eschatological glory to greater joy in the endtime. As a parallel to the exhortation not to be surprised in v. 12, believers are encouraged to rejoice instead. The basis for this injunction is interestingly expressed as follows: "in so far as you are sharing in the sufferings of Christ." The reason for this exhortation to rejoice in the face of present suffering is qualified by two important terms, one expressing degree or condition (*katho*) and the other expressing a relation of Christian suffering to that of Christ. The author is not speaking of joy in suffering in an anthropological sense but of suffering "in so far as" it is related to Christ's activity. To describe this relationship 1 Peter employs the verb *koinoneo* ("share"; see 5:1 for a similar use of the noun). But in what sense does the believer share in Christ's sufferings? While some interpreters have suggested that 1 Peter sees believers as united to Christ in mystical solidarity or even as sharing Christ's soteriological role, presumably under Pauline and Paulinist influence respectively, it seems best to view this sharing in a twofold way: first as a following in his footsteps and the acceptance of unavoidable suffering and secondly as the bearing of suffering in Christ's name (see vv. 14, 16). The logic of v. 13 suggests that joy in the present is the reasonable consequence of the christological paradigm; as Christ suffered innocently and is now enthroned in glory, so are believers, who are now subject to suffering, assured of eschatological glory and its present impact on Christian life, behavior, and their motivation. In light of this paradigm then, and its particular formulation in v. 13, one can see the logical development of vv. 13-16; because vv. 13 and 14 focus on the present impact of promised glory (joy and present glory, respectively) and vv. 15-16 reiterate what is already stated in the previous two verses, namely, that such suffering must be like that of Christ.

Verse 13 then focuses on joy as a proleptic reality, a reality that is assured on the one hand and on the other required of believers following in Christ's footsteps and, in the present context, sharing in his innocent, God-trusting confrontation with suffering (2:21-23). Indeed to heighten the effect of this claim and to add further assurance, 1 Peter insists not only that the assurance of future glory necessitates present rejoicing but also that such joy will lead to greater rejoicing ("shout for joy"—see BAGD 4 for combined use of *chairo* and *agalliao*; confer also 1:6-8 and Matt 5:12) when Christ's glory is revealed.

Christian Suffering and Present Glory (4:14-17a)

In grammatical terms the author embarks on a long series of parallel, complex "if" clauses (that extend as far as v. 18) but in thematic terms draws attention to some of the ideas noted in v. 13. The first two sets of "if" constructions form striking parallels and present interesting contrasts. The first of these (vv. 14-15) consists of a standard protasis or "if" clause and adjectival apodosis ("you are blessed"), a succeeding *hoti* clause that gives the reason for this affirmation of blessedness in the midst of abuse and a concluding injunction about merited punishment that contrasts with the initial "if" clause concerning innocent suffering. The second construction (vv. 16-17a) offers a similar yet contrasting structure. The opening "if" clause is apocapated ("yet if . . . as a Christian") and so presumes the theme of suffering from the previous construction and the apodosis is a contrasting (to blessedness in v. 14) negative injunction ("do not be ashamed"). Immediately there follows an antithetical injunction ("instead glorify God"), and the whole concludes with a *hoti* clause concerning divine judgment. Also marking off vv. 14-17a as a structural unit is the opening focus on the audience ("you are reviled") and on suffering "on account of the name of Christ" (v. 14) and the final reference to "glorify God through this name" and to the addressees as "the house of God" (vv. 16-17a).

Verse 14 continues the thematic development of the previous verse. What earlier had been expressed as "sharing the suffering of Christ" is now stated in the form of a hypothetical case as being "reviled (*oneidizo*) on account of Christ's name." While the ideas and the beatitude form are similar to those of 3:14 ("if you suffer for doing what is right, you are blessed"), the terminology is closer to the beatitude of the Q-source (Matt 5:11; Luke 6:22), where those who are "reviled or insulted" are declared "blessed." The author's choice of terminology again suggests verbal abuse rather than official or nonofficial persecution, and those so treated are called blessed for yet another reason, since already in the present they have God's Spirit, or the Spirit of glory, resting upon them. This new reason (presented as a *hoti* clause —"because . . . ") for Christian optimism is of interest on several counts. Seemingly 1 Peter employs an OT passage (Isa 11:2) both to present a traditional pneumatic theme and to formulate the statement in accordance with the letter's message and strategy. Employing an Isaian text that speaks of the Davidic heir who will bear God's spirit and relying on early Christian tradition that views new life as an infusion of the Spirit conferred by Christ (Mark 13:11 par; Acts 2:33), 1 Peter reminds the addressees that God's Spirit dwells within them. Interestingly the statement, related to Isa 11:2, has taken on a form that later scribes have found puzzling (see the textual discussion of *TCGNT* 695) but that makes sense in view of 1 Peter's thematic schema of suffering and glory. This Spirit, which Christians customarily identify as God's Spirit or the Holy Spirit (see 1:2, 11-12), is here characterized as the bearer of anticipated glory. Thus 1 Peter states: "you are blessed, because the Spirit of glory, that is, God's Spirit (*kai to tou theou*), rests upon you."

Promised glory, in the view of 1 Peter, impinges upon present existence; the addressees are blessed and must rejoice despite present suffering.

This first "if" construction is brought to a conclusion by an ominous contrasting injunction (v. 15) that underscores once again the innocent character of such suffering. In both negative and positive terms the addressees have been exhorted concerning such treatment (2:20 and 3:14). Further, this passage is an antithesis to the opening "if" clause of v. 14. Why then the emphasis on specific wrongdoing? A list of four activities is given, the first two of which are clearly designated as serious wrongdoing: murder and theft. Seemingly these are singled out as violations of the general respect owed to all human creatures (2:13, 17) on the one hand and as a betrayal of social responsibilities on the other; Christians like other wards of the Roman state would have been prosecuted in court for such offenses. Additionally such wrongdoing was listed among the major sins condemned by the Jewish decalogue (Exod 20:14; Deut 5:19). The third and fourth items of the list, however, present difficulty to the modern reader. The first of these (*kakopoios* —lit:, "evildoer") or its cognates appear frequently in 1 Peter (see discussion of 2:12, 14), but the term signifies general wrongdoing rather than a specific vice or criminal offense. What should its meaning be here in a series of specific activities? See a similar situation for the term *epithymia* in 4:2-3. The fourth term (*allotriepiskopos*) occurs only here in early biblical and Hellenistic literature, and its meaning has been much debated. While some, in considering the term's proximity to "thief" or "evildoer," have conjectured "concealer of stolen goods" or "mischief maker" (BAGD 40), the majority of scholars and translators, relying on the term's infrequent use in later Patristic literature (see *PGL* 77) and, etymologically on its seeming relationship both to the philosopher's claim to be overseer of the morals of others and to the theme of the "busybody," adopt the meaning "meddle in the affairs of others or being a busybody" (BAGD 40; *TDNT* 2:620-22). Thus it seems reasonable, in considering the double use of *hos* ("as") to introduce the first three as a unit and the fourth as a parallel to this list, to conclude, along with most scholars, that the author intends the following:

> Let none of you suffer:
>> as a murder, a thief, or (generally as) an evildoer,
>> nor as one who meddles in the affairs of others.

In this way the term "wrongdoer" would maintain its consistency in the author's varied descriptions of current behavior, while the last term "busybody" would introduce, with some specificity, a concern that is sometimes perceived in the letter's discussion of Gentile and Christian relations.

If we are correct in insisting on the meaning "busybody" for the last term of the list, then we would be justified in examining 1 Peter in light of such an admonition. From the outset, it is clear that the author is concerned about innocent suffering or maltreatment at the hands of pagan neighbors. But does careful reading not suggest possible provocation on the part of believers? The following factors might be seen as suggesting the author's concern about the Christians of Asia Minor as seeing themselves as the arbiters of current morality. Believers are to influence pagan behavior by their noble deeds instead of public speech (see 2:12; also 3:1-2); even where they are advised to speak, it is in self-defense (3:15). The language of 4:3-4 suggests not just an avoidance of earlier, pagan behavior but even a condemnation of such by the new converts. While the statement about nonretaliation (2:23; 3:9) and innocent suffering (2:20; 3:14, 16) clearly refers to maltreatment or undeserved verbal abuse, the author's insistence on "behaving honorably among the Gentiles" (2:12), on "not using (one's) freedom as a pretext for evil" (2:16), and on not reciprocating evil speech (2:12; 3:16) suggest less-than-gentle prior exchanges with Gentile neighbors about their beliefs and moral activities. In fact each discussion of evil speaking or slander, in light of nonretaliation statements, suggests some Christian provocation, an activity that the author explicitly classifies as interfering in their neighbors' business. Presumably the neighbors are now retaliating with corresponding verbal abuse or condemnation.

The second, parallel "if" construction (vv. 16-17a) is intimately connected with the preceding text. Not only is it introduced by *de* ("yet or for"), but also its structure and meaning presume the preceding verb: "yet if *you suffer* as a Christian." This protasis says essentially what was stated in that of 14a, suffering "as a Christian" being a restating of "on account of Christ's name." Interestingly believers are here identified by the name for which they suffer. The term *Christianos* to designate members of the Jesus movement occurs in the NT only here in 1 Peter and twice in Acts (11:26; 26:28). While it is often presumed that such a designation represents initially the derogatory viewpoint of Jewish and pagan outsiders, such a conclusion, though widely held, cannot be derived from analysis of either 1 Peter or Acts. For the latter the word, in narrative terms, is employed in one case to indicate official designation of the group (11:26) and in the other is placed in the mouth of an outsider (King Agrippa, a Jewish king appointed by Rome—26:28); in neither case is the term used in a derogatory way. Instead such usage fits Luke's attempt, among other goals, to present the Jesus movement as a law-abiding, world movement. In the case of 1 Peter the meaning is not that of suffering "for being a Christian" but of suffering as the result of upholding Christian values. Thus along with Acts, 1 Peter witnesses to early use by Christian writers of the term *Christianos* to designate the movement to which they belonged.

Following this initial "if" clause the addressees, in casuistic terms, are exhorted: "let them not be ashamed, instead let them glorify God through the name" or "in this manner" (see discussion below). The proximity of the term *aischyno* ("be ashamed") to the designation "Christian" has often led scholars to posit official, state persecution of believers as the context for 1 Peter. Thus they would assume that belonging to this movement meant public disgrace and condemnation of the "very name." As has been argued in the introduction and repeatedly in the commentary, the author's attitude toward Roman society does not reflect persecution but rather a realistic, yet optimistic exhortation to better relations between believers and their pagan neighbors. The shame about which the author speaks is not that which would be associated with belonging to an outlawed religious movement, but rather it, along with the concept of glorification, represents current anticipation of a future reality. Earlier in the letter, employing the term *kataischyno* (derived from Isa 28:16), 1 Peter insists that believers "will not be put to shame," while nonbelievers and those responsible for their abuse will be (see 2:6-7 and 3:16). Thus in the present, despite suffering or punishment that some might consider a source of shame, the addressees are to feel no shame for they are not destined for shameful condemnation but are called to God's "eternal glory." Indeed in contrast to shame they are to "glorify God" now in anticipation of the day of visitation when all beings are to acknowledge God's glory (see 2:12).

It is important to take note of a variant reading at the end of v. 16, whether one should glorify God "through this name" or "in this manner" (*onomati* or *merei*, respectively). On the one hand one could argue, both in structural and thematic terms, that just as believers are reviled "on account of Christ's name," so are they to glorify God "through this name" that they bear. So by acknowledging Christ's lordship (3:15), by following in his footsteps (2:21), by coming to him and being built into a spiritual house (2:4-5), the addressees already glorify God and stand as examples for their pagan neighbors that they might in their turn glorify the faithful creator. On the other hand, I am led to opt for the second reading (with the majority, though later manuscripts), since it is hard to see how a general expression like the latter would arise from a theologically pregnant phrase like the former. Besides, the latter provides additional insight for interpreting the remainder of the passage. Thus believers are to glorify God by means also of their suffering.

The reason for Christian joy and confidence in this instance is expressed by a *hoti* clause concerning judgment of God's house (v. 17a), a clause whose interpretation is crucial for the remainder of the passage. In this verse the terms *kairos* ("time") and *krima* ("judgment") can be viewed as technical, apocalyptic, or general terms, and in light of this two very different approaches are taken vis-à-vis vv. 17f.

By viewing the first term as a shortened form of "last or endtime" (see 1:5; also 5:6) and the second, used absolutely, as referring to final judgment, a number of scholars have proposed various apocalyptic interpretations for these verses. Against the background of the traditional scenario for the endtime (see Mark 13 and the book of Revelation) it has been proposed that the community's fiery ordeal represents the messianic woes or great tribulation of the elect prior to the final judgment, which in effect has already begun. Further they do not fail to note the term *telos* ("end or outcome") in 17b as confirming such an interpretation. Thus "the end of all things is near" (4:7); indeed the final act of the apocalyptic scenario has begun to unfold (see also 2 Thess 2:1-2), and the "end" here refers to the time of judgment that involves first God's house and then, more severely, the sinner and the godless. The principal objection to such an approach is the fact that apocalypticism, with its propensity for endtime speculation, pessimism, and aversion toward the outside world, and focus on suffering and vengeance, is adverse to the point of view of 1 Peter, which on the contrary lends attention to the time before the end ("remaining time in the flesh"—4:2) and to the proper conduct of believers within a reformable world. Like other NT authors, 1 Peter believes that the end is near and, like them also, is concerned with the believer's life in community and in society. This author in particular is concerned about and committed to Christian-pagan relations.

In effect recent commentators view v. 17a and the subsequent unit, which pursues the same theme, as concerned with the suffering of the righteous as it relates to divine judgment. The first term, *kairos*, as in 5:6, speaks of God's time or "due time," and the second, *krima*, as also the cognate verb (1:17; 2:23; and 4:4-5), refers to general or universal judgment; such is indeed confirmed by what follows. Important in this context are previous statements about suffering as a test for one's faith or as a purifying fire (1:7; 4:12), about universal judgment (see references given above), and about the believer's relation to God as manifested in behavior (holiness, purification, obedience, being conscious of God—1:15-16, 22; 2:19). As regards the last mentioned theme, 4:16b takes on a special meaning: the suffering believer is to glorify God precisely "in this manner," that is, through suffering "as a Christian." Verse 17a therefore presents an added reason why Christian suffering should bring joy in the present; indeed it marks the beginning of judgment or purification of God's house. Among other things present suffering is the beginning of eschatological judgment, to which all (1:17), both the living and the dead (4:5), the righteous and the ungodly (4:18), are subject. Divine mercy and patience (1:3; 2:10; 3:20; 4:3) notwithstanding, it is God's will that innocent suffering purify Christian faith in the present that it "might be found to result in praise, glory, and honor when Jesus Christ is revealed" (1:7). Judgment then begins for "God's house" (see 2:5 for discussion of this image and Ezek 9:6 for the terminology of the clause) in the present, for suffering is here presented as a means of purification.

Doing Good Despite Suffering (4:17b-19)

Having suggested that innocent suffering is under the purview of God's eschatological judgment, the author pursues this theme as it applies to the righteous and the godless. A new series of parallel "if" constructions contrasts the fate of the two by means of rhetorical questions (vv. 17b-18) and is brought to a proper conclusion on the theme of confidence or trust in "a faithful creator" (v. 19). Additionally the two "if" constructions are built on the same pattern: initial conditional clauses introduce ominous rhetorical questions concerning the fate of the disobedient or sinner, a pattern that is borrowed from Prov 11:31, itself cited verbatim in v. 18. The pattern of 17b therefore is built on that of the succeeding OT citation.

The first of these conditional-rhetorical constructions addresses the issue of judgment raised in the previous *hoti* clause (17a) and seemingly is an attempt to explain what was just said. In stating that eschatological judgment, in the form of purification, has already begun against the Christian community, 1 Peter employs an idiom, presumably from Ezek 9:6, *archomai apo*, that not only expresses "judgment against" but also judgment "beginning with" the house of God—the OT context suggests both ideas and may even have led the author in 5:1-5 to the discussion concerning elder and younger community members. In light then of this idiom, which is repeated in part: "if (it begins) against or with us," the author picks up the concept of present judgment of the holy in terms of purification and inducement to "rid oneself of all manner of malice" (2:1) and suggests that a more severe treatment of the wicked is yet to come. To the above phrase 1 Peter adds the term *proton* to insist not that judgment "begins *first* with" God's house, now qualified as "us" (a tautology no doubt), but rather that judgment "begins with us *in the present*" or "at the beginning" (LSJ 1535). This phrase would then form a contrast with the second part of the construction: "what will be the end (or "outcome"—*telos*) for the disobedient."

In relation to the above interpretation three important points should be made. First, the concept that judgment should begin with or from God's people, house, or elect would have been known to 1 Peter from OT and intertestamental literature, particularly the prophets who insist that judgment falls first on Israel to purify it of its sins and then on the nations (Isa 10:12; Jer 25:29; Mal 3:1-5; see also Amos 3:2) and later apocalyptic literature (see *2 Bar* 13:9-10: "he did not spare his own sons first, but afflicted them . . . that they might be forgiven"). Such a concept of successive judgment or punishment would have established a framework for the author's exhortatory contrast between present suffering and future condemnation for the godless.

Second, the above interpretation of *proton/telos* as suffering "in the present" for the righteous and "endtime" condemnation for the unrighteous agrees with the author's constant concern about the already and the not yet, whether it be salvation that is essentially future but that is already being received and is growing (1:9; 2:2) or glory that will be conferred at Jesus' coming but that (as Spirit of glory) already rests on those who believe. Thus present realities, whether suffering or joy, are explained in terms of eschatological promise. In this case the suffering of the innocent or righteous is explained as a foretaste of final judgment that purifies the believer's faith and thereby glorifies God, while endtime condemnation and presumably merited suffering are held out for the ungodly.

Third, to describe those who merit eschatological condemnation the author speaks of "those who do not obey the gospel of God," an expression that not only recalls "disobeying the word" (2:8; 3:1) in a Christian sense but also more generally all who oppose God's plan (3:20). The lack of precision here might lead one to envision only non-Christian opponents of the community as intended by the author, but the expansion of this group in v. 18 to include "the godless and the sinner" points more generally to the letter's purpose. First Peter is interested less in describing the end-day sufferings of unbelievers than in encouraging the addressees to remain firm despite their present suffering.

A second conditional-rhetorical construction (v. 18) follows, introduced only by a loose connective ("and") and reproducing verbatim the text of Prov 11:31. Its parallel structure and thematic context allow for a solid grasp of the author's message, since each term or theme of v. 18 is elucidated or supplemented by others either in v. 17b or the surrounding text. Thus "the righteous" (*ho dikaios*) mentioned in v. 18 corresponds to the "us" of the parallel statement and the earlier "house of God." Additionally in the overall context of the letter the term relates to those who are said to please God (3:12), to have been made "righteous" by God's righteous son (3:18), and to those who strive for righteousness or the doing of good (3:14; 4:19). The righteous are also those innocent ones "who suffer according to God's will" (v. 19). The expression "barely saved" focuses on the fate of the righteous in contrast to that, hinted at, of the unrighteous. Indeed there is no doubt that the just will be or are being saved (1:5, 9-10; 2:2; 3:21) but there is a point being made and emphasized, a point that is addressed to the audience's situation, namely, that the believer's part in the reception or growing into salvation (1:9; 2:2) is a difficult one. The seeming excesses of the unrighteous neighbors must not give the wrong impression to those undergoing suffering. Indeed the opponents, here qualified as "godless and sinner" (unique terms in 1 Peter—though see 2:20 on sin or wrongdoing), are also the disobedient ones, those who do not belong to God's house, those who nonetheless are threatened with an ominous fate (see also 2:8, 16; 3:12; 4:5)—in this case the OT imagery ("where will [they] appear") suggests the throne of judgment. Verses 17b and 18 may indeed sound ominous, but they are intended paraenetically as negative motivation for believers in the midst of bad times. Besides, the author is interested less in the suffering of the wicked than in the cessation of Christian suffering at the hands of Gentile neighbors and the glorification of God by all.

Following this forceful, negative motivation 1 Peter concludes ("so then" —*hoste kai*) the extended paraenesis on a note of comfort, trust, and practicality (v. 19). Interestingly the final exhortation is addressed to the entire community and is about innocent suffering—the author employs the third person plural imperative ("let those . . . entrust"). Not all are presumed to be suffering or at least are desperate under those circumstances. Nonetheless the situation is a major concern of the entire community, and those involved are characterized as "those who suffer according to God's will," an expression that reiterates the theme of innocent suffering, divine providence (see 1:6; 3:17), and especially the believer's daily experience as source of grace and as subject to God's judgment. Living according to God's will involves new loyalties, inspiration (2:15; 4:2), and trust in a judge who is both faithful creator and parent (1:17; 4:19).

It is in this vein that the author exhorts those who are suffering: they are to "entrust their entire being (*psyche*—see 1:9) to a faithful creator." In light of the exhortation to rejoice, to remember their blessed status, their duty to glorify God through suffering, and their encounter with God's demands

(4:12-18), they are to recall their longstanding hope and trust in God through Christ's agency and example (1:3, 21; 2:21-24) by now, in the extreme circumstances of their fiery ordeal, "entrusting their lives" in God's hands, since these sufferings conform to the divine will.

Two final, important issues should be noted in regard to this concluding exhortation, the first concerning 1 Peter's characterization of God as "faithful creator" and the second as expressing the believer's activity in light of an attitude of total trust.

Though one might insist on 1 Peter's unique use (in the NT) of *ktistes* or "creator" to speak of God, one might note that the theme is frequent nonetheless since other Christian writers favor the participle of the cognate verb or other circumlocutions (Rom 1:25; Col 3:10; Matt 19:4; Rev 10:6). Also one should note this author's passing interest in creation (1:20) and noteworthy use of the related term *ktisis* (see discussion of 2:13) to speak of the honor owed to God's "creatures." It is interesting then that God is addressed precisely as the lord and master of creation, the one who requires reverent fear (1:17; 2:17) and the one who is to be trusted. The choice of terms is one more indication of the author's concern for the community's Greco-Roman neighbors, since God is the creator of both believers and nonbelievers and requires their ultimate acknowledgment.

First Peter brings the exhortation to a close by insisting not only on proper attitude (trust in God) but also requisite activity. As noted earlier for all the addressees (1:13; 2:12), those undergoing suffering are to dedicate their energies to "doing good" (see discussion of 2:14). Thus consolation and exhortation on the part of the author are not meant as protection from menacing outsiders and much less as a prelude to martyrdom but rather as further motivation for involvement in contemporary society by means of honorable conduct.

Verses 12-19 in chapter 4 then open on a note of anguish concerning suffering that is testing the community's resolve and ends on an irenic theme since those who are suffering are exhorted to trust in "a faithful creator." Rather than choosing the apocalyptic road of separation from a hostile society, the community and its suffering members are to engage that society by "doing good" or conducting themselves honorably vis-à-vis God's creatures, all the while trusting the creator who is faithful despite unavoidable suffering. One could stop at this point and insist that this larger unit is about trust or hope in God's providence; however, one should look back to the author's reminder to the addressees that in accepting unmerited pain one is most like Christ, for one is then "sharing in his suffering," doing good toward God's creatures while awaiting Christ's bestowal of the crown of glory. Thus suffering and glory are at the basis of 1 Peter's exhortation to the troubled communities of Asia Minor.

Suggested Readings

Achtemeier, P. J. "Excursus: On the Meaning of *Allotriepiskopos*" in *1 Peter*. Minneapolis: Fortress, 1996, 311-13.
Chevallier, M. A. "Condition et vocation des chrétiens en diaspora: remarques exégétiques sur la 1re Epître de Pierre." *RSR* 48 (1974) 387-400.
de Villiers, J. L. "Joy and Suffering in 1 Peter." *Neot* 9 (1975) 64-86.
Filson, F. V. "Partakers with Christ: Suffering in First Peter." *Interp* 9 (1955) 400-12.
Michaels, J. R. "Eschatology in 1 Pet iii.17." *NTS* 13 (1966-67) 394-401.
Parker, D. C. "The Eschatology of 1 Peter." *BTB* 24 (1994) 27-32.
Richard, E. "The Functional Christology of First Peter" in *PFP*, 121-39

Community Code and Exhortation

(5:1-5)

A new and interesting section of 1 Peter follows what some scholars feel should have been a final exhortation. Instead the author returns to community concerns and seemingly now addresses Christian responsibilities. In historical terms this short passage has generated a large amount of literature since it is presumed to be an important statement concerning ecclesial structures and, in relation to this, concerning the development of the early church. The terminology employed has generated extensive comparisons with other NT works (particularly Acts 20 and the Pastorals) and early Patristic texts both to situate 1 Peter in ecclesiological terms and to trace the development of such structures within the early church. In addition there has been much discussion concerning the identity and function of the presbyter or fellow-elder.

In literary and thematic terms one notes immediate similarities to earlier discussions both of community issues as in 4:7-11 and of duties or responsibilities as in the duty code of 2:11–3:12, for there also one hears of ministry within the community and of mutual responsibilities and concern. Again the author speaks of the themes of suffering and glory, of imitation, of Jesus' final revelation, and of proper mind-set. Structurally the passage addresses first the presbyters or elders who are exhorted to proper care of the flock (vv. 1-4), then the younger members who are reminded of their duty toward the elders (v. 5a), and finally the whole community, which is to "clothe (it)self with humility" (v. 5b). Also, the passage bears some of the structural features and terminology of the earlier duty code.

In historical terms the major concern of many interpreters has been the assessment of data concerning early ecclesial structures. Thus they have focused on the passage's terminology, particularly *presbyteros* or "elder" as a technical term derived from Jewish tradition (as used in the Gospels) to designate a defined ministry in the community (see Acts 20:17; Titus 1:5; 2 John 1). In such usage they see a relatively well-developed ecclesial structure, a conclusion that is further indicated by other ministerial imagery and terminology: pastoral images (tending the flock, shepherd) and qualifications (regarding compulsion and greed) and the added concept of "overseer" (*episkopeo*—a textual variant).

From the above it is then concluded that the elders of vv. 1-5 are official ministers who exert leadership over individual communities and whose duties are here described in pastoral terms as "tending to God's flock." Beyond this, scholars employ these data in relation to other NT traditions to discern 1 Peter's position in the development of ecclesiastical structures. It is postulated that two basic types of community governance evolved within the church: a charismatic model that relied on ministerial functions or gifts (associated with the Pauline communities: Rom 12:18; 1 Cor 12:28) and an institutional model whose leadership was given to individuals or groups of elders (Acts 14:23; Jas 5:14). These scholars variously classify 1 Pet 5:1-5 as a model of the latter, as a later combination of the two types (accepting the variant reading of v. 2: "overseeing"—see also Acts 20:17; Titus 1:5), or Petrine usage more generally as reflecting both models (4:7-11 addressed to the first type and 5:1-5 to the second type).

Finally attention is given to the role that this passage, with its ministerial concerns and references to the author, plays in 1 Peter's paraenetic strategy. It is usually proposed that by assuming not only the office of apostle but also that of elder (*sympresbyteros*), the writer is able to legitimate the offices and authority of those being addressed and thereby to insist on proper order within the communities. The authority both of the author and of the elders would ultimately derive from Christ himself (see also Acts 20:28).

In turning to literary and thematic concerns one is quickly led to consider important objections to such conclusions. Perhaps the most basic problem is the assumption that *presbyteros* is a technical term for church office since its counterpart in the code structure of v. 5 is a term (*neoteros*: "younger") that cannot refer to an office but that must designate age (see discussion below); at best some scholars see the former as indicating both office and age. Moreover if one concludes that *episkopeo* of v. 2 is a later scribal expansion (see below), then there is even less reason for choosing the above line of interpretation.

In anticipation of the commentary the following observations are in order. Though various elements in vv. 2-4 clearly suggest that elders exercise leadership roles (shepherd imagery, themes of finance and reward, association of the elders with the writer), it is nonetheless the issue of age that governs the whole passage: older as opposed to younger members. The entire community is addressed concerning the responsibilities of its older members as ministers and models of fellow believers and the relationship of these to the community's younger members. Indeed all must adopt a proper mind-set in fostering mutual relations. Just as 1 Peter in 4:7-11 has discussed inter-community activity and behavior by schematically speaking of Christian activity as consisting either of speaking or serving (4:11), so here the community's membership is seen as consisting of older and younger members, whose responsibilities and needs vary considerably. The author's concern is not about positions of authority but with the proper inner workings of the community as its members face conflicts with their pagan neighbors. Those who, by virtue of their seniority in age and faith, exercise "stewardship of God's manifold grace" (4:10), are reminded that they are sharers, with the writer, in Christ's suffering and future glory and in their turn are to be models for those whom they serve. "In like manner" those thus served are to recognize their duty toward others who both follow in Christ's footsteps and act as his shepherds vis-à-vis God's flock. The contrast then between the terms *presbyteros* and *neoteros*, as demanded by the passage's code structure, points to the broader issue of the proper use of gifts or *charismata* within the community in view of divine judgment that begins even now with God's house. Indeed the passage, after underscoring the humble example of Christ as it affects all believers (apostles, leaders, community), closes on the theme of God's opposition to the arrogant and mercy to the humble (citation of Prov 3:34). Also it should be noted that the author's choice of terminology in 2:18 ("household members"), in 3:1-7 ("women/men" of the household), and 5:1-5 ("elder/younger members") reflects social-structural concerns, namely, household relations, gender concerns, and issues of seniority as providing the dynamics for Christian duty both toward outsiders and community members.

This section of 1 Peter consists of three grammatical units of varying lengths. The first, greater part (vv. 1-4) concerns elders and, in thematic and literary terms, forms a unified whole. Verse 1 consists of an extended, complex exhortation formula; vv. 2-3 are given to a lengthy imperative construction concerning the shepherding of God's flock; and v. 4 provides eschatological motivation in a concluding, paratactic statement. The second unit (v. 5a) is a brief exhortation addressed, in a manner similar to the code structure of 3:1 and 7, to the younger members of the community regarding their duty toward elders. The final unit (v. 5b) addresses once more the entire community and focuses on the theme of humility as the believer's proper mind-set before God.

Admonition to Elders (5:1-4)

The section addressed to the community elders is closely connected to the preceding by the conjunction "therefore" (*oun*) and so recalls the theme of judgment beginning with "the house of God." This connection also suggests the influence of Ezek 9:6 where God's judgment is said to begin with the elders of God's house (see discussion of 4:17). In light of this one should see the entire section on community duty as related to the themes of divine judgment and trust in "a faithful creator." Not only are elders being exhorted to proper pastoral care within the community, but also they are being reminded that this activity is under divine scrutiny.

The author introduces this extended exhortation with a lengthy, complex formula (v. 1). The governing term is the verb *parakaleo* ("exhort"), which also appears in 2:11; again its usage contrasts with other NT occurrences (see earlier discussion) and reveals 1 Peter's unique style and concerns. Here also 1 Peter favors a formal paraenetic introduction, employing the verb *parakaleo*, to underscore a subsequent imperative construction. Also of interest in each case is the author's attempt to situate the formula in its thematic context. In 2:11 the expression "as resident aliens and religious exiles" is added as an introduction to the extensive duty code concerning social-political and religious relations between Christian and non-Christian neighbors in Roman society. In 5:1 it is the double theme of Christ's suffering and consequent glory that is applied to give thematic context to the following imperative concerning appropriate pastoral ministry. The exhortation formula (also in 2:11), in a manner similar to the author's frequent use elsewhere of initial participial constructions (see discussion of 1:13f), provides texture and draws full attention to the paraenetic or subsequent imperative construction.

What then are the major themes and concerns of this introductory formula? From an early point one notes the author's elaborate self-designation: "fellow elder and witness of Christ's sufferings" and "sharer in (eschatological) glory." What is the meaning of these three terms, and what is their function in this paraenetic section of the letter? The first term *sympresbyteros* appears here for the first time in Greek literature and seemingly is an ad-hoc formulation similar to "fellow worker" or "fellow servant" (Rom 16:3; Matt

18:28) to establish a connection, on one level, between the writer and the groups within the community designated as "elders." While one could, in trying to understand this passage, appeal to later Patristic usage that interchanges the terms "apostle, disciple, and presbyter" to designate Jesus' early followers, one would still have to explain, in relation to 1 Pet 5:1, Luke's use of "elder" to distinguish a given group of leaders from the original disciples (Acts 11:30; 14:23; 15:2f). One probably needs to see the term "elder" as designating leadership in the early church (see earlier discussion) and view Luke, in theological terms, as anxious to isolate apostleship from general-church leadership and 1 Peter, in diplomatic or strategic terms, as intending the opposite. The author, while claiming to be Peter (1:1), nonetheless wishes to underscore a common bond of leadership or service within the community, a position that relates, in part, to seniority in faith. The second term *martys* refers not to martyrdom nor even to the claim of being an eyewitness but rather to the writer and addressees' roles as witnesses or bearers in word and behavior of Jesus' sufferings (BAGD 494.2c). Indeed the author's paratactic construction (*kai* and *ho* connecting "fellow elder" and "witness") implies that one should also read "fellow witness." The third term *ho . . . koinonos* ("one who shares") not only reiterates and further stresses the concept of common participation by all involved but also refers back to 4:15 where innocent sufferers are said to "share in Christ's suffering." Thus all three self-designations are terms of strategy that allow empathetic (the writer's personal involvement) yet catholic (the reality of all believers) treatment of the themes of suffering and glory. The author, like those being addressed, has responsibilities of leadership and like them, and all believers, is one who shares both Christ's sufferings and, already in the present (see 4:14), his glory, though it is a heavenly reality that is yet to be fully revealed. The author's self-designation, here as in 1:1 (see discussion of apostle as "one sent by Christ"), relates to the letter's paraenetic strategy; the author in offering advice to community leaders speaks from common experience and shared expectations.

Prominent also in this introductory formula is the dual theme of suffering and glory (see discussion of 1:11), whose introduction at this point serves several functions. Not only does the passage enhance the quality of the advice given by drawing a close connection between the writer's and community's experience of suffering and glory, but also it further stresses that innocent suffering should be no surprise (4:12) since both the writer and other believers experience the same kinds of suffering (5:9). Not only are suffering and consequent glory a common experience and anticipation of believers everywhere, but also they are especially related to service or leadership within the community, for presbyters are to be a "model for the flock" (5:3) like the suffering, gentle Christ (2:22-23) and are to be motivated by the promise of receiving "the unfading crown of glory" from the chief shepherd for their generous labors as shepherds of God's flock (5:2-4).

A final area of concern in discussing the introductory formula is the fact that a particular group within the community is addressed. Also important in this regard is the manner of address: "I exhort those who are elders among you." In structural terms vv. 1-5 are usually classified as a duty code, though 1 Peter does not use direct address as in 2:11–3:12 or in 5:5. Further no article is used with "elders" (this is true also of v. 5), and the author wishes to emphasize "among you" (*en hymin* is employed both in vv. 1 and 2). From these various clues one suspects that the author is less interested in ecclesial offices than in the well-being of the flock and its members as they encounter outside pressures. Indeed the communal terminology of the following verses ("flock of God," "allotted portions," "flock," and "all of you in your relations with each other") confirm such a conclusion. Those who are being counseled are those who, in Christian terms, are at the service of the members of the flock. Finally the author's address of "all of you" in v. 5b confirms this observation; it is the community and the well-being of its members that are foremost in the author's mind.

The advice given to the elders does in fact focus on proper pastoral behavior, a theme that is developed in vv. 2-3 in the form of a lengthy imperative construction whose second half consists of three successive "not/but" contrasts. The principal imagery here is that of "shepherding a flock" (*poimaino to poimnion*; see Isa 40:11; Jer 6:18; Mic 5:4). Similar imagery is employed in current literature for the Messiah (*PssSol* 17:40) and God's ministers (CD 13:7-12; Acts 20:28; see also John 21:15-17 and *1 Clement* 44:3; 54:2). Its use in 1 Peter seems formulaic and reflects the early Jesus tradition (Mark 6:34; 14:27; Matt 18:10-14 and Luke 15:4-7; Matt 10:6—see *TDNT* 6:487-90), where the figure of the shepherd implies safety, protection, and nurture. In the present case the term seemingly has a generic sense and envisions the overall activity of those in positions of leadership as analogous to the care and activity of shepherds (see further comments on the "chief shepherd" of v. 4). Additionally use of the aorist imperative, presumably a complexive-terminative type (BDF 337.2), underscores an activity that is to last until Christ's return. The terminology suggests the full scope of pastoral activity within the community, here described as "God's flock."

On the one hand, this traditional pastoral imagery further underscores the theological focus of the author, because although Christ is the chief shepherd (v. 4) and others act as his shepherds, the flock belongs to God. In this way 1 Peter recalls the long section on God's people (2:1-10) and the theme of new birth from an imperishable generation (1:3, 23). Also the fact that the leaders are tending "God's flock" brings specificity to the injunction; they are to provide for the flock what God wishes and to support it in accomplishing God's desires, whether this concerns protection, holy or honorable conduct, being built into God's house or people, honoring all, loving fellow believers, fearing God, and returning to their shepherd and guardian —in short, living according to God's will (4:2; see 1:5, 15-16, 22; 2:5, 9, 12, 17; 3:8; 5:10). On the other hand, the expression "in your midst" or "in your care" (*en hymin*) suggests a multiplicity of communities with their own leaders who are to focus on their "allotted portions" (see v. 3). The "flock of God" here refers to the general church and so those bearing responsibilities are reminded of their duties toward specific members of God's universal community (see the author's formulation of this concept in 5:9—the "brotherhood throughout the world").

There begins in v. 2b a series of "not/but" contrasts that deal with pastoral behavior. Before tackling these, however, it is necessary to discuss briefly a striking textual variant. While the majority of manuscripts read *episkopountes* ("being an overseer") prior to the series of contrasts, such important witnesses as B S* 33 and others omit this term. One could defend the former, longer text by appealing to the letter's tendency to expand imperative constructions with participial modifiers (see 1:17f) as well as its previous combination of shepherd-overseer imagery (2:25). By the same token one could appeal to these reasons to support scribal activity as resulting from exegetical expansion (see *TCGNT* 695-96). In this case it is probably preferable to opt for the latter, shorter text as being original and to view the longer version as owing to scribal activity and reflecting later ecclesial development (i.e., the added term would have a technical meaning: "to serve as overseer or bishop," as in later Christian literature).

If I am correct in omitting the expression "being an overseer," then the series of contrasts are intended as a commentary on the leadership's pastoral task. The first two consist of contrasting negative and positive adverbs and the third of antithetical participial constructions, the goal of each being to present negative approaches or abuses and to contrast these to ideal characteristics of pastoral care. Interestingly the directives concern not specific tasks but the manner in which pastoral care is to be carried out. The first pair contrasts relatively unusual terms: *anagkastos*, which refers to "compulsion" of a physical, metaphysical, or legal type (LSJ 100-1), and *hekousios*, which points to "willingness" or spontaneity (Heb 10:26). What exactly the author has in mind is hard to discern, though one probably should view the first as underscoring lack of freedom and so a type of "sad or begrudging necessity" and the second as stressing a joyful willingness to be at God's service without grumbling (see 4:9; cf. also Phlm 14). Also one should note the author's insistence, following the second term, that this "willingness" be "as God would have it" (*kata theon*; for the textual problem, see *TCGNT*, 696; see also 4:6). The freedom involved here, as in 2:16, derives from one's relationship to God and not from the compulsion of legal or social obligation incumbent on elected or chosen leaders and ministers.

The second pair contrasts another series of unusual terms: *aischrokerdos*, which relates to financial gain as motive for service, and *prothymos*, which underscores a theme similar to that of the second term in the first pair, namely, "willingness, goodwill, or eagerness." The first of these, though usually indicating "illegal gain," here seems to stress "the love of money" or reward as the reason for performing ministerial tasks (see also 1 Tim 3:8; Titus 1:7). Clearly such a statement presumes some monetary support for community work and at the same time points to abuses within the early church (see Acts 20:33; 1 Thess 2:5). In contrast to such unworthy motivation the author proposes eagerness for service as worthy of those charged with leadership and ministry within the community.

The third pair (v. 3), in a more complex manner, contrasts community ministry as the wielding of power, on the one hand, with service as the embodiment of humility and therefore as a model for others, on the other. In the place of adverbs the author employs contrasting participial constructions introduced by the particle *hos* once more to indicate a manner of acting. The first verb *katakyrieuo* indicates the use of power to rule over unwilling subjects. Such usage occurs in the LXX (Gen 1:28; Ps 118:133) and probably is derived by the author from its striking and suggestive use in the Jesus tradition (Mark 10:42; Matt 20:25). It is sometimes maintained that, owing to the letter's positive attitude toward contemporary secular culture, it is unlikely 1 Peter is contrasting secular power to Christian service as does Mark. On the contrary the term used indicates precisely what Christian ministry is not to be, that is, an attempt "to lord it over those in their charge." The term employed to express the object is *kleros*, a word that originally meant "lot or that which is assigned by lot" but here probably refers to that part of the flock to which various ministers are assigned (BAGD 435.2), that is, "your allotted portions." One suspects here a pointed reference to early abuses within the community whereby leaders appealed to divinely sanctioned roles as the basis for abusing rather than "tending God's flock." Indeed the parallel participial construction, as complemented by the theme of humility in v. 5, confirms this interpretation. The elders or those to whom ministerial functions are allotted are instead to "become models (*typoi*) for the flock." Though at this point the author does not explain the statement, it is clear from earlier comments that ministry is to be equated with service and that such service is made possible by the strength or grace that God gives to the humble (4:11; 5:5b). No doubt the author has in mind also the self-giving service of Christ (who is to be an "example"—*hypogrammon*) who sought not self-interest but the healing of others that they might live for righteousness (2:23-24).

Verses 2-3 therefore are an attempt on the author's part to characterize what is meant by "tending God's flock." In negative terms leadership, ministry, and stewardship are not to be motivated by a fateful sense of duty, or financial gain, or a love for power or control but, in positive terms, by a spirit of willing, eager, and self-effacing service that seeks God's glorification through Jesus Christ (4:11b). Service of community members and their needs in time of suffering is of primary concern to the author.

Finally in v. 4 an intriguing eschatological motive is given for encouraging proper pastoral behavior and activity. Reinforcing the original pastoral imagery of v. 2 and clarifying the nature of Christian authority (see also 2:25), the author characterizes Jesus as the "chief shepherd," thereby underscoring the role, responsibilities, and proper behavior expected of Christ's assistant shepherds. In this way 1 Peter delineates the full range of Christian authority: God as owner of the flock and Christ as chief shepherd doing God's work with the assistance of elders who act as guardians and minsters of the flock. Further stressing Christ's role, the author indicates once again that Christ is in heaven (3:22) and will be "made visible or manifested" (*phaneroo*; see 1:20; also Col 3:4) at the end when he will bestow a reward on his faithful assistants who will "receive" or "be awarded" (*komizo*; see 1:9; also 2 Cor 5:10; Eph 6:8) not "perishable silver or gold" (see v. 2) but "the unfading crown of glory" conferred on victors in the Greco-Roman world.

Description of the victor's crown or wreath (*TDNT* 7:629-31) as being "unfading" and "of glory" calls for comment. On the one hand, the first term *amarantinos*, like its synonyms in 1:4, underscores the eternal, otherworldly character of this reward, but here as a modifier of *stephanos* or "wreath" it possibly connotes "blossoming" (i.e., "a wreath of amaranthus"—see BAGD 42). On the other hand, by qualifying this reward as participating in "glory," 1 Peter refers to its heavenly, incorruptible character and draws a connection between the community's present suffering and its presbyters' sharing with Christ in future glory (see *T.Benjamin* 4:1; 1 Cor 9:25).

Admonition to Younger Members (5:5a)

The author turns in a more formal way to a code structure ("in like manner," direct address, use of the verb *hypotasso*—see 2:13f) to exhort a group called *neoteroi* or "those who are younger." The first expression, "in like manner" (*homoios*), as in its earlier use in 3:1 and 7, reiterates that the motivation cited for proper behavior as regards the elders applies to the new group addressed: they too are exhorted as sharers in Christ's suffering and glory (5:1); they too are to behave *kata theon* ("as God would have it"—2b); and, by implication, they are to imitate those whose service is modeled on that of the obedient Christ.

The new group being addressed is clearly a counterpart in terms of age to the earlier group called elders. There is ample evidence in the Pastorals for distinguishing groups, whether men and women, according to age and to address them in paraenetic discourse (1 Tim 5:1-2, 17; Titus 2:2-6; see also 1 QS 2:20-23; *1 Clement* 3:3). Since, however, it seems that the "elders" of vv. 1-4 are readily associated with positions of responsibility, authority, and ministry and since there are indications both that ministers were chosen from the earliest converts (1 Cor 16:15-16) and that positions of authority were not readily offered to recent converts (1 Tim 3:6), it would seem that the group of younger members would indicate more recent converts. Neither in vv. 1-4 nor in v. 5a does one get the impression that the "elders and younger members" constitute the entire community; seemingly they are two groups within the community that are singled out, prior to the general exhortation of 5b, for special consideration.

Finally the author's injunction to the younger members is brief and to the point: "recognize your duty (*hypotasso*) toward those who are presbyters" (in your midst). Use of this verb clearly indicates that the author wishes the reader to view this passage as a continuation or, better still, as a parallel to the earlier duty code (see 2:13 for discussion of this term). Here also it is doubtful that 1 Peter counsels submission, subordination, or obedience of the younger members to elders (even interpreted in a technical sense). Instead the younger members are to "recognize their duty" toward those who minister, those who deserve greater honor, or require assistance. One could view this duty in sociological and in ministerial terms. From the sociological viewpoint one could cite 1 Tim 5:1-2 as reflecting the duty of younger men and women toward the older and younger fellow believers:

> Do not speak harshly to an older man, but speak to him as to a father, to younger men as brothers, to older women as mothers, to younger women as sisters—with absolute purity.

Beyond this one could refer also to v. 17 where "elders who rule well" are said to "be worthy of double honor" (or compensation). In ministerial or functional terms younger members of the community or more recent converts are enjoined presumably to respect the elders as "stewards of the manifold grace of God" (4:10), gifts that have the community's service in view and God's glorification as the goal. Recent converts owe honor to those who "tend God's flock" as well as love since they too are members of "the brotherhood" (2:17). Additionally they are to recognize the elders' status as shepherds who model their lives on that of the chief shepherd and in their turn present themselves as models to the rest of the flock. One can only surmise how this injunction relates to the issue of the community's conflict with pagan neighbors. Whether it is the younger members who are surprised at the conflict (4:12) or who seek confrontation rather than gentle dialogue (3:14-16), it is nonetheless the assistant shepherds who are called upon to be models, like Christ, of nonretaliation, confidence, and support. The younger members, "in like manner," will be likewise motivated by the promise of eschatological glory. Last of all it might be noted that 1 Peter's use of *presbyteros* in v. 5a without the article suggests that the injunction to the younger members does not include the rest of the community (i.e., those who are not elders) but rather addresses those in the community who are relatively recent converts.

General Admonition to Humility (5:5b)

The final subunit of the community duty code not only pursues a definite code structure but also bears striking structural and thematic similarity to the conclusion of the earlier code. Both, in their final injunction, address the entire community ("all of you"—*pantes*), focus on mutual concern (unity, love, etc. vs "in your dealings with one another"), offer a participial or imperatival exhortation, and conclude with a *hoti* construction, which in the first case introduces a conclusion and a closing OT citation (3:9-12) and in the second case presents another OT citation as explanation of the injunction (5:5b). The concluding sections of the two codes then have the community's well being in mind, particularly its mutual relationships. In the first conclusion the author addresses the relations of believers and unbelievers both in the injunction and its concluding OT citation and in the second the issue of both injunction and OT citation is the community's mind-set involving mutual as well as divine relations.

The final injunction concerns all members of the community, including elders and younger believers, and involves mutual relations. In dealing with one another (*allelois*) the addressees are advised: "clothe yourselves with humility"; there then follows a citation of Prov 3:34 as justification for the injunction. Discussion then of this final exhortation can proceed in three parts: examination of the dressing imagery, of the relation between humility and community concerns, and of the form and function of the OT citation.

Though 1 Peter favors dressing or garment imagery (see 1:13 for "girding one's loins" or 4:1 for "arming oneself"), the terminology employed is nonetheless relatively rare in each instance. In place of the more frequent *endyo* for "putting on garments" or for "arming oneself," whether literally or metaphorically (see Mark 1:6; 6:9; Rom 13:12; 1 Cor 15:53; 1 Thess 5:8), the author employs the rare verb *egkomboomai*, which is derived from a common garment usually worn by slaves and so gives the meaning "binding oneself with" or "wearing constantly" (LSJ 473; BAGD 216). Its use here with "humility" (though see Col 3:12, which uses the more traditional verb) supports the servant interpretation that follows; namely, believers are servants of God and fellow servants of one another, a theme that is suggested by the clothing imagery and humility terminology employed.

The addressees are admonished to clothe themselves "with humility" (*tapeinophrosyne*), a theme that already appears in 3:8 in a discussion of the believer's mind-set as it relates to mutual concerns. There, without further explanation, the author insists that "oneness of mind" and "humble mindedness" are key factors in fostering a community where "sympathy, mutual love, and compassion" can flourish. Why, there as here, the insistence on humility as well as mutual concern when the former seemingly refers, in the Judeo-Christian tradition, to the human-divine relationship and, in Hellenistic society, to a servile or lowly status? Though the *tapeinos* word family was generally employed in a negative or disparaging sense by Greeks, its use by some writers to express obedience to the gods or true estimate of one's status probably led the LXX translators and other Hellenistic Jews to employ the word group to describe the human creature's right relation to or dependence on God (see *TDNT* 8:1-15). Thus for both Jewish and Christian writers "humility" addresses human-divine relations (a point that is borne out by 5:6-7) and the human need for salvation not relations between humans. The call therefore to make humility the standard of one's relationship to others is a striking one. While some have suggested that the author envisions service of other believers as requiring self-abasement (as in Mark 10:44-45—the one who is "the slave of all" or Jesus who girds himself to serve the disciples in John 13:4) or community problems as encountered by humility or viewing the interests of others first (Phil 2:3-4), it seems better to seek the important connection made here between humility and community life in the author's anthropology. As creatures of a faithful creator, believers owe honor to God's human creatures, love to fellow believers, as well as reverent fear to God (2:13-17), an attitude that is expressed in recognizing one's position or relation to God and therefore toward others (see also 3:8). Humility in 5:5b is the recognition of one's relation to God's other creatures. As God's servants, believers must use their freedom to honor and love, in short, to foster a loving relationship within the community of believers (2:16; 3:8; 5:5b).

The concluding text consists of a verbatim citation of Prov 3:34—only the original subject *kyrios* has been changed to *ho theos* (see also Jas 4:6). The OT text serves both as a conclusion to the subunit by discoursing on humility as a divinely approved mind-set and as a source for the major themes of the following section (humility as relation to God, opposition of the arrogant, and God's grace to believers).

First, the modification of the subject reemphasizes the document's consistent theocentric emphasis. Second, the citation's use of the categories "arrogant" and "humble" allows, initially, a ready identification of believers and their opponents as those, respectively, who receive God's favor or opposition. On the one hand, the term "arrogant" (*hyperephanos*) suggests opposition to God (see Mark 7:22 where it, along with blasphemy and folly, forms part of a trio of vices aimed at God) or, in the terms of 1 Peter, presumably those who are disobedient (2:8; 3:1, 22; 4:17; also 2:7), who live in "forbidden idolatry" (4:3), and oppose God's people (2:12; 3:13-16). On the other hand, the humble are the obedient (1:14, 22; 2:66-67) who address God as father and judge (1:17), who live in reverent fear before God (1:7; 2:17), and as servants of that faithful creator exercise their freedom by doing good and rendering honor to other human creatures (2:13-17) and by showing love, hospitality, and service vis-à-vis the family of believers (1:22; 2:17; 3:8; 4:8-11). Nonetheless it is the theme of humility that is of interest to the author (see further development in vv. 6-7); the theme of arrogance fits the situation less well since the hostile Greco-Roman neighbors are more readily described in less-severe terms as ignorant or foolish doers of evil who are given to sin and excess (1:14; 2:12, 15; 3:8, 10-12, 16; 4:3-4, 18—see discussion of the term "opponent" in 5:8). Third, appeal to the authority of the Scriptures underscores the importance of humility as the divinely-sanctioned mind-set that fosters mutual love among believers. Humility in one's dealings with other believers is enjoined because the creator, who expects trust, reverent fear, and holiness from human creatures (1:15-17, 21; 2:17), rejects the proud ("opposes the arrogant") as judge and showers the obedient with blessings ("gives grace to the humble") as father (see treatment of these themes below).

The duty code of 5:1-5 offers a marked contrast to that of 2:11–3:12. While both codes are addressed to the entire community, the earlier one focuses on situations between believers and nonbelievers that cause problems, and the present text deals with issues that concern the community itself. In the former the basis for resolving conflicts with outsiders is found in the respect creatures owe one another; in the latter it is found similarly in the humble recognition of one's relation to God as creature and to other believers as "being born anew . . . of imperishable generation" (1:23) and therefore all as children of a merciful God. This concept of humility as demanding equal honor and mutual love among God's children is further evidence of 1 Peter's refreshingly-positive anthropology and optimism vis-à-vis the church's ability to resolve its social problems. Indeed the author's call to older and younger members to recognize their respective duties in light of their common parentage speaks both of critical problems within the community in times of suffering and of an author's insightful paraenesis to addressees who are surprised at the fiery ordeal they are experiencing. Finally the closing citation from Prov 3:34, particularly its insistence that "God . . . gives grace to the humble," lays the groundwork for the concluding assurance that "the God of all grace" will sustain the community in its short-lived suffering (5:10).

Suggested Readings

Cothenet, E. "La première épître de Pierre" in *Le ministère et les ministères selon le NT.* Ed., J. Delorme. Paris: Declée, 1974, 138-52.

Elliott, J. H. "Ministry and Church Order in the New Testament: A Traditio-Historical Analysis (1 Pt 5,1-5 and Parallels)." *CBQ* 32 (1970) 367-91.

Hiebert, D. E. "Counsel for Christ's Undershepherds: An Exposition of 1 Peter 5:1-14." *BS* 139:556 (1982) 330-41.

Michl, J. "Die Presbyter des ersten Petrusbriefes" in *Ortskirche, Weltkirche.* Ed., H. Fleckenstein. Würzburg: Echter, 1973, 48-62.

Nauck, W. "Probleme des frühchristlichen Amtsverständnisses (1 Petr 5,2f)." *ZNTW* 48 (1957) 200-20.

Osborne, R. P. "L'utilization des citations de l'Ancien Testament dans la première épître de Pierre." *RTL* 12 (1981) 64-77.

Philipps, K. *Kirche in der Gesellschaft nach dem 1. Petrusbrief.* Gütersloh: Gerd Mohn, 1971.

Prostmeier, F. R. *Handlungsmodelle im ersten Petrusbrief.* Würzburg: Echter, 1990.

Schlosser, J. "Ancien Testament et christologie dans la Prima Petri" in *Etudes,* 65-96.

Spicq, C. "La place ou le rôle des jeunes dans certaines communautés néotestamentaires." *RB* 76 (1969) 508-27.

Closing Exhortation
(5:6-11)

The third major block of material in 1 Peter (4:12–5:11) is brought to a close by a brief, final exhortation that ends in a second, shortened doxology. This new subunit pursues the closing theme of the previous discussion, addresses further the community's suffering, and reassures the addressees once more of God's assistance and support. This unit opens and closes (vv. 6, 10) on the theme of divine care for those who are suffering, reassuring them that God will exalt them and give them glory.

While some scholars have proposed uniting vv. 5b-11 to what precedes, owing to the earlier treatment of humility and the address in v. 5b of the entire community (as opposed to the prior exhortations of elders and younger members), it seems best to posit a break between vv. 5 and 6. In this way the OT citation serves as a conclusion to the previous subunit, introduced as a *hoti* clause (see earlier discussion), and provides the themes around which the present exhortation is built. Additionally this unit as well as the previous one (5:1-5) are introduced by the inferential conjunction *oun* ("therefore"—see also 2:1; 4:1, 7). Also the unit opens on the theme of God's "mighty (*krataios*) hand" (v. 6) and closes on that of God's "dominion" (*kratos*—v. 11). Thus vv. 6-11 form a coherent unit in thematic and structural terms: vv. 6-7 reiterate the theme of humility as human dependence on God, vv. 8-9 direct attention to the arrogant opposition hinted at in the earlier citation, v. 10 returns more explicitly to the theme of grace noted at the end of the OT citation, and v. 11 brings the unit to a close in the form of divine praise.

Before proceeding with an analysis of the text it seems necessary briefly to consider the author's source and composition, especially since, on the one hand, several of the themes here discussed bear some resemblance to Jas 4:6-10 and, on the other, the present passage contains a number of disparate images whose sources are quite diverse. Indeed the text of James cites the same OT passage from Prov 3:34 (with the same change of subject: *ho theos* for *kyrios*) and along with it introduces the themes of grace, resisting the devil, humbling oneself before the Lord, and the promise of divine exaltation. The similarity is indeed striking, though the use the two authors make of this citation and the themes noted are also considerably different. In James the theme of grace serves as an introduction to the OT citation, while in 1 Peter it is that of humility that elicits a reference to the Jewish Scriptures. Additionally the two NT authors develop the themes in very different ways. Seemingly both have borrowed from a common paraenetic tradition, associated with the use of Prov 3:34, that dealt with submission to

God and resistance to the devil. Beyond this one should see 1 Peter's use of this paraenetic tradition in conjunction with other OT imagery (such as "God's mighty hand" and the "roaring lion") and themes from the Jesus tradition (about worrying and staying awake) to compose a final exhortation to a suffering community. In fact the passage ends (v. 10) on a familiar paraenetic note promising divine comfort and support. Verses 6-11 present a well-structured exhortation to the communities of Asia Minor who are reminded that other Christians are undergoing similar sufferings and that "the God of all grace . . . will restore (them) by making (them) firm, strong, and established" (v. 10) in their time of need.

Humility as Dependence on God (5:6-7)

The new injunction is introduced by "therefore" to underscore the connection between the two subunits, particularly the statement from Prov 3:34 on humility and the new exhortation to submit to God's care and protection. In grammatical terms the unit consists of an imperative construction followed by a *hina* clause and a familiar modifying participial statement, which in its turn is followed by a *hoti* clause. This relatively complex structure presents a number of themes whose function and interpretation are variously understood, whether it is the meaning of humility in this verse as it relates to its use in the injunction of v. 5b, the function of the word pair "humble-exalt" in v. 6a, the interpretation of *kairos* or "time" in v. 6b, or the relation of v. 6 on humility and exaltation to v. 7 on "casting . . . (one's) worries on (God)."

The overall interpretation of this paraenetic subunit depends seemingly on a number of considerations. From the outset it is clear that the theme of humility has a different focus in the injunctions of vv. 5b and 6a. In the first case the theme underscores mutual relations between fellow believers who, as children of God, owe each other respect, service, and mutual love; in the second case the theme points to the believer's proper, trusting relationship to God as creator and giver of new life. Thus the use of this theme in the two injunctions agrees with the overall emphasis of their respective contexts— 5:1-5 concerning community issues, conduct, and mutual treatment and 5:6-11 concerning the (suffering) believer's relationship to a God who cares and promises support (vv. 6, 10).

The antithetical word pair "humiliate or humble oneself" and "exalt" (*tapeinoo* and *hypsoo*, respectively) appears frequently in the OT to express the proverbial reversal of roles: the humiliation of the exalted and the exaltation of the lowly (1 Kgs 2:7-8; Isa 2:11). It is likewise employed in the Jesus tradition in the following formula: "all who exalt themselves will be humbled and those who humble themselves will be exalted" (Luke 14:11; 18:14; Matt 23:12; see also Luke 1:52). It is presumably from such usage that the paraenetic construction found here (humiliation and the promise of exaltation) in 1 Peter and Jas 4:10 arose: "humble yourselves . . . you may/will be exalted." For James the word pair illustrates how "double-minded" humans might gain a true sense of themselves, that is, humble recognition of their creature status vis-à-vis God. In the case of 1 Peter the antithetical pair allows the author the opportunity to discuss the addressees' situation in terms of trust in God's power and grace, for "humbling oneself" here means submission to God's power and care and believing in the promise of future exaltation.

The expression *en kairo* is variously rendered: in an indefinite way ("in due or at the appropriate time") or in an eschatological sense ("in the last time"). The latter is admittedly interpretive because the text reads literally: "in time." It is maintained, however, that the phrase is synonymous for "in the last time" of 1:5 and other expressions that allude to the parousia (1:7, 13; 4:7; 5:4). Thus v. 6 would be a statement of eschatological motivation. It is here suggested that the author is intentionally vague to express the optimism that, after a while (see v. 10), there will be a change in the community's fortune; God "will exalt you in due time." Such an interpretation will be borne out by discussion of v. 10 below and by consideration more generally of the author's optimistic expectations for Christian-Gentile relations.

Finally we might consider the interpretation of v. 7 and its relation to v. 6. The theme of not worrying because God provides for the future presumably derives from the Jesus tradition that recalls Jesus' teaching against anxiety (Matt 6:25-34; Luke 12:22-31). While both the theme of not worrying and that of divine care ("your Father knows that you need them") probably find their source in Jesus' teaching, their precise formulation has been suggested by the author's use of LXX idiom: Ps 54:23 ("cast your care on the Lord") for v. 7a and Wis 12:13 ("who cares for all") for 7b—this is further evidence to postulate an author who makes frequent meditative and pastoral use of the Jewish Scriptures. The author's meaning is quite clear: believers are to cast their every care on the merciful and caring God who provides what is needed. It is in light of this claim that one is to read the antithetical word pair ("humble-exalt") of v. 6. Humbling oneself under God's mighty hand (for the image, see Exod 3:19; 6:1; Deut 9:26; Jer 21:5) is not an image for submission to God's judgment (as in 4:19—see preceding verses) but rather the acknowledgment of God's dominion (see also vv. 10-11) and the promise of future exaltation. Humility is therefore the creature's submission and casting of all worry on a loving creator. Verses 6-7 therefore act as parallel statements concerning the believer's relation to God and provide the basis for Christian behavior and perseverance that rely on God's promise to "give grace to the humble" (v. 5c, citing Prov 3:34), for God is a creator and parent who cares.

Resistance against Arrogant Opposition (5:8-9)

The author now turns to a theme suggested by the OT citation of v. 5c, namely, that "God opposes the arrogant." In this way the author returns to the pressing issue of the community's suffering and the vigilance required for its survival. In the midst of a series of imperatives that offer some final advice, one encounters either the surprising identification of the community's opposition as satanic in character or the seemingly unique mention of the devil in the letter. At the same time one hears of universal Christian suffering.

The Opponent. In v. 8b 1 Peter introduces a character called the "opponent" (*antidikos*), a term that originally designated a legal opponent but that came more generally to signify any opposition. In its present context all legal overtones are gone (*TDNT* 1:374); instead the author focuses on its satanic character. Readers may be surprised at this direction in the author's thought because the Christians' sufferings have been seemingly laid at the feet of Gentile opponents or neighbors (2:12; 4:3) who are variously described as nonbelievers (2:6-7; 3:1), who are disobedient (2:8; 4:17), immersed in ignorance (1:14) and excesses of vice (4:4); they are identified also as the proud whom God opposes (5:5), a non-people (2:10) who malign, abuse (2:12; 3:9, 16; 4:14), demand answers of believers (3:15), and generally who are ungodly, sinners (4:18) and doers of evil (3:12). Why then at this point, as scholars suggest, does the author characterize the community's opposition ("your") as a single opponent who is immediately identified as "the devil" (*diabolos*—the term corresponds to the Semitic *satan*: "accuser") and whose activity, as expressed in v. 8b, is anything but verbal abuse and social maltreatment? Even if one does not identify or closely associate the two why the introduction of the "devil-opponent" at this point?

There are in effect three clues in the letter that contribute to a discussion of this issue. Twice 1 Peter speaks of the Christian situation in Asia Minor as *peirasmos*, a term that means either "trial" or "temptation." In both cases (1:6-7; 4:12) the author chooses to speak of Christian suffering as "trials" or a testing by fire that forms part of God's plan. At this point, however, it is not unreasonable to suggest that 1 Peter refers back to the earlier hints that these sufferings are indeed "temptations" or even "enticements" (see 4:4) to believers to return to their earlier desires or conduct (1:14, 18, 22). Another element in the letter that might be considered in such a discussion is the author's repeated use of the term *epithymia* or "desire" as a human or carnal force that works in opposition to God's will (4:2) and sometimes "wages war against the soul" (2:11; see also 1:14). Though an explicit connection is never made between this satanic adversary and loyalty to human desires, it is clear that both they and the devil are at work against God's plan for believers; conformity to such desires is the opposite of obedience to God (1:14); submitting to the devil is the antithesis of perseverance in the faith (5:9). Christian life demands loyalty to God rather than to the adversary of faith or to those human desires that spring from idolatry (4:2-3). A third clue relates to 1 Peter's treatment of the "disobedient spirits" in 3:19, 22 (see earlier discussion). The adversary of 5:8 is to be seen as the leader of the evil spirits, descendants of the original rebellious beings, who now dwell on and within the earth, pursuing their immoral activity against God's obedient children.

From these various clues we must conclude that the author's intention is not an identification of the pagan neighbors with satanic forces but rather the discussion of the devil and the role it plays in the community's crisis (see further discussion in relation to v. 9). The choice of terminology in describing this opponent points to the major theme of the unit and assists the reader in grasping more fully the author's message. By referring to the adversary and by further characterizing it as the "devil," 1 Peter leaves no doubt that the figure intended is God's opponent. In a passage that begins and ends on the theme of God's almighty power (vv. 6, 11) it is significant that the author situates the battle for human loyalty in the cosmic context of the ultimate contest between good and evil. This otherworldly opponent is described, in the words of a psalm well known to the Christian community, "as a roaring lion" (Ps 21:14; see Mark 15:34 par) in search of prey. Choice of this imagery can be explained as the author's attempt, under the influence of the psalm cited, to characterize the addressees again as innocent sufferers, in the manner of the OT Psalmist or Jesus during his passion, at the hands of the unrighteous. Or else one might more correctly view the choice as owing to the author's desire to present God's rival as a masterful lion in control of its earthly kingdom, roaming about (*peripateo*) seeking its prey at will ("seeking [someone] to devour").

Finally it should be stated that 1 Peter joins other NT authors, particularly Paul (1 Thess 2:18; 3:3; 1 Cor 5:5; 7:5; 2 Cor 2:11), in insisting that the devil or supernatural adversary plays a role in thwarting the divine plan by tempting believers away from their allegiance or by destroying them. Like

Paul also (Rom 16:20), 1 Peter looks forward to God's ultimate victory and dominion (v. 11).

Exhortation to Vigilance and Resistance. Verse 8 opens with a double imperative: "be self-controlled; be watchful" (*nepho* and *gregoreo*, respectively). Interestingly the first looks back to what has just been said concerning one's proper or humble relationship to God and the second, in light of this, prepares for the statement concerning the insidious opposition from God and the community. The first exhortation concerns mental balance in view of one's relation to God, described in vv. 6-7 as humility vis-à-vis and dependence upon a caring God. This exhortation repeats the earlier pleas for clear-minded, self-controlled action on the part of the addressees as they confront their current situation either with Jèsus' return in mind (1:13) or in view of their relation to God (4:7). The second injunction is an eschatological call for alertness. If one has a proper relation to God, one will readily see God's archenemy or master of evil at work in the threats to one's faith—spiritual discernment is vital. Like Paul in 1 Thess 5:6, the author exhorts the community to mental balance in assessing its eschatological situation and to vigilance in discerning the power and enticement of evil. Indeed this paraenetic imagery fits well the picture presented of a predator seeking unsuspecting victims. Thus the author begins the treatment of the opponent's role by advising vigilance and will follow the description of this satanic figure by enjoining proper behavior, first in the form of resistance (v. 9) and second by reminding the addressees of their relation to "the God of all grace" (v. 10), in the form of "casting (one's) worries on" the one Christians "invoke as father" (1:17; 5:7).

Following the presentation and description of the satanic opponent and its antagonism toward believers, the author again exhorts the readers to further action; they are to "resist him." The term in question, *anthistemi*, is employed in Matt 5:39 to discourage retaliation against an evildoer (see 1 Pet 3:9) but here as in Eph 6:13 and Jas 4:7 to characterize resistance or opposition to the evil one. What this resistance consists of is not easily discerned, though one can readily see similarities between the responses of Ephesians and 1 Peter. The former speaks metaphorically of employing "the whole armor of God" (truth, righteousness, the gospel of peace, faith, salvation, and the word of God) "to stand firm" (*hystemi*). In 1 Peter the injunction is followed immediately by a complementary adjectival construction: "being steadfast in the faith." Besides employing the cognate *stereos* ("being firm or steadfast") the author suggests both that the problem at issue is the possibility of apostasy (being lured away or devoured by God's enemy) and that the means of resistance is firmness of faith or commitment (on faith see earlier discussion of 1:5). Such an injunction, in the context of humble, balanced, and trusting relationship to God, underscores the author's initial assertion that the addressees "are being protected by the power of God through faith" (1:5).

In the second part of 5:9 the author offers further motivation for this spiritual battle by noting, seemingly in passing, that members of the Christian community throughout the world are experiencing the same kinds of sufferings. While some scholars have seized upon this passage to speak of widespread persecution, of apocalyptic woes announcing, in the author's mind, the end of the world, or even, by lending to the verb *epiteleo* the special meaning of "fulfil" or even "pay a tax of suffering," to speak of a diminishing quota of suffering that announces the end, it seems preferable to view this statement in relation to the author's strategy. The communities of Asia Minor, while being exhorted to resist the enemy of their faith, are assured (in fact "they know"—use of *oida*) that others throughout the Church are confronting the same sufferings and so are successfully resisting the temptation to deny their commitment, that there is a common bond of fellowship (*adelphotes*) between those everywhere who follow in Christ's footsteps, and finally that the "sufferings being perpetrated on" believers everywhere are well within the purview of a God who cares (3:17; 5:7) yet nonetheless tests those who have faith (1:7; 4:12).

Clearly then in vv. 8-9, 1 Peter draws special attention to a major problem the community is experiencing in relation to its suffering, namely, the threat of apostasy in reaction to its "fiery ordeal." On two previous occasions, 1:6-7 and 4:12, the issue was raised when these sufferings were called *peirasmos* ("trial" or "temptation"). In each case the author preferred classifying them as tests of faith allowed by God rather than dwelling on their character as enticements to abandon faith. In 5:6-11, devoted to God's almighty power (see vv. 6, 10-11), the author broaches the subject of apostasy or defection directly by speaking of the one who tempts believers or, in 1 Peter's terms, goes about arrogantly seeking, like a lion, believers to devour. The issue for 1 Peter is not that maltreatment by pagan neighbors is the work of the devil but that such suffering becomes the occasion of satanic enticement to believers to renounce their commitment to God. Indeed the author's injunction regarding treatment or resistance of this satanic adversary is not the avoidance of unfriendly neighbors or their treatment as allies of God's archenemy but the refusal to renounce their faith commitment, that is, remaining obedient or loyal to their faith. Further the injunction to resist this otherworldly opponent could seem presumptuous at first blush, but 1

Peter both emphasizes the assistance of the devil's all-powerful opponent and insists that although other believers worldwide have experienced such suffering, they have not given in to the devil's temptations to apostasy but have remained in the community of faith and thus are "steadfast in the faith."

At this point it would be most interesting to reread 1 Peter in light of 5:8-9, since one can now detect a leitmotif or subtext that runs throughout the document. The danger of apostasy viewed as a temptation by God's arch-enemy provides an added nuance to every promise of protection or reward, every mention of testing, of hope, and of perseverance. First Peter not only reinforces the addressees' sense of loyalty and commitment but also presents the community's troubles as difficulties to be overcome or, failing this, as trials that test the genuineness of their faith.

Assistance from the God of All Grace (5:10)

Having spoken of God's arrogant opponent who is also the enemy of the community and having exhorted the addressees to a firm resistance of its temptations, 1 Peter turns more directly to another theme introduced by the OT citation of 5:5, a theme that serves as further motivation for the suffering believers' perseverance. The promise that God "gives grace to the humble" provides 1 Peter the final and most basic guarantee for the letter's paraenesis. The verse in effect is a masterful statement of motivation for the addressees in their time of crisis, because it both speaks of past divine benefactions and reasserts the promise of future, imminent divine assistance from a God who cares.

The God of All Grace. Not only does the OT citation prepare for the reintroduction of the important theme of grace, but it also provides the means by which to characterize the one who has given new life and has shown mercy, for God is interestingly called "the God of all grace." This unique title (though see 2 Cor 1:3) is ready made for the present context, since the statement of motivation appeals to God's nature as one who provides benefactions. Not only is there a promise or call to future glory but also all gifts, whether life, new life, or charismatic gifts (see 2:3, 23; 2:9; 4:10, 19), find their source in the one who will afford a resolution to the community's fiery ordeal. First Peter clearly underscores the pervasive character of grace in the believers' lives (see also 5:12) and therefore its role as the solid basis for trust in God's care and promise (vv. 5-7). It is the God of grace who has and will provide for the humble, faithful, innocent sufferer.

A God Who Calls to Eternal Glory through Christ. Once again the theme of future glory is brought to bear on the author's exhortation to perseverance in the face of innocent suffering. Repeatedly believers have been promised the gift of glory and now are characterized as "called or destined" (*kaleo*) to share in God's being inasmuch as they have shared in Christ's suffering. In this statement several important points are made, whether about God as "the one who calls" (see also 1:15; 2:9), about believers as destined to return eternally to their creator, or about the christological means and medium for the achievement of this goal. God by nature is the one who calls out of darkness to light, now and in the eschatological future; believers therefore can cast their worries on such a God. Additionally the addressees are reminded of their vocation to return to the source of their goodness and being—not only are they called to be holy, like God, but also to share in God's eternal glory or being (see also 3:18). Finally the phrase *en Christo* signifies both the soteriological means and the paradigmatic model chosen by God for this purpose.

"After you have suffered for a little while." Situated after the long complex double subject characterizing the God who will act on the addressees' behalf is a short enigmatic parenthetical remark about the length of suffering. A similar, parallel statement appears in the letter's blessing section (1:6—see discussion). There as here this temporal statement about short-lived suffering (use of *oligon*) is usually interpreted as referring to the nearness of the parousia (see 1:5; 4:7; 5:6). Believers would be encouraged to persevere in view of Jesus' imminent return. However, the focus of both passages is not seemingly the imminent future but rather the addressees' current situation. In the first instance the context is the testing of one's faith (see also 4:12) in view of eschatological reward but nonetheless with joy at "receiving the (present) outcome of [their] faith" (1:9; see vv. 6-9). In this second statement about short-lived suffering, while one could ostensibly connect the remark with the preceding promise of "eternal glory" (after brief suffering), the more logical reading is to have this adverbial phrase modify the following series of verbs: God's activity will follow or bring about the cessation or reduction of the severe difficulties the community is experiencing. Again the temporal phrase concerns the present or immediate future and expresses the author's hope that the heightened tensions between Christians and non-Christians in Asia Minor will cease or be reduced in the not-too-distant future.

Assistance from a God Who Cares. Finally 1 Peter turns to the promised divine activity, for which four relatively rare terms are employed. Since all occur only here in 1 Peter, since each offers a range of meaning, and since the temporal context (whether present or future) is debated, there is considerable variety in the translation and interpretation of this paratactic verbal construct. The first term, *katartizo*, can mean "prepare" in view of or "complete" in reference to the eschaton, or else it can bear the meaning "restore," in a more idiomatic sense, to happier socioreligious circumstances. The second verb, *sterizo*, also presents a range of meaning, "support, confirm, establish, strengthen," but owing to its relation to v. 9 and the expression "being steadfast or firm in faith" (use of *stereos*), one should probably opt for being made "firm or strong." The third word, *stenoo*, offers less variety; its basic sense is that of "strengthening" or being made "strong." The final verb, *themelioo*, also has a more focused meaning since it relates to "foundation"; its meaning then is that of "laying a foundation" or "being established or firmly founded." The four terms fall into two groups: the first states an overall activity of "restoring to a former condition" (BAGD 417), while the last three express the means by which the communities will be restored. The text should probably be rendered: "God . . . will restore you by making you firm, strong, and established." The author then would be speaking of the near-future restoration of more amicable Christian-non-Christian relations in Asia Minor. The author promises that God, in due time (v. 6) or after the fiery ordeal has dissipated ("after a little while"—v. 10), will exalt the humble who trust in God's mighty hand by restoring the refreshing time (2:3) when the converts were steadfast in their faith (1:7), strong "with the strength that God supplies" (4:11), and firmly established stones in God's spiritual house (2:4-9). For those who have succumbed, for those who have been severely tempted or tested, and for those who had to bear the burden of support for those so tempted (reread 5:1-5), there is a promise of divine assistance that is founded on God's power and care to make use of that power on behalf of the beloved. Indeed by means of the emphatic pronoun *autos* ("he himself"—see 1 Thess 3:11; 5:23) 1 Peter stresses God's nearness to and care for those who have been called out of darkness to a new birth (1:3; 2:9).

Divine Praise (5:11)

The third major section of the letter ends like the second (see 4:11) with a doxology that reaffirms God's almighty power (see v. 6). Rather than the reaffirmation of the promise of eschatological glory (the term "glory" is not employed in this doxology; but see v. 10) there is a focus on divine power or dominion that not only anchors hope for a heavenly inheritance (1:4) but also provides confidence in or guarantees divine deliverance even during their "remaining time in the flesh" (4:2). The term *amen* once again (see 4:11) affirms the author's confidence in the "God of all grace" (5:10).

Suggested Readings

Bochert, G. L. "The Conduct of Christians in the Face of the 'Fiery Ordeal' (1 Pet 4:12-5:11)." *RE* 79 (1982) 451-62.

Boismard, M. E. "Je renonce à Satan, à ses pompes et à ses oeuvres." *LV* 26 (1956) 105-110.

Kendall, D. W. "The Literary and Theological Function of 1 Peter 1:3-12" in *PFP*, 103-20.

Lovestam, E. *Spiritual Wakefulness in the New Testament.* Lund: Gleerup, 1963.

Schwank, B. "Diabolus tamquam leo rugiens (1 Petr. 5:8)." *EA* 38 (1960) 5-12.

van Unnik, W. C. "Christianity According to 1 Peter." *ET* 68 (1956-57) 79-83.

Closing

(1 Peter 5:12-14)

First Peter is brought to a close in a distinct final unit that, on the one hand, bears many stereotyped features of traditional letter closings and, on the other, presents a tripartite structure that parallels the letter opening. Though ancient letters usually ended simply with the word "farewell" followed by an indication of the date of writing, many show considerable variety in closings by composing greetings and including various postscripts and requests. In the letters of Paul as here in 1 Peter one encounters the mention and commendation of messengers, whether letter carriers or not (Rom 16:1-2; 1 Cor 16:10-12, 15-18; 2 Cor 8:16-24; 1 Thess 3:1-6; Philm 10-16), a brief statement of the purpose of writing (2 Cor 9:1f; 13:10; Gal 5:2f; 6:11f; Phlm 21-22), a variety of greetings: church to church (Rom 16:16; 1 Cor 16:19; 2 Cor 13:12; Phil 4:21), from various colleagues (Rom 16:3-23; 1 Cor 16:19f; Phil 4:21-22), or "with a kiss" (Rom 16:16; 1 Cor 16:20; 2 Cor 13:12; 1 Thess 5:16), and a concluding, traditional benediction (most Pauline letters). One might also see 2 John 12 and 3 John 13 for references to the brevity of the letter being sent. Many of these formulaic features have parallels in Heb 13:22-25 and reappear in early Christian letters, particularly those of Ignatius of Antioch.

Although many of the features of this letter closing are traditional, their organization and the author's choice of themes relate closely to the purpose for writing and the strategy employed. Just as the letter opening presents three sections featuring the author, addressees, and greeting, so the closing focuses on the messenger (5:12), best wishes from the author's community (vv. 13-14a), and a final benediction (v. 14b). While in the opening a direct relationship is posited between the writer and Jesus as the basis for the presentation of the following paraenesis, in the closing another relationship is drawn between the writer and the faithful messenger who delivers and presumably correctly interprets the message of exhortation. Additionally this final unit reiterates the opening themes of grace, peace, exile ("exiles of the

dispersion" and "Babylon"), and divine election, each of which plays a significant role in the author's treatment of the community's socioreligious crisis.
Two final issues underscore the author's strategy. In the first place the mention of Silvanus and Mark, along with the cryptic reference to Rome
(Babylon), reemphasizes the pseudepigraphic strategy evident in the first
verse of the document (1:1), for they render presumed Petrine authorship
more plausible and acceptance of its paraenetic tradition more likely. Second,
the enigmatic statement of v. 12 concerning "God's true grace" refers a last
time to the community's innocent suffering as forming part of God's plan
and constitutes a final plea for remaining "steadfast in faith" (5:9).

The Letter, Its Carrier, and Its Purpose

(5:12)

The letter closes rather abruptly by introducing Silvanus, someone responsible for the letter's arrival, and by expressing briefly the author's purpose for
writing. Both topics have been the object of discussion or debate regarding
either the authorship of the letter or the meaning of the expression "God's
true grace."

Silvanus, the Letter Carrier

The Greek text reads simply: "through Silvanus (*dia Silouanou*) . . . I have
written briefly." The figure in question was a well-known missionary of the
apostolic period mentioned in Paul's letters (1 Thess 1:1; 2 Cor 1:19; see 2
Thess 1:1) and presumably called Silas in Acts 15–18. The role that the
expression "through Silvanus" is meant to express here has been much
debated in past discussions of authorship, since some have attributed the elevated Greek style of the letter to this figure as amanuensis or even co-author.
More recent examination of the evidence, authorship aside, shows that the
expression "to write through or by means of someone" indicates the use of a
messenger or letter carrier (Ignatius, *Romans* 10.1; *Philadelphians* 11.2;
Smyrnaeans 12.1; Polycarp, *Philippians* 14.1; see also Acts 15:23).

If therefore the expression "through Silvanus" indicates delivery rather
than composition, how does such information function in the author's strategy? The answer is related to the further characterization of the messenger as
"a faithful brother," a judgment ("as I think" or "in my judgment") that is
uttered by one who is presumed to be "an apostle of Jesus Christ" (1:1), as
well as a Roman "elder" (5:1). The expression *pistos adelphos*, as in the
Pauline tradition (see Col 4:9; also Eph 6:21; also 1 Cor 1:1; 2 Cor 1:1;

Phlm 1), probably designates a trusted or reliable co-worker who, in the context of the assumed author, would faithfully provide the hermeneutical context for the reading of the letter; that is, Silvanus would also bear the written document but provide oral instruction from its author (see similar situation in Acts 15:27 in regard to Silas and Judas). On the level of strategy the choice of Silvanus, as well as that of Mark (see below), is made to coincide with Petrine tradition, preserved in Acts 12–18, which counted him, along with Peter and others, among the leaders of the Jerusalem community (see 15:22). Silvanus then is presented as a valued co-worker of Peter's in Rome whose fidelity lends further credence to the document's apostolic authority.

Purpose for Writing

First Peter employs a traditional statement of purpose before bringing the letter to a close, a statement that usually engages the verb "to write" and sometimes underscores the brevity of the communication ("with few [letters]"—*di' oligon*). Though such language and sentiment are traditional, they do serve to introduce a self-conscious, though enigmatic statement concerning the letter's message. In typical fashion 1 Peter, for this purpose, employs a double participial construction that leads to a concluding exhortation for perseverance. To express this purpose 1 Peter employs the verbs "exhort" and "declare or witness that" (*parakaleo* and *epimartyreo* with an accusative infinitive construction, respectively). Together these two terms express the essence of the author's message. The first verb, which also occurs in 2:11 and 5:1 to introduce the two duty codes, allows the author to dwell on the community's twofold arena of battle: Christian-Gentile relations on the one hand and intracommunity concerns on the other. The exhortation is about proper, holy behavior vis-à-vis outsiders and insiders, behavior that will itself foster steadfastness in faith.

The exhortation to such behavior is placed in a particular context, expressed by the remainder of v. 12: "declaring that this is a true grace from God so that you might stand firm in it." This is clearly meant as a fundamental apostolic declaration (see also 5:1); the meaning of the declaration itself however is debated. It is particularly the term "this" (*tauten*) and its antecedent that lead to a variety of suggestions. Some see the entire letter and its message as the point of reference. In this way the author would recapitulate the document's extensive instruction concerning Christian new life and call and repeated injunctions to holy and honorable behavior. Others focus more particularly on the theme of grace as the proper antecedent. Thus the author would refer here to God's call and gift of new life, which makes conduct worthy of a holy God possible. These two options, however, are less than convincing since they do not focus sufficiently on the issue of innocent suffering and since both seem to express truisms: the first that the presumed author's writing or letter is the expression of "God's manifold grace" (4:10) and the second that the gift of grace is "God's true grace." A preferable option is to view the author as insisting that innocent suffering ("if suffering should be God's will") is a grace or gift from God that tests the genuineness of one's faith (1:6-7; 4:12) and need not be an enticement to renounce one's commitment to "the God of all grace." Analysis of 2:19-21 and 4:14 confirms such an interpretation. Thus innocent suffering is viewed as a further grace given by God (note that "true grace" bears no article and that "of God" should be read as a subjective genitive: "from God").

Finally, the concluding clause presents textual and grammatical difficulties. On the one hand, the majority of (but later) manuscripts read a perfect indicative, while the minority (but older) textual versions prefer an aorist imperative or subjunctive form (*estekate* and *stete*, respectively) of the verb *histemi*. On the other hand, in grammatical and stylistic terms, there seems to be a mistaken use of *eis* for *en*, as in the Greek vernacular (BDF 205), and a question concerning the interpretation of the clause as a statement, an injunction, or a wish. If we are correct in opting for the form *stete* on textual grounds, then we would have to choose between the imperative and subjunctive forms. While the structure of 5:9a, involving a relative pronoun introducing an imperative, would seem to suggest a similar situation in 5:12, the thematic context points to the use of a subjunctive to express a closing wish, because the author is "declaring" from personal experience ("as a witness of Christ's suffering"—5:1; both use cognates of *martyreo*) that the community's fiery ordeal is a blessing or grace and, it is hoped, that such knowledge will lead to perseverance in this time of difficulty ("in it" refers back to "grace" and *peirasmos* implies "trial and temptation").

Koinonia and Other Themes

(5:13-14a)

The second part of the letter closing is taken up with traditional greetings, whether from church to church and from a beloved individual, or a final injunction involving a symbolic act of mutual care. In anticipation of the analysis of the individual greetings of this subunit, one might describe its major theme as concerned with *koinonia* or relations between and within churches. The author clearly intends to strengthen the bonds between the communities of Asia Minor, called "elect exiles of the Dispersion," and that of the presumed writer, which is characterized as "co-elect" and residing in Babylon (see discussion below). Additionally the other greetings, from a well-known fellow-believer (Mark) and from the ranks of the communities, enhance the universal character of the local communities in their personal contact with one another and in their sharing of mutual love and hospitality.

The first of these greetings involves a figure described as "she who is in Babylon, elected along with you." Scholars, though with some uneasiness, generally view the statement as referring not to some otherwise unknown city called Babylon or to Peter's wife or other unknown woman as co-elect but rather to the Christian community of Rome. The objective of this initial greeting from one church to others, while drawing a relationship between the author's community and those of the addressees in terms of election, is to underscore the universal experience and care of the communities for one another. The second greeting, though more properly related to the issue of pseudepigrapha (see 5:10), also contributes to the universal sense that the author wishes to develop in the addressees since Mark, according to the tradition preserved in Acts, was involved, along with Paul, Barnabas, Silas, and others, in the universal mission that brought the good news to the provinces of Asia Minor (see 1:12). The third element of greeting consists of a traditional injunction to "greet one another with the kiss of love" (v. 14a), an injunction that seemingly focuses on relationships within and among the communities of the provinces addressed. The "kiss," a common custom among Greco-Roman and Jewish populations, was used to show affection toward family members and friends and honor toward people of higher rank. Placed on the cheeks, forehead, eyes, shoulders, hands, and feet and serving many purposes in various contexts, this custom apparently was adopted by early Christians to express their new family relationship with other believers (called *adelphoi* or "brothers and sisters"). In this instance the author seizes a last opportunity to encourage "constant love for one another" (4:8).

Within these traditional greeting forms one encounters many peculiarities that further indicate concerns of the author. The first greeting describes the community as residing in Babylon, the name of Israel's well-known historic destroyer and a name that, since the time of the book of Daniel, symbolically came to represent the eschatological world power that was in conflict with God's people. At a later period, in view of Rome's world domination and destruction of Jerusalem, the name was used in Jewish and Christian apocalyptic texts (*SibOr* 5:143, 159; *4 Ezra* 3:1-2, 28, 31; *2 Bar* 11:1-2; 67:7; Rev 14:8f) to identify Rome as the endtime world power that opposes the righteous. Its use here in 1 Peter does not seem to support such apocalyptic concerns but rather dwells on the name as suggesting the exilic theme noted at the beginning of the letter: "the exiles of the Dispersion." The Christian communities, whether of Rome, Asia Minor, or worldwide, are scattered among pagan neighbors as the result of their divine election. In fact the community of Rome is here characterized as "co-elect" or "chosen along with (the addressees)." Nonetheless, the choice of a political symbol reminds the audience that it also has a sociopolitical status and corresponding responsibilities (see 2:11–3:12). Thus the combination of sociopolitical and religious terminology allows the author the opportunity to refer back to the opening characterization of the addressees (1:1) and to reiterate the important designation of them as "resident aliens and religious exiles" (2:11).

Another unique feature employed within the greeting formulas is the choice of the traditional figure of Mark as one who also sends greetings. Early tradition regarding this early missionary is better known to us because not only does he figure prominently in Acts as a companion of Paul and Barnabas (12–15), but he also appears in the Pauline (Phlm 24) and Paulinist (Col 4:10; 2 Tim 4:11) correspondence. Also, tradition reported by Papias connects Mark with Peter and the writing of a Gospel (Eusebius, *EH* 2.15; 3.39.15). The author of the letter also associates Mark with Peter ostensibly to underscore further the claim of Petrine authorship (as earlier in the reference to Silvanus) and by the allusion to Mark as "my son" perhaps to appeal to his reputation as missionary and evangelist to claim him as disciple (see use of "son" in this way in Acts 23:6) or perhaps convert (see 1 Thess 2:11-12; Phm 10). In this way the author draws further connection between the Jesus tradition, the preaching of the good news to the inhabitants of Asia Minor (even by Mark: see Phlm 24), and the common experience of Christians worldwide as sharers of Christ's innocent suffering.

Finally, not only is the use of the "kiss" as a means of emphasizing Christian peace and unity a traditional motif in early epistolary literature (see earlier), but also its particular designation, not as a "holy kiss" as always in Paul but as a "kiss of love" in 1 Peter, calls for some comment. Use of the former would have been appropriate to characterize Christian relations to one another as exemplifying the divine injunction to holy conduct (1:15-16). Instead the author focuses on the crucial, repeated theme of mutual love among believers (see 1:22; 2:17; 3:8). But especially this modification of what is ostensibly traditional terminology ("holy kiss") points to the important, earlier discussions of community relations in 4:7-11 and 5:1-5— believers owe one another assistance especially in view of the fiery ordeal being experienced by many in the community. The weak need the love of the strong, and this love must be shown "without complaining" (4:9).

A Final Benediction

(5:14b)

The letter is brought to an end with a formal benediction that involves the traditional theme of "peace," which along with the immediately preceding references to "grace" (5:10, 12) forms a significant parallel with the opening greeting: "may grace and peace be yours in abundance" (see earlier discussion). Just as the earlier references to "grace" have been shown to apply directly to the community's situation and the author's strategy in dealing with that issue, so it can be demonstrated that the theme of peace relates both to Christian-Gentile relations and to community life. Not only does the theme of peace occur in the opening where there is the stated wish for an abundance of "grace and peace," but it also recurs, in the words of Ps 33:14, as a reality that is to be sought and pursued (3:11). In the context of that OT citation about "desiring life and . . . good days" (v. 10), it is clear that the author closes with the wish that there will be peace among neighbors and among brothers and sisters, a reality that will come about in as much as the addressees are and remain faithful ("who are in Christ') to the one they acknowledge as lord, shepherd, and guardian, to the one in whose footsteps they follow, to the one whose return they await (1:7, 13; 2:21, 25; 3:15; 4:13; 5:4, 10). Suffering as a Christian is possible because of divine grace; but peace and exaltation, in view of eternal glory, are the believer's reward from "the God of all grace." The author's words of consolation and pleas for perseverance rely ultimately on believers' fidelity to their christological model, the obedient and exalted Lord Jesus Christ, the one who experienced suffering and received eternal glory from a faithful, caring God.

Suggested Readings

Applegate, J. K. "The Co-Elect Woman of 1 Peter." *NTS* 38 (1992) 587-604.

Brox, N. *Der erste Petrusbrief.* Zurich: Benziger, 1979.

Doty, W. G. *Letters in Primitive Christianity.* Philadelphia: Fortress, 1973.

Elliott, J. H. "Silvanus and Mark in 1 Peter and Acts" in *Wort in der Zeit: Neutestamentlichen Studien.* Eds., Haubeck, W. & Backmann, M. Leiden: Brill, 1980, 250-67.

Fitzmyer, J. A. "Introduction to the New Testament Epistles" in *NJBC* 768-71.

Klassen, W. "The Sacred Kiss in the New Testament: An Example of Social Boundary Lines." *NTS* 39 (1993) 122-35.

Soards, M. L. "1 Peter, 2 Peter, and Jude as Evidence for a Petrine School" in *ANRW* 2.25.5 (1988) 3828-49.

Stowers, S. K. *Letter Writing in Greco-Roman Antiquity.* Philadelphia: Westminster, 1986.
White, J. L. *Light from Ancient Letters.* Philadelphia: Fortress, 1986.

Jude

Introduction

Lost toward the end of the NT collection of books, between the extensive and ponderous Pauline corpus and the strangely fascinating and lengthy book of Revelation, is a series of relatively unknown general letters and theological tracts. Among these general or "catholic epistles" perhaps the least conspicuous is the letter of Jude owing to its brevity (25 verses), obscure provenance (by "Jude . . . brother of James"), and seeming lack of context. Additionally the document has been a controversial one. Though the author of 2 Peter found the work appealing (see discussion below of 2 Peter's use of Jude), Christians through the centuries have reacted negatively to the work's polemic character, particularly its liking for condemnation rather than argumentation. Also, from the outset the author's undisguised use of the apocryphal books of *Enoch* and the *Assumption of Moses* as though they formed part of the scriptural canon was viewed with suspicion. Besides, the document has been criticized by many interpreters, especially the Reformers, as lacking in theological or edifying content. Modern scholarship, however, has taken a closer look at this forgotten book and has learned to appreciate its original context and its author's message. Before examining Jude's message, however, it is necessary to discuss its author, intended audience, and composition.

Author and Audience

In the letter opening one encounters a formulaic statement both about the author ("Jude, servant of Jesus Christ, that is, brother of James") and about the addressees ("to those who are called . . . "). To the extent that the vagueness of the latter leaves the modern reader perplexed, to an even greater degree does the specificity of the former cause problems for the scholar.

Author

The use of the name "Jude" (*Ioudas*) as self-designation calls for some comment both in terms of identification and purpose. The starting point for such discussion is usually the list of the five early Christians in the NT who bear the name of Jude or Judas: Judas the brother of Jesus and so brother of James, Joses, and Simon (Mark 6:3 par), Judas Iscariot (Mark 3:19 par), Judas the disciple with whom Paul stayed after his conversion (Acts 9:11), Judas Barsabbas, an early Christian leader (Acts 15:22f), or the apostle Judas, the son or brother of James (see Luke 6:16 and Acts 1:13—in place of Thaddaeus or Lebbaeus: Mark 3;18 par). Recent scholarship, usually with reluctance, considers either the first or last of these persons as the likely candidate—one would have to add the suggestion of some scholars that the figure intended is Judas Thomas ("the twin"—see *Gospel of Thomas*, prologue). By far the most usual choice is to consider Jude as the brother of Jesus, especially since the author also claims to be "the brother of James," who is then assumed to be James the Just, the Lord's brother. The major difficulty of course is not simply that the author does not claim to be "the Lord's brother" but more strangely claims to be the brother of the Lord's brother—an unusual statement under any circumstance. The major objection against the second option is that Jude does not employ the title of apostle. The third option does not really explain the fraternal relationship of Jude to James and appeals to later Gnostic tradition to explain the author's appeal to the authority of Jude to counter what is alleged to be Gnostic heresies.

Perhaps the problem with such discussion is that the starting point is wrong. The identity, real or alleged, of this Judas is to be determined not by considering known individuals of the NT period but by taking more seriously the author's attempt at self-identification. Whether or not the name of Jude is known to the addressees seems to be the point at issue, a point that the author clarifies by two successive phrases. The first phrase characterizes the author in Christian terms as a community leader (see comments below on "servant of Jesus Christ"), true also of James (1:1), while the second makes a further, explanatory statement (use of *de* not *kai*: BAGD 171.2—elsewhere only in Titus 1:1), "that is, (Jude is also) a brother of James." The former clarifies not the identity but expresses the author's claim of authority; the second seemingly addresses the issue of identity.

Why then the reference to James? Is the author making a historical point (self-identification) or establishing a basis for the subsequent polemics and paraenesis, that is, strategy? It is at this point that arguments against authenticity come into play, namely, the quality of the language of the document, the author's interest in tradition rather than personal authority (see vv. 3, 5, 17), and the letter's concern with heretical tendencies of the post-apostolic period. These issues point not to an early Aramaic disciple or relative of Jesus but to a later period (late first century) when tradition looms large in theological discussion and when pseudonymity becomes a popular defense or authenticating strategy. It is my conclusion here that Jude, in the letter opening, appeals not so much to the person of James, whether the apostle or the brother of Jesus, but to the successful pseudonymous letter of James to muster authority in a critical battle against opponents within the communities. Such a conclusion helps to explain both the author's non-use of more specific identification (apostle or brother of the Lord) and the quaintness of the characterization. In strategic terms Jude, like James, is presented as a figure from the early Christian generation who remembers and reminds the addressees of "the faith that was once-for-all handed over to the saints" (v. 3).

Beyond the authorial claim of v. 1a, Jude on two occasions employs the first person singular to speak as author, in the first case in relation to the paraenetic purpose for writing (v. 3) and in the second case to underscore the writer's authority as teacher of the community's tradition (v. 5). In the former case the author employs a complex writing formula to express both the urgency and the necessity for writing what can best be described as a polemical treatment of the community's situation. In the latter case Jude adopts the voice of tradition (see also v. 17). Use then of the first-person singular underscores on the one hand the author's strategy in addressing the community's problems and on the other the need to return to tradition as the repository of common belief and the safeguard of responsible behavior.

In more general terms the style and language of this pseudonymous author are those of a Hellenist whose appeal to the Hebrew Scriptures and to Jewish apocryphal works in their Greek form point to a Jewish writer of the Diaspora. The author's work is not lacking in literary grace; Jude shows a liking for repetition, particularly groupings of twos and threes (see examples of ancient sinners: vv. 5-7, 11). Further the author introduces the opponents as "certain ones" in v. 4 and then reintroduces them in five successive paragraphs as "these are" (use of *houtoi* in vv. 8, 10, 12, 16, 19). Additionally there is a conscious use of multiple images either to describe the opponents (whether as "irrational animals" in v. 10 or as "waterless clouds," "fruitless trees," or "waves of the sea" in vv. 12-13) or to contrast their godless behavior and forthcoming punishment with the protection promised those who "keep (themselves) in God's love" (play on the theme of "keeping" in vv. 1, 6, 13, 21, 24). The author then is a concerned leader of the Christian community, an educated one at that, who writes both in anger against opponents who are castigated for their heretical doctrine and immoral behavior and with concern for those being deceived and led astray by these godless, divisive malcontents.

Audience

Though the book of Jude is in large measure a series of condemning statements against members considered heretical, it is nonetheless written to people who are repeatedly addressed as "beloved" (vv. 3, 17, 20; see also v. 1). They are the ones who are "urged to fight for the faith" (v. 3) and who are exhorted as people of the Spirit to "build yourselves up on your most holy faith" (v. 20). They have been called by God and receive divine protection as they await Jesus' return (vv. 1, 21, 24). The letter is written for the faithful readers as warning against treacherous members, as exhortation to adhere to traditional Christian teaching and behavior, and as appeal to help those who are wavering. Though the polemical section of the letter, vv. 4-19, seems to dominate, the author is careful to focus the conclusion of the document (beginning actually at vv. 16 or 17) on what was, from the beginning, the intent of the letter: to "write . . . concerning (their) common salvation" (v. 3) or, more clearly, concerning God's activity as "Savior through Jesus Christ our Lord" (v. 25).

There is, however, in Jude the real possibility of a mirror reading; by examining the various statements concerning the opponents and allowing for their formulaic character, one can examine the ideal and even real characteristics of the faithful audience being addressed. The "beloved" are not interlopers or godless people "who transform God's grace into debauchery and disown the only Master and our Lord Jesus Christ" (v. 4). Indeed they are people of the Spirit who are exhorted to accept the community's tradition concerning God's lordship and saving activity. In addition they are exhorted to honorable behavior that recognizes God's loving assistance in Christ and to care for those who are wavering. The addressees are, like the author, fellow combatants for the faith who acknowledge the only God's assistance as father and savior in this battle for the hearts and minds of their fellow believers.

A distinction is apparently suggested between the author and audience on the one hand and the first generation of Christians on the other (vv. 3, 17). Besides, the letter addresses heretical tendencies of a later period. Jude, in the greeting, appeals to the successful pseudonymous letter of James to muster authority in a critical battle against errant teachers within the communities. Indeed "faith," for this author as for several other late NT writers, refers to content or true doctrine, namely, the community's tradition that requires defense (v. 3) and on which one must build one's life (v. 20).

Composition and Content

Jude has only the outward appearance of a letter: a standard greeting, a body, and a formulaic conclusion. Though its body opening employs a standard writing formula (v. 3), its concluding doxology relates more closely to a homiletic or liturgical form than to that of the letter. Its audience is rather general, and its treatment of the opponents lacks specifics—the latter draws readily from ancient descriptions of the ungodly. Thus many scholars describe Jude as a polemical tract, with an exhortatory conclusion, to which the author has given epistolary features.

The contents, found within vv. 4-23, present an interesting sixfold alternating pattern and shed further light on the genre and purpose of the document. Verse 4 introduces the opponents and their heresy (they are ungodly intruders who reject divine lordship and violate Christian mores), while vv. 5-7 give three groups that, owing to their evil deeds, underwent divine punishment: the unbelieving desert generation of Israelites, the fallen angels, and the immoral cities of Sodom and Gomorrah. The author then treats the activity of the opponents (both their denial of lordship and their immoral behavior—v. 8), but again focuses on the example of the devil to stress the divine nature of the condemnation (v. 9—use of *Assumption of Moses*). A third time Jude treats the opponents' activity (they are compared to "irrational animals"—v. 10) and concludes with three examples of ancient evildoers: the murderous Cain, the greedy Balaam, and the rebellious Korah (v. 11). In vv. 12-13 the activity of the teachers (selfish and polluting) along with their character ("waterless clouds," "fruitless trees," "wild waves," and "wandering stars") are again discussed, only to be excoriated by means of a citation from the *Book of Enoch* regarding the divine punishment of the ungodly (vv. 14-15). Verse 16 dwells again on the opponents (as malcontents and flatterers), who are identified, in the words of the apostles, with the ungodly scoffers of the endtime (vv. 17-18).

One notices a change in the last-mentioned passage, as well as the following, for the author no longer dwells on condemnation of the opponents but instead addresses the readers ("beloved" in vv. 17, 20). In this case the author draws attention to the ungodly behavior that the community is to avoid. In v. 19 also, after speaking a last time about the opponents (as divisive, "worldly people who do not have the Spirit"), Jude in vv. 20-23 advises the audience on proper doctrine and conduct. On the contrary they are to be people of the Spirit, who adhere to the "most holy faith" and who keep themselves "in God's love" in view of Jesus' return. Also, as they will then receive the mercy of Jesus, so are they now to show mercy to those at risk.

We can therefore propose the following outline for reading Jude:

Epistolary Opening (1-2) and Body Opening (3)   beloved
Six Alternating Patterns Regarding False Teachers (4-23)
    False Teachers, Charges, and Punishment (4-7)   a) certain
    Triple Charges and Prediction of Divine Punishment (8-9)   these
    Charges, Condemnation, and Divine Punishment (10-11)   these
    Multiple Charges and Prediction of Divine Punishment (12-15)   these
    Charges and Apostolic Predictions (16-18)   b) these/beloved
    Charges, Community Activity (19-23), Body Closing   these/beloved
Epistolary Closing (24-25)

From the above description one can easily see why Jude is best described as an exhortatory tract (see v. 3—use of *parakaleo*) written in letter form for the benefit of a community in the midst of a major crisis. In the first part of the document (vv. 4-15) the author addresses the opponents and their activity in an uncompromisingly polemic way before turning in the second part to the readers to appeal to their sense of apostolic tradition and godly behavior (vv. 16-23) in their joint battle "for the faith that was once-for-all handed over to the saints" (v. 3).

Strategy and Message

What, however, is the crisis that looms so large for the community and the author of this document? What are the issues involved, and how would one describe the author's strategy for counteracting these?

Heresy and Immoral Behavior

Despite earlier suggestions that the opponents were either Gnostic or proto-Gnostic intruders into the community (use of terminology from vv. 4 and 19: "sneak in" and "worldly people," respectively), it is best to recognize the formulaic nature of the author's descriptions and to investigate the repeated, twofold treatment of these heretical members. From the start they are called "godless or ungodly people" (*asebes*—v. 4) who are accused of violating both Christian tradition (by denying God's lordship and Christ's role in the quest for salvation) and moral standards and community fellowship (by living lives of debauchery and arrogance and by selfishly abusing fellowship). In short, like ancient sinners in their challenge of divine order and authority, they teach a doctrine of rebellion and live in rebellion, arrogance, and infidelity; and like these ancient sinners they risk losing the grace or salvation they have been granted (vv. 4-5) and taking the path of eternal punishment. Despite the stereotypical descriptions of these opponents, it is clear that both their teaching and their behavior are condemned, in the words of Enoch, as ungodly (vv. 14-15).

Theological and Christological Considerations

First and foremost Jude centers on divine activity, for it is God who judges and punishes. All the examples given by the author of the punishment that is to befall the opponents have God as their subject. The same one who saved the people from Egypt also punished the unbelievers of the desert generation (v. 5—see discussion of "lord" below). It is God who keeps the fallen angels in chains (v. 6). It is also the Lord God—not Michael the agent—who punishes (v. 9). In the citation from the *Book of Enoch* it is clearly God ("the Lord") who "executes judgment on all" (v. 15). Jude uses the divine passive (use of the passive with God understood as agent) in vv. 10 ("they are destroyed") and 13 ("for whom . . . darkness has been reserved"). Even impersonal constructions in vv. 7 and 11 indicate divine activity in meting out punishment. Furthermore the author is concerned with the divine plan: God is the one who calls and has once and for all "handed over" faith to the saints (vv. 1, 3; both divine passives) and guards or keeps safe the elect for the return and granting of mercy by the "Son" (vv. 1, 21, 24).

Jude's treatment of Jesus is also of interest; he is presented as the returning lord at the endtime. The beloved are kept by God for Jesus (v. 1); the beloved, while abiding in God's love, are to "wait for the mercy of our Lord Jesus Christ that leads to eternal life" (v. 21). While the document insists on the lordship of Jesus (vv. 7, 21, 25) and notes his soteriological role (v. 25), it is his apocalyptic function that is central to the author's strategy.

Author's Message and Apocalyptic Strategy

In an effort to combat the false teachers in the community, the author borrows from apocalyptic tradition. The community is a self-contained entity that is being secretly invaded from the outside (v. 4) and whose unity is being disrupted by the intruders (v. 19). The treatment of these opponents is situated in an eschatological context; they are said to be the scoffers of the end-days predicted by the apostles of Jesus (vv. 17-18). The author draws upon apocalyptic texts, *1 Enoch* and the *Assumption of Moses* (vv. 4, 6, 7, 9,

12, 14-15), to present suitable models for the impending judgment of the opponents. The fallen angels, the devil, Michael the archangel, and the people of Sodom and Gomorrah are familiar characters in apocalyptic stories of the intertestamental and early Christian periods. The punishment meted out to them involves eternal fire and chains. The teachers rebel against divine order, as did Cain, Balaam, and Korah (v. 11). They are accused of denying the lordship of God and the Messiah (v. 4) and of rejecting divine authority as well as that of the heavenly powers (v. 8b—see discussion below). Their activity is compared to all manner of apocalyptic abomination: perversion, licentiousness (vv. 4, 12, 16), rebellion against God and divine agents (vv. 4c, 8), animalistic behavior (vv. 10, 16), and ecological and cosmic phenomena (vv. 12-13). The author therefore has employed an apocalyptic schema to present the activity of the heretical opponents as the satanic activity of the end-days. God the Father, who has chosen a people, keeps them, and protects them until the coming of Jesus in glory. In the meantime "the beloved of God" (v. 1) must build upon their "most holy faith," pray in the Spirit, abide in the love of God, and await the mercy of the returning Lord Jesus (vv. 20-21). They must also extend a cautious, helping hand to the errant (vv. 22-23).

Jude, if read as strict polemics, may rank as the most negative book of the New Testament, but, if understood in light of the author's apocalyptic strategy, may offer a stern rebuke of atheistic doctrine and immoral and arrogant behavior within the community as it attempts to remain faithful to its tradition, that is, as it "fights for the faith that was once-for-all handed over to the saints" (v. 3).

Commentaries

Arichea, D. C., and H. A. Hatton. *A Handbook on the Letter from Jude and the Second Letter from Peter.* New York: UBS, 1993.

Bauckham, R. J. *Jude, 2 Peter.* Waco TX: Word Books, 1983.

Cantinat, J. *Les épîtres de saint Jacques et de saint Jude.* Paris: Gabalda, 1973.

Craddock, F. B. *First and Second Peter and Jude.* Louisville KY: Westminster/John Knox, 1995.

Elliott, J. H. *1-11 Peter/Jude* (with R. A. Martin. *James*). Minneapolis: Augsburg, 1982, 159-85.

Fuchs, E., and P. Reymond. *La deuxième épître de saint Pierre—L'epitre de saint Jude.* Geneva: Labor et Fides, 1988.

Kelly, J. N. D. *A Commentary on the Epistles of Peter and Jude.* Grand Rapids: Baker, 1982.

Kugelman, R. *James and Jude.* Wilmington DE: Glazier, 1980.

Neyrey, J. H. "The Epistle of Jude" in *NJBC*, 917-19.

__________. *2 Peter, Jude.* New York: Doubleday, 1993.

Perkins, P. *First and Second Peter, James, and Jude.* Louisville KY: John Knox, 1995.

Sidebottom, E. M. *James, Jude, 2 Peter.* Grand Rapids: Eerdmans, 1982.

Vögtle, A. *Der Judasbrief. Der 2 Petrusbrief.* Zurich: Benziger, 1994.

Watson, D. F. "The Letter of Jude" in *NIB*, 12:471-500.

Suggested Readings

Bauckham, R. J. "The Letter of Jude: A Survey of Research" in *Jude*, 134-78.

__________. *Jude and the Relatives of Jesus in the Early Church.* Edinburgh: T & T Clark, 1990.

Charles, J. D. *Literary Strategy in the Epistle of Jude.* Scranton PA: University of Scranton, 1993.

__________. "Jude's Use of Pseudepigraphical Source-Material as Part of a Literary Strategy." *NTS* 37 (1991) 130-45.

__________. "Literary Artifice in the Epistle of Jude." *ZNTW* 82 (1991) 106-24.

Dunnett, W. M. "The Hermeneutics of Jude and 2 Peter: The Use of Ancient Jewish Traditions." *JETS* 31 (1988) 287-92.

Eybers, I. H. "Aspects of the Background of the Letter of Jude." *Neot* 9 (1975) 113-23.

Ellis, E. E. "Prophecy and Hermeneutic in Jude" in *Prophecy and Hermeneutic in Early Christianity: New Testament Essays.* Tübingen: Mohr-Siebeck, 1978, 221-36.

Gunther, J. J. "The Alexandrian Epistle of Jude." *NTS* 30 (1984) 549-62.

Hahn, F. "Randbemerkungen zum Judasbrief." *TZ* 37 (1981) 209-18.

Heilgenthal, R. "Der Judasbrief: Aspekte der Forschung in den letzten Jahrzehnten." *TR* 51 (1986) 117-29.

Joubert, S. J. "Language, Ideology, and the Social Context of the Letter of Jude." *Neot* 24 (1990) 335-49.

__________. "Facing the Past: Transtextual Relationships and Historical Understanding in the Letter of Jude." *BZ* 42 (1998) 56-70.

Krodel, G. "The Letter of Jude" in *The General Letters: Hebrews, James, 1-2 Peter, Jude, 1-2-3 John.* Ed., G. Krodel. Philadelphia: Fortress, 1995, 94-109.

Lyle, K. R. *Ethical Admonition in the Epistle of Jude.* Bern: Lang, 1998.

Müller, P. "Der Judasbrief." *TR* 63 (1998) 267-89.

Rowston, D. J. "The Most Neglected Book in the New Testament." *NTS* 21 (1974-75) 554-63.

Sellin, G. "Die Häretiker des Judasbriefes." *ZNTW* 77 (1986) 206-25.

Watson, D. F. *Invention, Arrangement, and Style: Rhetorical Criticism of Jude and 2 Peter.* Atlanta: Scholars, 1986.

Webb, R. L. "The Eschatology of the Epistle of Jude and Its Rhetorical and Social Functions." *BBR* 6 (1996) 139-51.

Wisse, F. "The Epistle of Jude in the History of Heresiology" in *Essays on the Nag Hammadi Texts*. Ed., M. Krause. Leiden: Brill, 1972, 133-43.

Wolthuis, T. R. "Jude and Jewish Traditions." *CTJ* 22 (1987) 21-41.

__________. "Jude and Rhetoricism: A Dialogue on the Rhetorical Nature of the Epistle of Jude." *CTJ* 24 (1989) 126-34.

Opening

Jude presents a distinct, standard opening (vv. 1-2) and an equally discernible but less traditional closing (vv. 24-25). The former introduces the author and audience in terms that prepare for the document's message; namely, it focuses on the author's authority and on the addressees' privileged status.

Epistolary Opening

(1-2)

Though the opening of Jude follows the tripartite, stereotyped format of the ancient letter—author, to audience, greeting—its other features show that it is only superficially a letter. Indeed the closing (vv. 24-25) offers no standard epistolary features; instead one finds an extended doxology that brings the document to a close. Thus Jude has only the outward appearance of a letter: a standard greeting, a body, and a liturgical conclusion. Additionally there is no thanksgiving or blessing following the epistolary opening; instead Jude addresses the audience directly and turns to the purpose for writing (v. 3).

Author (1a)

The document opens with the claim that it is written by Jude or *Ioudas*, an individual whose identity and function are qualified by two subsequent phrases: "servant of Jesus Christ" and "brother of James" (for a list of the possible candidates for identifying Jude, see introduction). The first qualifying phrase is a traditional formula used in letter openings and elsewhere in epistolary documents usually to designate authoritative figures, whether missionaries and their envoys, or in a few instances to refer to Christians generally. While this title underscores the believer's acknowledgment of God's lordship (1 Cor 7:22-23; Eph 6:6), it is more readily used to stress the authority of apostolic or missionary figures (Rom 1:1; Phil 1:1; Gal l:10; Col 4:12; 2 Tim 2:24; 2 Pet 1:1). This phrase no doubt relates to the Jewish title "servant of God," which is frequently used for venerable leaders (Deut 34:5; Pss 89:3; 105:42; Neh 9:14; Dan 6:20) and is even employed for Christians (1 Pet 2:16; Rev 7:3). Indeed the opening of James (1:1—"servant of God and of the Lord Jesus Christ") shows how the two emerged side by side in early Christian literature. Thus it is to be assumed that the author's use of this title in the letter opening is intended to lay claim to ecclesial authority, whether in the role of apostle, missionary, or teacher. Choice of this title also supports the author's regular insistence on Christ's lordship; that is, calling oneself "servant of Jesus Christ" corresponds to the confession of him as "lord" (see use of "our Lord Jesus Christ" in all christological references after 1:4, 17, 21, 25).

The second qualifying phrase is connected not by *kai* but by *de* and thus functions as explanatory self-designation (BAGD 171.2): "that is, the brother of James." Because the term "brother" (*adelphos*) raises historical and literary concerns in this context, attempts have been made to interpret the word as designating a fellow believer or co-worker of James (as was Judas Barsabbas—Acts 15:22f). Nonetheless scholars more readily presume that the author claims a fraternal relationship to an early Christian by that name. In historical terms the author is understood as claiming to be a brother of James, that is, Jesus' brother (Mark 6:3) or of James the apostle (Luke 6:16; Acts 1:13)—ancient tradition has proposed both, though it and modern scholarship have generally favored the former. In literary terms it must be said on the one hand that the author makes no claim of apostleship (v. 17 seems to confirm such an impression), and on the other the claim to be a brother of Jesus' brother James (rather than "brother of the Lord") is a tortuous way to express such a fact. From this I therefore conclude that the second qualifying phrase, employing as its basis the traditional identification of James as either Jesus' brother or that of James the apostle, functions not primarily as a biographical statement but rather as a strategic claim to the authority of the successful pseudonymous letter of James to combat the heretical teachings of some within the community. The author's appeal to tradition and to the addressees' knowledge of the community's inherited teaching (see discussion of vv. 3, 5, 17) confirms such an interpretation.

Why then the choice of Jude as pseudonym of a letter whose purpose is the defense of tradition against new, heretical teachings? Such a question can be asked of other persons who are assigned early writings (Paul, Peter, and James), traditions, or ecclesial foundations. In the case of Jude the brother of Jesus there are ample stories told about him and his descendants (see

Eusebius, *EH* 1.7.14; 3.19.1-20.7); later traditions abound concerning various apostolic figures, including James and Jude. Ultimately the choice of such a figure centers on the author's need to bolster the authoritative voice of the statements condemning the errant teachers mentioned in the letter. Choice of the name of Jude harks back to the first generation in Palestine when Jesus' brothers and early disciples, in an idealized picture of the beginnings, possessed and preached the deposit of faith. Veneration of these early figures, who belonged to the apostolic age and, in the present case, who was intimately related to or associated with the author of the well-respected letter of James, led an early Christian leader to claim the voice of an early disciple of Jesus (from Palestine) to warn against the new teachings of errant teachers within the community. The author, like the venerable James, speaks with the voice of the apostolic generation (v. 17).

Audience (1b)

The intended readers of the letter are simply designated: "those who are called" or "the elect." Between the definite article and this substantivized adjective is a straightforward construction offering two qualifying statements: "those beloved of God the Father and kept safe for (by) Jesus Christ." While the title addresses the traditional theme of divine election, the two qualifying participial phrases focus more particularly on the addressees' situation by recalling the roles played by God and Jesus in the community's struggles against those slanderous intruders (vv. 4, 10).

In place of the Pauline "saints" (*hagioi*) or "elect or chosen out of" of other epistolary writers (*eklektoi*: Titus 1:1; 1 Pet 1:1; see also 2 John 1), Jude employs the substantivized adjective *klētoi*, derived from the verb *kaleo*. This common verb is frequently used in the OT to designate God's call or choice of Israel (see Isa 41:8-9 where the theme of God's love and protection are also prominent; also 42:1f) and in the Christian Scriptures becomes a technical term, along with its cognates, for God's gracious call to salvation (*TDNT* 3:488-96). Though Jude in v. 3 calls other believers "saints" as does Paul, one might suspect that the term used here in the letter opening has a bearing on the letter's strategy. Indeed just as use of the term "elect" by 1 Peter (1:1) underscores the community's alien or foreign status within Roman society (see also 2:12) or use of "holy one or saints" expresses a new anthropology on Paul's part (passim), so for Jude the term "call" stresses the divine origin of the believer's vocation (see discussion below of the author's theocentered perspective) and, from the outset, insists that the issue ultimately is in God's hands. Choice of terminology again has less to do with a presumed historical situation and relates more directly to the author's strategy in "fighting for the faith."

The first of the two phrases that modify the above designation of the addressees focuses further on God's role; its formulation and theme, however, call for some attention. The theme of divine choice recalls the traditional association that Second Isaiah (41:8-9; 43:1-4; 44:2; 51:2) readily makes with God's love for Israel. Likewise for Jude, God's choice of the addressees is made out of love, and so they are rightly called God's "beloved." Additionally it is the only place in the document where God is called "father," a title no doubt that underscores divine compassion and mercy. While some scholars render the statement as "beloved of or by God," many find the formulation with the preposition *en* anomalous (see *IBNTG* 47; *hypo* is used in Sir 45:1 and 1 Thess 1:4). Indeed, since the preceding passives ("called" and "beloved") already identify God as agent, one is led to interpret the construction differently. It is particularly the parallel statement of v. 21 ("keep yourselves in [*en*] the love of God") that suggests the meaning: "beloved in God" or, less literally, "live in the love of God the Father." Jude wishes here to stress the believer's intimate relationship to God as protection from and the antithesis of ungodly activity.

The second qualifying statement also requires some attention, in structural and thematic terms. It is debated whether perhaps the previous *en* might do double duty and indicate agency or whether the case is an instrumental dative or, more probably, a dative of advantage ("for Jesus Christ"). The last mentioned is the preference of many interpreters since it corresponds more exactly to the author's thinking. Protection is a present, divine activity and corresponds structurally and thematically to v. 21: "keep yourselves (in the present) in the love of God, as you wait (in the eschatological future) for the mercy of our Lord Jesus Christ that leads to eternal life." God's love and protection of the beloved is in view of Jesus' final coming. The author's perspective, in terms of strategy, is that of a community of righteous believers who are divinely protected in view of Jesus' victorious return in "the great day" (v. 6) to restore God's dominion.

Greeting (2)

This part of Jude is both more complex and different from the corresponding structures of other early Christian epistolary documents. Rather than the stark Hellenistic opening ("greeting"—see Acts 15:23; 23:26) or the standard Pauline greeting ("grace . . . and peace"; also 1 Pet 1:1), the author opts for a tripartite formula (see also 1 and 2 Tim 1:2: "grace, mercy, and peace") with an explicit wish (also 1 Pet 1:2; Polycarp, *Philippians*): "may mercy, peace, and love be yours in abundance"; interestingly the nearly contemporary *2 Bar* 78:3 offers a striking triple reference to grace or mercy, peace, and love in the author's letter opening. The multiple themes of the greeting are chosen with the document's message in mind. The mercy and love that are here desired for the addressees have their counterpart in the closing paraenesis of v. 21: "keep yourselves in the love of God, as you wait for the mercy of our Lord Jesus Christ that leads to eternal life." Additionally mercy is not only to be received but also to be shown to others (vv. 22-23). Peace is a state to be sought in the midst of perversion, slander, harsh words, and divisions (vv. 4, 10, 15, 19). And love, particularly as the theme is added to the traditional Jewish-Christian wish for grace and peace, becomes the key to community identity and perseverance; believers are repeatedly called "God's beloved" (vv. 1, 3, 17, 20) who are to engulf themselves in God's protective love (vv. 1, 21, 24).

The brief opening of Jude underscores with authority the document's positive goal. The author claims the authority of the early apostolic generation, particularly in strategic terms the weight of the letter of James, and addresses the audience as God's beloved children. From the outset one detects the author's apocalyptic strategy, for the community constitutes the righteous or God's beloved who receive divine protection against the ungodly who have invaded the community as they await the victorious return of the Lord Jesus Christ. In the meantime the author expresses the wish that mercy, peace, and love be granted to those chosen to share God's eternal glory (v. 24). From the outset also one detects the author's love of doublets ("servant of Jesus Christ and brother of James," also "beloved in God the Father and kept safe for Jesus Christ") and triplets ("mercy, peace, and love"), a feature that will be repeated often in the body of the letter.

Body Opening

(3)

Between the distinct opening and closing (vv. 1-2, 24-25, respectively) one discerns from vv. 3f what one must characterize as the body of the letter. Though, as noted earlier, there is no traditional thanksgiving or blessing, one finds at this point a concerted effort on the author's part to engage the audience in the letter's purpose and message. The body of the letter opens with direct address ("beloved"), introduces a complex double writing formula that expresses anxiety and the motive for writing ("being very eager to write you . . . , I found it necessary to write you . . . "), and closes with a request or petition for specific action on the audience's part ("urging you to fight for . . ."). In a formulaic manner the author alerts the readers to the tone and content of the letter; it is not to be a pastoral exposition of the beliefs they hold in common but rather a polemical treatment of the community's crisis and an exhortation to the addressees to resist these false members (vv. 4f), to adhere to the "most holy faith" (vv. 20f), and to assist those "who are wavering" (vv. 22-23). Verse 3 then consists of the body opening, which lays the foundation for the following sixfold treatment of the errant members and establishes direct, authoritative contact between the writer and addressees.

Our Common Salvation (3a)

Though the term "beloved" becomes a formulaic means of direct address in Christian circles, one suspects that its use here relates to the author's strategy. Thus on three occasions (vv. 3, 17, 20) the community members are addressed in this way, forms of address that both refer back to the letter opening and reiterate the apocalyptic theme suggested there. The audience is characterized as "those who are called," an appellation that is immediately described as owing to God's love and resulting in divine protection in view of Jesus' return. The term of address then underscores the special status of the righteous, whom the author presents as facing the scoffers and ungodly intruders of the end-days (vv. 4, 18).

The first part of the double writing formula employs a familiar Greek idiom *pasan spouden poieomai* ("having great eagerness" or "being very eager or anxious"), which could suggest either the author's desire or intention to write ("I wanted to" or "had already decided to") or the actual process of writing ("I had begun to" or "was in the process of"). Seizing upon these possibilities scholars have offered a variety of conjectures concerning the author's intended and actual letters. Seemingly Jude is not about the parties' "shared or common salvation" or even about the "faith . . . handed over to the saints"; rather it is an exhortation to the addressees to combat heretical members. Thus most scholars propose that the author intended to write a general pastoral letter (a document that either was never written or was latter composed—2 Peter and Hebrews have been suggested as candidates) but upon receiving alarming news from the audience decides to address their immediate concerns.

It is my suspicion that such a historical reconstruction takes too literally what appears to be a literary convention—some even use this writing formula of v. 3 to support a claim of authenticity. Instead the author of Jude counters what is perceived to be an unpleasant task on the writer's part and a cheerless message from the audience's point of view by insisting that it would be far more agreeable for author and addressees to discourse on the positive subject of Christian faith. In effect v. 3 is a self-serving defense made by the author to blunt the negative, polemic character of the letter that is being composed.

At the same time Jude's characterization of the Christian message as "our common or shared (*koinos*) salvation" calls for some attention both in terms of theological language and choice of terminology. On the one hand, choice of the term *koinos* speaks to the author's concern for orthodoxy. By insisting that author and audience share a "common" doctrinal deposit, the author prepares for what will subsequently be described and contrasted as aberrant teaching of ungodly outsiders. The appeal to apostolic tradition (see also later in the verse) thus sets the stage, in strategic terms, for a fierce condemnation of the opponents' unorthodox theological and christological beliefs.

On the other hand, the author's use of the expression "our . . . salvation" to speak of Christian faith has been the cause of acrimonious debate. Some interpreters have insisted that "salvation" for Jude is a present reality, a usage that therefore would point to late, "early Catholic" composition. In their estimation this letter lacks the eschatological or future sense that one discerns in Paul's concept of salvation. So Jude is seen as defending a stultifying set of doctrines (an established faith—v. 3b), among which doctrines is a concept of salvation seen as owing to a past event and bestowed in the present by the established church to its members. Such a reading of Jude is often reinforced by speaking of "the salvation we share." Others point to the author's complementary use of the term "save" (vv. 5, 23, 25) to insist that salvation is a future reality, much as it is in Paul. They note that v. 21 (future "mercy . . . that leads to eternal life") supports such a reading.

Unfortunately the discussion has centered on a defense of Jude being either early and traditional (in a Pauline sense) or late and orthodox (in an "early Catholic" sense) and, in light of this, one or the other interpretation of salvation has been proposed. In effect neither interpretation fits sufficiently either in contextual or thematic terms. Though many scholars insist that the context for interpreting the meaning of salvation is the presumed parallel between it and the following statement about faith, it seems ill-advised to adopt such a conclusion, since the former refers to a different topic (one the author would have liked to discuss) than the one addressed in the letter. Also one suspects that interpreters too easily apply the "once-for-all" character of faith (as expressed later) to their interpretation of salvation. Also, in thematic terms one sees from v. 5 that although salvation is a past event, it is not a "once-for-all" reality since it can be lost as the result of nonbelief. Thus at this point we might conclude that the author's concept of salvation is a broad one that encompasses divine initiative and compassion (vv. 21, 24-25) and human effort, activity, and assistance (vv. 5, 20-23). The author would have preferred writing about the positive, yet challenging common task of Christian living that looks to eternal life, but must instead attend to a more critical and pressing need.

Defense of the Christian Message   (3b)

The second part of the writing formula expresses forthrightly the author's basic purpose for composing the letter. While the first part of the formula, by employing a present infinitive, expresses a general attitude on the author's part, the second, by using an aorist instead, focuses on the concrete task at hand. This task is described as a necessity (*anagken echo*), an expression that here underscores responsibility (whether owing to position or inner compulsion) rather than divine necessity (see also Luke 14:18; Heb 7:27). Seemingly the author wishes to contrast the pleasantness of the first task to the less-agreeable nature of the second.

The remainder of v. 3 expresses in intriguing terms what the author considers to be the goal of the letter. Several of these terms require attention.

From the outset Jude states that the letter has exhortation as its goal, for the addressees are "urged to fight." Though one can hardly argue for the use here of a *parakaleo* formula (see 1 Thess 4:1; Rom 12:1-2; 15:30-32), one should note the author's diligence in addressing the audience ("beloved") and exhorting them to achieve the goal that the letter proposes (use of an infinitive of purpose).

The second term of interest is *epagonizomai*, a word that, along with the whole *agon* word group, suggests struggle or athletic competition. There is debate concerning the term's meaning in this context whether it implies a strictly defensive activity (in an "early Catholic" sense) or suggests a more offensive or missionary intent (as is more common in NT usage). Though this terminology is employed by contemporary philosophers to describe the moral contest of life and by NT authors (particularly Paul) to characterize the missionary struggle to establish communities of faith, its use in Jude takes a different direction, one that suggests defense of the faith and its doctrinal and moral precepts rather than its establishment and exemplification in lives worthy of the gospel (see Phil 1:27-30). On the one hand the defensive and polemic character of most of the letter is unmistakable because repeatedly (vv. 4f, 8f, 10f, 12f, 14f) the teachers are singled out for severe criticism and threatened with divine punishment for having perverted, abandoned, or abused the community's venerable traditions. On the other hand the addressees at the outset are exhorted to join in the defensive battle rather than being part of the problem (see vv. 22-23) and toward the end of the document are enjoined both to live consonant with their faith and to assist those who are vulnerable to the aberrant teachings in question (vv. 20-23). One detects in Jude not the defensive posture of a triumphant Church but a bitter internal struggle by the leadership of the community for the hearts and minds of its members (see v. 16).

The object that is to be so vigorously defended is curiously characterized as "the faith," an object that is further qualified as "once-for-all handed over to the saints." This description has been variously interpreted. Some scholars have insisted, in exaggerated fashion, that the term "faith" (*pistis*) refers to an orthodox creedal deposit or collection of confessional formulas that are said to have been given by Christ to the original apostles. Others have countered that the concepts of faith, tradition, and saints found in v. 3 are consistent with what one finds in Paul and other early NT writers. Indeed the term "faith" refers not to commitment or fidelity but to that which is believed or the message, a usage that is found in Paul (Gal 1:23; 1 Cor 16:13) and especially in later writers (Col 1:23; 1 Tim 3:9; Acts 6:7). More crucial for the reading of this long phrase is the interpretation of the terms modifying "faith," terms that are carefully placed between the article and noun. The deposit or message (note that Jude nowhere employs "gospel" but in v. 20 speaks of one's "most holy faith" as something on which to build) is characterized as "handed over or delivered (*paradidomi*) once and for all to the saints (*hagioi*)." Though some have proposed that Jude's conception here is that of Jesus handing over the deposit of faith to the apostles, it seems more correct, in accordance with NT usage of the verb *paradidomi* (1 Cor 11:2, 23; 15:3; 1 Thess 2:13), to view the process as involving the apostolic agents responsible for the communication and formulation of the church's tradition, particularly as it was received and preserved by believers, here called "saints" (as often in the NT: Paul, passim; Acts 9:13; Heb 6:10; Rev 5:8). This traditional deposit, comparable to Paul's one true "gospel of Christ" (Gal 1:6-10), is viewed by Jude as a sacred trust conferred "once for all" because it represents or encapsulates, in metonymic fashion, a "once-for-all" event, the Christ-event (see also Rom 6:10; 1 Pet 3:18). Finally, while it would be possible to interpret the term "saints" as designating the original followers of Jesus, it seems preferable to see the term, in traditional fashion, as referring to Christians generally. The addressees like others elsewhere in the church have the responsibility to defend the deposit of faith that has been given to all believers.

The body opening therefore addresses the main purpose of the document; it is a plea to the community to deal firmly with those who forsake the community's venerable traditions and an exhortation to all that they consider the situation a crisis that calls for bold action on their part, whether it be condemnation of the heretical members, lending a helping hand to those in the community who are wavering, or themselves adhering more rigorously to their "most holy faith." The body opening by means of its writing formulas sets the tone for the polemical letter that follows but also mitigates this severity by alluding to the community's common quest for salvation, a quest that requires the beloved to reach into the "fire" to rescue those who are perishing.

Suggested Readings

Bauckham, R. J. *Jude and the Relatives of Jesus in the Early Church.* Edinburgh: T&T Clark, 1990.

Doty, W. G. *Letters in Primitive Christianity.* Philadelphia: Fortress, 1973.

Fitzmyer, J. A. "Introduction to the New Testament Epistles" in *NJBC,* 768-71.

Hiebert, D. E. "Selected Studies from Jude: Part 1: An Exposition of Jude 3-4." *BS* 142 (1985) 142-51.

Webb, R. L. "The Eschatology of the Epistle of Jude and Its Rhetorical and Social Functions." *BBR* 6 (1996) 139-51.

White, J. L. "New Testament Epistolary Literature in the Framework of Ancient Epistolography." *ANRW* 25.2 (1984) 1730-56.

Six Alternating Patterns Regarding False Teachers

(Jude 4-23)

Proper analysis of the body of the letter requires consideration of several important structural and thematic factors. This is especially important since a variety of proposals have been made, employing some of these factors, to discern the document's train of thought and message. Relying on different types of evidence scholars have suggested three different approaches to the analysis of the structure of Jude.

The prominence of scriptural texts and motifs in vv. 5-19 has led some to conclude that these verses serve as a defense of the claim in v. 4 that the heretical members "were long ago foreordained for the condemnation," which is described in the remainder of the letter. This defense, it is suggested, takes the form of a midrashic development based on a variety of traditional scriptural citations and traditions. Others, relying on the letter's rhetorical features, propose that, following a brief presentation of the case against the opponents, the author devotes vv. 5-16 to proving the case against them. The document is then described in terms of deliberative rhetoric as *narratio* (v. 4), *probatio* (vv. 5-16), and *peroratio* (vv. 17f), with focus being on the second part or complex of proofs involving crimes and punishments. Still another approach takes into consideration the letter's typology of sinners and saints or godless intruders and beloved elect and proposes a twofold division, the first dealing with the deceivers and their punishment (vv. 4-16) and the second with exhortation for the faithful community (vv. 17-25).

Each of these approaches contributes to a better understanding of the structure and purpose of the document. In the first case it is significant that prediction terminology ("write beforehand"—v. 4) introduces the lengthy discussion of the ungodly teachers and that the treatment of these is done by means of ancient biblical traditions. It is questionable, however, whether one can argue for systematic midrashic treatment of specific OT texts. Instead one finds Jewish traditions drawn from a variety of OT and intertestamental sources whose examples of unrighteous behavior had become traditional in current paraenesis. Further it is equally significant that added prediction terminology ("speak beforehand"—v. 17) is used to introduce the second part of the document and that this paraenetic section appeals not to ancient Jewish writings but to more recent Christian oral tradition. Thus appeal to Jewish and Christian traditions both justifies the prediction theme of vv. 4 and 17 and serves a rhetorical function in the two parts of the document, a function related to the author's apocalyptic strategy.

In the second instance one can hardly deny that the author intends to discredit the opponents by dwelling on their activities and beliefs as owing to godlessness and by underscoring examples of divine condemnation for such unrighteous behavior. The claim, however, that vv. 5-16 serve as a series of proofs to discredit the opponents is both interesting and instructive on the one hand and limited and wrongly diagnosed on the other. Attacks on the opponents' character or ethos are not limited to these verses but instead are presented in six alternating statements beginning in v. 4 and ending in v. 19, where they are described as intruders, dreamers, slanderers, shameful people, grumblers and malcontents, and divisive individuals devoid of the Spirit (vv. 4, 8, 10, 12-13, 16, and 19, respectively). The descriptive language is exquisitely rhetorical, but the presentation in the intervening verses of past crime and punishment serves less to prove that crime is always punished as to underscore, first, the apocalyptic pattern established in vv. 4f, namely, that "endday scoffers" will be the object of similar divine condemnation and, secondly, the paraenetic message presented to the righteous in vv. 17f that the "beloved" rely on faith, the Spirit, and love of God and assist those who are wavering (vv. 20-22).

The third approach, by recognizing the important structural use of link words and themes in the two principal parts of the document, underscores the author's focus on both the heretical members and the faithful community. First, the community is addressed about the intruders and their godless activity ("beloved"—v. 3) and again in vv. 17f about its own desired reaction to these teachings ("beloved" in vv. 17, 20). Such an approach recognizes the epistolary features of the document as well as its dual focus on opponents and audience. It is less instructive, however, on the author's strategy and unusual interest in apocalyptic resources, themes, and patterns.

Three major features, it is proposed, contribute to a proper understanding of the document's structure and message. The body of the letter in thematic terms falls into two parts, one devoted to the errant teachers and examples of divine punishment for ungodly activity and a second offering advice and consolation to a beleaguered community. Such a division is further confirmed by linguistic and structural observations. It is hardly accidental that a cluster of terms in the first part of the letter reappears in the second section. Thus at the beginning one hears of the "beloved" (vv. 1, 3) who are "kept safe" (v. 1), for whom there is a wish for "mercy" and "love" (v. 2) and who possess "salvation" and "faith" (v. 3). There is also mention of "saints" (v. 3) and of the community that is "reminded" about ancient prophecy (v. 5) and is told about the "prediction" (v. 4) concerning the punishment of recent "intruders" (v. 4). From the outset of the second division of the letter one encounters a similar list of terms: "beloved" (vv. 17, 20), "keeping oneself in" (v. 21), "mercy' ("looking forward to mercy" and "showing mercy"—vv. 21-23), "love" (v. 21), God as "savior" (v. 25), "faith" (v. 20), "holy" ("holy faith" and "holy Spirit"—v. 20), "remembering" apostolic prophecy (v. 17), and "division" (v. 10; see reference in v. 4 to "intruders"). In effect the direct address of the community at the beginning of each section and the author's focus on similar themes underscore the parallel character of the two divisions of the letter and suggest complementary messages for these parts of the document.

A second major feature of Jude is the often-noted sixfold alternating pattern of vv. 4-23. In each case a statement is made about the opponents and there follow either examples, after the first four, of unrighteous behavior and divine punishment or statements, after the last two, of concern for the righteous addressees. In structural terms the six units are introduced first by an initial "certain" people (*tines*—v. 4) and then by five consecutive, iterative uses of the term "these" (*houtoi*—vv. 8, 10, 12, 16, 19). Clearly this repetitive structure unifies the two sections of the letter, while the second part of the unit falls into two types, thereby confirming the twofold thematic concerns of vv. 3-15 and 16-23.

The third crucial feature for interpreting the document concerns its overriding interest in apocalyptic resources, themes, and patterns. Not only does the letter of Jude focus on divine activity and authority as the guarantor of safety for the community and of punishment for the unrighteous members and on Christ's role as the returning lord of the endtime, but it also employs an apocalyptic strategy both to present these opponents and their merited punishment and to exhort the addressees to proper belief and behavior. The opponents are characterized as outsiders or "intruders" (v. 4) who seek to entice the righteous away from the "holy faith" that is under siege. Generous use is made of apocalyptic texts (*1 Enoch* and *Assumption of Moses* —see vv. 4, 6, 7, 9, 12, 14-15) and well-known stories about ungodly behavior from OT and intertestamental tradition, stories about fallen angels, the devil, Michael the archangel, the people of Sodom and Gomorrah, of the desert generation, and other ancient rebels. In effect the opponents are presented according to the typology of end-day satanic figures who rebel against God and of all manner of righteous belief and behavior. They are the ones about whom the apostles spoke: "in the last time there will be scoffers who follow their own ungodly desires" (v. 18). The community is reassured that God is keeping them safe for Jesus' return with mercy and eternal life (vv. 1, 21). But the addressees are also exhorted to keep themselves in God's love, to protect and build themselves up on the holy faith, and to assist those who are wavering in this battle (vv. 3, 20-23).

The structure of Jude therefore is a complex one that focuses on heretical members and righteous believers and that draws from Jewish and Christian traditions the weapons needed for fighting for the apostolic faith (v. 3). The use of a sixfold, alternating pattern both to characterize the opponents as endtime figures and to draw either punitive or exhortatory consequences for the addressees relies on apocalyptic typology that sees in the repetitive patterns of the past a basis for confidence or hope in the near future. The ungodly opponents will soon receive divine condemnation, and the righteous will continue to receive divine protection in view of the Lord Jesus' return to proclaim God's lordship.

Suggested Readings

Bauckham, R. J. *Jude, 2 Peter*. Waco TX: Word Books, 1983.

__________. "Jude's Exegesis" in *Jude*, 179-234.

Charles, J. D. *Literary Strategy in the Epistle of Jude*. Scranton PA: University of Scranton, 1993.

Ellis, E. E. "Prophecy and Hermeneutic in Jude" in *Prophecy and Hermeneutic in Early Christianity: New Testament Essays*. Tübingen: Mohr-Siebeck, 1978, 221-36.

Joubert, S. J. "Persuasion in the Letter of Jude." *JSNT* 58 (1995) 75-87.

Neyrey, J. H. *2 Peter, Jude*. New York: Doubleday, 1993.

Watson, D. F. *Invention, Arrangement, and Style: Rhetorical Criticism of Jude and 2 Peter*. Atlanta: Scholars, 1986.

Wendland, E. R. "A Comparative Study of 'Rhetorical Criticism,' Ancient and Modern—with Special Reference to the Larger Structure and Function of the Epistle of Jude." *Neot* 28 (1994) 193-228.

Wolthuis, T. R. "Jude and Rhetoricism: A Dialogue on the Rhetorical Nature of the Epistle of Jude." *CTJ* 24 (1989) 126-34.

False Teachers, Charges, and Punishment
(4-7)

Following the body opening (v. 3) one encounters the first of six alternating patterns dealing with the errant members. In terms of content v. 4 introduces these opponents and their heresy in a series of statements, while vv. 5-7 give three groups that, owing to their evil deeds, underwent divine punishment: the desert generation of Israelites, the fallen angels, and the cities of Sodom and Gomorrah. From the outset the author establishes the pattern that will be followed in the first four alternating statements; each statement of accusation or condemnation involving the opponents' beliefs or behavior is followed by examples of divine punishment.

The Opponents

The first of the alternating patterns not only introduces the culprits who are the cause of community division, but it also provides the justification for the acrimonious battle that will ensue. Indeed v. 4 is introduced by the only occurrence of the conjunction *gar* in Jude; the author thereby draws a close connection between the urgency for a defense of the apostolic faith and the presence and activity of the people mentioned in the successive statements of accusation.

(4a) Presentation of the Opponents. The first part of v. 4 insists on the reason and the urgency for the polemics that follow and also presents initial clues to the document's apocalyptic strategy. Not only are the opponents mentioned for the first time as "certain people" (*tines anthropoi*), a formula that is presumed by five subsequent "these" (*houtoi*) in the body of the letter, but also they are interestingly said to have "sneaked in" and to have "been foreordained long ago for . . . condemnation." The first expression, involving the rare verb *pareisdyno*, indicates the entry of outsiders into the community but may also suggest the nuance of "infiltration" or "sneaking in" (BAGD 624). Drawing upon this expression scholars have routinely suggested that Jude's opponents were itinerant preachers who had recently infiltrated the community of the addressees. Such groups, it is noted, appear frequently in early Christian texts where they are considered heretics or competing groups and are routinely compared to savage or ravenous wolves and called false apostles or teachers (Matt 7:15; Acts 20:29-30; 2 Cor 11:13-15; 2 Pet 2:1; 2 John 10-11; 3 John 5-8). Instead what one discerns in these texts is a typology that characterizes opponents or heretics as outsiders who invade holy communities and corrupt them with their teachings and practices rather than historical or sociological statements concerning charismatic or itinerant Christian teachers. Jude makes use of this typology to present the opposition as unholy outsiders that are corrupting the community of saints. Further, use of the cognate noun *pareisdysis* to describe the activity of Satan (as one who "causes error to creep in among us"—*Barnabas* 2:10; also 4:9) confirms such an interpretation and points as well to an apocalyptic perspective. Here, as elsewhere in Jude (vv. 1, 19, 21-23), the community is seen as a righteous minority, separate from a perishing world, united in its fidelity to "the only Master and (the) Lord Jesus Christ" (v. 4), and "kept safe" by God for Jesus Christ's return (v. 1b).

A second expression describes the opponents by means of prediction terminology; the statement, however, is variously explained by commentators. The verb *prographo*, which means literally "write beforehand," could ostensibly refer to an earlier statement by an author (see Eph 3:3), to proscription in a heavenly book or list (see *1 En* 108:7; also *TDNT* 1:771-72), or to the interpretation of OT tradition as "biblical prophecy." The term "long ago" eliminates the first from consideration, while the sequence of vv. 5-15 points less to the reality of heavenly books that record human deeds in view of eschatological judgment as to the reading of ancient episodes of divine punishment as paradigmatic for current, unrighteous behavior. Additionally in the expression "for this condemnation" the term *touto* refers to the following examples of divine condemnation written in the sacred books and traditions of God's people. The author insists then that examples of past ungodly behavior and divine punishment set the pattern for endtime scoffers.

(4b) The Teachers as Ungodly People. The second part of the verse presents an interesting characterization of the opponents, a characterization that some scholars see as a threefold accusation against them. This series of accusations would then be balanced by a threefold example of punishment of ancient evildoers in vv. 5-7. Such convenience of categorization, however, is not borne out by stylistic considerations. Indeed the first adjective *asebeis* stands alone as a characterization of the teachers who are then described by complex parallel participial phrases. Thus in stylistic and thematic terms the first expression acts as a general characterization of the opponents, while the participial phrases, in parallel fashion, define the meaning of the first expression.

The errant members therefore are described in ominous terms by the adjective *asebeis,* an expression whose word family originally characterized one's lack of relationship to the deity but whose Hellenistic usage became increasingly dominated by the behavior that ensued. While the term still referred to "godlessness," it then implied related sinful behavior. Such a nuance was conveyed either lexically by complementing the term with other expressions denoting consequent sinful behavior or contextually by describing the sinful conduct of people so characterized. In the first case one hears of "the ungodly and the sinners" as opposed to "the righteous" (Prov 11:31 cited by 1 Pet 4:18), of "ungodly sinners" and of "ungodly deeds" ("deeds of ungodliness" in the plural; both expressions are from *1 En* 1:9 and cited by Jude 15). In the second case the deeds as well as the "harsh words" uttered by the ungodly (Jude 15 = *1 En* 1:9), their debauchery and lusts (Jude 4, 18) are clearly related to the term *asebeis*. In addition this term had come to be used for Israel's apostasy and degeneracy in the endtimes (see *1 En* 1:9; *T.Levi* 10:2; 14:1; *T.Zebulon* 10:3; *T.Naphtali* 4:4-5). Thus the author's choice of this term to describe the opponents is consistent with intertestamental usage, particularly in apocalyptic literature, and was probably suggested by the Enoch passage cited later in v. 15, where both the atheistic beliefs and wicked behavior of the errant members are condemned. Finally it is no surprise that in the three occasions where the author employs predictive terminology—vv. 4, 14, and 17—that *asebeis* and cognates are used to describe the intruders, their beliefs, and activities.

Having therefore characterized the opposition as ungodly the author proceeds to describe first their wicked activity and then their theistic beliefs in parallel complex participial phrases. The first of these statements reads: "who transform the grace of our God into debauchery" or "insolence." The final term *aselgeia* could ostensibly be interpreted as expressing an insulting or insolent attitude toward the deity (LSJ 255; BAGD 114), an interpretation that would parallel the remainder of v. 4 as well as vv. 6, 8, and 15, or as describing the opponents' behavior in typological, sexual terms, a description that would agree with other passages in the letter (vv. 7, 8, 16, 18; also vv. 10, 12). While either option could be defended the latter seems more logical in the present context, because not only does *aselgeia* more readily indicate wanton, usually sexual, behavior, but also such an option underscores the dual meaning of *asebeis* as referring both to belief and consequent behavior. Thus the first statement would point to the opponents' behavior characterized as an abuse of God's grace. This grace or gift, which confers freedom on believers, becomes instead a pretext for licentiousness. They have "transformed" or "perverted" (*metatithemi*) their newly-gained freedom for their old slavery, which will finally destroy them (v. 10). While the focus of this statement is immoral behavior, it nonetheless has a direct relationship to *asebeis*, for the grace that is abused or perverted is precisely a gift from the one Christians acknowledge as "our God."

The second participial statement that characterizes the "ungodly" opponents reads: "who deny (or disown) the only Master and our Lord Jesus Christ." Two significant problems arise in the interpretation of this statement, namely, the meaning of the participle and the identity of its object. In the case of the latter does the Greek text indicate one object ("our only Master and Lord, Jesus Christ") or two (as translated above)? In grammatical terms both options are possible and indeed defended by scholars. In defending a christological reading of the statement (one object) scholars strive to defend the admittedly-stark use of the title *despotes* for Jesus and appeal readily to 2 Pet 2:1 either as a parallel usage or an early reading of Jude 4. Early passages that speak of Jesus as "master" are rare and questionable since these are figurative references in the parables to "master of the household" (Matt 13:27; Luke 13:25; see also Matt 10:25). Further the text of 2 Pet 2:1 says less about the author's interpretation of Jude than about that author's high christology (see discussion of 2 Peter). The evidence points to a joint reference to God and to Christ as objects. The term *despotes* designates God both in Jewish and early Christian literature, and its use with *monos* ("only Master"; see also v. 25: "the only God our Savior") points equally to such a conclusion. Perhaps the overwhelming reason for choosing this option is of a thematic nature, namely, how this passage fits into the author's theology and christology (see introduction). In terms of strategy the letter focuses on divine activity (see insistence in vv. 5-6, 9, 15 on God's role in imposing punishment) and thus finds reprehensible the opponents' challenge to divine authority. The author here insists that in questioning Jesus' lordship and teaching (the faith entrusted to the saints—v. 3) these opponents challenge divine sovereignty and will receive eternal punishment in return.

Thus the second issue, the interpretation of the verb *arneomai*, comes into focus. The denial of both the master and agent then does not involve an atheistic rejection of the deity and its envoy in some Gnostic or docetic sense but a questioning of God's soteriological plan that involved, through the Christ-event (v. 25), a divine call, a granting of grace, and an adhering to the venerable traditions "handed over once and for all to the saints" (vv. 1, 3, 4, 20). The author's characterization of God as "the only Master" and of Jesus Christ as "our Lord" adds further weight to this line of interpretation, because the teachers are said to "deny or disown" in practice not God but God's mastery over human destiny and not Jesus the founder of the community but his present lordship. Instead the author warns of future punishment for the intruders (v. 3) and extends a promise of mercy for the righteous (v. 21) who resist their divisive, corruptive influence.

Divine Punishment

After the introduction of the false teachers and a brief indictment of their beliefs and activities, the author turns to a first series of ancient examples of divine punishment. These are joined to the accusations by the particle *de* (see also vv. 9, 14, 17, and 20) to draw a clear connection between the new charges and the ancient examples of judgment. Additionally this first of four sequential judgment passages (vv. 5f, 9f, 11f, and 14f), like the first of the concluding paraenetic responses (vv. 17f, 20f), are introduced by "recall" formulas that direct the audience to remember the community's venerable tradition.

(5) The Desert Generation and Divine Punishment. The threefold example of divine punishment is introduced by a striking pair of paraenetic formulas, which in their turn are connected to the previous statement by *de* ("so"), implying a contrast between the opponents' rebellion and their divine condemnation. In this way the author wishes to stress the connection between the errant members' abuses and the concept of divine punishment that follows. In light of the abuses noted in v. 4 the author insists that the audience be "reminded" (*hypomimnesko*; see cognate at v. 17) of its earlier teaching concerning God's lordship. The term both underscores the traditional nature of what follows and provides the grammatical structure to connect the succeeding ancient examples of divine judgment ("I want to remind you . . . that the Lord . . ."). Also confirming the formulaic nature of the "remember" statement is a second remark of the author that the audience "knows all this" already (*oida*). This seemingly redundant emphasis underscores the author's strategy both in presenting the opponents as godless and in gaining the community's approval for the condemnation that follows. Believers know (perhaps "once for all": vv. 3, 5; see discussion below) what faith and rebellion mean in terms of reward and punishment—the consequences are a surprise to no one. Also, from such statements one may reasonably deduce that early Christian communities were conversant with intertestamental literature that dealt with the traditions cited in the remainder of the letter. Most probably the author is referring to the community's tradition that emphasizes divine sovereignty and Christ's role as lord of the community.

The first example of divine punishment cited by Jude is drawn from the Hebrew Scriptures and concerns the desert generation after its exodus from Egypt. The text states that though they were once freed or saved by God from the land of Egypt, they were nonetheless, because of their lack of faith, later destroyed by the one who had originally granted them freedom. The Jewish story is about Israel's rebellion against the community's duly appointed leaders, and the reason for their punishment, as here, is specifically stated as refusal "to believe" (Num 14:11). The parallel, seemingly, is that salvation or becoming God's people through grace can be lost, among other things by rebellion against God or by turning divine grace or freedom into reprehensible behavior. The desert generation was condemned to die in the wilderness (Num 14:33-35); the new rebels can look forward to a similar fate.

Finally v. 5 presents two problems that require a brief discussion. The first concerns the identity of the one who punishes the rebels, for the Greek text speaks simply of "the lord" (*kyrios*). Does this term refer to the one Christians call "lord," or does the author preserve OT usage here and elsewhere in the epistle (vv. 5, 9, 14) unless specifically naming Jesus Christ (vv. 4, 17, 21, 25)? While some scribes have attempted to sway the argument in the former direction by substituting "Jesus" for "lord" and while some scholars have argued for a reference to a preexistent Christ as the author of OT as well as NT salvation, Jude's overall treatment of theology and christology points to the latter. God the savior of Exodus is also the Christian savior, who through Jesus offers believers mercy that leads to eternal life (vv. 21, 25; see *TCGNT*, 725-26). Secondly a problem arises in deciding the placement of the term *hapax* in v. 5. Is it placed in and so modifies the participial statement ("you know all this *once and for all*"), or does it follow the subject of the *hoti* clause and so modify the following verb ("who *once* saved a people")? While it is tempting to read the two occurrences of the term in vv. 3 and 5 in the same way ("once for all") and to see the two statements as related, it is probably more reasonable to view *hapax* ("once") as a rhetorical parallel to *deuteron* ("on a second occasion") and to explain the variety in word order as a scribal attempt to read the two occurrences of *hapax* in a consistent way (*contra TCGNT*, 726). Thus the author's focus is not here on the once-and-for-all nature of the community's tradition but on the conditional character of grace or salvation.

(6) Divine Punishment of the Angels. Jude introduces a second example of divine punishment of evildoers, that of sinful angels and their punishment. At first glance and in agreement with scholarship of past generations one might suggest the traditional story of Satan's revolt against God, his defeat at the hands of the archangel Michael, and eternal punishment (see v. 9; also Rev 12:7f). While Jude's statement in v. 6 that these angels "did not keep their own domain" might be viewed as rebelling against God and while the description of the punishment would suit the traditional story, the further statement that they "abandoned their own abode" is unexplained. Besides, the backward reference in v. 7 to the sin of the angels as consisting of sexual aberrations (see discussion below) also rules out such a solution and instead points to the well-known biblical story about "the sons of God" who had children with "the daughters of humans" (Gen 6:1-4).

It is particularly this Genesis story as retold and expanded in *1 Enoch* that explains both the language and the themes one finds in Jude 6. These heavenly beings are variously called watchers, angels, or children of heaven (*1 En* 6:2; 10:9) and are described as heavenly inhabitants "who have abandoned the high heaven, the holy eternal place" (12:4) for a dwelling with humans. For this sin, which Jude identifies only in v. 7, they are banished from heaven and condemned to imprisonment in darkness within the earth with immense chains (10:4-6; 14:5; 54:3-5) until the ominous "great day of judgment" (10:12; 22:11).

Finally the author's twofold use and play on the word *tereo* ("keep") provides a clue for interpreting the exemplary character of the verse. Just as the angelic beings "did not keep their domain" of light and so are "kept" by God "in a place of darkness," so the opponents and those associated with them have abandoned, as apostates, their state of grace or enlightenment and will in their turn be condemned to punishment in "the deepest darkness" (v. 13 —see the reverse play on the same term in vv. 1 and 21).

(7) Eternal Punishment of Sodom and Gomorrah. In what may appear as an afterthought in grammatical terms, the author adds a third instance of sinful behavior and eternal punishment. This new example is also provided by early biblical tradition, that of Sodom, Gomorrah, and the other Cities of the Plain (Gen 19:1-29), but interestingly its meaning is explicitly related to that of the previous group: "likewise . . . in the same manner as the former [angels] . . . they serve as an example." The Genesis story of immoral behavior is simply described as "indulging in sexual immorality (*ekporneuo*) and going after other flesh." While the biblical story itself is variously interpreted in the tradition as focusing on the violation of hospitality, immoral behavior generally, or more rarely on the practice of homosexuality, the text of Jude merits careful attention both for its precise twofold characterization of the episode and its comparison to that of the angelic sin in the previous example. Ostensibly the first statement is a general expression of immoral sexual behavior, and the second is an attempt on the author's part to be more specific. The rendering of the expression of the second part as "pursuing unnatural lust or vice" (NRSV) may suggest homosexual behavior. It is the explicit comparison, however, with the previous angelic episode that suggests here in v. 7 humans desire intimacy with angelic beings in the way that in v. 6 heavenly beings sought sexual relations with humans. The denouement of the biblical story then provides the fiery imagery for eternal punishment both for Jude and for Jewish and Christian tradition.

We might conclude our discussion of this first of the six alternating patterns by dwelling first on the focus and function of the threefold examples of divine punishment and then on the likely source of these examples of divine judgment.

The first description of the opponents, which notes their failings in belief and behavior (v. 4), gives way to examples that have a bearing on the opponents' lack of faith, rebellion, and immoral behavior. In the first example the destruction or death of the desert generation warns of the present sinners' loss of eternal life (v. 21); in the second the abandonment of one's abode of light points to a loss of divine glory (v. 24); and in the third the pollution that ensues from the opponents' self-exaltation and challenge of the heavenly realm (see interpretation of v. 8 below) leads to a punishment by an eternal purifying fire (see the fire imagery of v. 23). Additionally the three examples of sin and punishment relate differently to the addressees. In the first case all believers, like the desert generation and now the opponents, are subject to a fall from grace. In the second example, the focus is on those who, having wilfully deserted their proper place, might be called apostates. Finally the third case involves those who, like Sodom and Gomorrah, challenge the heavenly realm, and bears a warning for their associates, that is, the cities or members "that surround them" (see vv. 22-23 for the author's treatment of those possible allies).

Scholars have routinely pointed both to the biblical texts that gave rise to the three examples cited by Jude in vv. 5-7 and to a variety of intertestamental texts (among others: Sir 16:6-14; *Jubilees* 20:2-7; *T.Naphtali* 3:1-4), which present all or some of these examples with other classical models of ancient sinners who received divine punishment. Examination of these shows no signs of literary borrowing by Jude. Instead one must conclude that the author employed paraenetic commonplaces that cited these cases, along with others, of ancient crime and punishment. In the case of v. 6, however, the direct relationship of the NT text to *1 Enoch* in literary and thematic terms, as well as the author's citation of that book in vv. 14-15, points to direct borrowing from the Enoch tradition.

Suggested Readings

Bauckham, R. J. "Jude's Christology" in *Jude*, 281-314.

Desjardins, M. "The Portrayal of the Dissidents in 2 Peter and Jude: Does It Tell Us More about the 'Godly' than the 'Ungodly'?" *JSNT* 30 (1987) 89-102.

Dubarle, A. M. "Le péché des anges dans *l'Epître* de Jude" in *Mémorial J. Chaine.* Lyons: Facultés catholiques, 1950, 145-48.

Dunnett, W. M. "The Hermeneutics of Jude and 2 Peter: The Use of Ancient Jewish Traditions." *JETS* 31 (1988) 287-92.

Feuillet, A. "Le péché évoqué aux chapitres 3 et 6 de la Genèse. Le péché des anges de l'Epître de Jude et de la Seconde Epître de Pierre." *Divinitas* 35 (1991) 207-229.

Fossum, J. "Kyrios Jesus as the Angel of the Lord in Jude 5-7." *NTS* 33 (1987) 226-43.

Klijn, A. K. J. "Jude 5 to 7" in *The New Testament Age: Essays.* Ed., W.C. Weinrich. Macon GA: Mercer University Press, 1984, 1:237-44.

Osburn, C. D. "The Text of Jude 5." *Bib* 62 (1981) 107-15.

Triple Charge and Prediction of Divine Punishment
(8-9)

Immediately after giving examples of divine judgment the author returns to the errant teachers in the first of five passages introduced by iterative "these" (*houtoi*—vv. 8, 10, 12, 16, 19), thereby underscoring the chief concerns of the letter, whether in condemning the beliefs and activities of these intruders with some specificity (vv. 4-15) or in exhorting the community members to remain faithful to the apostolic tradition and to assist the weak among them (vv. 16-23). In terms of content this literary unit reintroduces in v. 8 the opposition that is now characterized as dreamers whose activity once again involves sexual immorality and a challenge to divine lordship (see also v. 4). In contrast to this outrageous assault on divinely-established order the author offers the activity of two exalted figures, the devil who, by not keeping his own domain, like the false teachers, violated proper order and Michael who, by scrupulously observing the proper boundaries of divine authority ("did not dare"), both recognizes the absolute reaches of God's power and under-scores the inevitability of divine punishment for ungodliness. Again one encounters the pattern seen earlier; statements of accusation are followed by an example of divine punishment, which in this case counters directly the preceding accusation.

Further Description of the Opponents (8)

Verse 8 draws a direct relationship between the previous examples of ungodly behavior and what follows. At the same time the opposition, described simply as dreamers, are said to indulge in three related activities that are presented in a twofold classification, introduced by *men* and *de . . . de.* In this way the immoral activity of the first statement is counterbalanced by the following dual statement about authority or lordship—a similar twofold pattern of accusation occurs in v. 4.

This new section opens with three terms that have a bearing on the author's train of thought. The first of these *homoios* ("in like manner") underscores the close relationship intended between the previous examples of sinners and the new description of the opponents. Indeed the starting point for the new statement is precisely what has just been said about the inhabitants of Sodom in terms of sexual immorality and in their challenge of the heavenly realm. What happened in the past "in like manner" is occurring in the present. In view of this statement the second term, *mentoi* ("nevertheless"), takes on an added emphasis because it contrasts assured knowledge of past, similar sin and consequent punishment and states that the current offenders choose to act likewise despite the ominous consequences that will befall them. The third term, post-positive *kai* ("also"), introduces the new term that describes the opponents. Not only are they "ungodly" (v. 4), but they are "also dreamers." In this way the author underscores the cumulative effect and the crucial role played by the extended description of the false teachers.

As in v. 4 the author characterizes the opponents by a single descriptive term before focusing on their beliefs and activity. In this case, they are called "dreamers" (*enypniazomai*), a term that could also designate metaphorical sleep or blindness. On the one hand scholars often appeal to the term's use in Acts 2:17 (and generally) to underscore sleep as the medium for revelation (positively and negatively—used of false prophets in prophetic literature) and so speak of the sinful opponents as visionaries, who, in agreement with *1 En* 99:8, are easily blinded in the endtime by "the folly of their hearts" and "the visions of their dreams." On the other hand some interpreters view the common use of terms for sleep and dreaming as metaphorical statements of blindness and so consider the opponents blind or dead in moral terms and in relation to Christian tradition (*TDNT* 8:554). Since nothing in the letter supports the visionary option, it seems logical to opt for the meaning that depicts more succinctly the opponents' moral and intellectual bankruptcy (see vv. 10, 12-13, 16, 19).

After characterizing the opponents as blind and immoral, Jude proceeds to list their activity in three verbal statements. First, they are said to "defile the flesh," a statement that clearly parallels the earlier accusation of immorality in v. 4, recalls the ancient examples of sexual misconduct in vv. 6-7, and prepares for later, similar accusations. The expression, however, has broader implications both in terms of the verb employed and the variety of immoral behavior ascribed either to ancient or contemporary sinners. In the first instance the verb *miaino* ("defile") relates to ancient purity systems and so contrasts the defilement of the opponents with the ideal for believers who are to be without blemish and undefiled (see vv. 12, 23, 24). In the second instance one must consider the sexual conduct alluded to that either transgressed proper boundaries (humans and angels—vv. 6-7, animalistic—v. 10) or proper measure (vv. 12, 15, 16, 18). Defilement of the flesh then alludes to bodily behavior that pollutes the entire person and threatens the community of holy ones (v. 23). The expression then becomes an overall statement of the opponents' life of and love for vice or ungodliness (see interpretation of v. 18).

Secondly the opponents are said to "reject lordship or authority." Scholars hesitate both in translating and in interpreting this passage because it is not clear what the term *kyriotes* means in this context. Is the authority or lordship alluded to human, angelic, christological, or theological? Each of these options is indeed defended by scholars.

It has been suggested that the author intends here a challenge to human authority, particularly that of the leadership of the community, among whom one would include the writer of the letter. In support of such an option one could point to texts that see a challenge to duly authorized ecclesial authority as the rejection of heavenly (christological or theological) lordship (see Luke 10:16; 1 Thess 4:8). It has less often been proposed that the term *kyriotes* represents an angelic class (see Col 1:16; Eph 1:21) and so the issue concerns a challenge to angelic authority. There are basic problems, however, in such an interpretation; the term should be stated in the plural (some MSS have modified the text accordingly) and such a reading would probably be redundant in light of the following statement concerning angels. Most scholars see here a reference to the Lord's authority, most frequently viewed as that of Jesus (see interpretation of v. 4; also *Hermas, Similitudes* 5:6:1) or as that of God (see *Didache* 4:1).

Third, choice among these options is rendered more complex owing to one's decision concerning the interpretation of the following statement, which reads: who "revile or slander the glorious ones." Here also there is debate concerning the meaning and identity of the object: *doxai* (literally:

"glories"). Scholars are generally agreed that the term refers in a general way to celestial beings who reflect more directly divine glory, and in effect the term is employed for angelic beings in contemporary literature (1 QH 10:8; Philo *Special Laws* 1.8.45, *2 En* 22:7; *Ascension of Isaiah* 9:32). There is less agreement, however, in identifying these beings and the reason for the opponents' behavior toward them. From the outset one must conclude that these beings are good angels, at least from the author's perspective, unless one deduces from v. 9 that even wicked angels, like the devil, deserve respect (see below). Thus proposals that see the rejection by the opponents of demonic powers or Gnostic archons are not credible. What Jude seems to have in mind is a positive role of angelic beings that the opponents deny or dismiss.

There are two likely avenues for explaining both the identity and role of these beings that are the object of the opponents' scorn. On the one hand, it has been proposed that the opponents in rejecting the Mosaic Law or in claiming freedom from its demands have also dismissed the angelic beings as mediators of the Law (see *Jubilees* 1:27-29; Gal 3:19; Acts 7:38, 53; Heb 2:2). While one may see Paul's use of this tradition to bolster his argument for Christian freedom from the Law as similar or even consider his reference to dependence on the Law as enslavement to the elemental spirits of the world (Gal 4:3, 9), there is much difference in the present proposal. The opponents, in rejecting the moral authority of the Law, also dismiss its divine origin and role in God's plan. In support of such a proposal one might point to the author's concern for Moses (v. 9) and reference to rebellion against his authority by Korah (v. 11). Beyond this, however, one does not find in Jude much interest in the Mosaic Law. Presumably, the Torah would be viewed as a moral code, a code that is utterly rejected as applicable to Christian believers.

On the other hand, one might appeal to the role of celestial beings or angels in cosmic governance as providing the background for the accusation under discussion. These heavenly beings were present at creation and serve as its guardians: as watchers, as enforcers of divine order and of morality, as envoys, and even as participants in worshiping communities (Tob 12:12; 1 QM 7.6; 1 Cor 4:9; 11:10; Matt 18:10; 1 Tim 5:21; Heb 1:14; Rev 7:3— see *TDNT* 1:86). Clearly others in NT times associated angels with "the thrones, dominions, rulers, and powers" that govern the world according to Hellenistic belief (Rom 8:28; Col 1:16; 2:18; 1 Pet 3:22). One would probably be right in viewing the position of the opponents concerning the role of celestial beings as the antithesis of the views of the Colossian community. Whereas the latter sought the assistance of these celestial beings to the detriment of Christ's lordship, so the former denied them any respect or role in the scheme of world order and governance. As the Colossians adhered to all manner of ritual and moral observances to profit from the power of these beings, so Jude's opponents reject all natural and moral standards presumed to be associated with them. Both aberrations had their origins in varied notions of lordship. It is with this notion in mind that we return to the overall interpretation of v. 8. The verse concerns the rejection of divine lordship (*kyriotes*) and its various manifestations, whether in the heavenly or earthly realm. In the case of the earthly realm this perversion is described as a degradation of the human (see v. 10; also Rom 1:18f), and in the case of the heavenly domain this challenge is characterized as a wrongful denial (*blasphemeo*—"slander") of the role played by these divine agents in maintaining the established order (as guardians) and even in bringing about human salvation. Again it should be said that v. 8 is a further commentary on the thesis statement of v. 4 concerning lordship and grace.

Divine Order and Prediction of Divine Punishment (9)

Following a new indictment of the opponents Jude repeats the earlier pattern of focusing on a further example of divine punishment. As earlier (see v. 5) the two components of the pattern are joined by *de*, implying a close connection between the two. Also underscoring a close relationship between the accusations and the threatened condemnation is the use of the term *blasphemeo* and its cognate noun in vv. 8 and 9 (see also v. 10) and the author's concern about celestial figures in both verses. Clearly the example chosen for v. 9 is meant not only to reemphasize the inevitability of divine punishment but also to shed light on the accusations of the previous verse.

From the beginning one can insist that the example of Michael's confrontation with the devil is meant as a contrast ("not even," "but") to what the opponents believe and do in relation to divine lordship, particularly their treatment of heavenly beings. The example given, however, is an odd one on several counts and has generated discussion from the beginning. On the one hand, early Christian readers, both orthodox and heterodox (author of 2 Peter and Manichaeans, respectively) noted the relation between Jude 9 and an apocryphal work about Moses and either omitted the passage in the process of editing or rejected the work as canonical (see earlier comments on Jude's use of apocryphal resources).

On the other hand, determining the source and the exact text presupposed by Jude is difficult owing to the status of present scholarship. In antiquity it was assumed that Jude's source for the story of the battle over Moses' body was a lost Jewish work, the *Assumption of Moses*. While it was also known that there existed another work called the *Testament of Moses*, the discovery in the nineteenth century of a Latin, incomplete copy of what is ostensibly the latter has complicated matters considerably. Since the former no longer exists, since our copy of the latter does not contain the story in question, and since a variety of ancient references to the death and burial of Moses offer conflicting versions of the dispute between Michael and the devil, one can only speculate about the exact source and its wording. Clearly the context for this tradition was the biblical account of Moses' death on Mount Nebo and his burial in an unknown place (Deut 34:5-6). It is at this point that the confrontation between Michael and the devil occurs. As the heavenly host prepares to bury the body, Satan, as lord of matter or as accuser (according to varying tradition), objects to this burial. In the first case a Gnostic interpretation is given to the story whereby Satan is then accused of corrupting God's creation. It is more probable that Jude employed a text that relates the second version, namely, that the devil by accusing Moses of murder (see Exod 2:11-14) claims he is not deserving of burial. Such a conclusion is indicated by Jude's use of the term "slander" (*blasphemia*) in v. 9 to characterize the devil's charge.

Verse 9 therefore relates the story of Michael's encounter with the devil within a context that involves "slander" (see vv. 8 and 10) and somehow relates to the earlier accusation against the opponents that they "slander or revile the glorious ones." From the start the verse deals with two glorious beings, and readers are often tempted to suggest that Jude wishes to insist on respect even for such a fallen angel. That, however, does not seem to be the author's point because the terminology indicates both a judicial setting (*diakrino* and *dialego*: "debate" and "dispute," respectively) and a false or "slanderous" accusation. Michael, the head of the heavenly host or "archangel," is here seen as the principal opponent of the devil (Rev 12:7), who is also presented in his traditional role as accuser. The confrontation between the two figures concerns the worthiness of Moses. The devil has slandered him by accusing him (of murder), and so Michael as his advocate defends him; however, in keeping with the proper sense of cosmic order, he does not pass judgment ("does not dare") on this charge of blasphemy but, by citing Zech 3:2, appeals to the one who has the power to judge: "The Lord rebuke you." In contrast to the opponents who reject the proper boundaries of world order or lordship and deny even the role of the cosmic powers (and perhaps that of their lord—see v. 4; Col 2:15), Michael, even in the face of slander against the renown Moses, does not dare to violate the proper boundaries of cosmic order—God will pronounce judgment on such lawlessness. Michael is the antitype of those who violate or reject lordship. In the same breath the author underscores the inevitability of divine judgment of and punishment for such outrageous activity.

In structural terms therefore this second pattern (vv. 8-9) focuses once again on the teachers' beliefs and activity (rejection of lordship and consequent moral standards) and by means of an example of the rejection of lordship (blasphemous discarding of the role of the glorious ones) introduces a related instance of divine punishment. In this case, however, the example of Michael and the devil relates directly to the slandering of the glorious ones. Thus the term "slander" acts as a linking word between vv. 8-9 and draws a connection with the following pattern and its renewed accusations against the opponents.

Suggested Readings

Bauckham, R. J. "Jude and the Testament of Moses" in *Jude*, 235-80.
________. *Jude, 2 Peter*. Waco TX: Word Books, 1983, 42-76.
Charles, J. D. "Jude's Use of Pseudepigraphical Source-Material as Part of a Literary Strategy." *NTS* 37 (1991) 130-45.
Haacker, K., and P. Schäfer. "Nachbiblische Traditionen vom Tod des Mose" in *Josephus-Studien: Untersuchungen zu Josephus, dem antiken Judentum und dem Neuen Testament*. Eds., O Betz et al. Göttingen: Vandenhoek and Ruprecht, 1974, 147-74.
Loewenstamm, S. E. "The Death of Moses" in *Studies on the Testament of Abraham*. Ed., G. W. E. Nickelsburg. Missoula: Scholars, 1976, 185-217.
Reiche, Bo. "The Epistle of Jude" in *The Epistles of James, Peter, and Jude*. New York: Doubleday, 1964, 187-217.
Wolthuis, T. R. "Jude and Jewish Traditions." *CTJ* 22 (1987) 21-41.

Charges, Condemnation, and Divine Punishment
(10-11)

Following a clear assurance of divine punishment for the violation of the boundaries of lordship in v. 9, the author returns to the opponents in this new section by employing a second iterative "these" to lay further charges against them. This new unit again presents its data in a twofold manner; first, a charge is levelled against the opponents in v. 10, and then a series of examples of ancient evildoers is presented in v. 11. In the first case a close link is established with the preceding unit by repetition of the term "slander," and an even more striking connection is made between present evil activity and ancient punishment by the author's undisguised reference to the destruction of the opponents at the end of v. 10, a reference that leads directly to the triple example of divine punishment in the following verse.

New Charge and Condemnation (10)

The new section is introduced by postpositive *de*, a term that here indicates a contrast with what precedes ("but" or "on the contrary"). The previous verse had given a striking example of Michael as one who did not dare violate the boundaries of proper authority. At this point Jude offers the contrast of the opponents who both challenge lordship and speak against proper governance. Contrary to Michael these people violate and ridicule the standards that in effect they do not understand.

After reintroducing the opponents by means of iterative *houtoi* ("these people"; see also vv. 8, 12, 16, 19) the author presents a finely constructed but enigmatic parallel construction. In the first part the opponents are said to "blaspheme those things which they do not understand." Independently of the second part of the structure this statement is taken to refer either to the opponents' disregard of Moses and the Law or to their lack of understanding the roles of angelic beings as guardians of cosmic order (see vv. 8-9). The second statement, which concedes that these errant members have knowledge "by instinct as do irrational animals," claims that "they are destroyed" by that very knowledge. In interpreting the latter statement scholars either insist that Jude intends a parallel between "by instinct" and "defile the flesh" (v. 8) and so condemns the opponents' animalistic, sexual behavior or appeal to 2 Pet 2:12 to characterize the opponents as mere beasts whose fate is captivity and slaughter.

The verse's literary and thematic structure suggests that more careful attention be given to the overall character of the passage. On the one hand, the precisely formulated parallels direct attention to the contrasting content of the second part of both statements and on the other underscore the proverbial background of the two. After introducing the opponents ("these people" as subject) the author presents the following complementary statements:

a	on the one hand (*de*)
b	those things which (*hosa*)
c	they do not understand (*oida*)
d	they blaspheme
a'	on the other (*de*)
b'	those things which (*hosa*)
c'	by instinct as do irrational animals they do know
d'	by these very things they are destroyed.

The formulaic, identical nature of parts *a* and *b* direct the readers' attention to the parallel double verbal constructs of *c* and *d*.

Parts *d* and *d'* contrast what the opponents do in the first case ("they blaspheme") and what, in the second case, happens to them ("they are destroyed"). The content of *c* and *c'*, however, is far more complex and enigmatic, because use of the synonymous verbs *oida* and *epistamai* ("know or understand"), the first in the negative and the second in the positive, renders the meaning more elusive still. It is unclear in the case of the former what the opponents "do not understand" though one should probably look back to vv. 8-9 to explain the further use of "blaspheme" in v. 10a. There the false teachers are said to "defame or blaspheme" the cosmic beings that maintain the established order; in the present case the author seemingly accuses them of failing to understand what they, by their intellects, should know and thereby revile in their ignorance or haughtiness. In the case of the latter the author provides content to the contrasting statement; that is, what they do understand is characterized both as deriving from instinct (*physikos*) and being similar to what "irrational animals" grasp (*hos ta aloga zoa*). The contrast then is between the human being's higher and lower or rational and irrational natures. These opponents violate or disdain what their rational powers should acknowledge and so are subject to the lower instincts of their animal nature, instincts that bring about their downfall. Perhaps the proverbial statement of the seventeenth-century French philosopher Blaise Pascal captures this concept best: "the human being is neither angel nor beast, but the tragedy would have it that the one who strives to act like an angel ends up acting like a beast" (*Pensees* 678-358). The opponents are dreamers who by violating the dictates of their reason become subject to and destroyed by the urges of their instincts.

At this point one could appeal to the numerous references to sexual aberrations (vv. 4, 7, 8f) as indicating the author's train of thought in *c'*, but one might better appeal to the following examples of sinful behavior (v. 11) as providing the necessary clue. It is particularly the violent, rebellious activity of Cain and Korah that brought about their destruction. Indeed a well-known statement by Xenophon, to the effect that animals are violent by instinct (*Education of Cyrus* 2.3.9), confirms such an interpretation. The opponents are seen passively as people lacking in spirit (v. 19) and understanding and actively as people who disdain what they should understand and are dominated and destroyed by their violent instincts and uncontrollable lusts. Thus, rather than being able to claim special knowledge, they in effect abuse their rational nature, which in a proverbial manner becomes subject to irrational, destructive forces.

Prototypes of the Errant Members (11)

With a rhetorical flourish ("woe to them") the author joins the examples of condemnation to what precedes; the latter-day evildoers not only share in the punishment of their prototypes but also in the willful choice of their present, self-destructive behavior. Adopting a prophetic form of judgment oracle Jude addresses the opponents directly and compares their behavior to that of a well-known threesome of sinners from Jewish tradition (see *'Abot R. Nathan* 41; *Tosephta Sota* 4.9).

In the first case they are accused of "going or following the path of Cain," an expression that alludes not to the death but to the behavior of Adam's son. This biblical figure is best known in tradition as a murderer (see Gen 4:8; 1 John 3:12), but it is difficult to see how the teachers might be accused of similar behavior, though some have speculated that their divisive (v. 19) or licentious activity (vv. 4, 8) might have exposed the community to persecution and even martyrdom. Instead one should look to contemporary tradition where Cain is variously characterized as the prototypical sinner whether his vices be those of ungodliness, jealousy, envy, avarice, or egotism or whether he be viewed as a heretic who denies divine justice, defies cosmic order, and rejects the notion of future judgment (see Josephus, *JA* 1.52-66; Philo *The Worse Attacks the Better* 32, 50, 68, 78, 103, 119; *On the Posterity of Cain* 12, 21, 38-39, 42; *Jubilees* 4:5; *1 Clement* 4:7; targums to Gen 4:8). In this way Jude would be alluding to other characterizations of the opponents as ungodly, profit seeking, divisive, and shameful in their disregard for divine lordship and cosmic order (vv. 4, 8, 13, 15-16, 19).

Secondly the errant members are described as "having abandoned themselves to Balaam's error for the sake of gain." Once again the author appeals to contemporary tradition for the portrait it presents of the prophet Balaam, who is viewed as the personification of greed. Indeed he is characterized in later Jewish writings as having induced for profit the Israelites to sexual immorality and to apostasy (see Josephus, *JA* 4.118, 126-30; Philo, *Life of Moses* 1.266-68, 295-300; Ps-Philo, *Biblical Antiquities* 18.7, 13; see also Rev 2:14). Again the choice of such a traditional figure points to a variety of statements made about the opponents who stray and cause others to stray from the truth, who indulge in licentiousness, and seek their own advantage (vv. 3-4, 16).

Thirdly, the opponents are compared to still another traditional biblical figure and are said to "have been destroyed because of Korah's rebellion or controversy," a comparison that is based on the story of a rebellion against Moses and Aaron as related in Numbers 16. This dramatic episode is brought to a striking conclusion by stating that the "earth opened its mouth and swallowed up" the rebels (v. 32). Once again later tradition sheds light on the allusion as it appears in Jude, because it underscores the envy and ambition of the rebellious Korah (Sir 45:18; Josephus, *JA* 4.14f; *1 Clement* 51.1-4). Like the opponents he caused a schism within the community (v. 19) by his challenge of divinely established authority and order (vv. 4, 6, 8) and by his "bombastic speech" (v. 16—Jude employs the term *antilogia* or "dispute" to characterize Korah's rebellion).

Finally Jude's use of the aorist or past tense to speak of the opponents' punishment ("they have been destroyed") underscores the apocalyptic strategy of the letter, for these irrational, immoral, and ungodly people are destined for destruction by the very things they know and do by instinct (see v. 10b). Like the evildoers mentioned in v. 11, who have been cursed by God, killed in battle, or swallowed up into the earth (Gen 4:11-12; Num 31:8; 16:30-33), the opponents are already marked for punishment and are being destroyed by their worst instincts. Indeed they have already perished and are here condemned in a prophetic (woe) oracle.

Suggested Readings

Boobyer, G. H. "The Verbs in Jude 11." *NTS* 5 (1958) 45-47.

Charles, J. D. " 'Those' and 'These': The Use of the Old Testament in the Epistle of Jude." *JSNT* 38 (1990) 109-24.

Dunnett, W. M. "The Hermeneutics of Jude and 2 Peter: The Use of Ancient Jewish Traditions." *JETS* 31 (1988) 287-92.

Greene, J. T. *Balaam and His Interpreters: A Hermeneutical History of the Balaam Tradition.* Atlanta: Scholars, 1992.

Hiebert, D. E. "Selected Studies from Jude. Part 2: An Exposition of Jude 12-16." *BS* 142 (1985) 238-44.

Moore, M. S. *The Balaam Traditions: The Character and Development.* Atlanta: Scholars, 1990.

Sellin, G. "Die Haretiker des Judasbriefes." *ZNTW* 77 (1986) 206-25.

Vermes, G. "The Story of Balaam—the Scriptural Origin of Haggadah" in *Scripture and Tradition in Judaism: Haggadic Studies.* Leiden: Brill, 1961, 127-77.

__________. "The Targumic Versions of Genesis 4:3-16" in *Post-Biblical Jewish Studies.* Leiden: Brill, 1975, 92-126.

Wolthuis, T. R. "Jude and Jewish Traditions." *CTJ* 22 (1987) 21-41.

Multiple Charges and Prediction of Divine Punishment
(12-15)

A fourth series of charges is leveled against the author's opponents who are reintroduced by iterative "these" ("these people are"). In terms of content this new section focuses on the opponents' reprehensible behavior at the community's liturgical celebrations and then compares them to a series of unmanageable, barren elements of nature. As in previous units the initial series of charges is followed by a statement concerning divine punishment. To formulate this statement Jude borrows directly from *1 Enoch* the Lord's assurance that the ungodly will receive proper punishment. Further the author's threefold use of the root for "ungodly" in v. 15 underscores the previous characterization of these opponents as "ungodly" in v. 4 and their actualization of apostolic prediction in v. 18 by their behavior. In each case the term "ungodly" connotes "godlessness" and consequent sinful behavior (see comments on v. 4b).

Further Charges Against Opponents

This new section follows closely upon the preceding "woe" oracle leveled against the opponents. Indeed the author simply reintroduces them by iterative *houtoi* and proceeds to indict their behavior and unproductive activity. Just as the actions of the three previous OT figures (Cain, Balaam, and Korah) had gravely affected community practice, mores, and structures, so too that of the opponents who are described as subverting the community's sacred meals and as wild, sterile, and polluting agents who are destined for eternal punishment.

(12a) Blemishes on the Community's Reputation. In a lengthy substantive construction the author characterizes the opponents first as disruptive, self-centered participants at the community's sacred meals and secondly in the remainder of vv. 12-13, by means of stark natural imagery, as unproductive, shameful members of the fellowship. In the first case (v. 12a) several lexical difficulties render the interpretation unsure. The opponents are described initially as "*spilades* on your fellowship meals," a term that could be rendered "a hidden reef" or "a spot or stain" (BAGD 762). Thus they would be viewed either as a danger for unsuspecting believers (*spilas*) or as blemishes on the community's reputation (*spilos*). While the former agrees more naturally with Greek usage and would add another image from nature to Jude's description of the opponents, the latter seems preferable for several reasons. Such a reading agrees with 2 Peter's interpretation of the passage (see below); fits better with the other themes of v. 12a (especially that of communal behavior); forms a neat parallel with the author's use of *spiloo* in v. 23 ("stain or pollute") and other references to "perversion," sexual immorality, and shame (vv. 4, 7, 8, 13, 16); and is easily explained as a confusion between *spilas* and *spilos* (note the change from the former to the latter in 2 Pet 2:13).

These "blemishes" are said to affect the community's meals or "love feasts." The term employed is *agape* and seemingly is first used here to characterize the early church's custom of combining its liturgical services (especially the eucharist) with a community meal, a custom and terminology intended to express mutual love and sharing. Indeed this is the usage one finds in the early apostolic church (e.g., Ignatius of Antioch and Clement of Alexandria—see BAGD 6.II). One should probably remember here the problems encountered by Paul at Corinth where rich members ate and drank to excess all the while ignoring their less fortunate brothers and sisters (1 Cor 11:17-29). The parallel is rendered more plausible by the following statements made by Jude, for the opponents are further characterized by two participial constructions: "feasting together without scruple" ("without reverence"—see below) and "looking out only for themselves." The first, while often rendered "carousing together," simply describes the opponents' activity of eating as though they are part of the fellowship. Indeed *agape* connotes mutual love and sharing. The errant members, however, "care only for themselves." This second phrase, which employs the verb *poimaino*, could refer to the activity of shepherds who feed themselves rather than the sheep (see Ezek 34:2; also John 10:1-2, 9-10), but used with *heautous* probably refers less to irresponsible leaders than to selfish members who violate the nature of Christian fellowship (see also v. 16). Thus Jude accuses the opponents of "feasting together" with the rest of the community even though they selfishly violate the notion of Christian fellowship. Additionally, if one views *aphobos* as referring to reverential fear and thus lack of reverence for God (as is implied in v. 4), then one should find added support for the above interpretation. The opponents are not accused of public display or bravery as they eat with the rest of the community but of eating at a meal that by its very nature requires reverence for God and the Lord Jesus commemorated in the communal meal (see further discussion of *en phobo* in v. 23). They are an aberration or blemish on the community's reputation, especially as expressed in its "love feasts."

(12b-13) Unstable, Fruitless, Rebellious, and Defiling. Following an indictment of the errant members' behavior vis-a-vis the community, the author characterizes them more generally by means of a series of four complex substantive phrases, each of which employs stark images from nature. In structural terms each phrase introduces the central image, whether clouds, trees, waves, or stars, which are further qualified by a participial construction or relative clause. The choice of these four central images is usually explained as owing to two factors, namely, (1) Jude's appeal to the four regions of the world (air, earth, sea, sky) to characterize the seriousness of the opposition's teaching and behavior and (2) the probable influence of *1 En* 1:9–5:4 and 80:2-8. In the case of the latter factor Jude cites *1 En* 1:9 immediately following the accusations being discussed (vv. 14-15) and therefore knows the passage in question. Also, it seems that regularity of nature as described in *1 Enoch* 2-5 forms the contrast for the aberrant behavior of the opponents. It is less clear, however, to what extent they are to be compared to the rebellious nature of the end-days as described in *1 En* 80:2-8.

The first substantive clause describes the images as "waterless clouds driven by the winds." While the image of "wind-driven clouds" (see Jas 1:6) looks forward to the related themes of "uprooted trees," "wild waves," and "wandering stars" in the remainder of the passage, that of lack of moisture, probably related to the text of Prov 25:14 ("like clouds and wind without rain"—Jude is closer to the interpretation of the Hebrew text than that of the Greek), prepares more immediately for the second characterization of the opposition as unproductive and perhaps as deceitfully promising what they cannot deliver. Thus they are both clouds that do not bear the expected rain and that are blown aimlessly about.

They are further described as "fruitless trees of autumn that are twice dead, that is, uprooted." Again the author introduces first the nature imagery and then a significant qualifier. Employing traditional biblical imagery of a tree and its fruit (see Ps 1:3; Jer 17:8; Matt 3:10/Luke 3:9; Jas 3:12) Jude accuses the opponents of being sterile. They are unproductive trees in the autumn when they are expected to have fruit, because like waterless clouds they fail to deliver what is expected of them. The reason for their lack of production is not made explicit though the reader is provided with clues. Relying on the neighboring themes of wind and uprootedness one could liken the opponents to the imperfect trees of Wis 4:3-5 that fail to lay a foundation, do not produce, and are shaken and uprooted by the wind. Or one could appeal to the author's apocalyptic strategy and view the imagery in light of the endtime (see v. 18) disruption of nature when, among other phenomena, trees will not bear fruit in due season (*1 En* 80:3). While the latter provides a possible insight into the author's eschatology, the former seems to be supported by the following qualifying statement. Not only are the trees sterile or dead, but also they are "twice dead" since they are also "uprooted" and presumably cast about by the wind. Whether the author is referring to apostasy or apocalyptic condemnation (Rev 2:11; 20:6, 14; 21:8) as a "second death" it is clear that the intention is to characterize these people as both dead morally and already condemned to eternal death (see the concept of destruction in v. 11).

In a third compound statement Jude describes the opponents first as "wild waves of the sea." Again the author intends to emphasize the lack of stability and rootedness of these people; they are raging or roaring waves of a turbulent sea. The second part of the statement carries the imagery into another direction. While the previous accusation had underscored the opponents' instability as well as their lack of productivity, the new statement, drawing upon the character of the new imagery, insists that they are a source of danger because they pollute the community by their abominable activity. The imagery of the accusation is strikingly classical, although its inspiration is probably biblical. Jude seems to depend on Isa 57:20 ("the unrighteous shall be tossed by the rough seas [*klydonizomai*] . . . and its water shall toss up mire and mud"—the second part of the statement is found only in the Lucianic tradition of LXX manuscripts, following the Hebrew text) for the basic concepts (see also 1 QH 2:12-13; 8:15 for similar use of this OT passage) but formulates the statement in considerably more elegant Greek. "The wild or turbulent waves of the sea" now "spew up the foam (*epaphrizo*) of their own shameful activity." The new imagery takes on an active direction, for the opponents, represented as clouds or trees that were accused of being sterile, are now said to produce or toss up, like waves, all manner of "shameful" words and deeds (see vv. 4, 15) that defile members of the community, like so much "mire and mud."

Finally the opponents are compared to "wandering stars," an accusation no doubt that refers back to the example of the angels in v. 6 who did not keep their proper place. In following "the way of Cain," "the error (*plane*) of Balaam," and "the rebellion of Korah" (v. 11) they have become like the "errant or wandering (*planetes*) stars" or sinful angels (see Isa 24:21-22; *1 En* 18:13-16; 21:2-6; 86:1-3; 88:1-3) and will receive the same punishment: "eternal gloom of darkness" (see v. 6).

From the above we see that Jude's opponents are contrasted either to the stable and productive or the wild and rebellious elements of nature (see 1 En 2:1–5:4; 80:2-8). They provide no assistance (rain) to community members; instead they are fruitless because they are defective trees, and they pollute the community with their deeds and errors. In view of these characteristics then they are destined for condemnation as dead trees blown about by the wind and as stars whose light is extinguished in eternal darkness.

Prediction of Divine Punishment from *1 Enoch*

Having not only focused on accusations but also having insisted on punishment in vv. 12-13, Jude pursues now the theme of divine judgment by invoking the authority of ancient prophecy. The words of Enoch's prophecy are presented as confirmation ("so it was about these also") of the punishment previously noted.

(14a) The Prophecy of Enoch. Jude cites as Scripture an ancient text that many contemporaries viewed with great esteem. This pseudonymous text is written in the name of the Hebrew patriarch Enoch, who lived in the seventh generation after Adam and who is said not to have died (according to the genealogical pattern) but to have been taken up by God (Gen 5:24; see *1 En* 60:8; Heb 11:5). This loved one of God is portrayed as knowing the secrets of the heavens and through dreams and visions to be privy to God's judgment of the righteous and the ungodly. The work opens with a vision granted to Enoch about the blessedness of the righteous and the fate of the wicked. It is at this point that Jude borrows Enoch's pronouncement concerning final condemnation (*1 En* 1:9). Jude insists that the words of the ancient patriarch not only spoke of endtime evildoers in general but also specifically of the errant members (see v. 4) whose words and deeds are thereby subject to divine condemnation (see a similar concept as fundamental to the Qumran *Pesher on Habakkuk*). These words of prophecy, like those of the Lord Jesus (see Mark 8:38; 13:24; 14:62), describe the coming of the Lord (accompanied by angels) to judge the ungodly.

(14b-15) God's Judgment of the Ungodly. There follows a lengthy citation from *1 En* 1:9 that addresses the fate of the opponents. The modern reader, however, is confronted with several peculiarities of the passage that may or may not derive from the source being quoted, for it is debated whether Jude is citing from the original Aramaic or from a Greek version. On the one hand, the text of Jude 14b-15 differs from the Greek version on a number of textual points, some of which are unique to Jude ("lord" as subject) and others of which agree with other versions ("behold" at the beginning of the citation: in agreement with the Ethiopic and Latin of Pseudo-Cyprian or the shorter text, "with his countless holy ones," of the Ethiopic and Aramaic versions). But more important still is Jude's use of two infinitive phrases in the place of the three found in the other versions (the Aramaic is too fragmentary at this point) and a likely conflation of the second two on Jude's part. Lastly the conclusion of the Greek text is considerably longer than that of

Jude, which nonetheless follows the former's emphasis on the speech of the ungodly rather than the more abbreviated text represented by the Ethiopic version, which speaks only of deeds. On the other hand, though the citation of Jude favors the Semitic use of *en* in place of the Greek *syn* ("*with* his countless holy ones") and opts for the aorist ("the Lord has come") to render the Semitic "prophetic past" (*contra* the Greek and Ethiopic), it is nonetheless clearly related to the Greek version in terms of translation. Either the author modified the original Greek version by referring to the Aramaic or, more likely, had a less corrupt Greek version than the one presently available to us.

The citation opens with the formal and probably original prophetic utterance "behold," underscores the predictive sense of the statement by retaining or reinserting the Semitic past tense ("the Lord has come"), and stresses further its archaic character (and authority) by adopting the Hebraic use of *en* in place of *syn* ("with" in either case). In this way the reader is confronted with an endtime judgment scene, wherein God's agent, the risen Christ, is already present in the company of the heavenly host ("the holy ones"—see also 1 Thess 3:13; Mark 8:38).

The citation then turns to the twofold purpose for the Lord's coming: "to execute judgment on all and to convict all the ungodly." The first infinitive phrase corresponds exactly to the Greek version, but the second phrase results from a conflation of the second and third reasons given in the Greek text. Jude seemingly omits the second infinitive ("to destroy") and replaces it with the third ("to convict"—in some NT manuscripts the object of the third infinitive ["all flesh or everyone"] replaces that of the second). In this way, by omitting the concept of destruction, the author focuses less on the punishment than on the judicial process. Indeed the quotation addresses first the "judgment on all," both the righteous and the ungodly. In this way the author warns the whole community of pending judgment (see "those who are wavering" of v. 22) before turning to the condemnation of the culpable.

The second purpose for the Lord's coming is expressed in a parallel infinitive construction, which itself is modified by double statements. Each of these is introduced by the prepositional phrase "for all," and jointly they express the reason for the endtime condemnation. The verb *elegcho*, which usually involves rebuke as a call to repentance, here as in other eschatological texts (see *4 Ezra* 12:32-33; 13:37-38; *2 Bar* 83:3) refers to legal conviction and condemnation of the ungodly at the eschaton (*TDNT* 2:474-75). The focus of the author in this case is the divine confrontation of evil and its inevitable punishment in the endtime. Interestingly evildoers are characterized by the same ominous term used prominently in v. 4; they are characterized as "ungodly," meaning they challenge divine lordship both in their behavior and in their beliefs. Owing to Jude's editing of the Greek text of *1 En* 1:9 one finds an obvious stress on the concept of "ungodliness" (the root *asebeia* is employed four times in v. 15) and a clear attempt to describe this theme as involving the opponents' teaching and behavior.

The first prepositional phrase introduces and stresses the immoral activity or behavior of the opponents. By retaining the original, repetitive character of the source, Jude is able to insist not only that these people have performed ungodly deeds but also that they have done these with all abandon; that is, they were done in an "ungodly fashion." Like the ancient sinners noted earlier they willingly follow the path of godlessness by challenging divine order and by behaving according to their destructive, lower instincts (see v. 10b). By means of a parallel statement, introduced by an identical prepositional construction, Jude focuses likewise on the opponents' teaching; not only do they behave in an ungodly manner but, these people, described by the stark phrase "ungodly sinners," also "utter . . . harsh things against" God's Messiah. They are condemned for their denial of divine lordship (vv. 4, 8) and presumably of the Lord Jesus Christ's role as executor of divine judgment. They are said to utter "harsh or terrible things (*sklepos*) against" the Lord. For the interpretation of this accusation one should probably note the following clues. First, Jude is here following the lead of *1 En* 1:9f in describing the ungodly as transgressors of God's commands, as people who utter harsh words with their impure mouths, and as sinners addicted to wickedness and pride (5:4-8). Second, the character of their speech must be seen in light of their denials (v. 4), challenges to authority (v. 8), "bombastic speech" (v. 16), and description as "endtime scoffers" (v. 18). The opponents' doctrine therefore must be related to their stubborn resistance to God's plan for security (v. 1) and their prideful rejection of divine "mercy, peace, and love" through God's Messiah (see further discussion of vv. 16, 19, 24). Thus, employing the words of *1 Enoch*, Jude condemns the opponents for their ungodly behavior and arrogant teaching "disowning the only Master and (the) Lord Jesus Christ" (v. 4).

Suggested Readings

Bauckham, R. J. "A Note on a Problem in the Greek Version of 1 Enoch 1.9." *JTS* 32 (1981) 136-38.

__________. *Jude, 2 Peter*. Waco TX: Word Books, 1983, 93-101.

Black, M. "The Maranatha Invocation and Jude 14, 15 (1 Enoch 1:9)" in *Christ and Spirit in the New Testament*. Eds., B. Lindars and S. S. Smalley. Cambridge: Cambridge University, 1973, 189-96.

Charles, J. D. "Jude's Use of Pseudepigraphical Source-Material as Part of a Literary
    Strategy." *NTS* 37 (1991) 130-45.
Osburn, C. D. "The Christological Use of 1 Enoch I.9 in Jude 14-15." *NTS* 23
    (1976-77) 334-41.
________. "1 Enoch 80:2-8 (67:5-7) and Jude 12-13." *CBQ* 47 (1985) 296-303.
VanderKam, J. "The Theophany of Enoch 1 3b-7, 9." *VT* 23 (1973) 129-50.

Charges and Apostolic Predictions

(16-18)

After citing *1 Enoch* at length to underscore the inevitable divine judgment
that awaits "ungodly sinners," Jude returns more directly to the opponents
who are reintroduced by iterative "these." Following the pattern seen earlier
this new unit first presents accusations in a twofold structure against the
opponents (v. 16) and then invokes apostolic tradition to underscore the
apocalyptic strategy being employed to deal with these ungodly people (vv.
17-18). The opponents, in being accused of following their own desires
rather than those of God and indulging in arrogant speech, are identified
with endtime deceivers who are marked by their scoffing speech and ungodly
behavior.

Twofold Charge

The Greek text of v. 16 offers a variety of adjectival and participial forms
along with two finite verbs. Although translators often opt to render this
passage as a threefold series of accusations, it seems best to follow the
grammatical structure of the verse and to propose a twofold charge, each
introduced by an independent clause (connected by "and") and modified by
an adjectival or participial construction. Each charge then becomes a complex formulation of the indictment and corresponds to the following twofold
statement of accusation attributed to apostolic tradition. The new charges,
while focusing on behavior and speech, nonetheless involve the themes of
rebellion and personal gain.

(16a) Rebellion against Divine Order. This new section opens with the
familiar *houtoi* ("these people") and immediately reintroduces the opponents
who are the object of the author's condemnation. In the initial statement
they are characterized as "grumblers, that is, malcontents who follow their
own desires." The first term *goggustes* no doubt associates these people with
the "murmuring or grumbling" of the wilderness generation (use especially
of the verb), which expressed its displeasure or indeed its rebellion against

God and the community's divinely-appointed leaders (Exod 16:8; 1 Cor 10:10). Indeed the Israelites' lack of trust in Moses and Aaron and Korah's rebellion are both referred to as "grumbling or murmuring" in the LXX (see Num 14:2, 11; 16:11) and earlier cited by Jude as examples of ancient sinners (see vv. 5 and 11). The exact meaning of this "grumbling," however, is unclear since the lack of trust or rebellion could be seen as directed, as are the OT examples, either against community leaders or more seriously against God. Thus the second term *mempsimoiros* and its participial modifier give further specificity to the initial characterization. The "grumbling" is to be interpreted by the second term as "finding fault with fate" (the literal meaning of the compound word) or as rebellion against divine order. Thus, this second term is here translated as "malcontent" to express the opponents' rejection of God's moral order or restrictions and their choice to "follow their own desires." To describe the last mentioned term one might refer to v. 18 where the same participial construction is repeated in the apostolic citation but with the qualifier: "their own ungodly desires." The term *epithymia* in this instance refers not to sinful desire (a possible meaning) but to the opponents' rejection of God's will in favor of their own instinctive desire, which will, in the end, serve to destroy them (see v. 10). Verse 16a then characterizes the false teachers as disgruntled creatures who rebel against their creator in favor of their own interests and instinctive behavior.

(16b) Immoral Teaching and Flattering Attention. The second part of the verse expresses yet another accusation against the opponents; it is said that "their mouths utter haughty words while flattering people for their own advantage." One calls to mind immediately the author's repeated insistence that the opponents' wrongdoing involves both reprehensible behavior and objectionable speech (see 4, 8, 10, 15, 16, 18). So having addressed their self-centered behavior in the first part of the verse the author turns to their speech, which is characterized as *hyperogkos*. This adjective could refer to speech as "excessive, inflated, bombastic, or haughty" (BAGD 841), depending on the context and object of such address. While one could insist that the speech is directed to the community and that, by means of "inflated or excessive" claims, the opponents are ingratiating themselves or currying favor with some members of the community, it seems that the citation of v. 18, in speaking of "scoffers," demands that the speech involve theological issues or speech about God and divine order. Such an interpretation would also agree with the citation of *1 Enoch* in v. 15 where the ungodly are said to utter "harsh things against" the Lord.

It is preferable to view this speech, in light of vv. 4, 8, and 15 particularly, as referring to "haughty or bombastic" statements made against God and divinely established order. There is difficulty, however, in relating such speech to the remainder of v. 16b and its theme of currying favor with members of the community. Indeed the expression *thaumazo prosopa* (literally: "to admire someone") in view of its LXX usage (Gen 19:21; Lev 19:15; Deut 10:17) and negative context in Jude 16 ("for their own advantage or gain") seems to demand a sense of "fawning over, showing partiality, or flattering" (BAGD 352.1; see also Gal 2:6). What then is the relationship between denigrating speech about God and currying human favor? Presumably one could suggest that the challenge of the first leads to the second, whereby an attack against divine lordship and moral order would prepare for the errant members' abolition of moral restraints. Thus they act on two fronts at once: they reject the moral order, which belief in God as master and Jesus Christ as lord requires (vv. 4, 8—so their haughty words against God), and they become teachers for hire as they cater to the whims and lower instincts of their audiences (so they manipulate their hearers for their own interests—see v. 12).

The Endtime Scoffers of Apostolic Prediction

Having focused once more on accusations against the opponents in v. 16, Jude turns in a second section (vv. 17-18), addressed directly to the community ("but you, beloved"—the same is true of the sixth pattern; see v. 20), to the theme of prediction (see v. 4) by drawing from apostolic tradition. Clearly this forms part of the author's strategy as the letter draws from apocalyptic warnings about endtime deception of the elect. In this way the teaching and behavior of the opponents are linked directly with the ungodly, indeed satanic, activity of the final age of evil (see 2 Thess 2:1-5, 9-12; also Mark 13:22-23).

(17-18a) Apostolic Prediction. The opening terms "but you, beloved" (*hymeis de agapetoi*), as is true of v. 20, draws a contrast between the opponents addressed in v. 16 and the readers of the letter. Since in the preceding accusation they are said to have as their goal the deception of members of the community, Jude turns to the community's tradition about endtime activity. The author seems to have no specific text in mind (see Mark 13:22 and parallels), as the source is characterized as "the words spoken . . . by the apostles of our Lord Jesus Christ." Jude is less interested in specific predictions as in the danger of apostasy; this is borne out by the exhortation of vv. 20f. Employing predictive terminology once more (see also vv. 4 and 14) the author appeals to the Lord Jesus' teaching as preserved in apostolic tradition to condemn the teaching and behavior of the opponents. In this case one could either insist on the description of the apostles as sent by the "Lord Jesus Christ" and focus on Jesus' prediction of bad times after his death (Matt 24:11-12) or point to the apostles as sources about heresies within the community after they are gone (Acts 20:29; 2 Pet 3:2-3).

It has often been suggested that the language of v. 17, along with that of v. 3 (see earlier discussion), confirms a post-apostolic date for the composition of the letter. It is assumed that the verse speaks of the apostles as belonging to a past age. Such an observation is based more on impression than fact since the exhortation to remember what was foreannounced need not imply a long period but rather a developing tradition that is often repeated to communities (see 1 Thess 3:4; 2 Thess 2:5 as examples of repeated warnings). The focus of the letter is on tradition as "known" to the writer and addressees and as derived from the founders of the church; its concern is not the antiquity of the prediction. Additionally one might insist that the prediction is said to have been addressed to the hearers ("for they said to you") and so is presumed to be recent. One should be cautious in this regard, however, since ancient works or sayings are often presumed to have been addressed to contemporary audiences or about current issues (see v. 14; also v. 4). Finally the formula introducing the citation, by its use of the imperfect, stresses the repeated character of the warning: "for they often said to you."

(18b) The Coming of Endtime Scoffers. There follows a brief twofold statement allegedly taken from a collection of apostolic words or sayings. No such passage has ever been identified and, though its themes but not their formulation are frequent in current Jewish and Christian works, it is suggested that this particular passage is a construct of the author who wishes to summarize in a succinct way the activity of the opponents. The expression "in the last time" (use of *chronos* rather than *kairos*—see also 1 Pet 1:20) clearly underscores the author's apocalyptic strategy. Jude's use of the rare term "scoffers" (*empaiktes*—see also Isa 3:4; 2 Pet 3:3) to characterize the endtime deceivers is certainly motivated by the current situation, for the opponents are said to "challenge" or "mock" divine authority (vv. 4, 8) and to employ "harsh" or "haughty" words about God (vv. 15, 16). Additionally the author formulates the second part of the citation by modifying slightly an earlier accusation leveled against the opponents; only the ubiquitous term "ungodly" is added (see discussion of v. 4).

By means of this statement the author summarizes once again the twofold nature of the false teachers' ungodliness; they "transform the grace of our God into debauchery and disown the only Master and our Lord Jesus Christ" (v. 4). They scoff at divine authority and morality as they pursue their own selfish desires. They are newcomers or intruders who have introduced new ideas and ungodly behavior; but the community has been forewarned about this ungodliness and is reminded of its ancient tradition, which now must be defended (v. 3b).

Suggested Readings

Desjardins, M. "The Portrayal of the Dissidents in 2 Peter and Jude: Does It Tell Us More about the 'Godly' than the 'Ungodly'?" *JSNT* 30 (1987) 89-102.

Hiebert, D. E. "Selected Studies from Jude. Part 3: An Exposition of Jude 17-23." *BS* 142 (1985) 355-66.

Jeremias, J. *Unknown Sayings of Jesus.* London: SPCK, 1957.

Sellin, G. "Die Haretiker des Judasbriefes." *ZNTW* 77 (1986) 206-25.

Wisse, F. "The Epistle of Jude in the History of Heresiology" in *Essays in the Nag Hammadi Text.* Ed., M. Krause. Leiden: Brill, 1972, 133-43.

Charges, Community Activity, Body Closing
(19-23)

While the earlier sections of Jude focus on accusations against the opponents, the author's concern is to underscore the divine punishment that is sure to visit them. Indeed the reader of the letter is presented with a variety of ancient sinners who have received recompense for their ungodly deeds. There is a thematic shift in this section even if Jude follows in this case the pattern seen earlier. First, one encounters a statement of accusation introduced once more by iterative "these," and then there follows a second section that dwells not on divine punishment but on exhortation to the community members both to persevere in their faith and to treat erring members with mercy tempered with fear or caution. One notes, in terms of content, a shift from accusation to exhortation and, in terms of tone, a decided change from severity to love, mercy, and concern for those who waver.

Charge of Divisiveness (19)

The charge of divisiveness is clearly related to the preceding claim that the opponents are vying for the attention and favor of members of the community (see v. 16). In fact their activity is described in terms reminiscent of end-day deceivers who split communities apart by their arrogant speech, lax behavior, and selfish goals. The author turns then to the results that such speech and activity have on the community, for they are described as the cause of inner division. This accusation and further description of the opponents as devoid of the Spirit will lead Jude in vv. 20-23 to address a heartwarming exhortation to those who are faithful or at least receptive.

Once again the accusation section opens with the familiar *houtoi* ("these people"), a term that recalls the previous five sets of charges. From the outset they are characterized by the rare word *apodiorizo*, which means either "to make distinctions" or "to separate" (see BAGD 90). In the first case one could insist that the opponents "create divisions"; that is, they would belong to a spiritualist group that divided people into a pneumatic elite and a psychic general population. They would therefore have intentionally divided people according to whether they lived by the Spirit or by natural instincts. In the second case it is claimed that the errant members "caused divisions" by their teaching and reckless behavior. The divisions would be the result and not necessarily the intention of the opponents' teaching.

Both nuances are defended by scholars who either propose Gnostic influence, in the case of the former, or a less precise divisiveness, in the case of the latter, which would result from doctrinal and organizational disunity. The following characterization of the opponents as "worldly people who do not have the Spirit" provides further data for examining the nature of the divisions within the community and sheds light either on what these people thought of themselves or on how Jude chooses to describe them. In the first instance the term employed is *psychikos*, meaning a "nonspiritual, physical, or psychic person" in contrast to one who has or lives by the Spirit. In fact Jude follows this description by the further explanation that these people are "devoid of the Spirit."

Rather than seek in second and third-century Gnosticism parallels for Jude's "psychic and spiritual" distinction, one can hardly find a better comparison than Pauline usage in 1 Cor 2:14-16. Similar situations seem to be envisioned in both cases where people in the Christian community seemingly boast of a superior measure of the Spirit. In both cases Christians who make a special claim to spiritual power subject themselves to what is described by their opponents as immoral behavior. While one can reasonably presume in the Corinthian situation that Paul is using the spiritualists' own terminology, in the present case one should probably envision the terms of v. 19 as deriving from Jude who does not focus on the dualism of the language but rather denies emphatically the false teachers' spiritual claims. Rather than demonstrating that they are under the sway of the Spirit, their ungodly behavior and arrogant challenge of divine authority prove that they are worldly, morally blind, and rebellious malcontents who act according to their ungodly desires. Jude sees their teaching and behavior as proof not of spiritual prowess but of their godlessness and nonspiritual status. Their teaching and behavior, their claims of superiority, and their disregard for moral standards have brought about confusion, doubt, defilement, and arrogance that have ripped the community apart. Some members of the community have been tempted by such arrogance and debauchery and have put the "most holy faith" in jeopardy. Such activity is not the work of the Spirit but of worldly scoffers who are marked for condemnation.

Appeal to the Community "To Fight for the Faith"

Following a final accusation against the opponents, but one that affects the community's well-being or unity, Jude turns more directly to the addressees and their concerns. Employing a form of address used in v. 17 to introduce pertinent apostolic tradition ("but you, beloved") the author draws a sharp contrast between the psychic teachers who are "devoid of the Spirit" and the faithful who are to "pray in the Holy Spirit." In a series of exhortations the author counsels the addressees to remain faithful to God's grace, to attend to the unity and health of God's holy edifice, and to lend a merciful but discerning hand to wayward brothers and sisters.

(20-21) Exhortation to Perseverance. After drawing a sharp contrast between the worldly teachers and the receivers of the letter, Jude addresses the well-being of a community threatened by the disunity of boastful and reckless teaching and behavior within the group by some of its members. Verses 20-21, however, present an interesting problem. While they consist of two initial participial constructions followed by an imperative clause and terminate with a third participial statement, they are regularly interpreted as a series of four imperatives by recent translators and commentators. Based on the assumption that Jude, along with Paul (Rom 12:9-19) and 1 Peter (3:7-9; 4:7-10) among others, borrow paraenetic material that often lends imperatival force to participial constructions, scholars opt to render these exhortatory statements as a relatively independent series of commands. In effect, grammatically one must view v. 21a ("keep yourselves in God's love") as the principal clause of the complex sentence and consider the three participial constructions as modifiers that indicate either how the main action is to be accomplished (the first two) or the attendant circumstance or motivation for the activity (last construction). Thus one must view these statements as focused on the theme of love, a theme that has a great importance for the author's purpose in writing. Not only is the community (all Christians in this case) called "beloved of God," precisely as "father" (v. 1), but they are also movingly addressed three times by the author as "beloved" [of God] (vv. 3, 17, 20). In addition Jude's use of the term *agape* in vv. 2 and 12 call for further attention. In the case of the latter it is no surprise that the community's liturgical assembly is qualified as a "love or fellowship feast" since the participants have come together to share God's love through Christ. The former is of further interest since the greeting, in somewhat irregular form, addresses three important themes of the letter: peace, which is sorely lacking (vv. 2, 19); mercy, which is to be received as well as given (vv. 2, 21, 23); and especially divine love, which is the motive for election (v. 1), for gift (grace: v. 4), and for protection (vv. 1, 21). The focus then of vv. 20-21 is on faithfulness to God's love.

Before treating the three participial constructions we should look at the imperative clause that reads: "keep yourselves in the love of God." What does this seemingly straightforward-sounding statement mean? Is the qualifier "of God" a subjective or an objective genitive; that is, does Jude speak of God's love for humanity or the reverse? Is this an exhortation to fidelity to God's election or a plea to believers to remain true to their commitment in faith? It is more probable, along with most commentators, to view the former as the author's meaning since the notion of fidelity calls for action on the part of believers and so would imply a reaction to God's benevolence. Further it has been suggested that the exhortation is a call to the addressees either to avoid the false teachings described earlier or to allow the power of God's love to work within them ("keep yourselves from harm by making it possible for God to show his love for you in the future also"—see BAGD 815). Jude's use of the verb *tereo* here as in v. 1 suggests a different interpretation. God's love is seen not only as the source of election but also of protection for the faithful. The addressees are exhorted to remain in their proper place, in contrast to sinners who have not (see v. 6; also v. 11), because there they will receive protection in view of Jesus' return (contrast statements of v. 1b and the present verse). It should be noted that the theme of divine protection of the elect is another indication of the author's use of apocalyptic imagery as strategy (see Mark 13:20; Rev 12:14-17).

Further the addressees are exhorted to "keep . . . in God's love" by "building (them)selves up on the foundation of (their) most holy faith." Employing traditional architectural imagery to depict the community and its activity (see Rom 15:20; 1 Cor 3:9-15; Eph 2:19-22; 1 Pet 2:5-7) Jude insists that the work of believers is that of building up rather than tearing down, that of promoting unity rather than division (contra v. 19). The foundation of this building as well as its growth is precisely the "most holy faith" "that was handed over once-for-all to the saints" (v. 3b). As argued earlier this traditional deposit or gospel is seen by Jude as a holy or sacred trust and so is qualified as "your most holy faith," a statement that underscores the community's responsibility and fidelity as contrasted to the opponents' false teaching and ungodly behavior. Interestingly the author does not attempt to discuss the content of this holy tradition; of primary concern is the community's defense against the intruders. They are to protect themselves by acting as a community, by building on the sure foundation of the Christ-event, and further by "praying in the Holy Spirit."

This last participial construction is variously interpreted; the preposition phrase "in the Spirit," while meaning "under the power or inspiration of the Spirit," can designate a variety of situations. Does the author indicate charismatic prayer (including the "speaking in tongues"—1 Cor 14:15-16), apocalyptic fervor (2 Thess 2:2; Rev 1:10), or more generally the believer's life in the Spirit (Rom 8:9-11)? What is at stake here: the authenticating activity of the Spirit (1 Cor 12:3; 1 John 4:13) or the activity of the Spirit in believers that addresses God as father (see v. 1; also Rom 8:15-17)? It is the last mentioned that addresses the immediate context of v. 20. It is by means of prayerful invocation of God's Spirit that believers will remain in God's domain where they will receive protection in view of Jesus' return.

In effect Jude ends the complex structure of vv. 20-21 by insisting once more (see v. 1b) that believers are being "kept safe (by God) for Jesus Christ" or, in more judicial terms, for Jesus' bestowal of life-giving mercy upon his return. Jude employs the traditional language of eschatological expectation ("wait"—*prosdechomai*: see Mark 15:43; Luke 2:25; other terms are also used: Gal 5:5; 1 Thess 1:10) and interestingly characterizes Jesus' return as the granting of "mercy," in fact, a "mercy . . . that leads to eternal life." The choice of language is significant in this instance. Not only is the theme of hope or expectation emphasized here as motivation for perseverance in the "holy faith," but also the characterization of Jesus' return or judgment (see 2 Cor 5:10) as the granting of mercy points to the urgent need of addressing those who are faltering (see v. 22). On the one hand the language of mercy underscores the believer's need for forgiveness and this particular community's need to listen to the author's exhortation. On the other hand the note that such mercy "leads to eternal life" contrasts with the opponents who face the prospect of eternal damnation (vv. 7, 13). Only God's love can protect the community's members as they await Jesus' life-giving mercy.

(22-23) Exhortation to Mercy Mixed with Caution. After having addressed the entire community concerning its perseverance and fidelity to the apostolic tradition, Jude turns to the issue of wavering and erring members. In general terms the addressees are admonished to view them with "mercy mixed with caution." The precise formulation of this exhortation, however, offers some difficulties to the modern reader, since there exist two basic versions of the passage, a three-clause text and a shorter two-exhortation version, both of which reveal signs of scribal activity. Though translators usually opt for the longer, more commonly-attested version: "so on those who are wavering have mercy; but others save by snatching them from the fire; on still others have mercy mixed with caution"; it seems best on textual, stylistic, and contextual grounds to opt for the also well-attested, two-clause reading (P^{72}, B, C, some Church Fathers, as well as the early Syriac, Coptic, and Latin versions): "to be sure snatch some from the fire; but on those who are wavering have mercy mixed with caution, abhorring even the outer garment defiled by the flesh." Even though Jude has a predilection for triplets (see earlier list of sinners), it would seem that the repetition in the longer version of the theme of "mercy," as well as its clumsy attempt to join the three exhortations (*kai hous men . . . hous de . . . hous de*), and its indistinct grouping of three who are to be helped, among other reasons, suggest that the terse text of the recently discovered papyrus is to be preferred.

A careful examination of the textual variants that have arisen in both types further suggests an attempt on the part of scribes to distinguish between the various groups of offenders and their requisite treatment by the loyal community members. Additionally the uneasy reading in v. 22 of the participle *diakrenomenoi* as meaning either "debate" or "waver" called for different strategies on the part of scribes: either "convince" or "have mercy" (*elegchete* and *eleate* or *eleeite*, respectively). A more careful examination of the two-clause reading shows that Jude did not envision an extended list of people to be helped, but rather a general statement about assisting those who are being influenced by the opponents with the caution that those offering mercy not be themselves taken in by those who still show some defiance.

At the mention of "eternal life" in v. 21 Jude is led to advise the community to "snatch some from the (eternal) fire" (see v. 7). Such a descriptive statement as well as the final construction of v. 23, thus both the concepts of being "snatched from the fire" and that of "filthy garment," are drawn from Zech 3:2-4, a sequel to the passage already quoted in v. 9 (see earlier). Driving a wedge between the opponents and other members of the community who have been led astray, Jude advises the loyal members, in graphic terms, to reach out to brothers and sisters who are being engulfed in the fire of contamination or even condemnation and to assist them as concerned fellow believers. Aware no doubt of the danger of such activity, particularly in light of the extended descriptions of the opponents and their accomplishments, Jude exhorts the addressees to "show mercy mixed with caution on those who are wavering." Such an interpretation presupposes choices made regarding the meaning of two terms.

First, the participle *diakrinomenoi* can mean "those who are disputing" or "are wavering." While both meanings are possible here the first seems less likely since such community members are as unlikely to respond as are the opponents themselves. The second fits better in the context since "wavering" members might present a danger to the unweary brother or sister who lends a helping hand. Second, the prepositional phrase *en phobo* often means "out of reverence or divine fear," or it can refer to cautious activity. In the first case it would be suggested that the addressees not act like the opponents who have no reverence for God (v. 12: *aphobos*; see also v. 4) but should show mercy because they have such reverence. While this interpretation is indeed possible it seems more probable in relation to the concept of "wavering" members and in light of the remainder of the verse to argue less for the motivation of the mercy offered and more for the caution and care that should characterize the struggle for the faith that was noted in v. 3. At issue is fear of contamination.

The conclusion of v. 23 addresses precisely the theme of defilement or contamination. The loyal, concerned believer, in reaching out to such individuals, should "abhor even the outer garment defiled by the flesh." Interpretation of this statement and therefore discernment of the author's purpose is quite diverse. While some would see here a prohibition against contact with such sinners or heretics, the context, particularly as expressed by the two-exhortation version, seems to exclude such a conclusion, since mercy is to be shown them. Further there is debate concerning the meaning of the garment or tunic: does it refer to an outside source of pollution (the sinful world), to the body in terms of flesh as evil, or to the baptismal garment that reflects the reception of new life? Clearly the notion of defilement here favors the last mentioned for what was formerly pure has now been polluted by a return to life in the flesh. These people along with their teachers "have transformed God's grace into debauchery" (v. 4). That soiled tunic or "filthy garment," the symbol of ungodly desires and behavior, must be rejected and indeed replaced by clean apparel (see Zech 3:3-5). Caution and aversion to impurity are advised, but mercy must be shown to the wayward. The author fights for the faith by combatting uncompromisingly the source of heretical teaching and ungodly behavior, by exhorting the addressees to remember apostolic tradition and to persevere in God's protective love, and by enlisting their assistance in extending a helping hand to brothers and sisters who have been taken advantage of by the malcontents in their midst. Ultimately, in this final major section, Jude returns to the opening subject of the letter, namely, the community's "common salvation" or well-being (v. 3). Here the addressees are exhorted to unity, fidelity, and trust in God's assistance as they await the Lord Jesus' return to grant life-giving mercy.

Suggested Readings

Allen, J. S. "A New Possibility for the Three-Clause Format of Jude 22-23." *NTS* 44 (1998) 133-43.

Bieder, W. "Judas 22f.: *Hous de eate en phobo*." *TZ* 6 (1950) 75-77.

Birdsall, J. N. "The Text of Jude in P[72]." *JTS* 14 (1963) 394-99.

Horsley, R. A. "Pneumatikos vs. Psychikos Distinctions of Spiritual Status Among the Corinthians." *HTR* 69 (1976) 269-88.

Joubert, S. J. "Language, Ideology, and the Social Context of the Letter of Jude." *Neot* 24 (1990) 335-49.

Kubo, S. "Jude 22-23: Two-Division Form or Three?" in *New Testament Text Criticism: Its Significance for Exegesis*. Eds., E. J. Epp and G. D. Fee. Oxford: Clarendon, 1981, 239-53.

Lyle, K. R. *Ethical Admonition in the Epistle of Jude*. Bern: Lang, 1998.

Osburn, C. D. "The Text of Jude 22-23." *ZNTW* 63 (1972) 139-44.

Pearson, B. A. *The Pneumatikos-Psychikos Terminology in 1 Corinthians*. Missoula: Scholars, 1973.

Ross, J. M. "Church Discipline in Jude 22-23." *ET* 100 (1989) 297-98.

Webb, R. L. "The Eschatology of the Epistle of Jude and Its Rhetorical and Social Functions." *BBR* 6 (1996) 139-51.

Closing

(Jude 24-25)

In lieu of a traditional epistolary closing variously consisting of final greetings, prayer, injunctions, and a benediction (see 1 Thess 5:23-28; 1 Pet 5:12-14), Jude brings the letter to a close with an extended doxology. The form as well as the greater part of the content are traditional and so find numerous parallels in NT literature. On the one hand, the doxology of Jude 24-25 bears the characteristics of the traditional doxology (person addressed in the dative, praise expressed as glory, statement of temporal duration, and an affirmative "amen"). Though there are expansions of these various characteristics, whether further description of the one addressed or an extended list of themes added to the concept of glory, these are well attested in contemporary doxologies (1 Tim 1:17; Rev 5:13). On the other hand, Jude 24-25 is not unique in beginning the doxology "to the one who is able to . . . ," nor even in reiterating the address formula later as "to the only God . . . " (see Rom 16:25-27; Eph 3:20; also *Martyrdom of Polycarp* 20:2). Also, while doxologies usually occur at diverse points in early Christian documents, Jude again is not unique in placing this form at the very end (see Rom 16:25-27; 2 Pet 3:18; and later Christian texts).

In structural terms the doxology of vv. 24-25 falls into two parts, each introduced by an address formula. The first part (v. 24) focuses on a major theme of the letter, that of divine protection for the righteous, and the second (v. 25), by means of a resumptive construction, returns to the traditional form and function of the doxology.

Praise to God as Protector

(24)

The first part of the doxology is addressed to God precisely as "the one who is able" or has the power to do two things, both of which are introduced by infinitive constructions. The first of these states that God is able "to keep or protect you from stumbling." The theme of divine protection has already appeared at several points in the letter, indeed as early as v. 1 where the addressees are characterized as those "kept safe for Jesus Christ." Further they are exhorted to "keep themselves in the love of God," which protects them as they await Jesus' return (v. 21). No doubt Jude wishes to contrast the faithful, who depend on God's assistance, with ancient sinners and the problematic opponents who did not keep to their divinely assigned places but chose to follow their own ungodly desires in defiance of divinely established order (vv. 4, 6-7, 11-12, 16, 19). Furthermore this concept of divine protection of the righteous is both an apocalyptic and more general NT theme (2 Thess 3:3; Rev 3:10; 1 Pet 1:5; John 17:11). Lastly this protection focuses on the image of "stumbling" (*aptaistos*) or "falling." This rare term is similarly employed (use of the verb *ptaio*) in Rom 11:11 and 2 Pet 1:10 to describe deviation from the path of holiness and probably alludes to the more explicit "stumbling" terminology frequently encountered in the Psalms, which also portray God as guardian of the righteous (see 121:3-8; 140:4-8). In the present context the theme serves a paraenetic function by focusing on God's assistance to the beloved in their present situation. Thus God will provide the strength for them to keep themselves from harm or "in God's love" (v. 21).

The second infinitive phrase directs the reader's attention to the goal of present behavior, namely, that God is the one who "is able . . . to present you in the presence of his glory." Whereas in v. 1 God's present protection is said to have Jesus' return in view (see also v. 21, which speaks of "awaiting the Lord Jesus Christ's mercy"), in the present case the author focuses on formal admission (*histemi*) to the divine presence as the goal of Christian life. But it is not the actual arrival into the divine presence, here expressed as "glory" or divine radiance, which is the author's concern but, as an antithetical parallel to the preceding infinitive, the believer's presentation as either "blameless" or "unblemished" (*amomos*). The term could ostensibly refer back to v. 12, which describes the opponents as "blemishes," and even v. 23, which speaks of their "defiled tunics" and perhaps suggests a sacrificial nuance (see 1 Pet 1:19; Heb 9:14), but more probably it, along with other NT references (Phil 2:15; Col 1:22; Eph 1:4; 5:27; Rev 14:5), describes the righteousness or moral purity that is required of believers who both "fight for their common salvation" and "keep themselves in God's love" (vv. 3, 21; see also 1 Thess 5:23).

Finally the entire statement concerning Christian holiness and God's assistance in achieving this state ends on an eschatological note of joy; the loyal, the beloved will experience this glorious presentation "with rejoicing."

There will be great joy in the presence of the God of glory for the righteous (1 Pet 4:13; Matt 5:12; Rev 19:7; see also Isa 60:5; 61:10; *4 Ezra* 7:89).

A Closing Doxology

(25)

The second part of the closing, after the author's exhortatory statement concerning Christian holiness, returns more properly to the form and themes of the traditional doxology. Employing distinctive Jewish terminology Jude speaks on the one hand of "the only God" and on the other of the God who is also "our Savior through Jesus Christ our Lord." The first is a well-known Jewish confessional title employed by other NT doxologies (Rom 16:27; 1 Tim 1:17; see also 6:15-16; John 17:3). Its purpose here, along with the remainder of the statement, is seemingly to counteract the opponents' denial of "the only Master" and their challenge to divine, cosmic order (vv. 4, 8). The second title, also borrowed from Jewish tradition (Pss 64:6; 78:9; see also Luke 1:47; 1 Tim 1:1f; Titus 1:3f), speaks of God as "Savior," who not only punishes wayward behavior and demands lordship but also loves humanity and offers it salvation (v. 3).

There follows the prepositional phrase "through our Lord Jesus Christ," an expression that is connected by scholars either to the preceding title or the following divine attributes. In the case of the latter one could claim, with the support of the doxology of Rom 16:27 and other NT texts (see 1 Pet 4:11), that "glory . . . authority" are mediated through Christ. In the case of the former, owing to christological considerations, one would insist that God operates in human lives by means of the Christ-event. Not only does the author's low christology preclude Christ being mediator of such divine attributes "from every age" (in opposition to the latter), but also the author's insistence on divine lordship and on Christ's role as agent for God's activity (vv. 4, 8, 21) points to a reading whereby God's salvation is mediated through Christ.

Praise then is given to God, not only in terms of "glory," the usual attribute of doxologies, but also as "majesty, power, and authority." While the first and third (*doxa* and *kratos*, respectively) frequently appear, often together, in doxologies (1 Tim 6:16; 1 Pet 4:11; 5:11; Rev 1:6; 5:13 and in early Patristic texts), the other two, though designating divine attributes in Jewish and Christian literature, are rarely so used. Jude's purpose in providing such a striking list of attributes at the end of a letter, which underscores divine punishment for the ungodly and earnest pleading addressed to the faithful, stresses the author's vehement opposition to the errant members' doctrine that questions God's wisdom and lordship. The four attributes then reiterate for the author God's radiant being and eternal transcendence, as well as creative power and sovereign authority as ruler of the universe. This acknowledgment Jude insists is not only spatial but also temporal because it "always was, is now, and will be for all ages." To this solemn declaration of divine praise the author invites the addressees to join their resounding "amen."

Jude then begins and ends by appealing to "the only God," first as father who loves and calls humanity to a life of holiness and peace as it awaits the Lord's return to bestow mercy (vv. 1, 2, 21) and secondly as a savior God whose transcendence and dominion cannot be flouted with impunity and whose gift of salvation is accessible through the acknowledgment of Jesus Christ as Lord (vv. 4, 8, 24-25). Thus the reader of Jude, while painfully conscious of the importance of fidelity to tradition, moral integrity, and Christian unity (witness the relentless condemnation of the opponents), is reminded in closing that not only the intellectual and moral acknowledgment of "the only Master and our Lord Jesus Christ" (v. 4; also vv. 20-21) is required of the beloved but also the showing of "mercy mixed with caution" toward those who are at risk (vv. 22-23). The letter of Jude then is both a battle cry against heresy and a plea for "mercy, peace, and love" among "those whom God has called and keeps safe for Jesus Christ" (vv. 1-2).

Suggested Readings

Deichgräber, R. *Gotteshymnus und Christushymnus in der frühen Christenheit.* Göttingen: Vandenhoeck & Ruprecht, 1967.

Doty, W. G. *Letters in Primitive Christianity.* Philadelphia: Fortress, 1973.

Elliott, J. K. "The Language and Style of the Concluding Doxology to the Epistle to the Romans." *ZNTW* 72 (1981) 124-30.

Eybers, I. H. "Aspects of the Background of the Letter of Jude." *Neot* 9 (1975) 113-23.

Fitzmyer, J. A. "Introduction to the New Testament Epistles" in *NJBC* 768-71.

2 Peter

Redaction of Jude by 2 Peter

Even a cursory reading of Jude and 2 Peter reveals that there is a literary relation between these two documents. Even though the former made its way into the NT canon more quickly than did the latter, once the authority of the latter was established it became generally accepted, until recently, that Jude, the less prominent figure, borrowed generously from 2 Peter.

Since modern scholarship more readily considers or accepts the pseudonymity of both letters, more serious redactional study of their parallel passages is encountered in commentaries. One might consider the following texts as typical for studying the relationship between the two:

> <u>But these people</u>, on the one hand, <u>blaspheme</u> *those things which they do not understand*; but on the other, those things they know by <u>instinct</u>, <u>as</u> do <u>irrational animals</u>, by these very things they <u>are destroyed</u>. (Jude 10)

> <u>But these people</u>, <u>like</u> <u>irrational animals</u>, that is, creatures of <u>instinct</u> born for capture and destruction, who <u>blaspheme</u> *against things they do not comprehend*, in their destruction will also <u>be destroyed</u>, suffering wrong as payment for wrong-doing. (2 Pet 2:12-13)

The underlined terms and expressions indicate five verbal parallels. One less exact idiom is noted by italics (use of different verbs and grammatical structures). One can hardly doubt that one author borrows from the other, especially since the terms and themes are incorporated in unique stylistic structures: those of Jude in a contrastive construction ("on the one hand . . . but on the other") and of 2 Peter in a complex period whose subject is qualified by a series of adverbial and participial modifiers ("like . . . born for . . . who blaspheme . . . suffering"). Further, despite the great similarity of theme and terminology one detects here, as elsewhere, very different agenda on the part of the two authors. In the case of Jude the opponents are chided for the abuses of their rational nature, despite their claims to special knowledge, and thereby, in proverbial manner, to be subject to the irrational, destructive forces of their instincts (see earlier discussion). In the case of 2 Peter one finds an explicit statement on the fate of animals, the repetition (3x) of the theme of destruction, and the proverbial restatement of the law of the talion in v. 13a. One gets the impression here, as elsewhere, that 2 Peter employs terms and themes from Jude to compose a powerful condemnation of a new set of false teachers.

Owing to extensive analysis of this type it is generally agreed that 2 Peter borrowed from Jude and not the other way around. Certainly the editorial process strongly supports such a conclusion. It is estimated that 18 or 19 of the 25 verses of Jude have either been appropriated by the author of 2 Peter or have offered significant terms or ideas to that writer. While chapters 1 and 3 of 2 Peter reveal some dependence on Jude it is especially the relation of 2:1f to Jude 4f that is the clearest. In effect 2 Peter 2:1–3:3 is an undisguised rewriting of Jude 4-18. Both the order of the material and much of its terminology are seemingly dependent on the latter:

Jude	2 Peter	
4	2:1-2	edited/Egypt
5	2:3	edited/Egypt
6	2:4	angels
—	2:5	Noah
7	2:6	Sodom/Gomorrah
—	2:7-9	Lot
8	2:10	flesh/auth/glor ones
9	2:11	edited/Michael
10	2:12	irrational animals
11a	2:13a	woe/penalty
11b	2:14-16	Balaam
12a	2:13b	blemishes
12b	2:17a	nature
12c	—	—
13a	—	—
13b	2:17b	deepest darkness
14-15	—	Enoch citation
16	2:18	bombastic
17	3:1-2	apostles
18	3:3	scoff/lusts

It is clear from the above that the author of 2 Peter found Jude congenial, borrowed heavily, and, in a manner reminiscent of Matthew and Luke's use of Mark, reordered, added to, omitted from, and freely rewrote the main part of Jude to compose chapter 2 and the beginning of chapter 3 of this new document. Like Jude the author of 2 Peter was interested in combatting heretical teachers within the Christian community and found that text amenable to such a goal.

Finding the apocryphal material of the source embarrassing or distasteful, the author modifies greatly the text of Jude. Verses such as Jude 14-15, containing a citation from the *1 Enoch* and phrases in vv. 4 and 13 (about "foreordained condemnation" or "wandering stars"), are omitted. Terminology is toned down; for example, an account about sexual relations with angels in Jude 6 and 7 is rendered rather vaguely in 2 Pet 2:4 and 6 (see also Jude 12 and 16 for other examples). In other instances the source undergoes major changes as in v. 9 concerning Michael the archangel and the devil fighting over Moses' body (use of the apocryphal *Assumption of Moses*) or in v. 11 regarding Cain, Balaam, and Korah. Only the example of Balaam is retained and expanded in 2 Pet 2:15-16. In this editorial process the author of 2 Peter manifests a love for abstract terminology (Jude 7: "having . . . indulged in sexual immorality and having gone after other flesh" becomes "the ungodly" in 2 Pet 2:6 or Jude 8 "defile the flesh" becomes "follow the flesh with its desire for polution" in 2:10) as well as a fondness for OT examples not only to condemn the false teachers but also to defend the activity of true teachers (Noah, Lot, and Balaam in 2:5, 7-9, 15-16).

The author of 2 Peter then has borrowed much of the material for chapter 2 and the beginning of chapter 3 from Jude 4f, has retained many of its themes and terminology in the order of the source, and has greatly edited and expanded these for a new application. The sequence but not the structure of the source has been retained, for the sixfold pattern of Jude (see earlier) has virtually disappeared. In place of Jude's statement (v. 4) that "certain people have sneaked in," 2 Peter 2:1 speaks of false teachers who have appeared "among the people" and who will "bring swift destruction on themselves" (influence of the language of Jude 5). Second Peter then borrows various descriptions of Jude's opponents in the remainder of the chapter but abandons the alternating pattern (fivefold "these") of Jude 4-23. Thus the sequence and terminology of the source are employed and inserted in a new stylistic construct.

In the following study of 2 Peter, particularly of chapter 2, detailed attention will be given to the author's use of Jude's terms, themes, and images. It will be of interest to see how 2 Peter employs these in a new composition with a considerably different outlook and message.

Suggested Readings

Bauckham, R. J. *Jude, 2 Peter*. Waco TX: Word Books, 1983, 141-43, 245f.

Cavallin, H. C. C. "The False Teachers of 2 Pt as Pseudo-Prophets." *NovT* 21 (1979) 263-70.

Fornberg, T. *An Early Church in a Pluralistic Society: A Study of 2 Peter*. Lund: Gleerup, 1977, 33-59.

Neyrey, J. H. *2 Peter, Jude*. New York: Doubleday, 1993, 120-22, 187f.

Introduction

Also found among the general or "catholic epistles" is a second work that claims to have been written by the apostle Peter; indeed the author claims to be "Simeon Peter, servant and apostle of Jesus Christ." At a further remove from the canonical debate that took place within the early church, one might imagine that 2 Peter made its way easily, along with 1 Peter, into the community's official list of normative texts. Nothing is further from the truth, since this short document was slow in becoming known within the church and since that same institution was both slow and reluctant in granting it canonical status. Seemingly it was the influence of Jerome (*Epistles* 120.11) that finally led to its general acceptance within the universal church. Once accepted, however, it soon became associated with the other Petrine letter and its kindred spirit, Jude. Over the centuries it has had a mixed reception and in recent decades has been neglected, along with other general epistles, and relegated to the fringes of the church's canon. Modern scholarship has begun to look more closely at these early Christian texts in an effort to understand more fully their context, strategies, messages, and place in early Christian history. Having already examined 2 Peter's relation to Jude, it is now necessary to discuss its author, addressees, composition, and purpose.

Author and Audience

The opening of 2 Peter is interesting in several respects. On the one hand, the claim of authorship is unambiguous both in terms of names and titles. This specificity along with other authorial claims provides added importance to this feature of the letter. On the other hand, the vagueness of the statement concerning the audience will call for special attention.

Author

The writer of 2 Peter, possibly influenced by the group responsible for 1 Peter, draws on the reputation of the apostle to establish a new message to troubled Christian communities. While the first document had simply appealed to the authorship of Peter (1 Pet 1:1) and made brief reference to venerable members of the group (5:12-13), the second takes pains to underscore the Petrine tradition out of which its author writes or pretends to write. The author claims the titles of "servant" and "apostle," titles presumably borrowed from Jude and 1 Peter. The document also stresses the Petrine tradition and strives for authenticity by employing both the apostle's Semitic and Hellenistic names: "Simeon Peter" (1:1). Later in the chapter two scenes from the Jesus tradition in which the apostle Peter participated are invoked, namely, the foretelling of his death (1:13-15; see John 21:18-19) and the transfiguration (1:16-18; see Mark 9:2-8 and parallels). In 3:1 the author seemingly refers to 1 Peter: "this is now, beloved, the second letter I am writing to you." In both the events noted earlier and this particular reference to past correspondence the text underscores the alleged author's unerring connection with apostolic tradition and its promises. Finally at the end of the letter the author refers to "our beloved brother Paul" (3:15) in a further effort to solidify the writer's claim to knowledge of apostolic tradition (post-NT traditions also associate Peter and Paul).

There are other elements in the letter that point to pseudonymity. Not only is the style of 2 Peter very different from that of 1 Peter, but so are the two letters' treatment of problems. There is in the former a clearer indication of a lapse of time between the actual composition and the apostolic age than in both 1 Peter and Jude, because there is in 2 Peter a reference to a collection of Paul's letters that are now considered Scripture and that have been repeatedly misinterpreted (3:15-16). Further there are references to "your apostles," to the death of "our ancestors," and to promises that have seemingly not been fulfilled (see 1:4; 3:2, 4, 9, 13).

In general terms one can say that the style and language of this pseudonymous writer are those of an educated Hellenist. The style is complex and even convoluted (see 2:4-10a). The author's vocabulary, which contains a large number of unique terms, reveals an author who is acquainted both with biblical and pagan cultures. On the one hand, 2 Peter borrows many Jewish references from Jude but goes far beyond in modifying, developing, and adding to these. An example of this process is the author's use of Jude 11, which speaks of the murderous Cain, the greedy Balaam, and the rebellious Korah. What results in 2 Pet 2:15-16 is an elimination of the first and third figures and an extended treatment of Balaam to stress, by means of further biblical tradition (Num 22:21f), God's use of "a speechless beast of burden" to restrain the teachers' madness. On the other hand, 2 Peter seems to presuppose Christian biblical tradition: 1 Peter (see 3;1), James, some form of the Jesus tradition (perhaps Mark), and certainly Jude. Furthermore even the Jewish stories of Noah, the fallen angels, and creation seem to be related to the classical narratives of Deucalion and the flood story and the casting of the Titans into the underworld (Tartarus, 2:4) or Stoic cosmology and its version of the destruction and re-creation of the cosmos (3:10-13).

Audience

The letter is vaguely addressed "to those who have received a faith as precious as ours." From the outset it is clear that the formulation is not intended to offer specific information about the audience but rather to insist on the apostolic deposit that believers have received. Truly one looks throughout the document in vain for more exact details concerning the addressees. Clearly they are addressed as "brothers and sisters" (1:10) and as "beloved" of God (3:1, 8, 14, 17), as other believers would be, but they are also characterized as being exposed to "destructive opinions" by "false teachers" (2:1), as concerned members of the community who should recall the tradition that comes from "the Lord and Savior" (3:2), and finally as "forewarned" believers who should strive to preserve that precious faith as they await the fulfillment of the Lord's promises (3:13-14, 17). The addressees then are believers (location and specifics unknown to us) whose precious beliefs are threatened by false teachers whose doctrine and behavior lead others to licentiousness and loss of Christian freedom (2:18-19).

Genre, Content, and Structure

Despite its brevity, 2 Peter is a complex document that offers a challenge to commentator and reader. Not only does it bear the features of the traditional Greek letter, but it also has characteristics of a farewell discourse or testament. Also beyond these literary considerations one finds much debate concerning its structure and focus. In view of these observations, therefore, it will be necessary to discuss the genre, content, and structure of 2 Peter before addressing its author's message and strategy.

Genre

Study of 2 Peter's background and composition will help to clarify the document's purpose. In recent years the farewell-discourse genre has been proposed as shedding light on the form of 2 Peter and indeed serves as the setting for the author's message—the term "setting" is employed because the actual genre of 2 Peter is clearly epistolary. The farewell discourse has a long history in the biblical world, since it was customary for stories of great figures to terminate with such a discourse: Jacob (Gen 48–49), Moses (Deut 22–23), Joshua (Josh 22–24), and David (1 Chron 28–29). Tobit is also given such a discourse (Tobit 14), as are Rebecca and Isaac in the intertestamental book of *Jubilees* (35–36). The *Testament of the Twelve Patriarchs* are full-blown farewell discourses. The New Testament provides several examples; Jesus is given a farewell discourse in Mark 13 and parallels and an extended discourse in John 13–17, while Paul makes a farewell speech in Acts 20. The genre offers several important features:

- imminent death or departure of the speaker
- sorrowful reaction and consequent reassurance of the audience
- recitation of personal or national history and deeds
- the warning against deception
- the giving of advice
- exhortation to righteous conduct

When at the beginning of the letter the impending death of Peter, the alleged author, is stressed (1:13-14), reassurance is immediately provided: "so I will make every effort also to enable you always, after my departure, to recall these things" (v. 15). Second Peter more than any other pseudonymous NT writing, except perhaps 2 Timothy, takes pains to tell the story of its alleged writer. The author stresses God's benevolence for those destined to "become sharers of the divine nature" (1:3-4; see also 3:5f, 9), yet warnings against deception and false teachers permeate the letter (1:4, 16; 2:1f; 3:3f, 16). In fact the document ends with such a warning: "be on your guard lest, having been led away by the error of lawless people, you lose your own stability" (3:17). Finally the letter gives advice to its audience as regards false teachings and has recourse to the standard farewell advice about virtuous living (1:5-7) and keeping God's commandments (2:21; 3:2). Important for our purpose is appreciating the use that 2 Peter makes of farewell-discourse conventions in composing a letter to defend Christian prophecy against the proliferation of false teachings.

The genre more properly of 2 Peter is the letter form, but a letter that shares the tendencies of post-Pauline epistolary literature. Gone are the personal characteristics of earlier letters; instead one finds greater interest in general exhortation and, in the case of 2 Peter, in polemics against heretical tendencies. This document, as is true of 1 Peter and Jude, retains basic epistolary characteristics; it begins in typical epistolary fashion with a standard opening (sender, addressee, greeting) and ends in a less customary way, but in a fashion that approximates Jude, with a formal doxology. As do other letters it also regularly addresses its audience directly and occasionally as "brothers and sisters" (1:10) or as "beloved" (3:1, 8, 14, 17). In place of the usual thanksgiving or blessing of other NT letters or even of a proper writing formula (see Jude 3), the body of the letter presents an anomalous section that first acknowledges God's benefactions (1:3-4) and then addresses exhortatory concerns (vv. 5-9) with a formal, concluding appeal (vv. 10-11). Interestingly the letter ends on a similar exhortatory note, also with direct address (3:14-18).

Content and Structure

Beyond these basic epistolary features there is little agreement concerning the structure of the document, since the body of the letter continues to present problems for scholars interested in 2 Peter. Examination of several attempts to outline 2 Peter's train of thought will assist us in understanding its strategy and message.

Some interpreters have concluded that the whole of 2 Peter consists of three basic parts, each of which corresponds to one of the work's three chapters. The first focuses on the trustworthiness and power of God's promises; the second, on the deceitfulness and treachery of the false teachers; and the third, on the coming of the Lord's day. Such a thematic approach recognizes, with single-mindedness, the focus of 2 Peter on the delay of the parousia (see especially 3:4-5) as both a seeming nonrealization of God's promises (1:4; 3:4, 9, 13) and as the central issue of the polemic against the false teachers. One suspects, however, that the teaching of the opponents is more complex and that there is more inner unity of theme and function between the issues of true prophecy, the parousia, divine punishment, and apostolic tradition.

Another approach has focused on apostolic teaching or tradition as the unifying element. It is maintained that following a brief statement concerning God's call and an exhortation to godly conduct (1:3-11), the bulk of 2 Peter (1:12–3:13) is devoted to recalling apostolic tradition about the Lord's coming as the way of truth (1:12f), then castigating the false teachers' doctrine as the way of error (2:1f), and again recalling the tradition about the certainty of the parousia (3:1f); a final section is devoted to exhortation for those awaiting the Lord's return (3:14-18). The focus on apostolic tradition certainly is a major aspect of 2 Peter's strategy as well as the themes of truth and error, but here also the complexity both of the polemics and of the author's strategy needs more attention.

Several recent commentaries have proposed an intricate structure that sees 2 Peter as a letter with a testamentary setting designed to present an apology or series of responses to polemical statements by false teachers. For these the overall structure of 2 Peter is to be found in these various objections or replies (numbering 3, 4, or 5) to challenges leveled against traditional apostolic teaching. Statements about "cleverly devised myths" (1:16, NRSV), the value or confirmation of prophecy (1:19), the idle or nonexistent character of divine judgment (2:3), or the delay or non-coming of the Lord (3:4) are taken as indications of the teachers' challenges and either introduce (2:3f; 3:4f) or are enclosed in the author's responses. No doubt these statements and their surrounding narratives contribute to our broader understanding of the issues either being taught by the opponents or of concern to the author of 2 Peter, but it is hard to believe that these are all attributable to the teachers and that their surrounding narratives are in effect responses to the issues raised (why no response concerning Paul's letters as misunderstood?—see 3:15a-16). It seems more convincing to view the first two alleged responses (1:16 and 19) as related to the author's strategy and the second two (2:3; 3:4) as serving different functions in the author's polemic against the false teachers. Further there are structural indications in 2 Peter that point to the function these various statements play in the author's overall schema.

Between the epistolary opening with its anomalous thematic section (1:1-11) and the letter's closing (3:17-18) there is a long narrative whose structure calls for some attention. On the one hand, it is clear that the whole of chapter 2 is devoted to a polemical treatment of the false teachers and the certainty of their forthcoming punishment, the entire section of which is directly dependent on the text of Jude 4-16. Its function in the overall schema of 2 Peter is not well understood and rarely fits well into proposed outlines of the work. Clearly there is a break between it and the subject of 3:1f; there is, however, a close relationship intended between it and the ending of chapter 1, because the discussion of true prophecy in 1:19-21 leads directly to the contrasting development of the false teachers as "false prophets" who malign the way of truth (2:1-2). Chapter 2 then continues the discussion of the previous section. On the other hand, perhaps the clearest indicators of the letter's structure are to be found in 1:12-15 and 3:1-3.

Both emphasize the theme of "reminding or remembering" (1:12, 13, 15; 3:1, 2) and dwell on the addressees' knowledge of apostolic tradition. In the first case the complex recall formula introduces a long narrative contrasting the true source of the original apostolic tradition presented in the letter, that is, Peter as an inspired prophet or apostle of the Lord Jesus Christ (1:12f), and the false teachers who introduce destructive heresies and exploit the audience with their fabrications (2:1f). In the second case another recall formula, combined with a clever reference to a former letter (presumably 1 Peter) and employing further material from Jude (vv. 17-18), introduces more directly the primary issue of the polemics, namely, the delay of the parousia. The following overall outline is therefore suggested:

Epistolary Opening (1:1-2) and Body Opening (1:3-11)
True and False Prophecy (1:12–2:22)
    Peter and the Reliability of Apostolic Tradition (1:12-21)
    False Teachers: Their Deception and Punishment (2:1-22)
The Lord's Day: Promise, Providence, and Power (3:1-16)
    Delay of the Parousia, Repentance, Endtime (3:1-10)
    Final Exhortation about Holy Conduct (3:11-16)
Closing (3:17-18)

2 Peter then is a unified whole whose purpose is threefold: to establish the source and trustworthiness of apostolic tradition, to contrast this precious faith to the teaching and activity of the false teachers, and to discuss at some length the community's eschatology, particularly the delay of the parousia and consequent Christian behavior.

Strategy and Message

Peter's name and credentials are put forward to anchor the author's teaching, because Peter was an eyewitness that Jesus is the beloved Son and therefore the guarantor of the prophetic word (1:19). Thus the terms "remember" and "remind" (1:12f; 3:1f) are strategically employed as the author insists on the content of true Christian prophecy (1:19-21; 2:16; 3:2) or knowledge and wisdom (see 1:1-3f). In fact this deposit of faith (1:1) is said to have been given by the Lord Jesus to the apostles (1:14; 3:3) and is classified as Scripture that results from the guidance of the Holy Spirit (1:21). This too, along with the apologetic use of the transfiguration story as a promise of the Lord's return (1:16-18), forms part of the author's strategy.

In chapter 2 the author, in apocalyptic terms borrowed from Jude, terms very much in keeping with some farewell discourses (see especially Mark 13) but terms that also resonate with Stoic philosophy, takes the community's opponents to task. Divine judgment will be their reward as it was for figures of the past who violated God's commands. Though they, in Epicurean fashion, probably deny God's initiative in rendering judgment, 2 Peter assures the addressees that their "condemnation from long ago has not been idle nor their destruction asleep" (2:3b). Indeed the text of Jude is edited to underscore repeatedly the inevitability of divine punishment of the ungodly (see the use of "destruction" terminology in 2:1 and 12). There is hope, however, because even Balaam was ineffective when God used "a speechless beast of burden . . . [to] restrain the prophet's madness" (2:16). The false teachers' mocking denial of the parousia and of divine providence (3:3-4) merits the Lord's condemnation, for according to his promise there will be "new heavens and a new earth in which righteousness dwells" (3:13). Christian prophecy therefore is not the object of one's whims (1:20) but must be subject to authentic community tradition that is under the guidance of the Holy Spirit (1:21). The letter and its strategy therefore reveal an acute episode in the quest for authority in the midst of doctrinal and ecclesial strife.

Thus we are led to inquire about the nature of the heresy under scrutiny and to examine the author's strategy in combatting it. Three basic positions have been proposed for identifying these opponents and the doctrines they espouse.

Drawing upon similarities detected between the teachers of 2 Peter and the emergent Gnostic groups of the second century, a first group of scholars has proposed that the author is combatting a form of spiritualism that focuses on divine knowledge as granting moral freedom and rendering unnecessary eschatological doctrines of final judgment and future salvation. Also related to such claims is the further assertion that 2 Peter reveals a theological position that might best be described as "early Catholic" or rigid orthodoxy. Thus as Gnostics the opponents would espouse cosmic and moral dualism and assume a fully-realized eschatology. Second Peter would then respond by accepting a delayed parousia and by focusing on the community's tradition to foster doctrinal, ecclesial, and moral orthodoxy and to impose apostolic authority.

A second position draws its inspiration from contemporary Hellenistic culture and posits an Epicurean-like opposition that, like the teachers, deny divine providence, afterlife, and post-death retribution. These scholars see the most telling argument in the opponents' denial of divine providence and view the issues of delay of the parousia and the charge of immorality as owing to polemics against them and other Epicureans by defenders of traditional theodicy. Thus delay of the final conflagration would owe to divine compassion or forbearance rather than divine lack of care or involvement. Further it is pointed out, via Josephus' description of contemporary Jewish groups (*JW* 2.164-65; *JA* 13.297; 18.16), that similar views were espoused by the Sadducees and other Hellenistic Jews. Second Peter would then employ the terminology current in contemporary pagan and Jewish Hellenistic eschatological debates to defend traditional Christian beliefs about divine providence and judgment.

In a more traditional fashion a third position insists that the problem is more indigenous because it concerns eschatological skepticism and relates more directly to the issue of the delay of the parousia (see 3:4). Against the Christian teachers who mock the traditional belief about Christ's coming as unfulfilled and so based on human invention, 2 Peter insists that divine judgment is forthcoming, that they are bringing about their own destruction, and that the seeming delay of Christ's return owes to divine forbearance for the addressees. The author, they insist, is quick to point to the immoral excesses that result from the lack of eschatological motivation on the part of believers.

The first scenario is readily rejected by most scholars as unsatisfactorily explaining the context of the letter and as anachronistically reading later Gnostic developments into the late first- and early second-century circumstances of 2 Peter. The second proposal is certainly impressive in drawing similarities between the polemics of 2 Peter and contemporary defenders of divine providence. Nonetheless insufficient attention is given to the document's christological focus; divine judgment is at stake, but it is Christ's return that is the catalyst. In addition it is not God's existence or power that are denied; instead it is the "power and coming" (1:16) and the lordship of "the master who bought them" that are denied or challenged. The terminology and themes certainly conjure contemporary eschatological debates, but the context is more properly christological. The final proposal is probably more appropriate in explaining the Christian context of the author. With the passing away of the apostolic generation and the calling into question of eschatological motivation for righteous living, there certainly arose questions about final judgment, about unfulfilled promises, and the very nature of salvation, issues that undoubtedly called for the use and abuse of Pauline traditions. It is my conclusion therefore that the author borrowed from biblical tradition and Stoic philosophical debate to defend early Christian eschatology against disillusionment, whether delay of the parousia or the absence of divine judgment, and even against Epicurean pessimism that envisioned a noncaring divinity and denied afterlife and reward for the righteous.

Both the author's christology and strategy point to the above conclusion, namely, that the second and third options mentioned above offer combined assistance in appreciating the context of 2 Peter. While the document shows a certain familiarity with various elements of the Jesus tradition (the transfiguration story, the foretelling of Peter's death, the coming of the Lord's day like a thief, or the saying about the last state being worse than the first), it is nonetheless Jesus' soteriological and eschatological roles that predominate, especially as they relate to proper Christian behavior. Thus Jesus is frequently given the title "savior" and "the master who bought them" (1:1f; 2:1). He provides them with benefactions that "contribute to life and piety" (1:3). It is through "knowledge" of him that believers are true to their call and election and are fruitful or spotless in lieu of his return (1:2f, 8-9; 3:11, 14). Additionally he is repeatedly referred to as the present and eschatological "lord" (see 1:2f) who protects in the present and will exercise God's judgment on the last day.

Another important element of the author's christology needs elaboration here. A strong case can be made that 2 Peter has a high christology, a notion that here contributes to the document's strategy. On four occasions Jesus is given the title of "savior." In 2:1 the author intentionally modifies the text of Jude 4 where the opponents are accused of "disowning the only master and our Lord Jesus Christ" to "even disowning the master who bought them" (2:1). Only in 2 Peter is the divine title "master" used unambiguously of Jesus. Moreover the author's use of the transfiguration story (1:17) seems, in this Hellenistic setting, to insist on the special sonship of Jesus; only here, in 2 Peter, is God called "father." Also one must read 1:1 as "our God and Savior Jesus Christ" rather than the possible, alternate translation "our God and the Savior Jesus Christ." This is supported by the author's love for double titles for Jesus (1:11; 2:20; 3:18). This concept of divinization (Jesus "receives honor and glory from God the Father"—1:17) serves the author's purpose in defending Jesus' role in God's eschatological plan of salvation (see 1:16; 3:15). Indeed only 2 Peter has the phrase "the eternal kingdom of our Lord and Savior Jesus Christ" (1:11). The portrait that 2 Peter gives of Jesus, therefore, shows clear signs of development toward a high christology wherein the role of Christ rather than that of God receives increasing emphasis, and divine titles and attributes are freely conferred upon God's Son (1:17). Second Peter's argument or strategy is christological in its attempt to defend divine providence.

The last point brings us to a final note about the author's strategy. While it is probably true that the most basic and serious challenge to the Christian community and to the religious person generally, as it is expressed in 2 Peter, is that of denying divine providence ("all things continue as they were from the beginning of creation"—3:4b), it is nonetheless the first, interrogative statement of the false teachers that provides the author and the Christian's point of reference for such an eschatological debate: "where is the promise of his coming?" The issues of 2 Peter are christological in formulation since it is Jesus' lordship that is at stake; it is his return that motivates, at least in part, Christian behavior (see the addressees' question and its context in 3:11-13). As God's divine Son he is the promised one, who now provides assistance and protection, who will return to judge and to lead the righteous to his eternal kingdom (note that Jesus is here called "Lord and Savior"—1:11). Likewise since the promise can be traced through the eyewitnesses to the heavenly voice (1:16-18), the addressees can now believe Peter's final words (1:12-15) that the apostolic preaching about his "power and coming" (1:16) is "a very reliable prophetic message" (1:19) that dictates "what sort of persons [believers] ought to be in holy conduct and piety, while awaiting and hastening the coming of God's day" (3:11-12).

Both the negative and positive aspects of 2 Peter's exhortation require a serious audience. Whether a stern rebuke of false teachers (threatened with divine judgment) or a promise of Jesus' forbearance (time for repentance), the letter is a plea to the addressees to consider the gift of faith as something "precious" (1:1) and as something that needs to grow as "grace and knowledge of our Lord and Savior Jesus Christ" (3:18), the one who "received honor and glory from God the Father" (1:17).

Commentaries

Arichea, D. C., and H. A. Hatton. *A Handbook on the Letter from Jude and the Second Letter from Peter.* NY:UBS, 1993.

Bauckham, R. J. *Jude, 2 Peter.* Waco TX: Word Books, 1983.

Craddock, F. B. *First and Second Peter and Jude.* Louisville KY: Westminster/John Knox, 1995.

Elliott, J. H. *1-11 Peter/Jude* (with R. A. Martin, *James*). Minneapolis: Augsburg, 1982.

Fuchs, E., and P. Reymond. *La deuxième épître de saint Pierre—L'épître de saint Jude.* Geneva: Labor et Fides, 1988.

Kelly, J. N. D. *A Commentary on the Epistles of Peter and of Jude.* Grand Rapids: Baker, 1982.

Neyrey, J. H. "The Second Epistle of Peter" in *NJBC* 1017-22.

__________. *2 Peter, Jude.* New York: Doubleday, 1993.

Perkins, P. *First and Second Peter, James, and Jude.* Louisville KY: John Knox, 1995, 159-94.

Senior, D. *1 & 2 Peter*. Wilmington DE: Glazier, 1980.

Sidebottom, E. M. *James, Jude, 2 Peter*. Grand Rapids: Eerdmans, 1982.

Vögtle, A. *Der Judasbrief. Der 2 Petrusbrief.* Zurich: Benziger, 1994.

Watson, D. F. "The Second Letter of Peter" in *NIB*, 12:321-61.

Suggested Readings

Bauckham, R. J. "2 Peter: A Supplementary Bibliography." *JETS* 25 (1982) 91-93.

__________. "2 Peter: An Account of Research." *ANRW* 2.25.2 (1988) 3713-52.

__________. "Pseudo-Apostolic Letters." *JBL* 107 (1988) 469-94.

Boobyer, G. H. "The Indebtedness of 2 Peter to 1 Peter" in *New Testament Essays: Studies*. Ed., A. J. B. Higgins. Manchester: Manchester University, 1059, 34-53.

Charles, J. D. *Virtue amidst Vice: The Catalog of Virtues in 2 Peter 1*. Sheffield: Sheffield Academic, 1997.

Danker, F. W. "2 Peter" in *The General Letters: Hebrews, James, 1-2 Peter, Jude, 1-2-3 John*. Ed., G. Krodel. Minneapolis: Fortress, 1995, 84-93.

__________. "2 Peter: A Solemn Decree." *CBQ* 40 (1978) 64-82.

Dunnett, W. M. "The Hermeneutics of Jude and 2 Peter: The Use of Ancient Jewish Traditions." *JETS* 31 (1988) 287-92.

Farkasfalvy, D. "The Ecclesial Setting of Pseudepigraphy in Second Peter and Its Role in the Formation of the Canon." *SC* 5 (1985) 3-29.

Fornberg, T. *An Early Church in a Pluralistic Society*. Lund: Gleerup, 1977.

Käsemann, E. "An Apology for Primitive Christian Eschatology" in *Essays on New Testament Themes*. London: SCM, 1964, 169-95.

Knight, J. *2 Peter and Jude*. Sheffield: Sheffield Academic, 1995.

Lovestam, E. "Eschatologie und Tradition im 2. Petrusbrief" in *The New Testament Age: Essays*. Ed., W. C. Weinrich. Macon GA: Mercer University Press, 1984, 287-300.

Neyrey, J. H. "The Form and Background of the Polemic in 2 Peter." *JBL* 99 (1980) 407-31.

__________. "The Apologetic Use of the Transfiguration in 2 Peter 1:16-21." *CBQ* 42 (1980) 504-19.

Soards, M. L. "1 Peter, 2 Peter, and Jude As Evidence for a Petrine School." *ANRW* 2.25.5 (1988) 3828-49.

Watson, D. F. *Invention, Arrangement, and Style: Rhetorical Criticism of Jude and 2 Peter*. Atlanta: Scholars, 1986.

Opening

Second Peter presents a standard opening, but one that offers several hints concerning the letter's strategy and message. Following this brief opening the author substitutes an exhortatory unit for the traditional thanksgiving (here called the body opening). Both sections prepare the reader for the letter's content, the first by introducing the principal characters (alleged author, audience, and divine agent) and the second by establishing the basis for the addressees' hoped-for activity as they await the Lord Jesus' return (1:11; see also 3:12, 14).

Epistolary Opening
(1:1-2)

Like Jude, 2 Peter bears the features of post-Pauline letters. Thus its tripartite opening is short and formulaic, briefly presenting author and titles, unspecified addressees as receivers of divine benefaction, and a greeting that functions as a wish for abundant blessings. This opening bears similarities to 1 Pet 1:1-2 and Jude 1-2 (see below).

Author (1:1a)

Like the author of 1 Peter this writer claims Petrine authorship and presumably draws, from the reputation of the great apostle, authority for the message that is to follow. Thus the author claims to be "Simeon Peter," combining the Semitic and Hellenistic names of the alleged author. In further emphasizing this authorial claim 2 Peter employs, as does Luke-Acts often, the Semitic spelling "Simeon." If this is an archaizing touch it is clearly part of the author's strategy in emphasizing Petrine authority and drawing links between the letter's teaching and apostolic tradition.

Further the alleged author is described as "servant and apostle of Jesus Christ," titles found respectively in Jude 1 and 1 Pet 1:1. It is of less importance to claim that 2 Peter copies these titular statements from Jude and 1 Peter than to see here an indirect reference to two well-accepted writings of the Christian community. In this way the author not only appropriates the earlier titular statements but also prepares both for the extended treatment of the false teachers as having a precedent in Jude and for the explicit reference to an earlier Petrine letter in 3:1. As regards the first title one can assume a similar background and usage as in Jude 1 (see earlier comments), for here too it presumes a reference to an authoritative figure. Also as in Jude one sees here the author's insistence on Christ's lordship, since the title "servant . . . of Jesus Christ" corresponds to a formal confession of Christ as "lord" (see discussion of *kyrios* below). As regards the second title, that of apostle, several observations need to be made. While in 1 Pet 1:1 the term seems to suggest not only the exalted title of community leader but especially the nuance of "one sent by Christ" through the Spirit (1:1, 12), here in 2 Peter also there is a claim to being an authoritative voice, but especially there is emphasis on this figure as one who is both a reliable source and trustworthy transmitter of the community's tradition. Peter, the alleged author, remembers, was an eyewitness, was inspired by the Spirit, and was an apostle of "the Lord and Savior" who received the words, commands, and promises of the Lord Jesus (1:13-15, 16, 21; 3:1-2)—both Peter and Paul are seen as writers who have faithfully preserved the apostolic tradition for sincere and wise minds (3:1-2, 15-16). The author's claim then to be both "a servant and apostle of Jesus Christ" points to the crucial role of Christ's lordship, a theme challenged by the false teachers, and the importance of apostolic tradition as the standard by which new opinions are to be judged and as the antidote to the false teachers' doctrine and behavior.

Why then the choice of Peter as pseudonymous writer of an urgent letter whose purpose, in a fashion similar to that of Jude, is the defense of tradition against rampant heresy within the community? Though any response would be conjectural, as indeed it would be for other pseudonymous letters, such a response would have to consider both the author's discussion of true prophecy (1:16-21) and obvious reference to a previous letter. Though both the alleged writers of Jude and 1 Peter could claim to be eyewitnesses of the Jesus story and their texts qualify as the previous letter (3:1), both could not claim the same experience of Jesus' divine "honor and glory" (1:17). The very tradition employed to defend the trustworthiness of "the promise of [Jesus'] coming" (particularly the transfiguration episode—1:16-18) supports the logical nature of such a choice. Besides, 1 Peter, probably known to both sides of the debate, speaks of OT prophecy (1:10-12) and frequently of Jesus' final revelation or coming (1:5, 7, 13; 2:12; 3:18; 4:11, 13; 5:1, 4, 10). The choice of Peter as pseudonym therefore appeals to the authority of the venerable apostle, whom ecclesial tradition connected with the name of Paul, relates the community's present eschatological debates to themes already raised by 1 Peter and variously by Paul, and formulates a polemical strategy based on Petrine tradition whereby Peter will be able to speak to future generations regarding the truth of the promises given to the apostles by the Lord (see 1:15, 19).

Audience (1:1b)

The letter's recipients are designated rather generally as believers or people "who have received the faith." Such a general formula is not surprising when one considers other post-Pauline letters that either address large or undetermined groups of Christians (Jas 1:1; 1 Pet 1:1) or believers in general (Jude 1). Three elements of the formulation however merit some attention for the light they shed on the author's strategy.

First, the author's concept of faith approximates that of Jude (see discussion of v. 3) because it refers not to commitment or fidelity but to the message itself. The term seemingly replaces "gospel" and interestingly is here described in a subjective way as something "received." Additionally use of the rare term *lagchano*, as indicated by its other NT occurrences (Luke 1:9; John 19:24; Acts 1:17), stresses divine gift. Believers then are described as those who have willingly accepted a divine message or tradition, but a tradition that must be supported by righteous living (1:5).

Next, Second Peter qualifies this divine message first by a comparative adjective, *isotimos* ("as precious as" or "of equal privilege") and then by a lengthy prepositional phrase. The former focuses on the equality of status between the apostolic generation of believers, represented by the alleged writer, and those of a later time. They have received the same divine message. The latter proceeds to the reason for insisting on this equality, for it is of equal value or as precious as that received by the writer "owing to or through the righteousness of . . . Christ." The term *dikaiosyne* here as in other occurrences in 2 Peter (2:5, 21; 3:13) refers not to the right relationship that God bestows on believers but rather to moral activity. In the present case the author is not appealing to the Christ-event as the source of "equally precious faith" but to Jesus' upright and impartial bestowal of equal privilege to all believers. Finally, why the insistence that the beliefs of the addressees are as precious as those of the first generation of believers? Seemingly 2 Peter wishes to draw a close relationship between past and present, namely, the importance of the promise that Jesus will return in glory for both the original followers who have passed away and for those who are now hearing the author's words. Peter has experienced the Lord's glory, and the addressees will do so in the future, though they must await his return by "leading lives of holiness and godliness" (3:11). By insisting on the "equal quality" of the faith of past and present believers, 2 Peter underscores the continuity of apostolic tradition that involves past, present, and future realities. The Christ-event involves the salvific life of God's beloved son, "the master who bought them" (1:17; 2:1), includes the activity of God's agents and beloved ones, demands an unblemished life, and culminates in Jesus' "power and coming" and entry into his "eternal kingdom," which will involve "new heavens and a new earth in which righteousness dwells" (3:13; see also 1:11, 13, 16-17; 3:11-13).

Lastly, v. 1 ends with a series of genitive nouns that could be read as referring to one person, "of our God and Savior Jesus Christ" or as indicating two persons, "of our God and the Savior Jesus Christ." The first reading is favored by the majority of scholars, is suggested by the author's use of an article only before "God," and is supported by the author's love for double titles for Jesus (1:11; 2:20; 3:18). Therefore a strong case can be made that 2 Peter has a high christology (see discussion in introduction). One needs, however, to explain the author's striking reference to Jesus as "God and Savior." The second title is perhaps less startling since it is used of Jesus by several other NT writers (Phil 3:20; Luke 2:11; John 4:42; 2 Tim 1:10; 1 John 4:14, among others) and several other times in 2 Peter (1:11; 2:20; 3:2, 18: invariably as "our Lord and Savior Jesus Christ"). Clearly the title, originally a divine epithet, becomes at the end of the first century a means of underscoring Jesus' salvific role in God's plan. The first title is more troublesome. While one can point to other NT passages that employ similar language (John 20:28; Heb 1:8-9) and point to the development of a high christology, the usage of 2 Peter suggests not preexistence but deification of the Son who now possesses divine power (1:3), will share this divine nature with believers (1:4—use in both cases of the adjective *theios*), and has obtained an eternal kingdom and glory (1:11; 3:18). Such deification corresponds to current pagan usage and will be further examined later in relation to the expression "sharers of the divine nature" in 1:4. At this point it suffices to say that the risen Jesus is part of the divine world and exercises divine functions on the Father's behalf. Denial of Christ's power and salvific role by false teachers calls for an assertion of his lordship and of his role in the divine mission (see 2:1). The author insists that this divine agent acts as a savior through the message that has endured from apostolic times and that must now be defended. Denial of Jesus' present lordship and future coming with power contradicts the prophetic, apostolic message.

Greeting (1:2)

The author employs not the tripartite formula used by Jude but returns to the traditional Christian greeting of "grace and peace" with the wish that these be multiplied in the lives of the addressees. This formulation is identical to that of 1 Pet 1:2b, though a lengthy prepositional phrase is added. On the one hand, these are traditional concepts referred to in most NT letters. Thus grace and peace are divine gifts received through Christ, the first to make possible the initial and continued response to God's loving activity and the second a present and future state of well-being or reconciliation to God. On the other hand, use by 2 Peter of these two concepts reveals some specific nuances. These two gifts, as also in 1 Pet 1:2b and Jude 2, are able to be increased, presumably by God. Also these are related to knowledge (see later discussion). Both themes reappear at the end of the letter and thus reinforce the author's meaning that grace is to be found in Christian knowledge (3:18), that peace is a present reality for the believer (one that can be lost, 3:14), and that both are constituents of proper behavior that need to be increased and preserved.

To this traditional wish for an increase in grace and peace the author adds that this is to be achieved "through the knowledge of God and our Lord Jesus Christ." This last theme, expressed by the *ginosko* word group, is clearly an important (there are 12 occurrences of the word group in 2 Peter) and complex one (there has been much debate concerning the meaning of this theme and the contrasting nuances between the different usages). While the verbs *ginosko* and *gnorizo* represent standard lexical use ("to understand" and "make known"—1:20; 3:3 and 1:16, respectively), the other terms and their usage seem to indicate distinct nuances. The term *gnosis*, on the one hand, is not used negatively and thus does not suggest a polemical reference to Gnostic opponents, and on the other, is clearly related to human effort. In 1:5 and 6 "knowledge" forms part of a list of virtues and thus represents human effort. The same can be said of its occurrence in 3:18 where believers are exhorted to "grow in . . . knowledge"; consequently in that case it is a relative synonym for *epignosis* but serves to emphasize human effort. The verb *epignosko* and its noun *epignosis*, however, present a slightly different usage. It has been suggested that the prepositional augment *epi* gives the term an inceptive or ingressive sense ("to come or begin to know") and would therefore indicate conversion (a common usage in post-NT times; see already

Heb 10:26 and 1 Tim 2:4). Such an interpretation is borne out by the usage of both the verb and noun in 2:20-21 where becoming a Christian is described as "knowing the way of righteousness" and "fleeing the pollution of the world." The other uses seemingly indicate the state that begins with conversion and in which growth and godly, fruitful activity are possible (1:2, 3, 8; 2:20).

In the present case the term *epignosis* indicates the believer's turning to God and the recognition of Christ's lordship (in contrast to the false teachers who disown the salvific master—2:1) as God's messiah. It is the author's wish that owing to this state of enlightenment or knowledge believers may receive a greater portion of grace and peace, a peace that looks to an eschatological blessedness and holiness (3:14—see also 1 Thess 5:23) and grace that allows a firmer commitment and a more fruitful, godly life (1:3, 8, 10; 2:20-21). Finally it should be noted that while "knowledge" (use of *epignosis*) concerns Christ in 1:3, 8 and 2:20, here in 1:2 it involves both God and Christ. This is not an indication that the fundamental issue concerns God or theodicy but that the immediate and more pervasive issue is Christ's lordship, power, and return as judge and warrior.

The letter opening then serves several purposes. First, it accomplishes the several goals assigned to openings: it introduces the author and audience and presents a short formal greeting before turning to the matter at hand. Second, each of its formal segments hints to and prepares for the document's strategy and message. The author prepares both for the letter's Petrine strategy by insisting on the apostle's background and titles and for some of its major themes and emphases by insisting on apostolic tradition, on the nature of Christian life, and on Christ's divine, salvific mission. The addressees are reminded of their precious faith and its relation to the teaching of the Lord and Savior through his apostles, a faith that will allow them to overcome or avoid the destructive opinions, the licentious ways, and deceptive words of false teachers.

Body Opening

(1:3-11)

Following a formal opening 2 Peter presents an anomalous unit that, in grammatical and structural terms, is variously understood by scholars. Some interpret the initial *hos* followed by a participial construction in the genitive as a continuation of the preceding greeting and so view vv. 3-4 as a further amplification of the theme of knowledge just mentioned. Most scholars, however, consider v. 3 as a genitive absolute and interpret vv. 3-4 as the dependent first half of a complex sentence that is resumed somewhat awkwardly in vv. 5f. The second is preferable because it views 1:3-11 as a relatively brief unit that replaces the traditional thanksgiving or opening. Indeed the passage does not begin by thanking God (see 1 Pet 1:3f) or by speaking of the writing task (Jude 3), but instead it speaks of God's benefactions (vv. 3-4), human effort expected in response (vv. 5-10), and the eschatological goal and reward of the "call and election" (v. 11). This tripartite structure is usually viewed as a traditional homiletic pattern, used in farewell speeches (see *4 Ezra* 14:28-36), which here serves as an introduction to Peter's farewell advice to the addressees. Such a suggestion makes sense in structural terms and sheds further light on the unit's function.

Divine Benefactions (1:3-4)

Not only the grammar but also the intricate thematic interrelations are difficult to discern in these first two verses. Careful observation, however, suggests that the themes of piety, knowledge, Jesus' divine power, and escape from corruption are unified by the author's focus on benefactions and the means by which they are given or received.

Four benefactions are explicitly mentioned: "everything that contributes to life and piety," the believer's "call and election" (see also 1:10), "the precious and very great promises," and "becoming sharers of the divine nature." Interestingly the first focuses on ethical concerns and prepares for the letter's frequent exhortations. Believers are provided with the assistance needed to love "a life of piety" (literally: "life and piety"), that is, a moral life that derives from a proper relation to God. Immediately in vv. 5f the author will turn to these concerns. The second benefaction is mentioned in passing, since the call, as a past event, is the basis for the believer's present life of holiness. Surely that election has led to a state of knowledge or enlightenment for believers as members of God's beloved people, and they will be called upon "to make every effort to make (this) call and election firm" (1:10). Mention of the third benefaction prepares more directly for the letter's principal focus, namely, the eschatological "promises" that are being denied by the false teachers or "last-day scoffers." While at this point the promises are simply qualified as "precious and very great" and noted as leading to future benefaction, they will return as the object of concern as the author argues for their trustworthiness (1:12f), speaks of the danger and deceptive nature of the teachers' claims regarding these promises (2:1f), and insists on their slow but sure and their sudden but grandiose fulfillment in the power and coming of the Lord Jesus Christ (3:1f). Lastly, 2 Peter speaks of the ultimate eschatological benefaction, here described as "sharing in the divine nature" but elsewhere as "entry . . . into the eternal kingdom" (1:11) or experiencing "new heavens and a new earth in which righteousness dwells" (3:13). Thus the notion of benefaction involves the initial call and its cleansing; the promise of assistance in living a free, stable, and fruitful life; and the assurance that the eschatological promises made by the Lord and Savior to the apostles will be fulfilled and that those who are firm in their faith will share in God's immortality (see below for discussion of "divine nature").

The second major, unifying theme of vv. 3-4 concerns the means by which these benefactions are given or received. Second Peter states that the first of these was conferred by "his divine power." Though both a theological and a christological reading are possible, the latter seems preferable since the possessive pronoun should refer to the last mentioned person and since the author seems intent on underscoring Christ's role in relation to these various benefactions. In addition it should be noted that 2 Peter favors Hellenistic terminology (*theios*) to designate Christ's divine mission and activity. Further the author insists that this power operates through Christian knowledge or grace given through conversion (see discussion of 1:2). The second benefaction or call is said to have occurred "by or through the agency of his own glory and power." Several reasons suggest that this statement be read as a parallel or synonym of the earlier "his divine power." In the present case the terms used are *doxa* and *arete*. The second of these could be rendered "virtue or goodness" (see 1:5 below), but since the term by itself and as a pair in Hellenistic literature often stood for "manifestation of divine power" (*TDNT* 1:459-61), in the present context the two should be read as a restatement of the author's earlier statement. Further the author's insistence on "his own glory and power" prepares for Jesus' reception of "honor and glory from God the Father" in 1:17 and the doxology of 3:18b as well as for the intriguing reference to Jesus' "power and coming" (1:16) and his role as lord of the endtime (3:4f).

The other two benefactions, by means of *dia* phrases ("by which things" and "through these"), are also related to the dual references to divine power or glory, the first directly and the second via the great promises. Therefore these promises are mediated and their trustworthiness authenticated by divine glory given to him by the Father and witnessed by Peter the alleged writer (1:16-18). The final benefaction, participation in the divine nature, will see its realization through the Lord's promises, themselves given through the Lord's power and to be accomplished through the power and glory granted him by the Father.

A few final notes are needed regarding details of vv. 3-4. First, while some scholars hesitate to see Christ as "the one who calls," insisting that in early Christian tradition this activity is regularly attributed to God, it must be stated that here too additional divine activities are given to God's agent, because knowledge in 2 Peter is regularly "knowledge of the Lord Jesus Christ" (see 1:8; 2:20; note also 1:2), who also calls and acts as savior.

Second, in the past much attention has been given to the author's use of pronouns in vv. 3-4. Does "us" refer to the apostolic generation (as in v. 1) or to Christians generally (as in v. 2: "our Lord Jesus Christ")? Most scholars now assume that the latter is the case but variously explain the change in the middle of v. 4 to "you might become." The change from "us" to "you" is easily explained as a shift to direct address and is here motivated by the author's insistence that while all Christians, author included, are recipients of all divine benefactions, even the great promises, the success of the last mentioned as leading to their eschatological goal remains questionable as the author exhorts the audience ("you") to trust in the Lord's promises. The shift to "you" prepares directly for the paraenesis of vv. 5f.

Third, interestingly the two principal benefactions (principal in stylistic and thematic terms) are both introduced by the rare, formal term for gracious bounty (*doreomai*: vv. 3, 4) and further emphasize the author's dual concerns throughout the letter: behavior (a life of piety versus the licentiousness of the teachers) and the eschatological promises (hope or denial of Jesus' return).

Fourth, what does the author mean by "becoming sharers of the divine nature"? This controversial statement has been variously explained, whether in Platonic terms as a regaining of a lost divine state, in Gnostic terms as the attainment of divine knowledge, or from a more general Greek perspective as a sharing in the immortality of the gods. The terminology of "participation in the divine nature" (*theias koinonoi physeos*), though not as common as that of divinization or attainment of immortality, suggests human participation in the divine world of noncorruption and permanence. So, on the one hand, 2 Peter is able to employ Hellenistic terminology much as do Philo and Josephus (see *Abraham* 144 and *JA* 8.107, respectively) to describe human escape from the material world or the sharing of a heavenly one. Yet the author is perceptive enough to combine this daring statement with a more traditional view, on the other hand, a view that is underscored in the remainder of v. 4 and later in v. 11. Not only is the attainment of this "divine status" or immortality a promised, eschatological benefaction (use of the subjunctive of *ginomai*) but this change of status is further described as happening "after having escaped the corruption that is in the world because of evil desire." This "divine status" is the opposite of what believers experience in this world, which is now subject to corruption as the result of "evil desire." The world itself is not corrupt because of its materiality but, in Jewish terms, because of its "sinful desire," here interpreted as part of the traditional story of rebellion against God (Gen 3). Corruption (*phthora*—see also 2:12 and 19) is divine punishment from which believers escape when they attain immortality or participate in the divine world, a status that in v. 11 will be described as "entry into the eternal kingdom" (for further discussion of "escape" and "desire," see 2:10, 18, 20; 3:3). Only by faithfully awaiting for the realization of the Lord's great promises will the final escape from destruction and admission to the heavenly realm be achieved (3:13).

A fifth and final note is called for regarding the author's use of the term *cosmos* or "world." Seemingly 2 Peter envisions three distinct realities: the world of the ungodly destroyed by the flood (2:5; 3:6), the present world invaded by corruption (1:4; 2:20), and the eschatological reality—described as "new heavens and a new earth" or as "the eternal kingdom"—where the faithful will be sharers of the divine nature" (1:4, 11; 3:13). The first world was destroyed, along with the ungodly, by water; the second is to be annihilated by fire on the day of judgment, along with the destruction of the ungodly (3:6-7, 10-12), when the third will be established as the eternal home of righteousness (3:13).

Initial Exhortation (1:5-10)

This section of the text is marked off by a resumptive construction at the beginning of v. 5 ("and so for this very reason") and a concluding statement in v. 10 ("therefore, brothers and sisters"), both of which introduce the theme of "effort" and employ imperative constructions. In structural terms the section begins and closes with the theme of effort, dwells on a chain of virtues that are to characterize the believer's effort, and, by means of three resumptive statements ("these things"—use of *tauta* in vv. 8, 9, 10), makes further exhortatory observations.

Verse 5a, after referring back to the eschatological motivation of v. 4, introduces the theme of "effort," a theme that prepares for the following list of virtues and the author's exhortation to faithful, fruitful behavior. The stress on "making every effort" (*spoude*) is reinforced by the insistence in 1:10 that the addressees "make every effort" to be faithful to their "call and election" and in 3:14 to their time of waiting for the Lord's return. The theme of effort in vv. 5 and 10 then lends urgency to the author's exhortation to believers who are forgetting their cleansing from sin and their call to a life of holiness and godliness and to their entry into a kingdom or home of eternal righteousness (1:3, 9, 11; 3:11, 13).

The concept of effort is supplemented by a subsequent imperative that introduces a chain of virtues (vv. 5b-7). A list of eight virtues is governed by the verb *epichoregeo* ("add to or supplement"), suggesting that each of these is to be augmented by a following virtue. While no exact parallel list to this one is to be found in Hellenistic, Jewish, or early Christian literature, it is possible to find similar constructs, whether in virtue and vice catalogues or more particularly in what has been called a "sorites" or chain of things whereby successive items build upon one another to reach a climax. The text of 2 Pet 1:5b-7 is unique in many ways; on the one hand it employs terms and themes that are rare in the New Testament but frequent in moral writers of the period and yet on the other hand, more in tune with biblical tradition, begins and ends with the themes of "faith" and "love," respectively, and later concludes the exhortation on an eschatological note (see Wis 6:17-20; Rom 5:1-5; *Mishna: Sota* 9.15; and *Hermas: Visions* 3.8.7).

The list of virtues opens with the basic Christian concept of "faith" (*pistis*) or response to the divine call that has made possible all things necessary for a godly life (1:3). This divine gift, however, must be supplemented by a moral excellence or "virtue" (*arete*) that is characterized by holiness and godliness (3:11) and contrasts with the ungodly behavior of the false teachers. Moreover it calls for "knowledge" (*gnosis* rather than *epignosis*; see v. 2) that discerns and grows and that also contrasts with the ignorance and forgetfulness of the ungodly. Such a life also requires "self-control" and "endurance" (*egkrateia* and *hypomone*, respectively), virtues that stress self-mastery and stability in contrast to the licentious enslavement and defection of the false teachers and their followers. Instead 2 Peter stresses firmness in the truth and a life of "piety" or godliness (*eusebeia*—see 1:3 and 3:11) that derives from a proper relationship to the divinity. Nonetheless a stolid piety or a die-hard perseverance or endurance are insufficient for Christian lives of holiness and godliness. There must, in addition, be "mutual affection" (*philadelphia*), since Christian lives must be fruitful (see v. 8), conscious of divine mercy (v. 9), and aware of God's beloved within the community, that is, those who are called "brothers and sisters." Finally, and as climax, the faith of the community must aspire to or be supplemented by the greatest of all virtues, "love" (*agape*), "which" (in the words of Col 3:14) "binds everything together in perfect harmony."

There follow in 1:8-10 three successive statements that reiterate in positive and negative terms the author's exhortation to a godly life in view of the Lord's "precious and very great promises." Each statement refers back to the author's exhortation to a more virtuous effort by employing *tauta* or "these things." Verse 8 states in positive terms (actually there is use here of a striking litotes, literally: "render you not idle and unfruitful") the productive outcome of a virtuous Christian life. As a result of their Christian enlightenment or acknowledgment of Jesus' lordship (here described as "knowledge of our Lord Jesus Christ"—see discussion of *epignosis* at 1:2), their constant increase in virtuous activity cannot fail to be productive. In effect, v. 9 insists, failure to possess these qualities or virtues amounts to culpable blindness (a possible reference to conversion as enlightenment), owing to a weak faith that too easily forgets the cleansing or washing away of its sins in baptism. Such people are like the false teachers who return to their past sinful lives (2:21-22) and become slaves to corruption. Believers are to remember (they are to be "farsighted" or not "forgetful") their conversion from past sins. Indeed the author concludes (v. 10): they are to "make every effort to make (their) call and election firm." The author first returns to the theme of effort and reiterates that of divine election (v. 3) and then affirms in a bold way that such virtuous activity will prevent the believer from "stumbling" (*ptaio* as in Jude 24) as do some who are "led away by the error of lawless people and lose (their) own stability" (3:17). Verse 10 then ends by addressing the audience directly and pleading with them to apply themselves to a life of piety to which they have been called and for which they have been endowed.

Eschatological Goal (1:11)

The initial paraenetic section is brought to a close by a brief statement of eschatological motivation; the goal of such moral activity is "entry . . . into the eternal kingdom of our Lord and Savior Jesus Christ." Once again one should note the christological focus of the passage—the kingdom is here said to be that of Christ. One should also underscore the author's insistence on immortality, since the kingdom is characterized as being "eternal." Again one encounters the sublime titles of "Lord and Savior" as applied to Christ. "Entry into the kingdom" clearly alludes to the Jesus tradition and its statements about the kingdom, usually referred to as the "kingdom of God," in reference to conversion. The author here uses the idiom to refer to the eschatological kingdom and undoubtedly intends a reminder to the reader that the principal issue to be discussed is Jesus' eschatological role (see 3:4). Nonetheless the entire problem will be restated later as an issue involving theodicy (3:13).

Interestingly this paraenetic section begins and ends on a similar note of divine benefaction. Just as vv. 3-4 insist on a series of gifts received or promised to the believers, so v. 11, after stressing at great length the crucial issue of human effort and activity, stresses by a curious turn of phrase ("entry will be richly provided for you") the nature of eschatological salvation as gift. By means of a divine passive the author insists that, beyond human effort and cooperation, there is still the reality of divine bounty, for entry results from growth of grace abundantly given (1:2; 3:18).

Suggested Readings

Brown, R. E. et al, eds. *Peter in the New Testament.* Minneapolis: Augsburg, 1973.

Charles, J. D. "The Language and Logic of Virtue in 2 Peter 1:5-7." *BBR* 8 (1998) 55-73.

Danker, F. W. "2 Peter 1: A Solemn Decree." *CBQ* 40 (1978) 64-82.

Doty, W. G. *Letters in Primitive Christianity.* Philadelphia: Fortress, 1973.

Easton, B. S. "New Testament Ethical Lists." *JBL* 51 (1932) 1-12.

Fitzmyer, J. A. "The Name Simon" in *Essays on the Semitic Background of the New Testament.* Missoula: Scholars, 1974, 105-12.

Hiebert, D. E. "Selected Studies from 2 Peter. Part 1: The Necessary Growth in the Christian Life: An Exposition of 2 Peter 1:5-11." *BS* 141 (1984) 43-54.

Neyrey, J. H. "Without Beginning of Days or End of Life (Heb 7:3): Topos for a True Deity." *CBQ* 53 (1991) 441-46.

Picirelli, R. "The Meaning of 'Epignosis'." *EQ* 47 (1975) 85-93.

Wolters, A. " 'Partners of the Deity': A Covenantal Reading of 2 Peter 1:4." *CTJ* 25 (1990) 28-44.

True and False Prophecy

(2 Peter 1:12–2:22)

The author of 2 Peter clearly marks off two distinct parts of the document by extended, complex recall formulas in 1:12-15 and 3:1-3, each of which introduces the major parts of the discussion: 1:12–2:22 on true and false prophecy and 3:1-16 on the Lord's day and related issues of theodicy. In addition this first part focuses on two connected topics: Peter and the reliability of apostolic tradition in 1:12-21 and the deception and punishment of false teachers in 2:1-22, the latter of which is a substantial revision of the text of Jude 4f. Clearly the ending of chapter 1 on apostolic tradition and true prophecy (1:16-21) prepares for the discussion in chapter 2 of false prophets and teachers.

Peter and the Reliability of Apostolic Tradition

(1:12-21)

This new section, in terms of content, deals with the assumed author's forthcoming death and need to communicate to a future audience (vv. 12-15), with the writer's eyewitness acquaintance with Jesus the source of tradition (vv. 16-18), and with the nature of true prophecy (vv. 19-21). The first two sections relate "Peter" episodes; the first has Jesus predicting Peter's martyrdom (see John 21:18-19), and the second recounts his presence on the mountain of transfiguration (see Mark 9:2-8 and parallels). The former introduces the theme and genre of Peter's testament, and the latter prepares for the longer treatment of apostolic tradition and the focus in the third section on true prophecy, the last mentioned itself a prelude to the lengthy condemnation of the false teachers throughout chapter 2. All three units deal with the reliability of apostolic tradition and provide the authoritative voice for the author's condemnation of heresy and eschatological discussion.

Peter's Testament (1:12-15)

This short unit begins by "reminding" the audience "of these things" (v. 12) and closes in a similar vein: "recalling these things" (v. 15). Beyond these recall features there is also a rhetorical focus on the addressees' knowledge (v. 12) and the constant need for them to appeal to the apostolic past (v. 15). The principal function of the unit, however, is to be seen in its setting up of a testamentary context. While mention of Peter's imminent death or departure prepares for the urgency of the advice that follows, appeal to Jesus' prophetic word on the same subject underscores the theme of authentication that runs through the remainder of the chapter. Finally the entire unit provides the rationale for the composition of the document, which itself will survive the assumed author's death and be a continual reminder and source of apostolic tradition. Second Peter is intended to be a permanent, written record of "Peter's" teaching.

(1:12) Winning Addressees' Goodwill. After reminding the readers of their divine benefactions and the requisite response in terms of virtuous effort, the author turns more directly to the document's strategy. Plainly 2 Peter "intends" (future of *mello*) the letter to be a "perpetual" (see vv. 12, 15) source of advice, indeed as written testaments are intended to be. At this point one encounters the author's first use of "recall" terminology (*hypomimnesko*; see related terms in 1:13, 15; 3:1, 2) and a further occurrence of the expression "these things," a means no doubt to connect this new unit with the major themes of the letter opening (1:3-11).

In traditional epistolary fashion 2 Peter seeks to win the addressees' goodwill by complementing them that they "already know (these things) and are established in the truth (they) have." Reading of the remainder of the letter, especially 2:1-3, shows to what extend such a statement is rhetorical, but such a reading also shows that the author has some hope that the letter will be successful in its strategy. Being well grounded in the apostolic faith, here characterized as "the truth that you have" (see also 2:2; compare with Gal 2:5), is another indication of the author's focus on authentication. The community is or is to be grounded in the original gospel ("the truth that you have") that was preached to them at their conversion as contrasted to the new teachings that are running rampant in the community. There is a focus here less on a corpus of beliefs than on the community's fidelity to the apostolic preaching.

(1:13-14) Writer's Forthcoming Death. The author now turns more directly to the form and content of the testament. Employing a familiar Greek formula, "so I think it fitting" (*dikaion*), the author insists that, in the alleged Petrine context of imminent death and assumed authority, the writing of a testament to assist future generations is the proper thing for the chief apostle to do. This indirect use of authority underscores the author's pseudonymic strategy. To underscore the pathos required by the testament genre, twice 2 Peter emphasizes the nearness of death: "as long as I am" alive (v. 13) and since death "is imminent" (v. 14). The insistence on this theme both stresses the text's function as testament and prepares further for its use by an alleged future audience. The author's purpose is "to stir or arouse" (*diegeiro*) the audience from its moral stupor or forgetfulness (see 3:1; also 1:9), a common motivation for the deathbed advice of great figures of the past. Once again the author invokes the theme of "reminding" as a way to underscore the role that apostolic tradition is to play in the combatting of heresy. The author does not pretend to offer new solutions to the community's problem but rather to remind the addressees of the doctrine or "truth" they already possess. Verse 14 suggests that the alleged author approaches death as an old person and that this death had been the subject of Jesus' comments. For the latter 2 Peter probably draws from well-known Petrine tradition the fact that the chief apostle had not only betrayed the master but had also died a martyr's death, both events of which had been foretold by Jesus (see Mark 14:30-31; John 13:36; and especially 21:18; see also the "Quo Vadis?" story from the *Acts of Peter*). Clearly the author's appeal to biblical tradition reinforces the text's claim to apostolic authority. Additionally it should be noted that the confirmation of Peter as a true disciple, after his denial, is done precisely by the one who is acknowledged as "our Lord Jesus Christ."

Finally a word should be said about the author's choice of imagery; being alive is characterized as "being in this tent (*skenoma*)" and dying as "the divesting (*apothesis*) of the tent" (vv. 13, 14). Much has been said about this imagery: 2 Peter espouses a radical dualism whereby at death the immortal soul leaves the mortal body seen as a dwelling place or tent (Wis 9:15), or instead the author employs Hellenistic terminology, much as does Paul in 2 Cor 5:1-5, to contrast earthly existence and its vicissitudes to an eternal, heavenly existence (see 1:4, 11; 3:13), where the earthly tents will be exchanged, in Lukan terms (16:9), for "heavenly tents." It is the latter that explains better the author's emotional suggestion that the elderly Peter has one last, major task to accomplish before his "entry into the eternal kingdom." One can only conjecture, however, at the reason for the author's choice of such poetic imagery, for there is no further attempt in 2 Peter to develop this line of thought.

(1:15) A Perpetual Means of Recall. Verse 15 brings to a conclusion the author's focus on Peter's testament by reiterating the principal themes of the unit: insistence on intention and effort, recall of apostolic tradition and a perpetual means ("enable you") for doing so, and the apostle's forthcoming death (here characterized as "departure"). The verse however adds something new to the author's discussion. The author clearly indicates that the time envisioned for the assistance follows Peter's death—the letter will be a per-petual source of access to the community's early tradition. By the addition of post-positive *kai* ("also") the author notes that both addressees and author have to make "every effort." By employing the future tense "I will make every effort" the letter points to the ensuing text and perhaps other Petrine tradition (see note on "second letter" at 3:1; also the early ascription of gospel tradition to Peter via Mark) and expresses the fond wish that the community will receive the assistance needed to resist the teachers' deceptive and destructive doctrine and behavior. In the context of v. 15, however, the focus is less on the false teachers as on the final words of the verse: "to recall these things," a phrase that refers back to v. 12 and even further back to the anaphoric use of "these things" in vv. 4 (*bis*), 8, 9, 10. In this way the author stresses both the community's virtuous effort and memory of its bene-factions, particularly the promise of Jesus' return (1:3-11).

Apostolic Eyewitnesses of God's Revelation (1:16-18)

The unit of vv. 16-18 is a complex, convoluted construct. Verse 16 consists of two contrasting participial constructions that frame the principal clause, while vv. 17 and 18 either consist of incomplete sentences (*anacolutha*) or function as further attempts to qualify the author's principal claim concern-ing Jesus' coming in v. 16b. Moreover the unit presents a familiar but abbreviated version of the transfiguration story from the Jesus tradition (see Mark 9:2-9 and parallels) and relates this episode both to the preaching of early Christian eschatology and the theme of ancient mythology. Discussion of the unit, however, has focused on two issues: the author's intention in referring to "myths" and the form of and the function played by the trans-figuration story.

The unit opens with a striking statement, usually rendered: "we did not follow cleverly devised myths" (NRSV). Scholarship has been virtually unanimous in discerning traces of polemics in this statement, particularly since the author continues: "but we had been eyewitnesses." While earlier scholars suggested that 2 Peter was attempting to characterize the false teachers' doctrine as Gnostic formulations, more recent studies see 2 Peter as responding here and in later passages to accusations made against traditional eschatological doctrine. Instead of viewing the author's reference to "myths" as an accusation against the false teachers or as a response against their accusations, it seems preferable to situate the theme within the unit's overall function, namely, 2 Peter's insistence that eschatological teaching is based on revelation from God given to Christ and witnessed by the apostles and not on myths and their wise interpretation, an interpretation that the false teachers perhaps use as the basis for their "specious arguments" (see comments on both 1:16 and 2:3). Further there seems to be no real polemics in 2 Peter against mythology as such but rather a focus on the authentic, divine nature of apostolic teaching.

Clearly 2 Peter employs an abbreviated version of the transfiguration story and focuses particularly on the words spoken by the heavenly voice. Nonetheless the author retains the original tradition's characterization of the event as a theophany that occurs on a mountain before eyewitnesses, who experience otherworldly glory or light as they are commissioned by God or the heavenly voice (compare with Mark 9:2-8; Matt 17:1-9; Luke 9:28-36). Though the text of 2 Peter is closest to that of Matt 17:5 (itself a conflation of the baptismal and transfiguration statements of the heavenly voice), its reading, with textual variants, diverges from all three Synoptic versions. Perhaps the variations in the statement of the voice are to be explained in relation to the function these heavenly messages played in the early Jesus tradition. In effect there are several attested uses of the heavenly statement: a first is employed at Jesus' baptism (see Mark 1:11; Matt 3:17; Luke 3:22), a second at his transfiguration (Mark 9:7; Matt 17:5; Luke 9:35), and a third is variously attached to parousia traditions. The last mentioned group includes, of course, 2 Pet 1:16-18 but also the *Apocalypse of Peter*. The last mentioned, roughly contemporary to 2 Peter, presents a version of the transfiguration in what is seemingly a post-resurrection context that involves a discussion of the end of the world (ch. 1) and reward of the just and punishment of the wicked (chs. 2–14). Indeed, the second part of the work (chs. 15–17) is set on a "holy mountain," includes visions of Moses and Elijah, a familiar statement by the heavenly voice, and Jesus' departure into heaven. This work like 2 Peter employs the transfiguration story as the basis for acceptance of the tradition's promise of Jesus' return. The words of the heavenly voice then have been appropriated and edited for a variety of purposes.

In considering the overall message of this unit some exegetical analysis is required. Certainly the themes of eyewitness, divine glory, and the teaching about Jesus' return are central to the author's purpose, but their relation to that of myth and to the transfiguration remain to be explained. Also the overall unit's relation to the previous section on Peter's testament and to the following discussion of prophecy will require further attention.

(1:16) Not from Myths but from Eyewitnesses. The author makes three statements in this verse, two of which are contrasting participial constructions ("not . . . but"), that sandwich and depend on a straightforward comment about apostolic preaching.

Not by Myths. Owing to 2 Peter's negative reference to myths and positive appeal to eyewitness accounts, it has usually been assumed that the verse treats myths polemically. Beyond the fact that *ouk . . . alla* ("not . . . but") is a favorite stylistic feature of the author (1:16, 21; 2:4, 5; 3:9, 9) and does not usually introduce polemical statements, and beyond the fact that mythology or related themes are mentioned nowhere else in 2 Peter, there is reason to reexamine the present statement about myths. The author employs the idiom "to follow or appeal to the authority of myths" (*mythois exakaloutheo*). It is stated simply, by means of a contrasting statement, that apostolic tradition derives from eyewitness authority. The noun *mythos*, however, is modified by a curious participial adjective: *sesophismenos*. This relatively rare verb from the *sophia* word family means "to make wise" but owing to its present assumed negative context (that of "myth-making"), its passive form, and its negative use by some contemporaries, it is concluded that "with a derogatory wave of the hand the author is dismissing the errors as 'cunningly devised myths' " (*TDNT* 7:527) or is rejecting the teachers' slander against the prophecy about the Lord's return as myths cleverly devised for the purpose of deception. Both terms require some attention.

In the Hellenistic world "myth" was most commonly used to indicate story as opposed to logical argument (*mythos* as opposed to *logos*). Though some ancient philosophers labeled them fantastic stories invented or fabricated for the naive masses (use of the verb *plasso* to characterize "myth-making," but see the term *plastos* in 2:3), their function was widely recognized as supporting the piety and moral behavior of the populace. Reference to "myth," whether in 2 Peter or contemporary literature, need not indicate a hostile or polemic intention but rather a recognition (perhaps begrudging on the part of monotheists) that such stories were an accepted means of expressing universal truths (see discussion of 2:3).

Use of the term *sophizo*, while routinely assumed here to mean "fabricate," "craftily devise," or even "invent to deceive," does not suffice to read the participial construct as "deceptive myth-making," whether on the part of the teachers or the orthodox believers. Instead the term probably points to the use of myths or stories as a source of wisdom or as a means of instruction (see 2 Tim 3:15 for a positive use of the only other use of *sophizo* in the NT). A well-known passage from Josephus (*JA* 1.18-26) supports such a reading, because in contrasting the beginning of his treatment of Moses as legislator, he insists that he is not "following myths" or appealing to their authority (1:22; same expression as used by 2 Peter) as do other legislators but instead will recount the biblical narrative, as did Moses, as prelude and basis for discussing divine law. Just as Josephus is led to reject classical myths as a reliable guide for a discussion of divine law and chooses instead the narratives of God's dealings with humanity for that purpose, so 2 Peter will not appeal to pagan myths to defend the reliability of the promise of divine reward and punishment at the hands of the returning messiah but rather will appeal to apostolic witness to divine revelation, that is, the wisdom that God gives (see 3:15b). Seemingly the false teachers deny both the community's eschatological stories and their ethical significance.

In this first participial construction then 2 Peter states that the apostolic preachers "did not appeal to the authority of (the classical) myths as a source of wisdom" as did the Hellenistic moralists, the ancient philosophers, or even some of the community's teachers; instead they appealed to apostolic experience and tradition.

But as Eyewitnesses. The second, contrasting participial construct states that the apostolic preachers "were acting as eyewitnesses of [the Lord Jesus Christ's] majesty," that is, the authority for their preaching derived from their experience on the holy mountain, an experience that is related in the traditional story that follows. Three terms require some comment. First, the word translated "eyewitness" (*epoptes*, meaning "observer") was often used to describe one who experienced visions in ceremonies of the divine (especially Eleusian) mysteries (BAGD 305.2). It is probable that 2 Peter uses this term here, along with other terminology, to underscore the privileged revelation received by Jesus' apostles who experienced the transfiguration. Second, the term rendered "majesty" (*megaleiotes*) is used in the Septuagint and inter-testamental literature mainly for divine grandeur or magnificence (see Josephus, *JA* 1:24; Luke 9:43) and here further confirms Jesus' special status as one who has been elevated to divine majesty. Third, the author's use of *ekeinos* ("that one's"), referring back to "our Lord Jesus Christ," prepares for what will be said in v. 17, namely, that Jesus has received divine "honor and glory" from God. Jesus not only acts in God's name but also shares divine attributes.

The Lord's Power and Coming. While attention is usually directed to the contrasting participial constructions, it is usually not stressed that the main clause is the focus of v. 16. Indeed the former presents the basis for the apostolic message and its credibility. Thus it is as eyewitnesses of divine activity that the author can claim, in the name of apostolic preachers, "we made known the power and coming of our Lord Jesus Christ." The verb here used for the apostolic preaching is *gnorizo*, a term that suggests divine revelation (see also Luke 2:17; Rom 16:26). Already, in this statement it is implied that the eschatological promise at issue (see 3:4), Jesus' return as warrior and judge, derives from divine revelation, a revelation communicated to special devotees or eyewitnesses. Second Peter also speaks of Jesus' "power and coming" (*dynamis kai parousia*), a curious phrase that provides a clue for the document's overall interpretation. On the one hand, the term *parousia* (see also 3:4, 12) is the traditional term used early in Paul's career (see 1 Thess 2:19; 3:13; 4:15; 5:23) for comparing Jesus' endtime coming as judge to the pomp and circumstance accompanying official or imperial visits of the Roman period. But the author's addition of the theme of "power," on the other hand, stresses also his role as one exercising divine power either as endtime warrior or more specifically as one who will not leave the ungodly unpunished. This note about divine power, expressed as a christological issue, relates directly to 2:1 and the claim that the false teachers "even deny the Master." It is Jesus' divine power, not directly that of God, that is being challenged. In this way the emphasis on Jesus' ("that one's") "majesty," "power," and sonship reinforce the christological character of the teachers' heresy. The issue is one of theodicy but more particularly theodicy in a Christian key. Finally the powerful one who is due to return is described specifically as "our Lord Jesus Christ," namely, the same Jesus whose death and resurrection brings about human salvation (2:1; see use of "savior" title —1:1f) and whose acknowledgment as lord constitutes the believer's profession of faith in God's salvific and eschatological agent.

(1:17) Revelation of Jesus' Honor and Glory. Verse 17 oddly appears as an independent nominative participial construction and so either looks forward to an unexpressed main clause or is to be read as a nominal clause with unexpressed copula: "for (he had) received honor and glory from God the Father." The latter seems more probable. This new statement clearly serves as an explanation (use of *gar*) of the previous claim that the apostles had "acted as eyewitnesses of (Christ's) majesty." Therefore its principal theme is once again that of divine benefaction (see 1:3f). Jesus possesses divine grandeur because it was bestowed upon him by "God the Father," a benefaction now described as "honor and glory" (*time kai doxa*). Use of the first term focuses on supernatural dignity or grandeur and serves more properly as a synonym of "majesty" in the previous verse, while the second reiterates the concept of divine or royal power already developed in 1:3. Jesus, whether at his heavenly enthronement or proleptically on the mountain of transfiguration, has been given a share in God's dignity and authority. In this way he possesses the divine majesty of his Father.

At this point the author appeals to the traditional story of the transfiguration as the occasion and, more properly, as evidence of the granting of divine status to Jesus; that is, he is invested with divine majesty or honor and divine power or glory as preparation for his return as lord to judge and reign over his kingdom (1:11). The heavenly voice, with terminology drawn from tradition, is interestingly presented as "coming forth to him from the majestic Glory." Both this description of the voice's descent and of the divine origin of the message reveal an author's care to protect divine transcendence and to underscore its magnificence—God is simply called "the splendid or majestic Glory."

The voice is sent to Jesus ("came to him") and proclaims the words familiar to the addressees from the Jesus tradition: "This is my son, my beloved, with whom I am well pleased." Interestingly, however, it is not a revelation to Jesus (as is the heavenly message in Mark 1:11) but seemingly a public proclamation of Jesus' sonship as well as his appointment as eschatological lord. Relying on a messianic reading of Ps 2:7, in accordance with the Jesus tradition generally, the author cites a version of the heavenly message that agrees most closely with Matt 17:5. Jesus is appointed and proclaimed God's messianic king, the one who is now proclaimed lord by all believers and will return with power that was given to him. His present majesty, his status as "beloved son," supports the teaching concerning his return in power to exercise divine lordship. Finally it should be noted that 2 Peter retains the voice's note on Jesus' divine election ("with whom I am well pleased"), for this forms a neat parallel with 1:3 and the insistence on the believer's call by Jesus' "own glory and power"—note that 2 Peter adds an intensive pronoun ("with whom *I* [*ego*] am well pleased") to stress further the divine source as well as beneficence ("beloved") of this revelation.

(1:18) From a Heavenly Source. Parallel to the event just described is the statement of the apostolic reaction to the heavenly voice (the two verses are joined by the coordinating conjunction *kai*: "and"). This meaning is further borne out by 2 Peter's use of two intensive terms: "we *ourselves* heard *this* voice." The stress therefore is both on being witnesses, that is, being disciples who saw Jesus' majesty and heard the heavenly voice, and the fact that it is that very voice that provides divine authority. Indeed the author states further that the voice had a heavenly origin ("come from heaven") and that the apostles were with Jesus.

A final note is required here concerning the revelatory character of this episode. From the outset 2 Peter insists, by choice of terminology, that the revelation that the apostles witnessed as privileged devotees was made known in their preaching of Jesus' return in power. It was not the examination of ancient stories about the gods and human destiny that served as the basis of Christian preaching but the foretaste of Jesus' sharing of divine majesty. In that experience wherein God's revelation was made known through divine benefactions to Jesus and a heavenly statement to him, the apostles were told and reassured about Jesus' "power and coming." Finally the author insists that this revelation originated from heaven and was granted both to Jesus and to the apostles "on the holy mountain," the perennial site of theophanies and revelations where humans commune with God. The author's reference to "*the* holy mountain" seemingly lays a strong claim to the authority of the community's tradition that invariably spoke of Jesus' and the apostles' revelatory experience on the mountain of transfiguration.

Reliability and Origin of Prophecy (1:19-21)

Treatment of this passage is rendered difficult owing to the diversity of opinion concerning various issues and the seeming lack of consensus regarding the author's overall meaning. Does the expression "the prophetic message" refer generally to Old or New Testament prophecies, to specific eschatological predictions from the NT Scriptures, or specifically to the promise of Jesus' coming as related to the transfiguration? Thus the importance of that message, as noted in v. 19, would vary according to one's interpretive choice. Are vv. 19-21 about true prophecy and the ramification of this for the following treatment of the false teachers who are likened to "false prophets" (2:1)? How does the issue of interpretation relate to the reliability of prophecy? Also, whose interpretation is intended in v. 20—that of the reader or of the prophet? Finally, should this section of the letter be seen as a response to a further denial by the false teachers? Answers to these questions must be found in the clues provided by the text.

(1:19) Attention to This Reliable Message. The new section introduces the topic of prophetic speech. The idiom used (*exo . . . bebaioteron*) means not legal "confirmation" (see NRSV) but "possession of something very reliable" (BAGD 138.2); note that the comparative form of the adjective, here as often in Hellenistic Greek, has a superlative sense. Hence the passage opens by stating simply: "and so we possess a very reliable prophetic message." The major difficulty in interpreting this passage, however, is discerning what the phrase "the prophetic message" (*ho prophetikos logos*) designates in the present context. This rare expression can hardly be classified as a technical phrase to designate the Old or New Testament Scriptures, though sometimes so employed by Philo (*On Plants* 117; *Allegorical Laws* 3:43) and some early Christian writers. Instead one must look in the text of 2 Peter for the most logical referent. While there will be explicit citations or allusions later to the Hebrew Scriptures, to dominical sayings, and even to Paul designated as "Scripture," it seems that vv. 20-21 serve more logically to introduce, by means of a different expression ("scriptural prophecy"), these scriptural subjects (see below). Verse 19 then functions as a conclusion to the preceding discussion of the transfiguration as the basis for the apostolic teaching on the parousia. In stylistic terms vv. 17-19 present three successive and complementary statements. Verse 17 describes the transfiguration as Jesus' investment with divine majesty, while vv. 18 and 19 present two complementary passages, each introduced by *kai*, to establish the importance of this revelatory event. Verse 18 reiterates (see eyewitness theme of v. 16) that the apostles witnessed this otherworldly event, and v. 19 concludes further that the community's prophetic message (the apostolic "revelation of the power and coming of our Lord Jesus Christ") is most reliable since it meets the burden of forensic proof. On the one hand the apostles were witnesses of the manifestations and words of the event, an event that underscores the divine authority of the transfiguration as prophecy of Jesus' return in power. The opening statement of v. 19 then is a conclusion that the author draws about the forensic value of the transfiguration as witnessed by the apostles. On the other hand, these verses underscore Peter's role (he is present at the revelatory event according to tradition—see Mark 9:2) and so develop further the document's testamentary characteristics.

Second Peter follows this logical assertion with a brief paraenetic statement: the audience "would do well to attend to" this "reliable prophetic message." It is precisely the teachers' refusal to look to the Lord's return as motivation for godly behavior that leads them to return to their pre-conversion days of darkness and ungodliness (2:20-22). This paraenetic aside leads the author to describe, via striking light imagery, the effect this enlightening message should have on receptive believers. Second Peter, employing common biblical imagery (see Job 29:3; John 5:35), compares this revelatory message "to a lamp shining in a dark place." Presumably the world that Christians came from or live in is a place of darkness needing otherworldly light (see 1:4 and 2:19f for the author's vision of an unenlightened world). Furthermore 2 Peter uses a double statement to describe the function of this enlightening process. First of all, these statements are governed by a temporal qualifier "until" (*heos hou*); thus they involve the interim period before the Lord's day, a theme that runs implicitly and explicitly throughout the letter (1:3f; 2:19f; 3:11f). The "most reliable prophetic message" is to serve as a light or as hope in a dark world as believers await the Lord's coming. Secondly the end of that process is described as "the day that dawns," that is, the Lord's day or day of salvation (Luke 1:78), which supersedes the temporary light of the promise. Thirdly 2 Peter reaffirms, by means of light imagery, the letter's principal claim that the day of salvation is to be ushered in by the "lightbringer" (*phosphoros*), "the day-star," Jesus the star that "rises in (their) hearts." Drawing upon the intertestamental tradition (*T.Levi* 18:3; *T.Juda* 24:1) that interpreted "the rising star" of Num 24:17 as referring to the coming messiah, 2 Peter portrays Jesus, by means of Hellenistic imagery usually applied to Venus, as the one who will establish the eternal light in the hearts of all believers. Christians are people of the light or of the day not of darkness or of the night (see also 1 Thess 5:5, 8). So, while they are to live now in the temporary light of hope, based on "a most reliable prophetic message," in the endtime that lamp will be replaced by the light that the Lord will provide both in a cosmic (3:7-13) and deeply personal sense ("in your hearts").

(1:20-21) Reliability of Apostolic Witness to God's Prophetic Message. The final verses of the section, in actuality a participial extension of the statement begun in v. 19, present a challenge to the modern reader. Indeed many scholars insist that 2 Peter is concerned about two important themes in these verses: proper interpretation of Scripture in v. 20 and the true origin of prophecy in v. 21. Also it is common for scholars to view either or both verses as polemics against accusations by the false teachers. Finally, in most discussions of this section of 2 Peter, it is difficult to see how these verses either fit into the author's testamental use of the transfiguration story or prepare for the lengthy treatment of the false teachers in chapter 2.

Most of the discussion centers on the admittedly difficult and unfamiliar idioms of v. 20. First, one encounters the expression *idia epilypsis*, which means "one's own interpretation or explanation." The term *idios* could refer to "private" interpretation or to the prophet's meaning. Therefore the expression could refer either to the concept of private interpretation (to condemn the idiosyncratic and self-serving scriptural interpretation of the false teachers) or to the idea of personal interpretation (as a means to define prophecy not as human but as God-inspired speech). The verbal expression *ou ginomai* with the genitive is usually rendered "is not a matter of" (BAGD 160.II2a). The vagueness of the expression, in Greek as well as in English, leads scholars to view the idiom as referring to private interpretation or to the origin of prophetic interpretation. Another feature of v. 20 adds to the difficulty of proper interpretation, namely the meaning of "prophecy of scripture." Does the expression refer to the prophetic writings or Scripture more generally, or does it serve as a generalized synonym for the earlier "prophetic message" (v. 19)?

Perhaps the best clue for making sense of this verse and its surrounding context is found in the opening idiom of v. 20: "understanding first of all that . . . " (*touto proton ginoskontes hoti*). Since the same expression is used again in 3:3, it seems logical to seek clarification by comparing the usage in each case. In the latter the expression explains what has just been said about the past discourse of the prophets and apostles concerning the end-days; in the former the new verses return to the theme of reliability of the prophetic message. Verse 20 then is not about private or personal interpretation but about the origin of the prophetic message derived from the transfiguration experience. Thus 2 Peter's use of the adjective *idios* underscores not "private" or prophetic interpretation but God's message (contemporary usage supports this reading). Also the term *epilypsis* suggests not so much the sense of "interpretation" as that of "explanation" wherein the transfiguration is seen as prophecy of the parousia. Furthermore the author, in v. 20, is referring to the origin and not the interpretation of the prophetic message. Lastly the expression "the prophecy of scripture" refers back to the "reliable prophetic message," itself an attempt to characterize the transfiguration as the basis for the apostolic preaching about the parousia (see vv. 16, 19). In effect, in v. 20, 2 Peter insists that the apostolic preaching about Jesus' return is reliable because "no prophecy of scripture derives from personal explanation." This statement is seemingly not a response to accusations leveled against orthodox preaching but rather an attempt on 2 Peter's part to underscore the apostolic authority of the community's eschatological beliefs.

This line of defense, particularly the author's reliance on the testament as genre, raised a possible problem in terms of strategy. By insisting so forcefully that the reliability of the parousia was based in large part on Petrine involvement as eyewitness (see use of "Peter" episodes in vv. 12-15, 16-18) the author risked suggesting that the community's eschatological beliefs were Peter's personal explanations of past events rather than God's prophetic message. Verse 20 then is a first attempt to explain the parousia as a divinely inspired promise. The ambiguity, however, of this first response (see earlier discussion of the terminology of v. 20) has led the author in the following verse to restate in clearer and more formalized terminology a position on the origin and nature of "prophecy" more generally.

Verse 21 is expressed in formal negative and positive contrasting terms ("not . . . but"). In short the author insists that prophecy derives not from a human but from a divine source, but notes nonetheless that the medium of this prophecy is human speech. Several interesting final points need to be made regarding this verse. The author's use of *phero* in both segments of the verse is hardly accidental; prophecy is said "not to *come from* the human will" but instead to derive from human speech "*moved or impelled by* the Holy Spirit" (the italicized terms represent use of the verb *phero*). No doubt, an intentional connection is being made with the heavenly voice that "came" upon him, from heaven (use of *phero* both in vv. 17 and 18). Use of this term along with the focus on speech in both passages underscores the author's point that prophecy ultimately consists of divine speech, whether in the form of a heavenly voice or human speech that, under the impulse of the Holy Spirit, speaks the things of God (*apo theou*).

Additionally the author's use of prophetic terminology is instructive in understanding the section's overall function. In v. 19 prophetic terminology is employed a first time to characterize the transfiguration and its relation to the preaching of the parousia as "a reliable prophetic message"; thus the entire discussion up to this point is placed under this particular rubric. In v. 20 the term "prophecy" is used to describe the community's belief in the parousia as a particular example of scriptural prophecy. Finally in v. 21 "prophecy" now becomes a general term for divine revelation. In this discussion the author slowly moves from a consideration of a particular prophetic episode to a defense of the reliability and the nature of prophecy generally; this last point will lead to a lengthy discussion of false prophets or teachers in chapter 2.

The community's tradition concerning the Lord Jesus' coming in power is a reliable prophetic message, the author insists, one that comes from a heavenly source and that is embedded in the original apostolic preaching and indeed one that must serve now as a shining lamp for those who await the lightbearer's return on the Lord's day. Peter and the other apostles have and continue to serve as reliable witnesses to God's prophetic message concerning the community's eschatological beliefs.

Suggested Readings

Aune, D. E. *Prophecy in Early Christianity and the Ancient Mediterranean World.* Grand Rapids: Eerdmans, 1983.

Bauckham, R. J. "Pseudo-Apostolic Letters." *JBL* 107 (1988) 469-94.

Collins, J. J. "The Testamentary Literature in Recent Scholarship" in *Early Judaism and Its Modern Interpreters.* Eds., R. A. Kraft and G. W E. Nickelsburg. Atlanta: Scholars, 1986, 268-85.

Harvey, A. E. "The Testament of Simeon Peter" in *Essays on Jewish and Christian Literature and History.* Eds., P. R. Davies and R. T. White. Sheffield: JSOT, 1990, 339-54.

Hiebert, D. E. "Selected Studies from 2 Peter. Part 2: The Prophetic Foundation for the Christian Life: An Exposition of 2 Peter 1:19-21." *BS* 141 (1984) 158-68.

Knoch, O. "Das Vermächtnis des Petrus: Der 2. Petrusbrief" in *Wort Gottes in der Zeit.* Eds., H. Feld and J. Nolte. Düsseldorf: Patmos, 1973, 149-65.

Kolenkow, A. B. "The Genre Testament and Forecasts of the Future in the Hellenistic Jewish Milieu." *JSJ* 6 (1975) 57-71.

Neyrey, J. H. "The Apologetic Use of the Transfiguration in 2 Peter 1:16-21." *CBQ* 42 (1980) 504-19.

Nineham, D. E. "Eyewitness Testimony and the Gospel Tradition III." *JTS* 11 (1960) 254-64.

Vögtle, A. "Die Schriftwerdung der Apostolischen Paradosis nach 2. Petr 1,12-15" in *Neues Testament und Geschichte.* Eds., H. Baltensweider & B. Reiche. Tübingen: Mohr-Siebeck, 1972, 297-305.

Zmijewski, J. "Apostolische Paradosis und Pseudepigraphie im Neuen Testament: 'Durch Erinnerung wachhalten' (2 Petr 1, 13; 3, 1)." *BZ* 23 (1979) 161-71.

False Teachers: Their Deception and Punishment
(2:1-22)

After having discussed at some length the reliability of the apostolic preaching about Jesus' coming and after having focused on the nature and origin of true prophecy, the author turns rather abruptly to a treatment of people who are characterized as false teachers and are compared to false prophets who in ancient times lived among the people of Israel. Clearly the theme of prophecy treated immediately at the end of chapter 1 leads to that of false prophets at the beginning of chapter 2. To the extent that the apostolic witnesses are presented as reliable mediums of God's prophetic message to the addressees, to an even greater extent the opponents are condemned as false prophet-like teachers who deceive, teach false doctrine, and indulge in licentious practices. As has already been noted and discussed at some length, this entire section of 2 Peter is heavily dependent on the text of Jude 4f. The author has borrowed words, themes, and entire textual units to construct a bitter condemnation of the opponents' deceptive teaching and behavior and to insist on the divine punishment that awaits these ungodly people.

The severe treatment of the false teachers extends throughout the chapter, most units of which owe some elements to the text of Jude. Already in 2:1-3, 2 Peter borrows several themes from Jude 4, but this dependence ceases in vv. 17-18 only to resume briefly at the beginning of chapter 3. Interestingly this borrowing is not structural because 2 Peter does not follow the sixfold alternating pattern of Jude 4-23. Indeed the striking "certain people" and the subsequent fivefold use of "these" (*houtoi*) in Jude (4, 8, 10, 12, 16, 19) disappear. Only in 2 Pet 2:12 and 17 does one find trances of Jude's iterative use of *houtoi*. Beyond these structural indicators scholars have also sought in 2 Peter's dependence on Jude other clues to understanding the construction of the chapter. Since 2:4 (on punishment of the angels), v. 10b (on slandering the glorious beings), and v. 17 (on nature imagery) all relate to specific texts of Jude and introduce blocks of material from that source, some scholars have tended to employ these to determine the structural units of chapter 2 (see NRSV). Nonetheless grammatical and thematic considerations have led to a disconcerting variety of proposals for understanding the unity of the chapter. Recent commentators have insisted that 3b prepares for the theme of judgment that is treated in vv. 4f, while other scholars have proposed a unit beginning with vv. 10, 10b, or 12. In addition 2 Peter has been much criticized for the grammatical difficulties and ambiguity presented by the chapter as well as for its repetitive treatment of themes.

These difficulties seemingly derive from a desire to relate the composition of 2 Peter to a redactional use of Jude's material. It would seem, however, that one should seek the text's structure and meaning in relation to its own grammatical features and stylistic indicators. Considerations of these last-mentioned factors lead me to propose a tripartite structure whose parts are loosely interrelated units. The first of these (vv. 1-10a) introduces the opponents specifically as "false teachers" and, by comparing them to the "false prophets" of old, prepares for the generous use of OT examples in chapter 2 of divine judgment and punishment of the ungodly. In terms of content vv. 1-3 introduce the teachers, insist on their doctrinal and moral errors, and underscore their just punishment. Verses 4f provide a list, in the spirit of Jude 5-7, of both godly and ungodly figures from the past and their respective treatment by God. It has been proposed that a new subunit begins at 3b; in effect the second half of the verse is seen as introducing the theme of divine punishment, which is further developed in vv. 4f. Such a conclusion is based more on considerations of content than on structural features. Verse 3b consists of a relative clause and must be joined to the first part of the verse. Overall, vv. 1-10a consist of two types of grammatical structures: vv. 1-3 present a series of three independent clauses, interconnected by *de . . . kai . . . kai,* and vv. 4-9 involve a lengthy conditional sentence whose protasis (vv. 4-8: consisting of 4 clauses introduced by *ei* and continued by 3 successive uses of *kai*) is balanced by a concluding apodosis (vv. 9-10a). Interestingly each of the three independent clauses of vv. 1-3 is modified by a dependent relative clause: "people such as," "on account of whom," and "whose condemnation." Obviously the three constructions form a grammatical unit, a unit whose content (focused on divine judgment) is then developed by a series of OT examples. Thus the section begins by introducing the false teachers and their activity and by insisting on the certainty of their punishment and then presents a series of good and evil people and their respective treatment by God.

The second unit (vv. 10b-14b) begins ominously by characterizing the teachers as "bold, audacious" people. Immediately they are accused of "maligning glorious beings," an accusation that is developed in relation to an ancient Jewish story concerning angels. Second Peter resumes in v. 12 the polemic against the teachers by borrowing directly from Jude 10 the following statement: "but these people are like irrational animals." The remainder of the unit consists of a series of loosely-related, sometimes complex participial constructions: "maligning things" (v. 12b), "regarding as pleasure" (v. 13b), "having eyes full of" (v. 14a), and "having hearts" (v. 14b). From beginning to end the unit focuses on accusations against the false teachers.

The third unit (vv. 14c-22) presents an overall structure similar to that of the previous passage: an initial polemical characterization of the teachers ("accursed lot"—v. 14c), a statement of accusation against them ("forsaking the straight path") related to an OT story (that of Balaam and the speaking beast of burden—vv. 15-16), a resumption of the polemic by a similar statement (also borrowed from Jude 12: "these people are waterless springs"), and a series of loosely connected, complex statements (all introduced by post-positive *gar:* vv. 18-19, 20, 21-22) related to the theme of divine punishment.

The three units then show the progression of the author's thought from the introduction of the false teachers and certitude of divine judgment (vv.

1-10a) to the polemical treatment of these opponents' teaching and activity (vv. 10b-14b) to the harsh reality of enticement to apostasy and debauchery, which is the lot of the accursed (vv. 14b-22). From beginning to end the section focuses on the reality and fate of the false teachers.

False Teachers and Divine Judgment (2:1-10a)

The first unit of chapter 2 introduces the opponents and the danger of their activity among the addressees. A first part presents a series of statements regarding them and their influence, while a second illustrates God's treatment of the devout, who are rescued from trials, and of the unrighteous, who are punished even now in view of the day of judgment.

(2:1-3) False Teachers, Their Error, and Their Punishment. Chapter 2 opens with a brief introduction to the opponents and their activity. Three successive statements—the last two joined loosely by the conjunction "and" —are made about them, and in each case the author draws an important conclusion by means of a relative construction.

The first statement (v. 1) is clearly connected stylistically and thematically to the previous discussion of true prophecy. Second Peter's opening clause, "but there also arose false prophets among the people," stresses this connection. There were both true and false prophets in Israel. Hence the earlier discussion of prophecy leads the author to set up an ancient as well as a contemporary contrast, a typology that will allow for a condemnation of the teachers who are compared to Israel's false prophets and for an extended use of OT stories as evidence of God's just judgment as prophecy. The opening statement of v. 1, however, draws an interesting comparison between ancient false prophets and contemporary opponents who are labeled "false teachers." This comparison no doubt builds on the previous discussion wherein 2 Peter characterized the apostolic witnesses as bearers of a "reliable prophetic message." Just as the apostles in their preaching (1:16) are comparable to the OT prophets (1:20-21), so are the present heretical opponents like the false prophets of OT times in their erroneous and destructive teaching. The comparison goes further; in 2:1 the author implies that just as there "arose" falsehood within the context of divine revelation in the past, so in the future, despite and indeed as a challenge to a new prophetic message, there will appear similar agents of falsehood.

Consideration of this initial statement of v. 1 calls for comment on two other issues. The first concerns the author's continued use of the testament genre that is here underscored, on the one hand, by the future tense employed by the dying apostle ("there will be among you") and, on the other, by the use of the traditional theme of troubled times awaiting the addressees (see *T.Levi* 14:1f; *T.Judah* 18:1f; Acts 20:29f). The second issue involves the author's characterization of the opponents not as false prophets, as is often the case in literature influenced by apocalyptic thought (*T.Judah* 21:9; Mark 13:22; 1 John 4:1; Rev 19:20), but as false teachers. Presumably the avoidance of the former indicates that the focus of the comparison is neither on the false promises or claims of authority one would expect of OT pseudoprophets nor on the satanic challenge to divine power in the endtime by apocalyptic false prophets but rather on the false content of the opponents' message. Presumably also these people are actual teachers, and the author's goal is not to dispute their positions but to discredit their teaching and its immoral consequences. Thus neither their prophetic characteristics (though see the comments about Balaam in vv. 15-16) nor their authoritative roles in the community (they participate in ecclesial activities and influence fellow believers—see 2:2-3, 14, 18-19) are stressed but rather the devastating consequence of their eschatological teaching.

The second part of the statement, as is true of vv. 2 and 3, consists of a complex relative clause that either develops further or draws consequences about the initial comments. In the case of v. 1 the relative construction is extended by two participial clauses. Therefore three additional comments are made about the opponents who have just been introduced. First, by employing vague, future terminology ("people such as will"—*hotines*) to lend verisimilitude to the testament theme, the author describes what being "false teachers" means; they "will bring in destructive opinions." While the verb *pareisago* could suggest "malicious or secretive" action, its sense here is probably neutral and so refers to the introduction of nontraditional, indeed non-Christian ideas into the community's discussions. Additionally the term *hairesis* could refer to schools of thought, fairly-developed heretical positions, or more generally to dogmas or opinions (BAGD 23-24). The last mentioned fits the context best because the author is referring to their teaching or doctrine that is qualified as "destructive" (lit. "of destruction"—*apoleias*). This last term characterizes not a doctrine of cosmic and personal destruction—the teachers promise freedom from these (2:19; 3:4f)—but rather a doctrinal stance that ironically leads, via false argumentation and immoral behavior, to eschatological destruction (see 3:7).

Secondly, to explain these alleged "destructive opinions," the false teachers are said to "disown the master who bought them," a statement whose terminology is partly derived from Jude 4: "*disown* our only *master* and Lord Jesus Christ" (use of *arneomai* and *despotes*—underlined terms respectively).

Clearly the terms have a christological application in 2 Peter, a conclusion indicated especially by the soteriological description (on the ransom terminology, see 1 Pet 1:18; 1 Cor 6:20; 7:23) of the one designated "master." The verb *arneomai*, here as in Jude 4, means not "to deny" but to "disown or reject" the master's lordship. In addition, while the characterization of Jesus as *despotes* (for discussion of this divine title, see Jude 4) points to a high christology, use of "buying" and "master" terminology further underscores the author's interest in the issue of lordship. Jesus is God's agent of manumission, and believers, like the author of the letter, are "servants or slaves of Jesus Christ" (1:1; see *TDNT* 1:124-28). They owe him the honor of lordship. Finally 2 Peter's combination of themes in this segment of v. 1 further confirms our understanding of the letter's strategy and purpose. The basic issue is a christological one, namely, the teachers' rejection of the notion of parousia, here described in terms of lordship and related to Jesus' role as lord of believers. By questioning Jesus' coming they thereby deny his power (1:16), the same power given to him by God as salvific agent (ransom and savior terminology). Ultimately then this denial is a challenge of divine providence.

Thirdly, the author is led once again to emphasize the destructive consequences of the teachers' doctrine and behavior; only in this case the element of "self-destruction" is stressed. The audience no doubt will perceive the irony of 2 Peter's claim that those who complain of the slow arrival of the endtime will themselves receive a "swift" judgment and punishment. There is the implication in this verse that the destruction here noted not only refers to endtime condemnation but also to present destruction or punishment, whether as implied earlier in the expression "destructive opinions" and then described as debauchery that is likened to dog's vomit or a pig's wallowing in the mud (2:2, 22) or as present punishment of the unrighteous in view of the day of judgment (2:10a). A life of debauchery is itself seen as a form of destruction (see discussion of 2:2, 10a, 18).

The second statement (v. 2), also consisting of an initial comment followed by a complementary relative clause, develops further the issue of the destructive consequences of the teachers' opinions. Not only do they indulge in self-destruction, but also they lead others into "debauchery" (*aselgeia*; see also 2:7, 18). The term is borrowed from Jude 4 and has a similar meaning and slightly different function in 2 Peter. Thus in both texts the term designates wanton behavior, but whereas in Jude it describes the behavior that flows from ungodly beliefs (use of *asebeis* in Jude 4), in 2 Peter it indicates the destructive consequences of the opponents' eschatological teaching. Debauchery becomes for 2 Peter an enslavement to destruction (2:19). It is in this sense that "many will follow them in their debauchery." Indeed the rare verb "follow" (*exakoloutheo*), already employed in 1:16 in a similar context, suggests that many believers (this is the only place where a large number is indicated) will follow their authority as teachers and will indulge in what is described later as "desires of the flesh" (2:10, 18). The opponents then are seen as dangerous in regard to their teaching and its consequent behavior, because the students follow the logic of their masters. But like them they will be headed not for freedom but for a similar enslavement in the guise of debauchery.

This second statement is further qualified by a relative clause, whose function is to refocus the discussion on the opponents' teaching and its broader consequences, consequences that are described as follows: "on account of whom the way of truth will be maligned." Three elements need attention to discern correctly the author's meaning.

The term "whom" could ostensibly refer to the "many" who follow or even involve both the teachers and their followers but more logically concerns the teachers who are the object of the author's polemics in all three initial verses.

The expression "the way of truth" (*he hodos tes aletheias*) is a striking one, which has been variously interpreted by scholars who have favored reading the term "way" either in the general ethical sense of walk or behavior (often in Jewish literature; see *TDNT* 5:50f) or in its more technical use to designate a group and its beliefs and way of life (1 QS 8:13-14; 9:17-18 and Acts 9:2; 19:9—see BAGD 554.2c). In defense of the first option scholars point to the prior reference in the verse to debauchery and to an assumed parallel in 2:21 in the phrase "the way of righteousness" (see below). Thus the phrase would refer to an authentic, virtuous moral life. Others propose that 2 Peter employs "the way" here and elsewhere in the letter (2:15, 15, 21) to designate the Christian movement not as a corpus of teachings but as a way of life that involves both beliefs and behavior that derive from God. The latter is preferable here since the modifier "the truth" refers back to 1:12 where the term designates "the Gospel" or divine revelation and so in 2:2 indicates Christian tradition as a true prophetic message. In the present context the author insists that just as the teachers' "destructive opinions" lead to wanton behavior, so does that behavior serve to discredit the Christian movement in the eyes of nonbelievers.

The verb rendered "malign" represents the Greek term *blasphemeo* (see also 2:10-12) and probably alludes, as does Paul in Rom 2:22-23, to God's plaint in Isa 52:5 (LXX): "on account of you my name is constantly maligned among the Gentiles." The false teachers will not only cause divisions within the community but will also by their godless behavior open the community to public ridicule. The author, like Paul in 1 Thess 4:10b-12, is concerned about the community's image and reputation.

The third statement (v. 3) lays against the opponents an accusation that relates directly to their function as teachers, teachers of the Hellenistic marketplace who sell their facile ideas to the rowdy crowds and highest bidders. Consequently they are placed in the category of cunning sophists who manipulate their audiences for financial gain. While the theme of "greed" (*pleonexia*) is traditionally used in polemical texts (see 1 Thess 2:3f), the author's return to this issue in vv. 14 and 15 indicates more than formulaic use. Instead this theme along with others in the statement characterize the teachers as operating with false motives, goals, and arguments. Indeed the verb generally rendered "exploit" (*emporeuomai*) means to "do business" and here further suggests financial exploitation of or catering to the crowds as a means of monetary support.

The teachers are condemned for the methods they employ in their exploitation. The expression *plastois logois*, literally "with made-up or false words," is rendered in a variety of ways: "deceptive words," "fabrications," or "made-up stories." While the verb *plasso* suggests falsehood or fabrication, the noun *logos* in the plural idiomatically refers to speech and, in contrast with the reference in 1:16 to "myth," probably means "argument." Few scholars have failed to note the relationship between the two, even insisting that they express the same accusation in different terms. Nonetheless the contrast between *mythos* and *logos* suggests that 1:16 concerns "story," and 2:3 refers to "argument." It has already been stated in discussing the former that 2 Peter declines to employ the classical myths to explain eschatological realities but chooses divine revelation and its stories to defend the promise of Jesus' return. In 2:3 the author accuses the teachers of using "specious or false arguments" in their explanation of these same realities. The result seemingly, as one deduces from reading 3:3f, is that they explain away, through false explanations or arguments, Jesus' return and God's cosmic lordship as human inventions in the style of the classical myths for the purpose of controlling public behavior. The author will insist that apostolic tradition is reliable and its eschatological teaching genuine as reality and promise, while the false teaching of the opponents exploits fellow believers and, by robbing them of their eschatological motivation (3:14), leads them also to destruction.

Following the initial statement about the teachers' destructive activity, the author once again by means of a relative construction dwells on their inevitable punishment. Not satisfied with insisting on the future character of this judgment the author will now, by appealing to providential considera-tions, turn to its origin in the divine plan. Borrowing from Jude the theme of "foreordained condemnation," as well as some of its terminology (*krima*: "condemnation" and *ekpalai* for *palai*: "long ago"), 2 Peter recasts the con-cept in imagery that has Jewish as well as Hellenistic parallels. Thus the phrase "people who long ago were foreordained for this condemnation" (Jude 4) becomes "whose condemnation from long ago has not been idle" and is further characterized: "and their destruction is not asleep." Jewish lore about slumbering gods, even the God of Israel, who is called upon to arise and to grant assistance or just judgment (Pss 3:7; 12:5; 44:23-26; 121:4), no doubt provides the background for such imagery. But it is also probable that the author is here responding to the teachers' mockery about a slow or sleeping deity who is allowing "things to continue as they were from the beginning of creation" (3:4, 9). It has been convincingly shown that the teachers are here employing the tactics of Epicurean critics of Stoic and Christian theodicy, wherein they mockingly speak of sleeping deities and idle providence (Cicero, *Nature of the Gods* 1.21-11; Origen, *Against Celsus* 6.78). Second Peter's response is to personify God's judgment and its consequent punishment and to present them as active divine agents, the first as working throughout history ("from long ago"—see following examples from Jewish lore) and the second as presently effective (use of the present; see also 2:9 and the discussion above about debauchery as present destruction) and eschato-logically threatening (3:7). The response then that divine punishment or condemnation is not idle will be treated in vv. 4-8, and the further insistence that this punishment or destruction is not asleep but indeed active even now will form the conclusion of the author's treatment of ancient models of devout and unrighteous people and their just treatment by God (2:9-10).

(2:4-10a) God's Treatment of the Ungodly and the Righteous. The remainder of this unit about the false teachers consists of a lengthy, complex conditional sentence that presents an alternating series of ungodly and right-eous figures to show how God dealt with such issues in the past. Following the fourfold protasis (vv. 4, 5, 6, 7-8) the author introduces pertinent con-clusions for the addressees concerning the fate of the devout and the unrighteous (v. 9). The passage ends by reiterating the dual heresy of the opponents (v. 10). The list of ancient models is clearly related to that of Jude 5-7 (desert generation, angels, Sodom and Gomorrah), but 2 Peter selects the last two and places these negative examples, along with two positive ones (Noah and Lot), in chronological and evil/good alternating order: the angels (v. 4), Noah and the ungodly flood generation (v. 5), Sodom and Gomorrah

(v. 6), and Lot and the lawless people of his day (vv. 7-8). Two further points should be made concerning the author's redactional work. On the one hand, the two new, positive examples (vv. 5, 7-8) also address the ungodly contemporaries of the good models and, on the other, the two negative examples drawn from Jude are edited either to underscore the model's mention of present punishment (v. 4) or to add a note on future destruction (v. 6).

A short note is required here to point out 2 Peter's striking similarity to Sir 16:6-23. The latter presents, in the first part of the text, examples of ungodly behavior and insists (v. 8) that God "did not spare" these people but instead provided just judgment (vv. 6-16). As in 2 Pet 2:4f such discussion is a clear response to those, cited in 16:17f, who challenge divine retribution. Both authors present a defense of traditional theodicy by appealing to past examples of divine judgment and by pointing to God's cosmic lordship (see 2 Pet 3:3f).

Verse 4 presents a first example, a primordial one, of ungodly figures who did not escape divine punishment. Its elements are drawn from Jude 6 and some of its vocabulary ("angels," "gloom," "keep,' "for judgment"). Uninterested in the details of the offense committed, the author states simply that they are angelic figures "who sinned." Further, seemingly to add a Hellenistic note to the discussion, 2 Peter points out that they were "held captive in Tartarus" (*tartaroo*), thereby alluding to the frequent comparison made between the fall of the Watchers (*1 Enoch* 6f; see Gen 6) and the imprisonment in Tartarus of the Titans of Greek mythology (Josephus, *JA* 1.73; see Hesiod, *Theognis* 617f). Second Peter insists, in the manner of Sir 16:8, that God "did not spare" them but instead "handed them over to chains [variant: "pits"] of gloom to be kept for judgment." The theme of preeschatological punishment appears in Jude 4 and provides for the author another opportunity to note that divine punishment or self-inflicted destruction begins in the present as the unrighteous become slaves of the things that defeat them (2:19; see discussion of v. 9 below). The angelic imprisonment in the netherworld serves as a model for the sinner's present enslavement to destruction. The focus of this statement then is present punishment as a pledge of eschatological or final judgment, which will itself be a punishment in "the gloom of darkness" (2:17).

A second protasis (v. 5), introduced by *kai* and implied *ei* ("and if"—see v. 4), offers a second example of an ancient figure confronted with God's just judgment. Before presenting the positive example of divine protection of Noah, 2 Peter insists that God "did not spare the ancient world," his contemporaries, characterized later in the verse as "the world of the ungodly" (see 1:4 for a discussion of "world" in 2 Peter). Indeed Noah's generation, introduced to Jewish readers as "corrupt" and "filled with violence" (Gen 6:11), became known in later tradition as the personification of debauchery and licentiousness (Matt 24:38; Luke 17:27), while Noah, the righteous one (Gen 7:1), acquired the reputation of teacher or "preacher of righteousness" to an unrepentant generation (Josephus, *JA* 1:74; *SibOr* 1.125-95). The focus of v. 5 then is the author's insistence on the inevitability of divine punishment for the ungodly (God "did not spare" and "brought a deluge on" them—see Gen 6:17), on the one hand, and divine care and protection for the righteous, on the other. The term "protect" (*phyllasso*) speaks in generic terms (as does "rescue" in vv. 7, 9) of divine care to suggest in this case the story of the ark and the rescue of Noah's family from the cataclysm. Finally 2 Peter's reference to Noah as "the eighth," often rendered "together with seven others," has suggested a number of conjectures, none of which are really convincing. One should probably view this detail simply as part of the Noah tradition (see 1 Pet 3:20) and consider instead the author's note that Noah was a "preacher of righteousness" as a symbolic reference to his function as preparing for the age of righteousness, exemplified by the Jesus movement as "the way of righteousness" (2:21) and for the promised eschatological realm of righteousness (3:13).

Verse 6 consists of a third protasis ("and if" as in v. 5) and presents another example from Jewish lore of divine judgment. Second Peter borrows and greatly reduces the text of Jude 7. Gone are the references to surrounding cities and sexual sin. Instead the author retains the concept of "punishment of eternal fire" by alluding simply to the cities' "reduction to ashes," thereby pointing to the eschatological end of the earth and the heavens (3:7f) and indulging in some etymological fun, for the area was called "the land of ashes." Furthermore the author builds on the model's reference to Sodom and Gomorrah as an example (*hypodeigma* for *deigma*) of divine retribution by insisting that God "condemned them as an example of what is coming to the ungodly" (in defense of this reading, see *TCGNT* 702). In this way the ancient example becomes an explicit warning to all that their time of waiting is to be well spent "in leading lives of holiness and godliness" (3:11f). Thus this third example focuses exclusively on the divine punishment and omits mention of the offense and Lot.

A fourth and final protasis (vv. 7-8), however, introduces the example of Abraham's nephew and his contemporaries. Though some scholars see this reference to Lot as an extension of the previous illustration and speak of three ancient examples, the author's style demands that vv. 7-8 be seen as a fourth statement of divine judgment. Second Peter follows contemporary tradition in viewing Lot as a righteous person, perhaps modeled after Noah the preacher of righteousness and one who likewise contrasts sharply with his lawless neighbors (Wis 10:6; Philo, *Life of Moses* 2.58; Luke 17:26-30). Also to be compared with the earlier statement about Noah (use of "protect") is the vague term "rescue" (*rhyomai*; see also v. 9) used to describe divine assistance implied in the OT story. Again 2 Peter is less interested in the details of the story than in divine judgment and assistance. Of particular interest in this example is Lot's relationship to his contemporaries. On the one hand the neighbors are characterized as "lawless people" who exhibit "debauched behavior," and on the other hand Lot is said to be "oppressed" or "distressed" by this behavior. While some scholars stress the first meaning of the verb (*kataponeo*), it is probably more correct to view the passage as implying inner distress rather than outer conflict or persecution. Indeed v. 8, treated correctly by most scholars as an explanatory parenthesis, demands such an interpretation, since the verse seems designed to underscore the righteous person's situation as one of daily, mental challenge by unrighteous beliefs and behavior. Verse 8 repeats the characterization of Lot as righteous, mentions his ill-treatment at the hands of "lawless people" (use of synonyms: *athesmos* and *anomos*—see further discussion at 2:16; 3:17), and lays stress on the debauched behavior or deeds of these lawless people; but the verse also adds new elements. Presumably, to connect explicitly the example of Lot to that of the addressees, 2 Peter emphasizes the daily challenge ("living among them day after day") of living in a world of corruption wherein righteous persons are tormented ("torture of a righteous soul") both by what they hear and see. In this way the author prepares further for discussion of the dangerous influence of the false teachers' doctrine and behavior (2:10f) and for the exhortation given at the letter's close to the addressees who risk losing their purity and stability (3:14, 17).

Finally, in vv. 9-10a the author brings the lengthy conditional sentence to a close: "if God did such and such (vv. 4f) . . . then the Lord knows how to . . . (v. 9)." The apodosis introduces God's consequent activity as involving both the good and the evil. The former, characterized as "devout" (*eusebes*—see 1:3), will be "rescued . . . from trials" by God. The general term for divine assistance ("rescue") is repeated from the Lot episode but now introduces the traditional and much-used noun *peirasmos* (see especially Sir 33:1; Matt 6:13/Luke 11:4). Rather than refer to "temptation" to sin, whether alluding to daily or eschatalogical situations, the term here probably suggests the experience of the righteous person in the face of ungodly people and their licentious behavior (see Luke 8:13; Acts 20:19; 1 Pet 1:6). It is especially in view of the examples of Noah and Lot and the presumed situation of the addressees in the face of evil contemporaries that the author envisions divine assistance for those who strive for lives of holiness and god-liness while awaiting the Lord's return (3:11-14). One sees here as elsewhere in 2 Peter a strong emphasis on exhortation and a positive view of the outcome as regards the addressees.

Following the brief treatment of the devout, the author turns to the fate of the ungodly. Interestingly the author insists that these are being subjected to a state of punishment prior to the final judgment. They, like the angels, are already being punished. While some have attempted to focus this statement on the final judgment, it seems instead, following the generally accepted interpretation, that 2 Peter follows an old biblical tradition that insists that either God sends upon sinners a "deluding influence" or that these simply "delight in wickedness" (both expressions from 2 Thess 2:11; see also Ps 81:12; Ezek 14:9; Rom 1:24f). In this particular instance the teachers' opinions are said to be "(self-destructive" (2:1) and their behavior "enslaving" (2:19f) as they and their followers return to the corruption of evil desires (1:4; 2:20-22).

Finally the author borrows elements from Jude 7-8 to reformulate in v. 10a the opponents' dual error. On the one hand, the behavior that results from their theological and christological doctrine is described as an enslavement to the flesh ("following the flesh") and as typified in depravity (or "polluted desire"). On the other hand, their basic religious stance is stated as "despising or looking down on lordship." The expression (with the verb *kataphroneo*) serves as a parallel to 2:1 ("disowning the Master") and probably is a rewriting of Jude's similar statement about "flouting lordship" (*atheteo*). In the case of 2 Peter the accusation, as retained from Jude, certainly refers primarily to a denial of Christ's lordship as the returning lord (3:3f—also God's sovereignty), but probably also alludes to the role of angels in the apocalyptic scenario (see vv. 10b-11 below).

Accusations (2:10b-14b)

At this point the author introduces a pattern that will be repeated in the next section: a vivid characterization of the opponents ("bold, audacious people") followed by an initial accusation illustrated by a story from ancient tradition (the angels in vv. 10b-11 and Balaam in vv. 15-16) and a reintroduction of the teachers by the expression: "these people are . . ." (vv. 12, 17). In this case the author focuses especially on accusations displaying boldness, recklessness, and greed, accusations that are formulated as a series of complex participial constructions (2:12b-14b).

(2:10b-11) Bold and Audacious People. Taking a clue from Jude 9 concerning Michael's respectful caution ("did not dare"—use of verb *tolmao*), 2 Peter characterizes the opponents as the very opposite; they are "bold or insolent" (*tolmetes*) as well as "audacious or arrogant" (*authades*). These descriptive terms flow directly from the author's previous accusation concerning the opponents' defiance of lordship (2:1, 10a) and prepare for the immediately following story about the angels.

First, the author brings an accusation against them and then contrasts with their audacious behavior that of the very beings they malign. The terminology for this charge is drawn from Jude 8: "they malign or slander the glorious ones." As in Jude one presumes that these "glorious beings" are God's cosmic agents who play a role as guardians of established order (see comments on Jude 8) and, in the case of 2 Peter, especially who participate in the apocalyptic scenario when the risen lord, returning as Son of Man, does battle with the satanic forces, executes judgment on the ungodly, and gathers the elect from the four ends of the earth (see Mark 13:26-27; Rev 14:14-20; Jude 14-15). In more contextual terms the author insists on the teachers' arrogance by noting that "they are not afraid" (*tremo*) to act in such a foolhardy way.

Verse 11 introduces angelic characters and their respectful attitude toward judgment. With this statement the author clearly intends to contrast ("whereas"—*hopou*) the audacious teaching and behavior of the opponents. Interpretation of the verse, however, is problematic for source, stylistic, and contextual reasons. From the outset one must view this verse as a heavily redacted version of Jude 9 and its telling of the confrontation between Michael and the devil regarding the body of Moses. Thus scholars are divided on whether the interpretation of 2 Pet 2:11 depends on the author's and audience's knowledge and perhaps even misinterpretation of the apocryphal source used or whether the new text is to be interpreted entirely from contextual clues. In stylistic terms it is unclear what the relationship is between the "glorious ones" of v. 10b and the "angels" of v. 11. Further it is not certain whether the phrase "against them" implies a condemnation by the "angels" of the "glorious ones" or of the false teachers. If the "angels" and the "glorious ones" are distinct groups, especially if the latter are evil spirits or fallen angels (see *1 En* 10.1f; 12.3f), then one could consider the "angels" as not wishing to condemn their fellow spirits—the issue of greater strength, however, seems problematic. Again, decisions regarding these ambiguities are frequently resolved by having recourse to the author's apocryphal source. While scholars sometimes relegate v. 11 to the author's poor and misinterpreted use of a source, they usually fail to note that the author's choice to retain this text as well as its radical rewriting suggest deliberate, contextual use. Whether or not 2 Peter knew the original apocryphal story or even misunderstood Jude's nebulous summary of the event in question, it seems best to focus on the author's composition as it would have been heard by an audience that had only the text of 2 Peter as context.

Nothing in vv. 10b-11 suggests a negative identification either of the "glorious beings" (*doxai*) or the "angels." Only if one views the phrase "against them" as referring to the former, is it necessary to characterize them as malevolent beings. On the contrary the term *doxai* suggests a positive reading, one that envisions the spirit world as reflecting divine glory and power. It seems best to view the accusation of v. 10b as representing the opponents' challenge of angelic roles in salvific and eschatological contexts and to read v. 11 as characterizing the teachers' claims as the height of folly. The term "angels" is a synonym for the *doxai* and these otherworldly figures serve as models of proper behavior vis-à-vis God's domain. Truly there is a certain irony that the powerful angelic beings ("greater in strength and power") are more respectful and less audacious than the false teachers. Though insulted by them they will not respond in kind (with "a maligning or insulting judgment") in their roles as God's agents ("from the Lord"). That task, as noted in the previous section, is God's alone.

(2:12a) Like Irrational Animals. The author returns more directly to vehement accusations. First, there is a substantive clause ("these people [are] like . . .") that compares the opponents to nonrational beings, and this is followed by a series of nominative participial construction in vv. 12b, 13b, 14a, and 14b (note that the participle in each case is in post-position), which introduce added accusations. Second Peter borrows generously terms and themes from Jude 10 to construct the whole of v. 12: the derogatory "these people," "like irrational animals," creatures of "instinct," "blaspheming or maligning things they do not [understand]," and ultimate "destruction." The overall structure and meaning of the passage, however, are quite different from those of the source used. While Jude wishes to emphasize that the opponents' downfall results from their ironic reliance on their lower instincts ("like irrational animals"—see Jude 10), 2 Peter employs the theme of "the irrational animal" as a central image to reinforce the original characterization of the teachers as "bold, audacious people" (v. 10b) and to introduce a series of related accusations. So from the outset 2 Peter insists on the controlling image; they are "like irrational animals" whose tendencies and activities are best described in a bestial way.

The author employs the concept of "animal" to describe the false teachers and further characterizes this image by several other phrases. Borrowing the term from Jude 10, the author calls them *alogos*, meaning "speechless" or "irrational." Though the former is possible (see v. 16 for a clearer use of such a concept), the latter fits the context more closely, because 2 Peter, like Jude, wishes to underscore the irrational character of the opponents' behavior. Also they are described as "creatures of instinct" (*physikos*—see related term of Jude 10) to emphasize overindulgence and tendency to violence and greed. Finally they are characterized, in contrast to Jude's usage, as "born for capture and destruction" (rather than "decadence"—see also later in v. 12). Just as they naturally seek prey for their survival, so they themselves become the objects of capture and death. In this opening statement then the author prepares for the list of accusations that follow.

(2:12b-14b) They Destroy and Are Destroyed. Though borrowing several themes from Jude 10, 2 Peter restructures the material so that the initial comment of v. 12a prepares for a series of charges against the teachers, charges that are introduced by participial constructions and various modifiers. A first accusation (v. 12b) focuses on the irrational behavior of the teachers: "they malign things they do not understand." The choice of the verb *agnoeo* rather than retention of *oida* of the source might suggest further that the teachers have "never understood" or "come to know" the basic truths of the community's tradition (see discussion of *epignosko* at 1:2). In spite of their claims to knowledge they are like irrational beings that do not understand such things and, in their folly, even mock the forces that will bring about their destruction.

This first accusation is followed by two brief statements, the first of which is difficult to interpret. Literally the Greek text states: "in their destruction they will also be destroyed"; that is, either "by their destruction (of others) they will be destroyed" or "they will perish in the same way that these (beasts) perish." Choice of the first reading seemingly anticipates the following statement regarding "payment for wrongdoing," while the second underscores the comparison drawn at the beginning of v. 12 (they are "like animals"). The second statement (v. 13a) expresses a form of the law of the talion: "suffering wrong as payment for wrongdoing," and thereby underscores both the themes of destruction and divine punishment in the context of animal behavior.

A second accusation concerning debauchery or indulgence follows in the remainder of v. 13. Clearly this lengthy charge is related to the first half of Jude 12, but once again the differences are considerable. Indeed 2 Peter borrows the terminology of "feasting with" (*syneuocheomai*) and the general notion of pollution from Jude and develops a charge against the opponents that contains several descriptive elements. While the focus of the source was on selfish, irreligious abuse of the community's fellowship meals, the interest of the new composition is considerably different, because the author omits reference to these meals (see below) and directs the addressees' attention more generally to the theme of debauchery: "they regard as pleasure daytime indulgence." Several rhetorical points are made here and reiterated in the remainder of the verse and in the following accusations. Not only does the author employ the characteristic term *hedone* to designate exquisite "pleasure" but also suggests that "dissipation or indulgence" (*tryphe*) constitutes the opponents' very idea of enjoyment. Additionally 2 Peter insists that the opponents' self-indulgence be qualified as the height of degeneracy, that is, daytime dissipation (see Acts 2:13-15; Qoh 10:16; Isa 5:11).

Owing to their mindless pursuit of pleasure (see Philo, *Allegorical Laws* 3.116, who describes pleasure as the antithesis of reason), they are described as "blots and blemishes" (see discussion of Jude 12), the opposite of what faithful believers should be who await the Lord's return (3:14). They violate the purity of the community by "revelling or indulging (*entryphao*) in their lusts or deceptions" (*apate* for *agape* or "fellowship meals" of Jude 12). Indeed they pretend to feast or to share in fellowship with other believers but instead practice deception and dissipation. They are deemed "worst than animals" (*4 Ezra* 8.30) in their behavior within the community.

In v. 14a the author returns to the attack by describing the opponents as "having eyes full of adultery" (lit.: "adulteress") that "unceasingly look for sin." Both expressions designate the profligate with an eye cast for every possible occasion for sin. The first idiom probably relates to an ancient saying that the profligate "has harlots not maidens in his eyes" (the latter plays on the term *karai*, which designates "pupils of the eye" as well as "maiden"—see Plutarch, *Morals* 528e). The second simply portrays the opponents as being on the lookout for or unable to resist sin. Sin, like prey and violence for the animal, has become a matter of instinct for these teachers; they sin even with their eyes (see Matt 5:28). In this way, the author adds, they "entice or snare unstable people." The imagery used is that of hunting or fishing with bait (*deleazo*), the bait and the method of enticement being described in some detail later in v. 18. These false teachers prey on the unsteady (*asteriktos*), those who, like themselves (3:16), either lack the stability of true commitment or are in serious danger of losing it (1:12; 3:17). The author's use here of the term "unsteady" to characterize the opponents' potential victims lends greater urgency and hope to the final wish that the addressees "not lose (their) own stability" (3:17). Lastly the author's use of hunting imagery can only underscore the irony that the teachers have become like animals, themselves "born for capture and destruction" (2:12a), and are already enslaved to debauchery and error (2:18-19).

A final, brief accusation (v. 14b) brings the section to a close; the opponents are charged with "having hearts trained in greed." This statement looks both backward and forward—backward as it recalls the earlier charge that the teachers act like cunning sophists who sell their ideas to the highest bidders in a public forum (2:3a) and forward as it prepares for the story of Balaam the mercenary prophet (2:15-16) and the discussion of the havoc brought about by professional hucksters on the unweary and the inexperienced (2:18-20). Like athletes, they "are trained" (*gymnazo*) and, like the sophists they are, they know how to turn a profit.

Further Accusations (2:14c-22)

One encounters once again the pattern seen earlier at 2:10b and following. First the false teachers are characterized by a striking epithet ("accursed lot"); secondly an initial accusation is illustrated by the story of Balaam from the Jewish Scriptures (vv. 15-16), thirdly, the false teachers are reintroduced by the expression "these people are . . ." (v. 17); and lastly, the author's discussion is presented as a series of three *gar* ("for") clauses—vv. 18-19, 20, 21-22—which focus on the situation of the false teachers as people under God's curse.

(2:14c-16) Accursed Lot. The opening epithet *kataras tekna* (v. 14c), often translated literally as "children of the curse" or "accursed children," must be understood as a Hebraism wherein personal terms, such as "son," "children," "lord," etc. are modified adjectivally by a noun in the genitive to express a person's relation to a class or abstract concept. In this case the teachers are said to be worthy of or destined for a curse (*BG* 43-44). Indeed they are "an accursed lot" whose lives are under a curse because they are enslaved to every form of debauchery and are destined for eternal darkness or destruction. Seemingly the entire section describes the lot or destiny of these hapless, unstable people.

Immediately 2 Peter explains the epithet by charging that "they have gone astray by forsaking the straight path" (v. 15a). Like Israel of old, the false teachers are under a *curse* for *going astray* by forsaking *the path*, described as disobeying God's *commandments*. The italicized words correspond to terms found in Deut 11:28 and employed in 2 Pet 2:14, 15a, and

21 (also 3:2) and so suggest LXX influence on the construction of this unit. Further, one must also reckon with the author's use of Jude 11 for this passage ("astray" for "error"—same root in Greek) as well as the remainder of vv. 15 and 16 concerning Balaam. The opponents' error ("going astray"—see also 2:18; 3:17) is characterized as abandoning the community's tradition, which is here called "the straight path" (a common LXX phrase: see Ps 106:7; Isa 33:15) or elsewhere "the path or way of truth" or "of righteousness" (2:2 and 21 respectively). Again "the path" seems to refer both to the community's teachings and its mores.

Second Peter follows this general accusation by drawing upon the story of Balaam (vv. 15b-16) to characterize further the opponents' error as owing to mercenary considerations. Already in 2:2-3 it has been stated that these people act out of greed in their roles as teachers of false doctrine and debauchery. Omitting the examples of Cain and Korah as found in Jude 11, 2 Peter focuses on Balaam as a mad prophet whose behavior and fate illustrate the situation of the false teachers. To establish the relation between these, 2 Peter asserts that in straying from the straight path they have "followed persistently (*exakoloutheo*—see also 1:16; 2:2) the path of Balaam," the antithesis of the former. While, in trying to discern what is meant by this path, one could speculate by examining later tradition about Balaam (whether about his greed, deception, divination, or immorality—see Numbers 22–24; Deut 23:4-5; Josh 13:22; and especially the targums to the pertinent chapters of Numbers), it seems best to examine what 2 Peter suggests about the Balaam story. Employing contemporary tradition the author focuses on two aspects of the story. First, retaining Jude's characterization of Balaam as a mercenary (see discussion of v. 11), 2 Peter portrays him, in terms already used of the false teachers in 2:13 ("suffering wrong as payment for wrongdoing"), as one "who loved payment for wrongdoing." Unfortunately commentators often interpret v. 15c in light of 13a and see here an ironic twist wherein Balaam in being put to the sword by the Israelites is in fact receiving "payment for his wrongdoing" (see Num 31:8 and later Jewish tradition). The author's point is not Balaam's ultimate punishment but rather his perversity, because, like the teachers (see 2:13b), he found pleasure in wickedness (see 2 Thess 2:12) and, in this case, in its reward (see 2:3, 14b). As earlier the nature of the "wrongdoing" is unspecified.

Secondly 2 Peter employs a new element from the Balaam tradition to address the prophet's error. In place of (contrastive *de*) the reward he so desired, the prophet "received a rebuke for his lawlessness (*paranomia*)" (v. 16a). Once again without specifying the nature of the ancient prophet's activity (see also 2:8 for "lawless deeds") the author focuses on a curious episode wherein a brute or speechless animal, even provided with a human voice, "restrains the prophet's madness" (v. 16b). Ignoring the often conflicting reports of this episode (nature and author of the rebuke), 2 Peter seemingly focuses on the lowly character of the beast of burden as God's agent. No doubt the author saw the irony of an "irrational animal" showing greater insight than one who claimed divine knowledge (see Philo, *Life of Moses* 1.272) and playfully suggests that, if in ancient times the words of an unreasoning animal were able to restrain a mad prophet, God could and would in the present, by means of the words of the prophets and the holy apostles (3:2), counteract the irrational teaching and behavior of greedy teachers. The rhetoric and OT example then not only heighten the polemic against the opponents but also advance the author's strategy in suggesting that the false teachers' madness or error can be restrained and that the addressees will not lose their stability (3:17).

(2:17) Like Waterless Springs and Wind-Driven Mists. The author returns more directly to the characterization of the opponents by drawing once more from Jude, quoting verbatim from the beginning of v. 12 and the end of v. 13 and borrowing water imagery from the former. The opponents are reintroduced by a phrase from Jude 12: "these people are . . ." (see earlier at 2:12) and are described as "waterless springs and mists driven by the whirlwind." In contrast to the cosmic imagery of Jude 12b-13 involving air, earth, sea, and sky, 2 Peter retains elements from the first ("waterless" and synonyms of "driven" and "wind") to construct two new nature images. Gone are the oblique references to *1 Enoch* 2-5 (note that the citation from *1 En* 1:9 in Jude 14-15 is also omitted) concerning cosmic irregularities of the endtimes. In their place one finds images that scholars find striking but rarely germane. Clearly a "waterless spring" is a symbol of empty promises; but what does "the mist" (*homichle*) designate? Is the term to be distinguished from "dew" or "rain clouds" or, owing to its being wind-driven, would it suggest an insubstantial or fickle source of water? If one is to judge from its LXX usage, *homichle* designates "mist" as a beneficial source of water or refreshment (Ps 147:16; Sir 43:22) and becomes an image of transitoriness owing to its contextual use (vanishing with the sun or wind: Job 24:20; Wis 2:4; and here). Thus both images indicate a possible source of water or nourishment; the first is a broken or dried-out "cistern or spring" (Jer 2:13) and the second an unusable water resource. Both bear eschatological connotations. In the first case the term *pege* ("spring or cistern") is used in eschatological promises where Israel will be "like a spring of water whose waters never fail" (Isa 59:11; also 35:7; 41:18-19; 49:10, or negatively Jer

2:13; 51:36); in the second case the water source or "mist" is threatened by the endtime "whirlwind" (*lailaps*; see Jer 25:32; Wis 5:23; also Job 21:18). Thus in the author's usage the teachers are accused both of promising what they cannot give (see 2:19: promise of freedom but delivery of slavery) and of taking away what had already been gained (see 2:20-22: divine knowledge is given up for earlier error). The images are chosen in view of the author's basic accusations against the opponents.

The charge is brought to a close by 2 Peter's statement, borrowed verbatim from Jude 13, that these are people "for whom the gloom of darkness has been reserved." It is always pointed out, correctly, that this statement fits better as an image in its original setting where "wandering stars" are the direct antecedent and also that the statement had by then become a standard eschatological idiom. Verse 17 then serves as a general accusation against the false teachers for the havoc they have caused in the community and insists on the effectiveness of divine judgment on these accursed people.

(2:18-22) They Entice and Are Enslaved. Immediately following, the author strives in a series of three *gar* statements to provide explanations for the enigmatic accusation concerning empty teaching and false promises. Additionally each of these makes use of proverbial or formulaic constructions to bring the author's statement to a close. The first complex statement (vv. 18-19) returns to the theme of enticement or exploitation of unweary converts (2:3, 14; see also 3:17) and dwells particularly on the themes of false promises and self-destruction, the former of which relates to that of "waterless springs." Borrowing from Jude 16 the terms *hyperogkos* (here indicating "high-sounding or boastful" speech) and "desires" (see 1:4; 2:10; 3:3), the author constructs a two-part statement that dwells first on the teachers' methods of deception (v. 18) and then, with the help of a proverbial saying, on the ultimate irony of their accursed existence (v. 19). Just as 2 Peter has already accused them in 2:14 of "enticing unstable people" by means of their sinful, lustful activity, so again they are said "to entice" their prey by two important, interrelated means: "by uttering high-sounding, empty words" and by offering "desires of the flesh, that is, debauchery" as allurement. In the first case 2 Peter renews earlier statements about the opponents as teachers. From the outset of chapter 2 the opponents are called "false teachers" who introduce "destructive opinions" (see v. 1). Without questioning their teaching role the author challenges and indeed condemns their doctrine, which is said to lead to their own destruction. But more important they employ "specious arguments" in their greedy efforts to exploit their fellow believers (v. 3). It is probably in relation to the last mentioned that one must consider their empty, deceptive speech as able to lead the addressees astray (3:17). Their speech then is characterized in sophisticated terms as inflated, bombastic, and motivated by mercenary considerations. In the second case they seemingly offer a sense of moral freedom (explained more fully in the following verse), that the author calls debauchery (see earlier at 2:2) or more graphically, following the lead of Jude 16, as "desires of the flesh." They are here accused of compromising the community's moral standards, standards that are contrasted to pre-Christian mores. This is particularly clear when the teachers' victims are called "those who are just barely escaping those who are living in error." The addressees, especially those who are victims, are unstable converts whose pagan ways are recent memories and whose conversion was earlier called "an escape from corruption" (1:4). Thus the opponents are presented as offering moral freedom (called licentiousness) as bait or enticement (see discussion of 2:14) to an unweary audience.

The second part of the statement (v. 19) introduces what scholars have come to view as an important clue about the opponents' teaching. Though expressed in polemical terms, 2 Peter's statement that the teachers "promise them freedom" resonates with Pauline (Rom 3:8; 6:15; Gal 5:13) and other NT passages that address similar notions of exaggerated freedom or licentiousness. Of particular interest are 1 Pet 2:16, which warns believers of "using (their) freedom as a pretext for evil," and Jude 4, which accuses similar opponents of "transforming God's grace into debauchery." Indeed, in claiming freedom from moral constraints the teachers may well have appealed to the Pauline writings, as the enigmatic reference to Paul in 3:15-16 suggests. What the opponents' notion of freedom or of salvation (see 3:15a) would have been, however, is hard to discern. While various scholars have proposed that the opponents promised freedom either from the moral law, the authority of otherworldly beings, the threat of judgment, or destruction or corruption, one runs into the problem of verifying such proposals. Second Peter, in responding to the opponents, rarely speaks of the law as such and usually views immorality as a result either of denying eschatological judgment or as related to a disdain for lordship. Since one can only know what 2 Peter says about the issue, one is probably best advised to look to 2:19 and its context for an interpretation of this passage.

From the outset it should be stated that v. 19 is not about the opponents' teaching generally, but about how they entice new converts (see v. 18). They claim freedom from moral restraints and so are accused by 2 Peter of enticing former pagans with the licentious behavior of their former error. The remainder of v. 19 seems to confirm that this freedom is indeed related to the theme of *phthora,* meaning both "corruption" and "destruction." By claiming freedom from moral restraints they seemingly deny the need for divine assistance or benefactions "that contribute to life and piety" (1:3) and underestimate the Christian belief that conversion is an "escape from the corruption that is in the world" (1:4; see also 2:18). In their folly they reengage ("entangle"—see 2:20) the corruption they have just escaped and are defeated by these forces and thereby become "themselves slaves of destruction." It is at this point that 2 Peter appeals to what is seemingly a proverb: "by whatever people are defeated, by that they are enslaved." Employing military imagery the author envisions the teachers as reengaging foolishly with the error they have just escaped and now find themselves enslaved to "the defilements of the world" (see vv. 20f). The teachers' promise of freedom is not only an unfulfilled promise (see use of cognate term in opponents' accusations concerning eschatological promises: 3:4, 19) but a perverse loss of freedom or return to pre-Christian mores.

A second *gar* construction in the form of an extended conditional sentence (v. 20) extends the previous discussion of the teachers' defeat and, by means of a dominical saying, dwells on their accursed situation. The protasis offers contrasting participial constructions, the first describing conversion as "escaping the defilements of the world" and the second characterizing the teachers' error as "being entangled once again in them." The first recalls two previous statements that speak of conversions as "escape" either from the world's corruption (1:4) or from error (2:18). In this case the pre-Christian existence is described as being subject to defilement and conversion not as being "free from" but as "fleeing from" such defilement by turning to God through Jesus Christ ("knowledge of") and by recognizing his lordship and his salvific role (see discussion of 1:2, 11). With this goal of "fleeing from," the second participial clause contrasts the teachers' folly of becoming involved or entangled once more with evil desires that bring defilement. The protasis then describes a process we must call apostasy (Matt 12:43-45; Rom 6:6-11; Heb 6:1-6), a turning away from enlightenment, a process that is the result of rashness, which has brought about defeat, and leads to self-destruction.

The author concludes in the apodosis, citing verbatim a saying of Jesus (Matt 12:45; Luke 11:26), that "the last state has become worse for them than the first." This proverbial saying, cited in the Jesus tradition as a conclusion to the story of the unclean spirit's return, is here employed to contrast pre-conversion to apostate states; as bad as the condition of the unenlightened person is, that of the renegade is far worse since it involves culpable choice.

The final *gar* construction (vv. 21-22) focuses on the topic of apostasy. Just as the proverbial saying of v. 19 about defeat and enslavement has led in v. 20 to further discussion of the theme of defeat, so at the end of v. 20 the proverbial statement about the apostate's worsened state leads in this verse to added discussion of what the author labels a better alternative. To express this concept 2 Peter employs in v. 21 what scholars call a Tobspruch or "better . . . than" construct, a popular wisdom form often used in early Jewish and Christian literature (Prov 15:16, 17; Qoh 7:1, 2, 5; Mark 9:43; 1 Pet 3:17) to contrast forms of behavior and to admonish against hideous courses of action. Once again the author's contrast is between the pre-conversion status ("not to have known the way of righteousness") and the rejection of Christian commitment ("to turn back from the holy rule"). In the first case acceptance of the gospel is described as "knowledge" (see discussion of 1:2) or commitment to the Christian way of life, earlier called the "way of truth," and "the straight way or path" (2:2 and 15 respectively) but here characterized as that "of righteousness." Apparently 2 Peter, by using this term, wishes on the one hand to underscore the theme of behavior (see 2:5-6), which dominates the entire section, and to relate it on the other to more doctrinal concerns later in the verse. In the second case the false teachers' ultimate error is that of turning their backs on God's rule (*entole* as referring to the Christian dispensation—BAGD 269.2f). Additionally the author underscores its divine origin ("handed down"—see Jude 3) and thus its reliability. As was implied at the end of v. 20, 2 Peter again insists, in agreement with other NT writers, that refusal through ignorance is far more understandable than is the willful refusal of the gift of salvation (see Mark 14:21).

As was the case in the two previous *gar* constructions, this one (v. 22) is brought to a climax by appealing to common wisdom. Indeed the author explicitly enlists the wisdom of the past as applicable to the false teachers: "that which is found in the proverb has truly happened to them"—the proverb then serves an exemplary function. Interestingly, however, the author employs the singular for the term "proverb," thereby suggesting that the following double proverb formed a single unit (see Matt 7:6 for a joint reference to the same animals). Regardless the proverb concerning the dog ("a dog returns to its own vomit") derives from a Jewish source: Prov 26:16, while that about the pig ("a sow is washed only to wallow in the mud") resembles one found in Oriental and Greek sources (*Ahikar* 8:15; Heraclitus, *Fragments*; Sextus Empiricus, *Pyrrhoneioi Hypotyposeis* 1.56). Both proverbs address the issue of apostasy in terms of animal behavior, that of the dog stressing the concept of "turning back" (cognates of *strepho* in vv. 21, 22) to uncleanness and that of the pig alluding to the rejection of past washing. The teachers then act like unclean animals that have "forgotten the cleansing of their past sins" (1:9), because like dogs they have returned to the filth they once emitted and like hedonistic pigs they have preferred to wallow once again in the mud.

This verse brings the author's lengthy condemnation of the false teachers to a close on a note of apprehension and revulsion. These dangerous exploiters (2:1-3) are like unclean animals (v. 22) who epitomize and foster the licentiousness of the Gentile world, but they are also like irrational animals whose destiny is "capture and destruction" (v. 12). The severity of the condemnation of the teachers can be understood only in light of their refusal to understand and accept God's promise and is indeed softened in light of the author's discussion later of God's "forbearance or patience" (3:8-9, 15).

Suggested Readings

Alexander, T. D. "Lot's Hospitality: A Clue to His Righteousness." *JBL* 104 (1985) 289-91.

Bauckham, R. J. *Jude, 2 Peter*. Waco TX: Word Books, 1983.

Cavallin, H. C. C. "The False Teachers of 2 Pt as Pseudo-Prophets." *NovT* 21 (1979) 263-70.

Desjardins, M. "The Portrayal of the Dissidents in 2 Peter and Jude: Does It Tell Us More About the 'Godly' Than the 'Ungodly'?" *JSNT* 30 (1987) 89-102.

Dunham, D. A. "An Exegetical Study of 2 Peter 2:18-22." *BS* 140 (1983) 40-54.

Dunnett, W. M. "The Hermeneutics of Jude and 2 Peter: The Use of Ancient Jewish Traditions." *JETS* 31 (1988) 287-92.

Feuillet, A. "Le péché évoqué aux chapitres 3 et 6 de la Genèse. Le péché des anges de l'Epître de Jude et de la Seconde Epître de Pierre." *Divinitas* 35 (1991) 207-229.

Fornberg, T. *An Early Church in a Pluralistic Society*. Lund: Gleerup, 1977.

Greene, J.T. *Balaam and His Interpreters: A Hermeneutical History of the Balaam Tradition*. Atlanta: Scholars, 1992.

Hiebert, D. E. "Selected Studies from 2 Peter. Part 3: A Portrayal of False Teachers: An Exposition of 2 Peter 2:1-3." *SC* 141 (1984) 255-65.

Lewis, J. *A Study of the Interpretation of Noah and the Flood in Jewish and Christian Literature*. Leiden: Brill, 1968.

Moore, M. S. *The Balaam Traditions: The Character and Development*. Atlanta: Scholars, 1990.

Neyrey, J. H. "The Form and Background of the Polemic in 2 Peter." *JBL* 99 (1980) 407-31.

Pearson, B. "A Reminiscence of Classical Myth at II Peter 2.4." *GRBS* 10 (1969) 71-80.

Schlosser, J. "Les jours de Noé et de Lot. A propos de Luc, XVII,26-30." *RB* 80 (1973) 13-36.
Skehan, P. "A Note on 2 Pe 2,13." *Bib* 41 (1960) 69-71.
Snyder, G. F. "The *Tobspruch* in the New Testament." *NTS* 23 (1977) 117-20.
Vermes, G. "The Story of Balaam—The Scriptural Origin of Haggadah" in *Scripture and Tradition in Judaism: Haggadic Studies*. Leiden: Brill, 1961, 127-77.

The Lord's Day: Promise, Providence, and Power

(2 Peter 3:1-16)

Following upon a long, first section on true and false prophecy, focusing on the reliability of apostolic tradition and the false teachers' deception and punishment, the author now turns to the immediate issue of concern, namely, questions about the Lord's day specifically and more generally about theodicy. Like the introduction to the first part (1:12-15), the opening of this section is marked by easily-identifiable recall formulas, involving the terms "remember," "recall," and "understand" (3:1-3). Additionally the author claims that the current letter is a second attempt to discuss the issues at hand with the community. The remainder of the letter is devoted to two related topics: the delay of the parousia, repentance, and the endtime (3:1-10) and eschatological exhortation, including a brief note about Pauline interpretation (3:11-16). It should be noted that the various subsections, along with the epistolary closing, are marked by the same term of direct address: "beloved" (3:1, 8, 14, 17).

Delay of the Parousia, Repentance, Endtime
(3:1-10)

After having hinted on several occasions concerning the community's most pressing problem, namely, the undermining of its eschatological beliefs by teachers active within its ranks, the author, after strongly urging the addressees to recall its prophetic and apostolic tradition (vv. 1-2), cites what seemingly are the words of the opponents concerning Jesus' return and more generally about divine providence (vv. 3-4). There then follows a first response concerning the teachers' error, a response that focuses on God's power to create and destroy the earth and the heavens (vv. 5-7). In this way 2 Peter responds to the second statement (v. 4b) allegedly made by the opponents to the effect that there is no divine providence ("things continue as they were from the beginning of creation"). Thus vv. 1-7 constitute a first subsection.

In v. 8, introduced also by "beloved," 2 Peter addresses the community members directly. Employing a similar expression as in v. 5 to the effect that the teachers "fail to notice" their theological error, the author now warns the addressees in their turn "not to fail to notice" God's sense of time. Indeed, vv. 8f address the first mocking statement (v. 4a) made by the opponents concerning the delay of Jesus' return. So, in this second subsection one encounters several issues that relate both to the themes of delay and repentance (vv. 8-9) and to the sureness and stark nature of the end-day (v. 10). Both units then deal with the community's eschatological doctrine as this relates to the false teachers' challenges regarding the parousia and divine providence.

Eschatological Challenge and Divine Providence (3:1-7)

This first unit, in preparation for its discussion of the teachers' eschatological errors, appeals urgently to the audience's loyalty to tradition by claiming apostolic authority (reference to second letter), by stressing continuity with the Old and New Testament prophetic and apostolic tradition, and by characterizing the teachers, in apocalyptic terms, as "end-day scoffers." The author then formulates, in the opponents' words, the community's principal christological and theological concerns. After this first subunit (vv. 1-4) the author focuses on the teachers' errors by discussing God's relation to creation and its eschatological ramifications (vv. 5-7).

(3:1-4) The False Teachers' Errors. This introductory subunit falls easily, in terms of function, into two parts: vv. 1-2, which appeal for the audience's attention and loyalty, and vv. 3-4, which present the opponents' views in the form of direct citations. This new section opens with an ominous statement that has been much discussed, namely, that the present document "is now the second letter" the author is writing (v. 1a). This claim is variously explained as referring to Jude, to a lost letter, or to 1 Peter. The last mentioned is more plausible since such a claim fits more readily into the author' Petrine strategy (see discussion of 1:1, 12f). In this way the readers' consciousness is brought back, after a long break, to the letter's testament setting.

The author proceeds immediately (v. 1b) to propose the reason for writing, in a manner similar to and employing comparable terminology to that used in the introduction to the first major section (1:12-13). While in the first case the author's main concern is that of introducing the testament form to establish the alleged writer's apostolic authority (see discussion of v. 13), in this case the goal is to prepare the addressees for a discussion of the community's eschatological doctrine.

First, the author states, "in these I am stirring up your pure disposition (*eilikrines dianoia*) by way of reminder" (see 1:13). Both the meaning and function of this statement, however, are debated. Some wish to see the term *dianoia* as referring to "mind or understanding" and therefore to view the passage as referring to an understanding of the issues that the community once had, at least prior to its contact with the false teachers. The goal then of the community would be to remember the "pure or uncontaminated" doctrine that it once possessed. Comparison of this passage with 1:12-13 suggests, however, that the author intends the statement to win the addressees' goodwill (see 1:12), and so *dianoia* refers instead, as many translators also suggest, to "disposition." The addressees as converts had a "pure disposition," one that is now dormant, and it is to this original commitment to apostolic tradition that the author appeals.

Secondly the author turns explicitly to tradition as the source of orthodoxy. Employing the text of Jude 17 ("remembering the words spoken before hand by the apostles of our Lord Jesus Christ"), the author appeals once again (see 1:16-21) to OT prophets and apostolic witnesses to validate the community's eschatological beliefs. A new reference is made to the "holy prophets" as well as to a "command" from Jesus, who is once again called "Lord and Savior" (see 1:11). Both "the reminder" about an original open or pure disposition on the addressees' part and the appeal to the community's apostolic preaching prepare for the casting of the teachers' eschatological affirmations as the work of endtime scoffers who seek to lead the faithful astray.

The second part of this subunit (vv. 3-4), borrowing a last time from Jude (v. 18), first casts the opponents as licentious endtime scoffers and then formulates their principal challenges to Christian eschatology in the form of a taunting question and a statement challenging divine providence. This new subsection opens with a striking comment, one that has already appeared verbatim at 1:20 (see discussion), "understand first of all that." Presumably the author insists that what follows immediately is the principal conclusion to be drawn from the preceding discussion; if one looks carefully at the ancient prophets and apostolic tradition one will have to view the opponents in the following way. Thus borrowing generously from Jude 18 the author then envisions Peter, the alleged writer, as addressing the movement's future, endtime problems, namely, "that in the last days scoffers will come to scoff, living according to their own desires." This first element of the unit (v. 3), which characterizes the opponents as apocalyptic figures, remains true to the source being used by emphasizing their activity as scoffing or mockery and their behavior as selfish indulgence (see discussion of Jude 18).

It is particularly their alleged speech (v. 4) that becomes the focus of the remainder of the letter. First, they are cited as asking: "where is the promise of his coming?" Both the themes of "promise" and *parousia* have already figured prominently in the author's discussion (see especially comments on 1:4, 11, 16) and become the focal point of the teachers' eschatological position. The form used in the rhetorical question betrays a heightened sense of mockery, one frequently used in the Jewish Scriptures to express the taunts of the wicked or of Israel's enemies: "where is your or their God?" (see Pss 41:4; 78:10; Joel 2:17; Jer 17:15). In this case the rhetorical question is particularly appropriate as it dismisses mockingly the promise that Jesus would return on the clouds as Son of Man (see Mark 14:62 and parallels) to render judgment on good and bad alike. That the author here refers to Jesus' role as judge is confirmed by the earlier statement concerning Jesus' "power and coming" (1:16). The author will return to this theme in vv. 8f by focusing on the issue of delay and its implications for Christian living.

Secondly the teachers' accompanying statement, "for since (our) forefathers fell asleep, all things continue as they were from the beginning of creation," calls for some discussion. No doubt the expression "fall asleep" (*koimaomai*) is a common ancient euphemism for death, used from the time of Homer for the sleep of death whether in inscriptions, epitaphs, and biblical and Hellenistic literature (BAGD 437.2). The reason for its use in this particular context is rarely discussed. The idiom, "the fathers or forefathers," has been explained as either a reference to OT times or to the apostolic generation. In the first case the teachers would be making a claim to the nonfulfillment of ancient prophecy and in the second to the delay or nonactualization of the parousia. Objections are raised against both, because Christians maintained that ancient prophecy was fulfilled in the life of Jesus and his followers, on the one hand, and that early Jesus tradition, in its belief in an imminent parousia, on the other, postulated Jesus' return before the death of the early followers (see Mark 9:1 and 13:30 and parallels). Thus the first identification seems excluded by the teachers' and writer's Christian context, and the second, following the standard interpretation of v. 4b, is rendered most difficult. The following considerations then are in order.

The false teachers' second statement (v. 4b) must be understood in relation to their mocking question about the parousia and indeed its promise, for it serves (use of *gar*) as a justification for their scoffing nonbelief in apostolic teaching about "the Lord Jesus Christ's power and coming" (1:16). Both the death of the first generation of believers and the seeming nonintervention of God in human history are cited as proof why the promise of his return remains unfulfilled and that the promised accompanying benefits (see 3:13) will never be a reality.

The first part of v. 4b focuses on the death of the early generation of believers as a contradiction of the promise of an imminent return (see references above) and may even have in view, at least in part, a problem similar to that encountered by Paul in 1 Thess 4:13-18. Interestingly 2 Peter, like Paul, speaks not of "death" but of "falling asleep." It is here proposed that the author in both parts of v. 4b is challenging statements of the teachers, which are in their turn a polemical restatement of accepted traditional views. In the first case the term "sleep" is chosen in place of "die" to modify the accepted notion of "sleep with the ancestors or forefathers" (see Gen 47:30) into a statement about death as eternal sleep. Thus it is claimed that death becomes endless sleep or inevitable fate (see Seneca, *Epistle 99: On Consolation to the Bereaved* and Lucretius, *On the Nature of Things* 3), and there will be no rescue of these by a returning lord. 2 Peter will respond to this charge both in speaking of repentance (3:8, 15) and more directly in addressing the concept of new life in 3:13 (see also 1:4, 11).

The second part of the verse, in stating that nothing changes, seemingly appeals to notions of the immutability of the universe to counteract the commonly accepted axiom that "everything is flux" and thereby to deny the possibility of divine intervention in cosmic and human affairs (see Philo, *On the Eternity of the World* 7f; *On Dreams* 2.283; Plutarch against Epicurean claims in *On the Delays of the Divine Vengeance*, passim, see especially 560F-68). Such a position presupposes a God who is indifferent and distant from the world and casts doubt on the very notion of divine punishment. Second Peter will turn immediately to this last notion to challenge the teachers' statement that things have been thus "from the beginning of creation."

(3:5-7) A First Response—Regarding Divine Providence. The author begins by noting the teachers' lack of logic ("it escapes their notice"—BAGD 466), insisting that their stated position ("for in maintaining this") ignores the known facts of past (biblical) history. The remainder of the unit is a review, in cosmological terms, of God's relationship to created reality, beginning with creation and ending with "the day of judgment and destruction." Verses 5-6 deal with the world prior to its destruction by the flood, and v. 7 is devoted to the present universe. The primary function of the passage is to demonstrate God's active role vis-à-vis the cosmos. The first issue raised is divine intervention in creation (v. 5). Following the lead of the Genesis account the author insists that this cosmic event occurred "by means of God's word" (see Gen 1:3f; also Ps 33:6, 9; Wis 9:1; Heb 11:3), which divided the primal waters and by means of or in the midst of this watery chaos produced a heavenly firmament and dry land in the midst of the waters (Gen 1:6-10: "out of water and through water" as the author states). God's involvement in and control of the creative process forms for the author the starting point for belief in divine providence. God's involvement in the world and especially in that of human behavior is underscored by the flood episode (v. 6), which demonstrates divine judgment on the ungodly (see the reference back to 2:5—"deluge" and "cosmos"). Second Peter insists that this punishment is also accomplished by "God's word" and once again by means of water.

But just as "the former world" was subject to the divine creative power in creation and destruction, so "the present heavens and earth" are under God's ruling power, that is, subject to "the same word" (v. 7). Rather than focusing on God's sustaining and protective role (see 2:9), 2 Peter dwells on the cataclysmic parallelism between the old and the present world. Just as the former was destroyed by water, so the present, in Stoic and traditional apocalyptic terms (Lucretius, *On the Nature of Things* 5; Isa 66:15-16; Mal 3:19; *SibOr* 2. 196-213), is to meet a fiery conclusion (see vv. 10, 12 below). In this way the author draws a further parallel between God's past treatment of the ungodly both by water and by fire (see 2:5-6; also Josephus, *JA* 1.70). Additionally "the present heavens and earth" are said to be "reserved or marked for fire," a curious expression that is further explained as "being kept for the day of judgment and destruction of ungodly people." While some scholars appeal to God's treasury of good and evil (use of *thesaurizo*) to explain this passage (see Philo, *Allegorical Laws* 3.105-6), it seems instead to focus on the cosmos itself (grammatically), which, according to divine decree, will be engulfed in an eschatological fire of destruction. Thus 2 Peter's goal in this passage is to focus on biblical and contemporary cosmology as it confirms God's involvement in human affairs and especially as it underscores the inevitability of divine judgment of the ungodly. Verses 5-7, after all, are a response to the false teachers' taunting statement and conclusion that, since "nothing has changed since the beginning of the world," God's condemnation and destruction have indeed been idle or asleep (2:3). The author insists: the opposite is the case.

Delay and Repentance, Certitude and
Starkness of the Endtime (3:8-10)

A second subunit is clearly marked off in stylistic and thematic terms. Like the section above it opens with the term "beloved," repeats the earlier expression "escape . . . notice" (v. 5), and turns from a response to the teachers' challenge to a plea addressed to the community. After having responded to the statement that "nothing changes," 2 Peter now focuses on the theme of the Lord's return in terms of "delay," provides a reason for this divine respite, and then reminds the addressees of the certitude of the Lord's coming and of the stark nature of that day.

(3:8-9) A Second Response—Regarding the Lord's Coming. The author now turns to the teachers' mocking question: "where is the promise of his coming?" In contrast to the opponents who ignore (seemingly an intentional activity) certain basic facts, the community is exhorted (use of the imperative) to consider an important fact in response to the question just cited. From this point on the tone of the letter becomes more positive and is increasingly that of exhortation. The point that the addressees are asked to consider seriously (v. 8) concerns time as seen from a divine perspective. To express this concept the author employs what is seemingly a citation or reformulation of Ps 89:4. A text ("a thousand years in your eyes are like yesterday which is past"), which ancient Jewish and Christian writers employed in various chronological ways to determine the time and length of creation or the eschatological timetable (*Jubilees* 4.29-30; *Barnabas* 15.4; Irenaeus *Against Heresies* 5.23; *Genesis Rabbah* 8.2), becomes in the hands of 2 Peter a twofold statement about time from God's perspective and the relation of each of these to human activity (similar statements can be found in Sir 18:9-11 and *2 Bar* 48:12-13). The first part of the double statement, "with the Lord one day is like a thousand years," prepares for the discussion of divine delay and its purpose (v. 9); the second part, "and a thousand years like one day," warns about the end coming unexpectedly (v. 10), especially for the unrepentant. By relativizing the concept of time in this way the author insists that the problem of time is a human one and does not provide a basis for questioning divine providence.

Indeed in v. 9 the author turns to the problem of "delay" and its purpose in God's plan. The theme itself is common in contemporary literature where authors insist that "the Lord will not delay" (Sir 32:22; see also Hab 2:3; Isa 13:22; *2 Bar* 48:39; Heb 10:37). In the hands of 2 Peter the theme serves two important purposes. In v. 9a it is combined with that of "promise" to counteract the false teachers' claim that, since the lord's return is allegedly overdue (the early Christians have passed away), the promise will never be kept. Instead, Jesus, who is called "the lord of the promise" (the genitive is explained otherwise by various scholars), does not delay as the opponents would have it ("as some people consider 'delay' "). Instead Jesus will come ("like a thief"—see v. 10), and the promise both of his coming and of its promise of new life (v. 13; see also 1:4, 11) will be fulfilled. Thus the author employs the opponents' terminology and robs it of its power. The promise is indeed "a reliable prophetic message" that must be understood properly (see 1:19-21).

In v. 9b one encounters the important theme of God's "forbearance or mercy" (*makrothymia*; see also 3:15). The time between Jesus' first and second coming, a time that the opponents increasingly call "a delay" or even dismiss as a non-promise, is in reality a part of God's salvific plan because it is designated as the time "of forbearance." "The lord of the promise," "the master who bought them" (2:1), "does not wish that any be destroyed but that all should reach repentance." Several themes from this passage call for attention.

First, divine "forbearance or patience" is a major OT theme that relates to the Jewish concept of God's very being as "merciful and gracious, slow to anger" (Exod 34:6). Consequently God's judgment and wrath are tempered by the desire that sinners repent and, especially in apocalyptic literature, this forbearance is seen as bringing about a delay of final judgment in view of repentance (see *4 Ezra* 3:30; 7:132f; *2 Bar* 21:20-21; 24:2; 85:8).

Second, the theme of forbearance in this case relates to Christ and his role as savior. The author regularly describes Christ as "lord and savior" (1:11; 2:20; 3:2, 18; see also 1:1) and in striking terminology calls him "the master who bought them" (2:1). It is no surprise then here also to have such terminology attributed to the divinized Christ, who as risen lord desires the salvation of all and wishes that every opportunity be given for repentance. The focus at this point on christology is important because in this way the author brings the addressees' attention back to the community's tradition that underscores Christ's lordship. Christ will return and guide believers into his eternal kingdom (1:11), but in the meantime they are "not to be idle and unfruitful in the knowledge of (the) Lord Jesus Christ" (1:8). The lord of the promise will keep his promise but, out of forbearance, awaits the proper moment, dictated by universal repentance.

Finally 2 Peter's expressed desire for universal salvation, whether that "none be destroyed" or that "all reach repentance," should not be overlooked as one examines the author's overall perspective. The letter, despite its severity toward the teachers and their followers, expresses a degree of optimism both that the addressees will be true to their "call and election" (1:10) and that universal repentance will be possible. No doubt 2 Peter would agree with Joel's sense of divine patience and repentance, namely, that all return to a gracious and merciful God, who is "slow to anger, and abounding in steadfast love, and relents from punishing" (2:12-14) and, in Christian terms, a God whose agent bought them back and assists them (1:3; 2:1) in being found "without spot or blemish" in anticipation of his return (3:14; on divine kindness and human repentance, see Rom 2:4).

(3:10) Sureness and Stark Nature of the Lord's Day. After dwelling on the theme of mercy or forbearance as the reason for eschatological "delay" (in accordance with human reckoning), the author in v. 10 returns uncompromisingly to the community's traditional teaching concerning the Lord's day. If complaint about delay or a misreading of divine time and purpose might be reasonably offset by the theme of mercy and the desire for universal repentance, the same cannot be said about the illusion that many have about limitless time. In fact what seems like a thousand years in anticipation will be no more than a day in reality (see v. 8b). The author insists both that the time of the Lord's day is unknown and that it will arrive unexpectedly. Either citing early Jesus tradition (Matt 24:42-44; Luke 12:39-40) or, more likely, borrowing from Paul (1 Thess 5:2; see discussion below of 3:15-16), 2 Peter compares the coming of the Lord's day to the unpleasant and unexpected arrival of a thief. For all, both righteous and ungodly, it will come suddenly and unavoidably, but for the unrepentant it will be most unwelcome and unpleasant. The statement serves as a warning and as an exhortation to both.

To the above attempt to counterbalance the description of the Lord's day as one of judgment (v. 10a) and of mercy (v. 9), 2 Peter adds three further statements to underscore the former. These are connected to the original statement about the coming of the Lord's day by a temporal connective ("when") and so provide a series of events that are to occur on that occasion. Although all three present serious lexical or textual problems to the modern reader, they nonetheless provide interesting comments on the Lord's day, since they encompass the fate of the whole cosmos and focus on eschatological judgment and punishment.

First, it is said that the heavens will "pass away with a roar." Using the traditional terminology of the Jesus material ("pass away"—Mark 13:31 and parallels; Matt 5:18/Luke 16:17) the author speaks of the endtime annihilation of the heavenly bodies (or heavens) with what is presumably a "rushing or roaring sound" (*rhoizedon*—a rare onomatopoeic term) to denote either cosmic attention or temporal suddenness. All will see or be aware of the cosmic dimensions of the great event. Secondly the author states that "the elements will be destroyed by burning" (BAGD 425). The theme of destruction by fire reiterates what is said at 3:7 and 12 (see also 2:6), but identification of "the elements" (*stoicheion*—also v. 12) is much discussed, because the term can refer to the elemental substances of matter, to the heavenly bodies, or to angelic or spiritual powers. Each could be defended, but the first seemingly fits best in the present context and so serves as a synonym for "earth." In this way the two first statements address the destruction of the entire cosmos, the heavens and the elements/earth. Indeed v. 12 offers a close parallel where again the heavens and elements/earth, in complementary clauses, are said to be destroyed by fire and heat. Thirdly the author now focuses on human activity by stating that "the earth and its works will be disclosed." This translation presumes the best attested reading *heurethesetai* ("will be found"—see *TCGNT* 705-6) and, in agreement with many recent commentators and translators, suggests the forensic sense of "disclosure" or "being found out" in both a positive and a negative sense. Such a meaning resembles other NT usage. Thus in Paul one can "be found a sinner" (Gal 2:17) or a "trustworthy" servant (1 Cor 4:2—see also Luke 23:4; John 18:38; Acts 13:28; Phil 3:9; 1 Pet 1:7; and *Pss Sol* 17:8). The clause then would designate eschatological judgment of the righteous and ungodly according to their works, a task that is traditionally assigned to the returning lord.

Suggested Readings

Allmen, D. von, "L'apocalyptique juive et le retard de la parousie en II Pierre 3:1-13." *RTP* 16 (1966) 255-74.

Bauckham, R. J. "The Delay of the Parousia." *TB* 31 (1980) 3-36.

Cavallin, H. C. C. "The False Teachers of 2 Pt as Pseudo-prophets." *NovT* 21 (1979) 263-70.

Chaine, J. "Cosmogonie aquatique et conflagration finale d'après la Secunda Petri." *RB* 46 (1937) 207-16.

Dupont-Roc, R. "Le motif de la création selon 2 Pierre 3." *RB* 101 (1994) 95-114.

Meier, S. "2 Peter 3:3-7—an Early Jewish and Christian Response to Eschatological Skepticism." *BZ* 32 (1988) 255-57.

Neyrey, J. H. "The Form and Background of the Polemic in 2 Peter." *JBL* 99 (1980) 407-31.

Riesner, R. "Der zweite Petrusbrief und die Eschatologie" in *Zukunftserwartung in biblischer Sicht. Beiträge zur Eschatologie.* Ed., G. Maier. Wuppertal: Brockhaus, 1984, 124-43.

Smitmans, A. "Das Gleichnis vom Dieb" in *Wort Gottes in der Zeit*. Eds., H. Feld & J. Nolte. Düsseldorf: Patmos, 1973, 43-68.
Talbert, C. H. "II Peter and the Delay of the Parousia." *VC* 20 (1966) 137-45.
Vogtle, A. "Die Parousie- und Gerichtsapologetik 2 P 3" in *Das Neue Testament und die Zukunft des Kosmos*. Düsseldorf: Patmos, 1970, 121-42.
Wenham, D. "Being 'Found' on the Last Day: New Light on 2 Peter 3:10 and 2 Corinthians 5:3." *NTS* 33 (1989) 477-79.
Zmijewski, J. "Apostolische Paradosis und Pseudepigraphie im Neuen Testament. 'Durch Erinnerung wachhalten' (2 Petr 1, 13; 3, 1)." *BZ* 23 (1979) 161-71.

Final Exhortation about Holy Conduct

(3:11-16)

Having insisted in forceful terms on the false teachers' misreading of divine time and intervention as related to the theme of repentance and having underscored the sudden, certain, and unpleasant character of the parousia, the author in a final movement of the letter turns more specifically to the issue of conduct and its motivation. While one might be tempted to join 3:11-13 to the previous discussion about the delay of the endtime and to see the segment as providing contrasting eschatological motivation for Christian behavior, it seems best to view vv. 11-16 as a complex unit dealing with the community's behavior and thus to qualify the overall unit as a final exhortation to the addressees. The section itself seems to have two subunits. The first (vv. 11-13), beginning with "therefore" (reading of *oun* rather than *houtos*: "thus"), deals with a question from the community about holy conduct and piety. The second (vv. 14-16), opening with "therefore (*dio*) beloved," focuses on forbearance, salvation, and tradition. The last mentioned also discusses the community's misuse of the Pauline writings. More important, in structural terms, is the parallel with 3:1f where a question and statement from the false teachers serves as an introduction to the author's discussion of the parousia, delay, and forbearance (vv. 5f). Here also a question, in this case from the members of the community and related to the behavior espoused by the teachers, again introduces a discussion of righteous living and its traditional foundation. The last mentioned points to the community's misuse of the Pauline writings in this regard.

Question about Behavior and Its Motivation (3:11-13)

This first unit prepares for the author's specific exhortation to an unblemished life (vv. 14f) by posing a question on that very subject. The query, however, is situated in the context of cosmic conflagration and seemingly challenges or at least calls into question the reason for righteous living. The author responds in v. 13 by restating God's eschatological promise (see also 1:11).

The above interpretation of the concluding clause of v. 10 (about judgment rather than fiery punishment—see discussion of textual problem) is further confirmed by the following unit, which speaks not only of cosmic destruction (and by implication destruction of the ungodly—see v. 7) but also of holy works or conduct for those who await the coming of the Lord's day. This subunit consists of two structural segments, the first a complex exhortatory question that situates present behavior in the context of cosmic eschatological destruction (vv. 11-12) and a contrasting, concluding statement that holds out the promise of cosmic righteousness for proper behavior (v. 13).

(3:11-12) Proper Behavior in View of Just Judgment. These verses, by their reference back to cosmic destruction ("since these things are to be destroyed") and by their repeated description of the end-day both as "God's day" and the entire universe (in terms parallel to v. 10) as being engulfed by fire, present a curious setting for the intriguing question about appropriate behavior. Are the addressees being advised about proper behavior in view of God's just judgment, as is often maintained, or is the author reflecting a hesitant question on the part of the intended audience? Surely the members of the community seemingly are asking: "what sort of persons ought [we] be in holy conduct and piety while waiting for and hastening the coming of God's day?" Such a question would be appropriate not only for people who rejected afterlife as a "sharing of the divine nature" (1:4) and so would act like the false teachers, but also for people who are told that the cosmos is destined for a fiery destruction. It is in light of this that the contrasting statement of v. 13 must be interpreted (see below).

The author's stress in vv. 11-12 on destruction by fire not only reiterates earlier statements (2:6; 3:7, 10) but also allows for an interesting blending of Jewish and Greek imagery in describing eschatological realities, particularly the association of a conflagration by fire with divine judgment (see Isa 66:15-18; Mal 4:1; *1 En* 1:6-7; *SibOr* 3:71-92; 4:171-78; Cicero, *On the Nature of the Gods* 2.46.118; Lucretius, *On the Nature of Things* 5.381-410). A contemporary reader would have found these associations quite intelligible. The concept of regeneration found in v. 13 would also have been familiar to a Hellenistic audience (*1 En* 45:4-5; Philo, *Special Laws* 1.208; *On the Eternity of the Universe* 89; *4 Ezra* 7:30-31; Rom 8:21).

Additionally the themes of "holy conduct" and "piety" noted in v. 11b point back to earlier discussions of virtuous activity (1:3f) and ungodly behavior (2:2f) and prepare for the final exhortation of 3:14f. Further the first part of v. 12 needs some comment, since the faithful are said to "wait for and hasten the coming of God's day." The theme of "waiting" (*prodokeo*) is so crucial here that the author will again employ the term in v. 13 to speak of "awaiting new heavens and a new earth" and in v. 14 of "awaiting these things." No doubt 2 Peter wishes to underscore the interim period and its moral obligations, the object of the community's question (see especially 1:3-11 on virtuous effort and 2:5-9 on the righteous behavior of Noah and Lot). By use of this verb the author at this point wishes to stress both the temporal aspect of the situation and moral readiness. By use of the concept of "hastening," a traditional apocalyptic theme (Isa 60:22; *2 Bar* 20:1-2; 83:1; *Barnabas* 4:3) that relates back to vv. 8-9 concerning repentance, the author points in anticipation to the following exhortation, which will again mention forbearance. Finally, 2 Peter speaks not of "the Lord's day," as elsewhere (see v. 10), but of "the coming of God's day." While one could suggest stylistic variation as the reason for this usage, it seems more likely that the author wishes at this point to stress God's creative power, God as the one who both annihilates the present cosmos and recreates "new heavens and a new earth."

(3:13) Eschatological Motivation for a Life of Righteousness. The above comment leads us to a discussion of the unit's concluding statement. Verses 11-12, with their challenging question about a moral response in view of such a bleak future, lead the author to restate the tradition's proper eschatological motivation for a life of righteousness. Yes, the present world will be destroyed, like the pre-flood earth (3:6-7), but, according to the divine promise (Isa 65:17; 66:22 and often in apocalyptic and intertestamental literature), the faithful (perhaps walking unharmed through fire—Isa 43:2) can look forward to "new heavens and a new earth, in which righteousness dwells." Proper behavior is to be motivated eschatologically both by the prospect of cosmic annihilation and by the promise of a new paradise-like creation, a new age characterized by righteousness (Isa 11:4-5; *1 En* 10:20-21; 91:17; *4 Ezra* 7:112-15; Rom 14:17)—it should be noted that the Christian movement is itself characterized in 2:21 as "the way of righteousness." Therefore the "promise" of v. 13 is also God's promise, one that is reliable and contradicts the false teachers' claim that "all things continue as they were from the beginning of creation" (3:4). Indeed there will even be a new creation.

Forbearance, Salvation, Tradition (3:14-16)

This second subunit is delineated from and related to what precedes by its obvious stylistic features. By the use of "therefore" the author wishes to designate the function of what follows as a result of the previously stated eschatological motivation. Even moreso the concept of "waiting" is reiterated from the previous discussion (vv. 12-13), and the theme of proper behavior is developed at greater length. This section also opens with the important term of direct address "beloved" (see 3:1, 8, 17). Finally the author returns to the themes of forbearance and salvation and, in relation to these, warns against misinterpretation of Pauline tradition, which presumably some in the community misconstrue to their own advantage.

(3:14-15a) Present Behavior. The unit opens on the theme of waiting ("since you await these things") and therefore directs its attention to interim behavior. The expression "these things" indicates an emphasis on dual motivation: human behavior as being both subject to just judgment and as destined for an afterlife of righteousness. Having established this eschatological motivation, however, the author focuses on present behavior and exhorts the addressees by means of two imperative clauses. The first encourages the community to exert maximum effort (*spoudazo*) in view of their goal. The theme of effort has appeared prominently in 1:5 in a discussion of virtuous activity and v. 10 in a statement about being faithful to one's call and election. In this case the term underscores the human effort required to reach the stated goal. By use of this general term the author refers back to the extended discussion of chapter 1 with its chain of virtues. This effort points to the extensive human activity that supplements faith, temperance, piety, and love of others (1:5-7).

The goal of this activity is stated as "being found by him spotless and unblemished," that is, "at peace." First, "being found by him" indicates the juridical situation of appearing before the returning lord as judge, who will come "like a thief at night." Clearly the author intends the theme of just judgment to be a strong motive for righteous activity. Secondly the desired state of the devout person is stated in terms diametrically opposed to the earlier description of the false teachers. Just as they are "spots and blemishes" (2:13), so are the devout to be "spotless and unblemished" (see 1 Pet 1:19; Jude 12, 23-24). Thus, they are to be both ritually and morally pure, because they were bought by the lord and cleansed of their sins (1:9; 2:1) and with the help of divine benefaction are to live fruitful lives of righteousness (1:3, 8). Thirdly the phrase "at peace" (*en eirene*) is probably to be viewed as explaining the overall state of believers; it is an appositive statement that summarizes their relation to God and the Lord Jesus (piety as the acknowledgment of lordship) and their consequent behavior (holy conduct—see v. 11). Thus it describes their present state of well-being vis-à-vis God (see 1:2).

The second imperative (v. 15a) pleads for the addressees' understanding of a point already made (3:9) and of a deeper sense of the meaning of salvation. They are exhorted: "regard the Lord's forbearance as salvation." The present time, viewed once again as divine respite, is both further opportunity for repentance and piety and proof of divine benefaction "that contributes to life and piety" (1:3) through God's agent as savior. As the false teachers considered the seeming nonoccurrence of the parousia ("consider 'delay' ") as proof of God's lack of care, so the addressees are urged instead to regard the "delay" as evidence of divine forbearance and thus salvation ("consider salvation") as a process that might best be described, in the author's words, as grace from God and peace in the knowledge of the Lord Jesus Christ.

A final point should be made here concerning the theme of salvation. While the author's immediate goal in this second imperative clause is to urge the addressees once more to view the present time of respite as part of God's salvific plan, it is also the author's intention to refocus the audience's attention on Jesus' salvific role in the lives of believers. In five instances Jesus is called Savior. The context of each of these usages provides a rich texture for viewing the author's sense of salvation as it applies to the lives of the addressees. The gifts of grace, peace, knowledge, and other benefactions, as well as their growth, are explicitly related to Jesus' role as savior (1:1-3, 8; 3:18). Through knowledge of him one flees from the pollution of the world (2:20); one becomes acquainted with the way of righteousness and receives his holy commands (2:20; 3:2). As he has acquired them for his own (2:1), so he provides them richly with everything that contributes to a life of righteousness that will assure them entry into his eternal kingdom (1:3, 11). At this point 2 Peter also wishes the addressees to view the time that the Lord graciously gives them as further evidence of God's power at work among them. That too, in answer to the false teachers' mockery, is part of the salvific process.

(3:15b-16) Proper Use of the Community's Scriptures. The remainder of this unit though devoted to a relatively independent topic, the misinterpretation of Paul's letters, is not an autonomous or simple section in grammatical terms. On the one hand the material is loosely connected to the two previous imperatives and provides added confirmation for these exhortations. Consequently considerable debate has taken place concerning the precise antecedent for this Pauline discussion, as well as Pauline parallels for these, whether delay as forbearance (Rom 2:4; 3:25; 9:22-23; 11:22-23), moral preparation for the parousia (Rom 13:11-14; 1 Cor 7:27-35; 1 Thess 5:4-11), or salvation more generally (see below). One should probably understand both imperatives as designating the antecedent for the Pauline reference, especially if one considers the first as summed up by the phrase "in peace" and the second as characterized by the concept of salvation. Thus the author wishes to enlist the authority of Paul in the document's discussion of salvation in all its facets (see discussion above of vv. 14b-15a). Indeed all of Paul's letters are concerned with human relations to God and consequent righteous behavior. At this point one might inquire about which letters of Paul the author would have used. The best candidates, as indicated by the themes of 2:19; 3:10, and 15, are Romans and 1 Thessalonians. Such a conclusion, however, is far from certain.

On the other hand the passage is complex and seemingly redundant, because it speaks first of Paul writing to the addressees and then of the teaching of his various letters. Following this the author claims both that the letters are difficult to understand and that they are being misinterpreted. Finally the would-be exegetes are said also to distort the other Scriptures. In grappling with the meaning and function of the entire passage scholars usually propose that it is the false teachers' misuse of Paul that brings about a defense of his letters as inspired Scripture. These opponents are accused of misinterpreting an admittedly- difficult Paul, along with other Scriptures. Thus 2 Peter presents a defense of Paul as being part of a unified apostolic tradition and his letters as already forming part of a collection with quasicanonical status.

More careful attention to the structure of this Pauline unit suggests a complex situation, because while most commentators focus on the concluding part of the unit concerning the misuse of the Pauline letters, there are really three important segments to examine. The first is introduced by "as also" (*kathos kai*) and speaks of Paul writing to the addressees; the second, also beginning with "as also" (*hos kai*), involves the subject matter of the entire Pauline corpus; and the third, in the form of a complex relative clause ("in which [letters]"), treats the subject of misinterpretation of Paul's letters. Each of these segments contributes to our understanding of the unit's meaning and function.

The first unit (v. 15b) states straightforwardly that Paul composed a letter to the addressees. Viewed from a historical perspective one is led either to seek a candidate for it among Paul's letters or to interpret the "you" of address in universal terms and to coalesce the first two statements about the letters. Such an approach is questionable since this passage parallels that of 3:1, has a similar context, and serves an analogous function. Just as the author can claim, in pseudepigraphic terms, to be writing the addressees a second letter, without undue concern about producing a letter with a specific designation and audience, so the author can again maintain that Paul has already written the addressees about the subject at issue. Besides, just as Peter, the alleged writer, can claim divine inspiration and authority for the letter being written (1:12-21), so again can the author claim, in Pauline terms (Rom 12:3; 1 Cor 3:10; Gal 2:9; 1 Thess 2:4), that the apostle ("our beloved brother Paul"—a fellow apostle) "was given wisdom" by God (see 1 Cor 12:8) when corresponding with them. Both Peter and Paul, as distant figures of the first generation, are witnesses to the reliability of the apostolic tradition. Also, by insisting on direct contact between Paul and the addressees it is probable that 2 Peter is suggesting that the community involved is Paulinist and that the Pauline tradition is very much part of the present controversy. Thus reference here to Paul lends further credence to the author's pseudepigraphic strategy both in terms of authorship and of authentication of apostolic tradition.

A second unit (v. 16a) presents a seemingly redundant series of prepositional phrases that translators usually conflate: "speaking of this as he does in all his letters" (NRSV). The passage, as is suggested by its structure, is a parallel to 15b and should be rendered: "as also (he has written) in all his letters, speaking in them about these things." Not only does the new statement suggest a Pauline collection of letters known to author and audience, but also it seemingly broadens the discussion about tradition. Just as Paul is said to have written the community with divine wisdom, so is his entire corpus, indeed Pauline tradition itself, said to have been the product of inspiration ("all his letters"). Further the author adds a general statement about Paul's method and content. He discusses or speaks about these many things and is indeed subject to misinterpretation and misuse. Thus the statement prepares for the final accusation against the false teachers and leaves open the range of subjects involved.

The author concludes the statement on the authenticity of Pauline tradition by focusing on what was probably a major problem, namely, the opponents' alleged misuse of Paul and other sacred writings (v. 16b). It is conceded that the Pauline texts contain "obscure or difficult" passages, a point with which ancients, Paul among them (1 Cor 2:14-3:4), as well as moderns would agree. The earlier hint about Paul's method of discussion ("speaking about") assists us in understanding how statements of Paul were easily taken out of the context of his discussion of issues and made into slogans about new life, freedom, and a host of half truths whose contexts were discarded. Community members, presumably the false teachers, who do such things are said to "distort or twist out of shape" Paul's statements to their own advantage or, in the author's polemical terms, "to their own destruction" (see discussion of 2:1). Further they are characterized as "ignorant and unstable," terms that, on the one hand, focus on misunderstanding (as does "obscure") and, on the other, qualify them as insufficiently grounded in the community's tradition (see 1:12; 2:14). They are false teachers because they lack both the instruction and the background to interpret either Paul or "the other Scriptures."

The expression "the other Scriptures" is an intriguing concept whose content and usage here is much discussed. That the author means to include in this category the OT Scriptures is obvious, but beyond that it is unclear what Christian works would have been thus labeled. Regardless, 2 Peter is here referring to the community's sacred, foundational works, both Jewish and Christian, that were read for worship and studied for spiritual edification. The importance of this reference is of course the claim and the reality that the letters of Paul were soon recognized, by both opponents and the orthodox writer of 2 Peter, as authoritative writings. One sees here an excellent example of the (Christian) canonical process at work in its early stages of development.

Closing

Contrary to Jude (vv. 24-25), which employs an extended doxology as conclusion, 2 Peter follows a more traditional epistolary convention, consisting of direct address ("beloved"), brief negative and positive exhortations, and an even shorter, concluding doxology. The epistolary closing is carefully constructed to underscore both the negative and positive tone of the document and ends optimistically on a positive note as it gives praise to Jesus Christ as lord and savior. In structural terms the unit consists of a transitional address formula, a testamentary warning that introduces two imperative, hortatory constructions, and a final, brief doxology.

Final Exhortation

(3:17-18a)

The final unit of the letter is clearly marked as a conclusion ("therefore"—*dio*) to the author's overall strategy and message. Also the author, a last time, addresses the audience with the endearing term "beloved" (3:1, 8, 14). Thus, returning explicitly to the testamentary genre, the author expresses a final warning about the bleak days ahead; the addressees (emphatic "you") are "forewarned." Adopting once more the testamentary convention of predicting the future (see 2:1f), the author speaks a final time about the false teachers who will arise like wild animals in the community (see the "savage wolves" of Act 20:29-30). But the warning is also a reminder of what the community knows in more positive terms about its commitment to the truth (1:12-15).

The first of the two imperatives resumes the negative part of the letter's strategy. Recalling the preceding severe treatment of the false teachers, their doctrine, and their behavior, the author warns the addressees a last time: "be on your guard" (*phylasso*). The opponents, who are portrayed as wild animals seeking prey and as debauched people who entice the unstable (2:2-3, 14), are dangerous, so the devout, who will receive protection from the Lord (2:9), need to be vigilant, rejecting their enticements and making every effort to be firm in their call and election (1:5, 10; 2:18). Specifically they are warned about "being carried away by the error of lawless people" and thereby "losing (their) stability." These future, dangerous people are described in terms employed earlier about the false teachers. They are described as "lawless" or lacking in moral restraint (2:7 about Lot's contemporaries as examples of the opponents) and as people who are in "error" or have gone astray (see 2:15 where the verb is employed of the teachers who "go astray by forsaking the straight path"). By the use once again of this terminology the author is able to subsume in a final warning the earlier descriptions of the community's dangers. Also the addressees are warned against "being led or carried away" by the teachers' "destructive opinions" (2:1) and enticements (2:14, 18). Interestingly the terminology used in this exhortation under-scores further the imagery of the Christian movement as "a path" from which one can wander or deviate. Finally the author describes the danger of apostasy as a loss of one's stability. Just as Christian commitment was described as "being established (*sterizo*) in the truth" (1:12) or well grounded in the apostolic faith, so the ultimate danger is for the believer to lose that firm grounding and, like the false teachers, to become unstable and to stray from the straight path of truth and righteousness (2:2, 15, 21).

The initial negative exhortation is immediately counterbalanced ("instead") by a positive one (v. 18a) that recapitulates the benefaction and growth themes of chapter 1. The addressees are exhorted to "grow in the grace and knowledge of our Lord and Savior Jesus Christ." Though the term "grow" (*auxano*) is employed only here, the author has earlier developed this theme as "abundance of grace and peace through knowledge" (1:2), as "making every effort to supplement" (v. 5, also v. 10), as "increasing" and "being fruitful" (v. 8), and as "doing . . . things so as never to stumble" (v. 10). Also the focus is on the benefactions received and the human response to these, in this case "grace and knowledge" (see 1:2 and more fully 1:3f), the first as a divine gift that makes possible and constitutes the continued response to God's loving activity ("grace of or given by"—subjective genitive) and the second as the human turning to and commitment to God and acceptance of Christ's lordship as God's messiah (objective genitive). It should be noted that the author's use here of *gnosis* rather than the more frequent *epignosis* emphasizes the themes of effort and growth (see discussion of 1:2).

An important final note is needed here about the author's christological focus, because, while 1:2 speaks of "abundance through the knowledge of God and our Lord Jesus," in the present case the author associates "growth in grace and knowledge" to the "Lord and Savior Jesus Christ." In fact the entire letter ends on a christological note (see also v. 18b). One probably should conclude from this that the key issues being debated, namely, the present lordship and future return of the Lord Jesus, have influenced the author's construction even of this conclusion. At stake is Jesus' salvific role in the life of believers (see discussion of 1:1; 3:15) and the exercise of his power as present lord and returning judge. His grace in this case then refers particularly to his forbearance that allows repentance and continued commitment and to knowledge of him that recognizes his lordship and looks forward, through a time of holy conduct and piety, to his coming.

A Closing Doxology

(3:18b)

Finally the letter is brought to a close not with the more usual benediction (see Phlm 25; 1 Pet 5:14b) but with a doxology (Rom 16:25-27; Jud 24-25). In this case 2 Peter follows the standard conventions of the form: person addressed in the dative ("to him"), praise expressed as "glory" (*doxa*), statement of temporal duration, and perhaps an affirmative "amen" (the reading is textually questionable; see *TCGNT*, 707). The doxology is addressed simply "to him," that is, to Jesus Christ, as lord and savior. Though this practice is rare in early Christian literature (also 2 Tim 4:18; Rev 1:5-6), praise is here directed to Jesus in divine terms. Indeed, since glory is regularly reserved for the divinity (see 1 Cor 10:31; Phil 1:11), its usage in this passage is significant. On the one hand, its use by 2 Peter further confirms the high christology of the document, but a christology nonetheless that points to deification. Jesus can and should be glorified, because God, as was noted earlier in the letter, has given him "honor and glory" (1:17). On the other hand, the ascription of divine glory to Christ can only be meant to underscore the author's profound sense of Jesus' salvific role and power, both in the present as lord and savior who rescues the devout and in the future on the day of God as the one who exercises divine judgment, which leads to the destruction of the ungodly and to the entry of the beloved into his eternal kingdom (1:11; 2:7).

Finally the temporal element of the doxology is of more than passing interest. First, the author seemingly transforms the tripartite formula of Jude 25 ("from every age, is now, and will be for all ages") into an emphatic binary one ("both now and on the day of eternity"—*kai . . . kai*). In this way one again encounters the author's concern about Christ's present and future role in the life of believers. Secondly the unusual expression "the day of eternity" (see Sir 18:10) is probably a subtle reference to the Lord's day that will soon dawn (1:19), to the divine reckoning of time (3:9), and to the Lord Jesus' eternal kingdom (1:11).

Second Peter then begins and ends by appealing to Jesus' lordship, the denial of which, as is seen repeatedly in the letter (see 2:1, 10; 3:4), is the major concern addressed. Thus the letter opens by characterizing Peter as "servant and apostle of Jesus Christ" (1:1) and closes by ascribing glory or lordship to him both in the present and for eternity. Employing the testament form, 2 Peter presents the community's apostolic tradition in the words of the soon-to-depart Peter (1:12-15) and warns, in graphic detail, about false teachers who propagate their destructive opinions and lead many, themselves included, on the path of destruction (2:1f). The addressees are assured that the community's eschatological teaching is reliable and inspired; the Lord's promises are based on the prophets, witnessed by the apostolic generation, and communicated by their lord and savior (1:16, 19; 3:2). They must, in their time of waiting for the lord's return, employ the time graciously given to them to remain pure, to avoid the enticements of the unscrupulous teachers, and to remain true to their commitment to God and to the Lord Jesus Christ. Christ has provided for their success and demands a firm effort on their part (1:3-10). The letter of 2 Peter, like its predecessor and benefactor Jude, reveals a fierce struggle against people judged to be false teachers and becomes a plea for eschatological and moral orthodoxy. The letter reveals some of the growth pains the early church experienced as it moved out into the Greek world and as its members dialogued with its contemporaries, striving all the while to protect the truth of its beliefs and the integrity of its morality.

Suggested Readings

Allmen, D. von. "L'apocalyptique juive et le retard de la parousie en II Pierre 3:1-13." *RTP* 16 (1966) 255-74.

Conti, M. "La Sophia di 2 Petr. 3.15." *RivB* 17 (1969) 121-38.

Doty, W. G. *Letters in Primitive Christianity.* Philadelphia: Fortress, 1973.

Elliott, J. K. "The Language and Style of the Concluding Doxology to the Epistle to the Romans." *ZNTW* 72 (1981) 124-30.

Hiebert, D. E. "Selected Studies from 2 Peter. Part 4: Directives for Living in Dangerous Days: An Exposition of 2 Peter 3:14-18a." *BS* 141 (1984) 330-40.

Overstreet, R .L. "A Study of 2 Peter 3:10-13." *BS* 137 (1980) 354-71.

White, J. L. *Light from Ancient Letters.* Philadelphia: Fortress, 1986.